ASPEN PUBLISHERS

CORPORATIONS

FOURTH EDITION

STEVEN L. EMANUEL

Harvard Law School, J.D. 1976
Member, NY, CT, MD and VA Bars

The *CrunchTime* Series

Wolters Kluwer
Law & Business

AUSTIN   BOSTON   CHICAGO   NEW YORK   THE NETHERLANDS

No part of this publication may be reproduced or transmitted in any form
or by any means, electronic or mechanical, including photocopy, recording,
or any information storage and retrieval system, without permission
in writing from the publisher. Requests for permission to make copies
of any part of this publication should be mailed to:

    Aspen Publishers
    Attn: Permissions Department
    76 Ninth Avenue, 7th Floor
    New York, NY   10011-5201

To contact Customer Care, e-mail customer.care@aspenpublishers.com,
call 1-800-234-1660, fax 1-800-901-9075, or mail correspondence to:

    Aspen Publishers
    Attn: Order Department
    PO Box 990
    Frederick, MD 21705

Printed in the United States of America.

1 2 3 4 5 6 7 8 9 0

ISBN 978-0-7355-7229-4

This book is intended as a general review of a legal subject. It is not intended as a source for advice for the solution of legal matters or problems. For advice on legal matters, the reader should consult an attorney.

About Wolters Kluwer Law & Business

Wolters Kluwer Law & Business is a leading provider of research information and workflow solutions in key specialty areas. The strengths of the individual brands of Aspen Publishers, CCH, Kluwer Law International and Loislaw are aligned within Wolters Kluwer Law & Business to provide comprehensive, in-depth solutions and expert-authored content for the legal, professional and education markets.

CCH was founded in 1913 and has served more than four generations of business professionals and their clients. The CCH products in the Wolters Kluwer Law & Business group are highly regarded electronic and print resources for legal, securities, antitrust and trade regulation, government contracting, banking, pension, payroll, employment and labor, and healthcare reimbursement and compliance professionals.

Aspen Publishers is a leading information provider for attorneys, business professionals and law students. Written by preeminent authorities, Aspen products offer analytical and practical information in a range of specialty practice areas from securities law and intellectual property to mergers and acquisitions and pension/benefits. Aspen's trusted legal education resources provide professors and students with high-quality, up-to-date and effective resources for successful instruction and study in all areas of the law.

Kluwer Law International supplies the global business community with comprehensive English-language international legal information. Legal practitioners, corporate counsel and business executives around the world rely on the Kluwer Law International journals, loose-leafs, books and electronic products for authoritative information in many areas of international legal practice.

Loislaw is a premier provider of digitized legal content to small law firm practitioners of various specializations. Loislaw provides attorneys with the ability to quickly and efficiently find the necessary legal information they need, when and where they need it, by facilitating access to primary law as well as state-specific law, records, forms and treatises.

Wolters Kluwer Law & Business, a unit of Wolters Kluwer, is headquartered in New York and Riverwoods, Illinois. Wolters Kluwer is a leading multinational publisher and information services company.

TABLE OF CONTENTS

Preface

Thank you for buying this book.

The *CrunchTime* Series is intended for people who want Emanuel quality, but don't have the time or money to buy and use the full-length *Emanuel Law Outline* on a subject. We've designed the Series to be used in the last few weeks (or even less) before your final exams.

This book includes the following features, some of which have been extracted from the corresponding *Emanuel Law Outline*:

- *Flow Charts* — We've reduced most principles of *Corporations* to a series of 17 Flow Charts, not published in the full-length Emanuel or elsewhere. We think these will be especially useful on open-book exams. The Flow Charts are numbered to correspond to the chapter number in the Capsule Summary for the chapter dealing with the same topic. A list of all the Flow Charts is printed on p. 2.

- *Capsule Summary* — This is a 100-page or so summary of the subject. We've carefully crafted it to cover the things you're most likely to be asked on an exam. The Capsule Summary starts on p. 29.

- *Exam Tips* — We've compiled these by reviewing dozens of actual past essay and multiple-choice questions asked in past law-school and bar exams, and extracting the issues and "tricks" that surface most often on exams. The Exam Tips start on p. 139.

- *Short-Answer* questions — These questions are generally in a Yes/No format, with a "mini-essay" explaining each one. They've been adapted from our *Law in a Flash* Series. The questions start on p. 187.

- *Multiple-Choice* questions — These are in a Multistate-Bar-Exam style, and were created especially for this book. They start on p. 243.

- *Essay* questions — These questions are actual ones asked on bar exams, and are adapted from a series we publish called *Siegel's Essay and Multiple-Choice Questions and Answers*. The questions start on p. 269.

I hope you find this book helpful and instructive. Good luck.

If you'd like any other Aspen publication, you can find it at your bookstore or at **http://lawschool.aspenpublishers.com**.

Steve Emanuel
Larchmont, NY
January 2009

FLOW CHARTS

TABLE OF CONTENTS
to
FLOW CHARTS

Note: The cross-references in the Flow Charts' footnotes (e.g., "See Ch.6, V(B)") are to the full-length *Emanuel Law Outline* on Corporations (2009 Ed.) Where no chapter is included in the cross-reference (e.g., "See III(C)(1)"), the reference is to a place in the chapter corresponding to the Flow Chart. (E.g.: if the Flow Chart is "Figure 3-4," a reference in it to "III(C)(1)" is to section III in Chapter 3 of the *Emanuel Law Outline*.)

Figure 2-1
Pre-Incorporation Transactions by Promoters

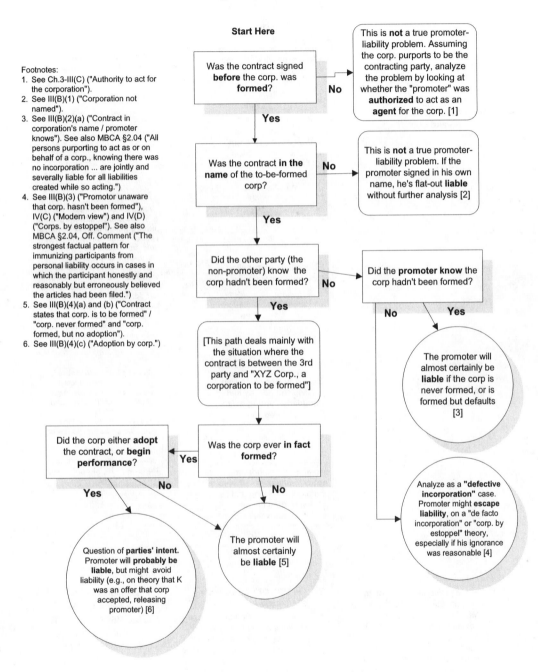

Footnotes:
1. See Ch.3-III(C) ("Authority to act for the corporation").
2. See III(B)(1) ("Corporation not named").
3. See III(B)(2)(a) ("Contract in corporation's name / promoter knows"). See also MBCA §2.04 ("All persons purporting to act as or on behalf of a corp., knowing there was no incorporation ... are jointly and severally liable for all liabilities created while so acting.")
4. See III(B)(3) ("Promotor unaware that corp. hasn't been formed"), IV(C) ("Modern view") and IV(D) ("Corps. by estoppel"). See also MBCA §2.04, Off. Comment ("The strongest factual pattern for immunizing participants from personal liability occurs in cases in which the participant honestly and reasonably but erroneously believed the articles had been filed.")
5. See III(B)(4)(a) and (b) ("Contract states that corp. is to be formed" / "corp. never formed" and "corp. formed, but no adoption").
6. See III(B)(4)(c) ("Adoption by corp.")

Start Here

Was the contract signed **before** the corp. was **formed**?

No → This is **not** a true promoter-liability problem. Assuming the corp. purports to be the contracting party, analyze the problem by looking at whether the "promoter" was **authorized** to act as an **agent** for the corp. [1]

Yes

Was the contract **in the name** of the to-be-formed corp?

No → This is **not** a true promoter-liability problem. If the promoter signed in his own name, he's flat-out **liable** without further analysis [2]

Yes

Did the other party (the non-promoter) know the corp hadn't been formed?

No → Did the **promoter know** the corp hadn't been formed?

No   **Yes**

Yes

[This path deals mainly with the situation where the contract is between the 3rd party and "XYZ Corp., a corporation to be formed"]

The promoter will almost certainly be **liable** if the corp is never formed, or is formed but defaults [3]

Did the corp either **adopt** the contract, or **begin performance**?

Yes ← Was the corp ever **in fact formed**?

No   **No**

Yes

Question of **parties' intent**. Promoter will **probably be liable**, but might avoid liability (e.g., on theory that K was an offer that corp accepted, releasing promoter) [6]

The promoter will almost certainly be **liable** [5]

Analyze as a **"defective incorporation"** case. Promoter might **escape liability**, on a "de facto incorporation" or "corp. by estoppel" theory, especially if his ignorance was reasonable [4]

Figure 3-1
Election of Directors
(under the MBCA)[1]

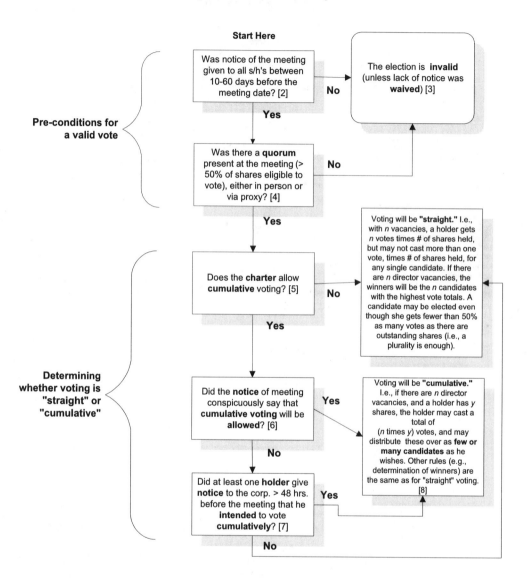

1. Some provisions shown on this diagram are particular to the MBCA (e.g., the precise advance period for notice of the meeting), but most are comparable to those found in most states (e.g., the requirement of a quorum, or how cumulative voting works).

2. See MBCA §7.05(a). "s/h" = "shareholder."

3. Waiver will occur if either: (a) the s/h signs a document waiving notice; or (b) the s/h attends the meeting without objecting, at the beginning of the meeting, to the lack of notice. See MBCA §7.06.

4. See MBCA §7.25(a).
5. See MBCA §7.28(b).
6. See MBCA §7.28(d)(1)
7. See MBCA §7.28(d)(2)
8. See MBCA §7.28(c).

Figure 3-2
Removal of a Director
(under the MBCA)

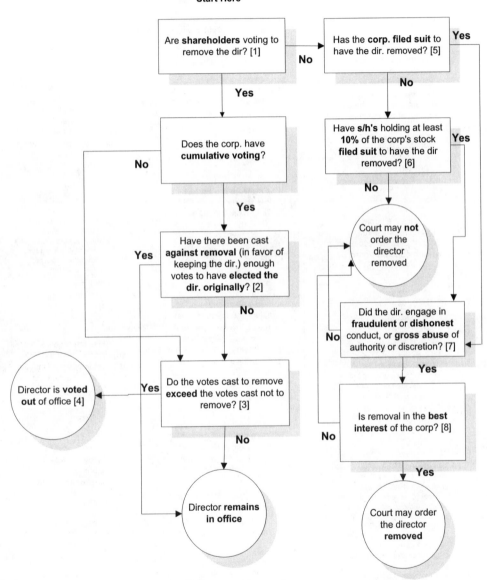

Start Here

Footnotes:

1. All the usual formalities for s/h action (notice; quorum, etc.) apply to a vote to remove a dir. Also, the notice of meeting must state that the purpose is to remove the director. See MBCA §8.08(d).

2. This is necessary to prevent the removal power from being used to negate the effect of cumulative voting. See MBCA §8.08(c), 1st sent.

3. See MBCA §8.08(c), 2d sent. Notice that a plurality of shares outstanding can remove a director, if the turnout is light.

4. Notice that the s/h do not have to have "cause" for removal.

5. This will presumably have to be done by board action, i.e., by a majority of those voting, when a quorum of the board is present. Presumably the director to be removed may vote against the filing of the suit.

6. See MBCA §8.09(a).

7. Id.

8. Id.

Figure 3-3
Formalities for Board Action
(under the MBCA)

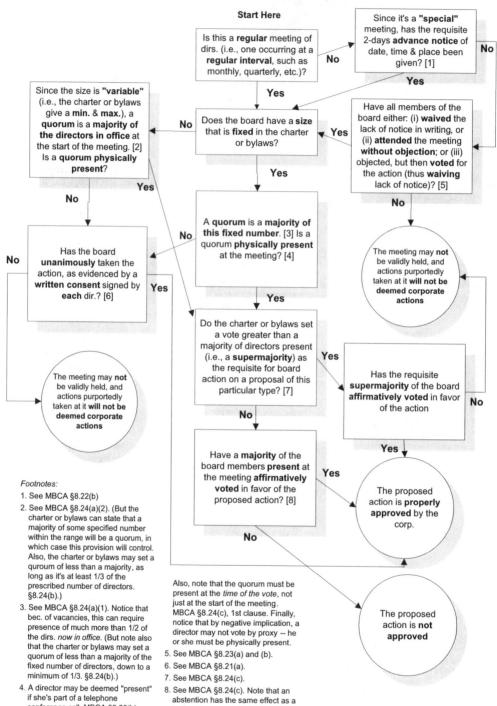

Footnotes:

1. See MBCA §8.22(b)

2. See MBCA §8.24(a)(2). (But the charter or bylaws can state that a majority of some specified number within the range will be a quorum, in which case this provision will control. Also, the charter or bylaws may set a quorum of less than a majority, as long as it's at least 1/3 of the prescribed number of directors. §8.24(b).)

3. See MBCA §8.24(a)(1). Notice that bec. of vacancies, this can require presence of much more than 1/2 of the dirs. *now in office*. (But note also that the charter or bylaws may set a quorum of less than a majority of the fixed number of directors, down to a minimum of 1/3. §8.24(b).)

4. A director may be deemed "present" if she's part of a telephone conference call. MBCA §8.20(b).

Also, note that the quorum must be present at the *time of the vote*, not just at the start of the meeting. MBCA §8.24(c), 1st clause. Finally, notice that by negative implication, a director may not vote by proxy -- he or she must be physically present.

5. See MBCA §8.23(a) and (b).

6. See MBCA §8.21(a).

7. See MBCA §8.24(c).

8. See MBCA §8.24(c). Note that an abstention has the same effect as a "no" vote.

Figure 3-4
When Does a Person Have
Authority to Act for a Corporation?

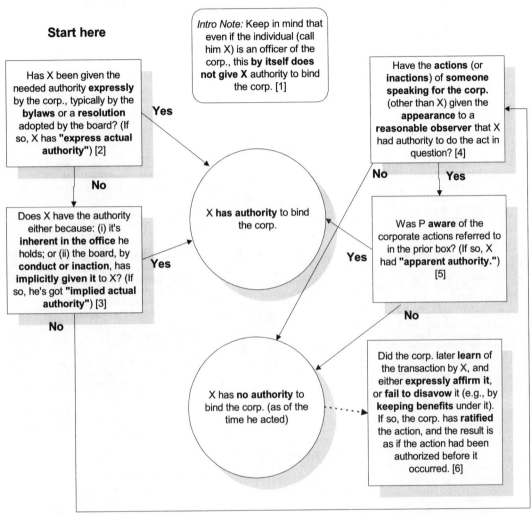

Start here

Has X been given the needed authority **expressly** by the corp., typically by the **bylaws** or a **resolution** adopted by the board? (If so, X has **"express actual authority"**) [2]

Intro Note: Keep in mind that even if the individual (call him X) is an officer of the corp., this **by itself does not give X** authority to bind the corp. [1]

Have the **actions** (or **inactions**) of **someone speaking for the corp.** (other than X) given the **appearance** to a **reasonable observer** that X had authority to do the act in question? [4]

Yes

No

Does X have the authority either because: (i) it's **inherent in the office** he holds; or (ii) the board, by **conduct or inaction**, has **implicitly given it** to X? (If so, he's got **implied actual authority**") [3]

X **has authority** to bind the corp.

No   **Yes**

Was P **aware** of the corporate actions referred to in the prior box? (If so, X had **"apparent authority."**) [5]

Yes   **Yes**

No

No

X has **no authority** to bind the corp. (as of the time he acted)

Did the corp. later **learn** of the transaction by X, and either **expressly affirm it**, or **fail to disavow** it (e.g., by **keeping benefits** under it). If so, the corp. has **ratified** the action, and the result is as if the action had been authorized before it occurred. [6]

Footnotes:
1. See III(C)(1).
2. See III(C)(3).
3. See III(C)(4)(a) and (b).

4. See III(C)(5)(a).
5. *Id.*
6. See III(C)(6).

Figure 6-1

Has the Director Satisfied Her Duty of Care?

(ALI Approach[1])

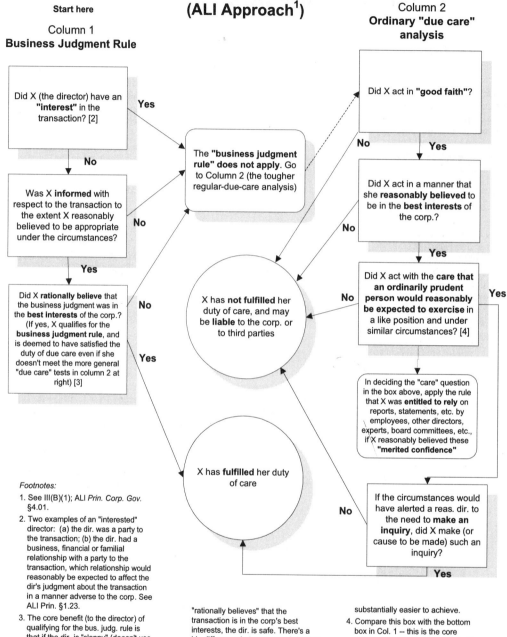

Footnotes:

1. See III(B)(1); ALI *Prin. Corp. Gov.* §4.01.

2. Two examples of an "interested" director: (a) the dir. was a party to the transaction; (b) the dir. had a business, financial or familial relationship with a party to the transaction, which relationship would reasonably be expected to affect the dir's judgment about the transaction in a manner adverse to the corp. See ALI Prin. §1.23.

3. The core benefit (to the director) of qualifying for the bus. judg. rule is that if the dir. is "sloppy" (doesn't use "the care of an ordinarily prudent person,") but the dir. nonetheless "rationally believes" that the transaction is in the corp's best interests, the dir. is safe. There's a big difference between merely having a "rational belief" and taking "ordinary care" -- the former is substantially easier to achieve.

4. Compare this box with the bottom box in Col. 1 -- this is the core difference between qualifying for the bus. judg. rule and not doing so (as described further in note 3 above.)

Figure 7-1
Self-Dealing Transactions
(ALI Approach[1])

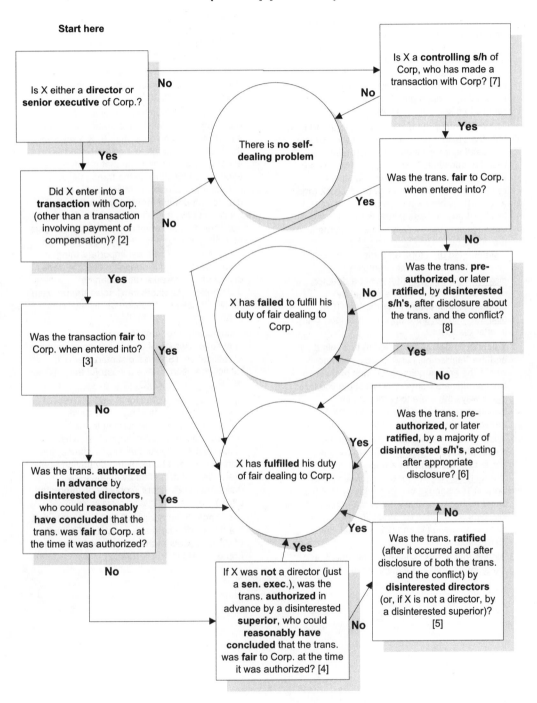

Start here

Is X either a **director** or **senior executive** of Corp.?

Is X a **controlling s/h** of Corp, who has made a transaction with Corp? [7]

Did X enter into a **transaction** with Corp. (other than a transaction involving payment of compensation)? [2]

There is **no self-dealing problem**

Was the trans. **fair** to Corp. when entered into?

Was the transaction **fair** to Corp. when entered into? [3]

X has **failed** to fulfill his duty of fair dealing to Corp.

Was the trans. **pre-authorized**, or later **ratified**, by **disinterested s/h's**, after disclosure about the trans. and the conflict? [8]

Was the trans. **authorized in advance** by **disinterested directors**, who could **reasonably have concluded** that the trans. was **fair** to Corp. at the time it was authorized?

X has **fulfilled** his duty of fair dealing to Corp.

Was the trans. pre-**authorized**, or later **ratified**, by a majority of **disinterested s/h's**, acting after appropriate disclosure? [6]

If X was **not** a director (just a **sen. exec.**), was the trans. **authorized** in advance by a disinterested **superior**, who could **reasonably have concluded** that the trans. was **fair** to Corp. at the time it was authorized? [4]

Was the trans. **ratified** (after it occurred and after disclosure of both the trans. and the conflict) by **disinterested directors** (or, if X is not a director, by a disinterested superior)? [5]

See footnotes on next page

Notes to
Figure 7-1

Footnotes:

1. See ALI Prin. Corp. Gov., §5.02 and §5.10. The ALI approach is considerably tougher on the Key Player (shown here as X) than the approach of the RMBCA or that of most courts. For instance, if the conflict is not disclosed in advance, it's much tougher to get it insulated through post-transaction ratification; see note 5 below.

   The most important basic concept to get from this chart is that there are a number of ways a self-dealing transaction can nonetheless be found to constitute "fair dealing." Thus where X is a director or senior exec. (but isn't a controlling s/h), the transaction will be ok (and X won't be liable for breach of his duty of loyalty) if any of these things is true: (1) the transaction is fair to Corp., in the judgment of the court; (2) it's pre-authorized by disinterested directors, after disclosure of the conflict; (3) it's pre-authorized by a disinterested superior (if X is not a director, only a senior exec.); (4) it's ratified by disinterested directors after the fact; (5) disinterested s/h's pre-approve it or later ratify it, after disclosure.

   You should look at the "failed to fulfill his duty" and the "fulfilled his duty" circles, and see where the arrows pointing to each of these circles originate from -- this will show you how many ways there are to immunize the transaction, and how few ways to have the transaction be a breach of the duty of loyalty.

2. Examples of transactions that would trigger these rules: (1) X sells property to (or buys property from) Corp; (2) X makes a contract to supply services to (or buy services from) Corp.; (3) A spouse or close relative of X (i.e., one who has essentially the same economic interests as X) does a transaction with Corp. such as those in (1) and (2). See ALI Prin., §5.02, Note c.

3. Notice that a "yes" answer to this question pretty much ends the inquiry: if the court thinks the transaction was "fair" to Corp., it doesn't matter that there was no advance disclosure to Corp., or advance approval by disinterested directors or s/h's.

4. If X was a director, go directly to the "ratification" box, which is to the right (and which has note [5] in it).

5. Actually, in addition to the requirements for post-transaction ratification stated in the box, it must also be the case that: (i) X disclosed the then-known facts to a disinterested senior exec. before the trans., (ii) that disinterested exec. acted for Corp. in the trans.; (iii) X did not act unreasonably in failing to get board or disinterested-superior approval before the trans.; and (iv) the failure to get pre-trans. approval did not "adversely affect the interests of [Corp.] in a significant way." See ALI Prin. §5.02(a)(2)(C). The most important thing to note here is that if X doesn't make pre-trans. disclosure to anyone, ratification by disinterested directors can't solve the problem (only fairness or ratification by disinterested shareholders can do that).

6. Additionally, the transaction must not constitute a waste of Corp's assets at the time of ratification. (So even distinterested-s/h ratification cannot save a wasteful trans.) See ALI Prin. §5.02(a)(2)(D).

7. If X is both: (a) a director or senior exec. of Corp. and (b) a controlling s/h of Corp., analyze the problem according to the "controlling s/h" (right-column) test, which is similar but slightly stricter. (For instance, the transaction can't be insulated by having been pre-approved or ratified by supposedly disinterested directors -- only by disinterested s/h's.)

8. As in note 6, an additional requirement is that the transaction not have constituted a waste of Corp's assets at the time of ratification or approval. ALI Prin. §5.10(a)(2).

Figure 7-2
Sale-of-Control Transactions

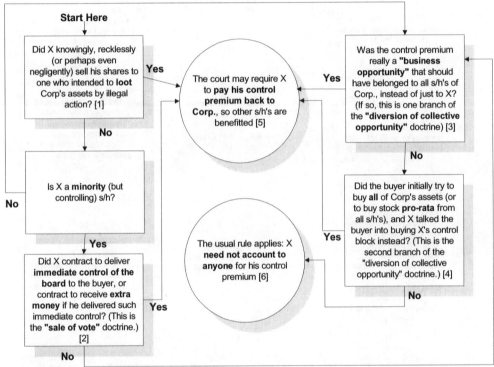

Use this flowchart whenever a **controlling shareholder** (called X in this chart) has **sold his "control block"** for a **"premium,"** i.e., for a high per-share amount in a transaction where other s/h's didn't have the same opportunity to sell

Start Here

Did X knowingly, recklessly (or perhaps even negligently) sell his shares to one who intended to **loot** Corp's assets by illegal action? [1]

Yes

The court may require X to **pay his control premium back to Corp.**, so other s/h's are benefitted [5]

Yes

Was the control premium really a **"business opportunity"** that should have belonged to all s/h's of Corp., instead of just to X? (If so, this is one branch of the **"diversion of collective opportunity"** doctrine) [3]

No

Is X a **minority** (but controlling) s/h?

No

Yes

Did X contract to deliver **immediate control of the board** to the buyer, or contract to receive **extra money** if he delivered such immediate control? (This is the **"sale of vote"** doctrine.) [2]

Yes

No

The usual rule applies: X **need not account to anyone** for his control premium [6]

Did the buyer initially try to buy **all** of Corp's assets (or to buy stock **pro-rata** from all s/h's), and X talked the buyer into buying X's control block instead? (This is the second branch of the "diversion of collective opportunity" doctrine.) [4]

Yes

No

Footnotes:

1. See V(B). Be most alert to this box when the business has a lot of easily-liquidated assets (e.g., an investment company).

2. See V(C). Be especially alert to this possibility when the directors resign *seriatim* right after the sale, and the buyer therefore gets board control even though he has only a minority of the stock. See V(C)(3)(a). (But if buyer retains control at the next regular s/h meeting, this will probably ratify the change of control, and the "sale of vote" doctrine probably won't apply. See V(C)(5).)

"sale of vote" doctrine probably won't apply. See V(C)(5).)

3. See V(D)(1). This is the situation illustrated by <u>Perlman v. Feldmann</u>. It will be an unusual exam fact-pattern that will make a strong case for applying the rule in this box (since <u>Perlman</u> is practically unique).

4. See V(D)(2).

5. The disadvantage of this remedy is that the buyer (who may well have been a semi-wrongdoer) gets a windfall, since he owns a significant

part of Corp. and Corp. is getting this court-ordered "rebate" from X.
Therefore, the court may instead order payments by X directly to the non-controlling s/h's. See V(F)(2).

6. In other words, only if one of the three special exceptions shown in the chart applies (looting, sale-of-vote, or diversion-of-collective-opportunity), may X be forced to disgorge his premium. Thus in the "ordinary" case, X gets to keep the premium.

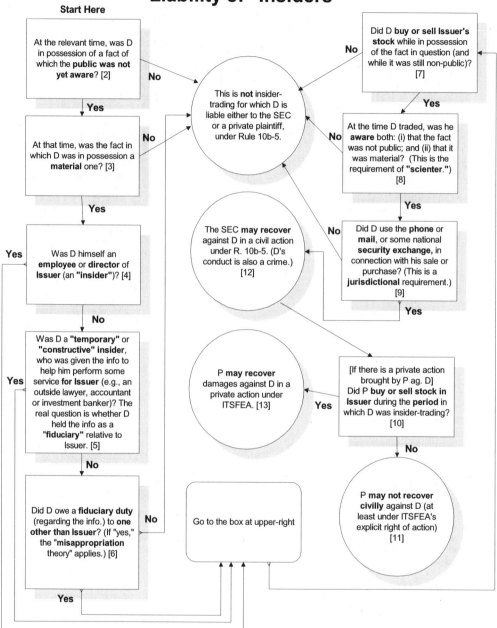

Figure 8-1
Insider Trading:
Liability of "Insiders"[1]

See footnotes on next page

Notes to
Figure 8-1

Footnotes:

1. This chart deals only with the problem in which D is an "<u>insider</u>" (employee, director, temporary professional, etc.) of the Issuer. In other words, it does not deal with the situation in which D is a "<u>tippee</u>." Nor does it deal with the situation in which D, an insider, is liable as a <u>tipper</u> rather than as one who himself buys or sells. See Fig. 8-2 for how to analyze tipper/tippee problems.

2. This is the requirement of "non-public" information. See III(F)(4).

3. See III(F)(3).

4. See III(G)(3).

5. See IV(F).

6. See IV(H)(2), for a discussion of the "<u>misappropriation</u> theory," now accepted by the Supreme Court. Be alert to the misappropriation theory in any fact pattern involving a <u>reporter</u> (who learns the info from his employer, while covering a story on the issuer), <u>printer</u>, <u>professional</u> working for an <u>acquirer</u>, or other person who learns something about the issuer while on the job for an employer other than the issuer.

7. Notice that this chart covers only "insider trading," not other forms of 10b-5 liability. So D can't be liable if he never buys or sells the issuer's stock. (By contrast, if D makes a false statement about Issuer's stock, he can be liable under 10b-5 for the affirmative misstatement, but this isn't insider-trading. See See III(E)(5).) Also, note that this chart only deals with Insider's liability as "principal," i.e., as the one who did the buying and selling. If Insider is a <u>tipper</u>, he might be liable as such even though only the tippee did any buying or selling. For the tipper's liability, see Fig. 8-2, nn. 5, 6 and 10.

Finally, note that <u>mere possession</u> of the inside info is <u>enough</u> for a "yes" answer -- there's no requirement that the inside info have <u>caused</u> the purchase or sale (so D can't argue, "I would have bought [or sold] anyway, even without the info.") SEC Rule 10b-5-1. (But if D had <u>irrevocably committed</u> to the purchase or sale before getting possession of the inside info, then answer "no," because of SEC Rule 10b-5-1's "safe harbor" for pre-planned trading programs.) See III(F).

8. For the requirement of scienter, see III(H)(5).

9. See III(D)(7).

10. For the requirement that P buy or sell, generally, see III(E), including <u>Blue Chip Stamps</u>. For the "contemporaneous trader" requirement imposed by ITSFEA, see III(L)(1)(b).

11. At least, P may not recover under the ITSFEA (Insider Trading and Securities Fraud Enforcement Act of 1988), which gives an express private right of action for contemporaneous traders victimized by 10b-5 violations. A court might still grant an <u>implied</u> private right of action to one who was hurt by insider trading but who did not trade contemporaneously (e.g., an <u>acquirer</u> of Issuer, who bought some shares before the insider traded and then had to pay more for shares acquired after the insider traded.) See IV(H)(2)(e).

12. D's conduct is almost certainly a criminal violation of the federal mail- and wire-fraud statutes. See IV(H)(1).

13. But P's recovery is probably the <u>lesser</u> of: (i) P's actual damages; and (ii) D's gains made (or losses avoided) by virtue of the insider-trading. See III(M)(2)(a).

Figure 8-2
Insider Trading:
Liability of "Tippees" under 10b-5[1]

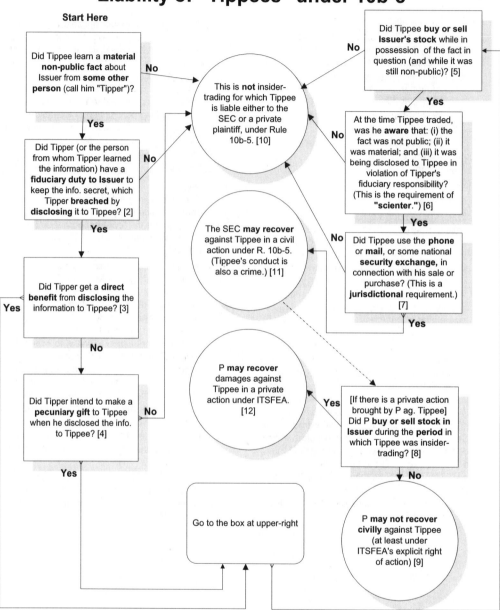

Start Here

Did Tippee learn a **material non-public fact** about Issuer from **some other person** (call him "Tipper")?

No →

Yes ↓

Did Tipper (or the person from whom Tipper learned the information) have a **fiduciary duty to Issuer** to keep the info. secret, which Tipper **breached** by **disclosing** it to Tippee? [2]

No →

Yes ↓

Did Tipper get a **direct benefit** from **disclosing** the information to Tippee? [3]

Yes ←

No ↓

Did Tipper intend to make a **pecuniary gift** to Tippee when he disclosed the info. to Tippee? [4]

No →

Yes ↓

This is **not** insider-trading for which Tippee is liable either to the SEC or a private plaintiff, under Rule 10b-5. [10]

Did Tippee **buy or sell Issuer's stock** while in possession of the fact in question (and while it was still non-public)? [5]

No →

Yes ↓

At the time Tippee traded, was he **aware** that: (i) the fact was not public; (ii) it was material; and (iii) it was being disclosed to Tippee in violation of Tipper's fiduciary responsibility? (This is the requirement of **"scienter."**) [6]

No →

Yes ↓

Did Tippee use the **phone** or **mail**, or some national **security exchange, in** connection with his sale or purchase? (This is a **jurisdictional** requirement.) [7]

No →

Yes ↓

The SEC **may recover** against Tippee in a civil action under R. 10b-5. (Tippee's conduct is also a crime.) [11]

P **may recover** damages against Tippee in a private action under ITSFEA. [12]

Yes ←

[If there is a private action brought by P ag. Tippee] Did P **buy or sell stock in Issuer** during the **period** in which Tippee was insider-trading? [8]

No ↓

P **may not recover civilly** against Tippee (at least under ITSFEA's explicit right of action) [9]

Go to the box at upper-right

See footnotes on next page

Notes to
Figure 8-2

Footnotes:

1. This chart deals only with the problem in which D is an "tippee," i.e., one who learned the information directly or indirectly from an "insider" of the issuer. That is, it does not deal with the situation in which D is himself an insider. See Fig. 8-1 for how to analyze insider problems.

2. If the tipper had no fiduciary duty, nothing the tippee does or thinks can make the tippee liable under 10b-5. See Dirks v. SEC; also III(G)(4)(c) and IV(B)(1). If the tipper had a fiduciary duty to someone other than the issuer (e.g., tipper was a reporter for a newspaper which had secret info about the Issuer), the tippee might be liable under the "misappropriation theory"; see Fig. 8-1, n. 6; also IV(H)(2)(f). For this chart, treat the situation in which the tipper had a duty to a non-issuer who gave him the information the same as if the tipper had a duty to the issuer.

3. The tipper must either get a personal benefit from the disclosure (this box) or intend to confer a pecuniary benefit on the tippee (the next box). See Dirks v. SEC; also III(G)(4)(c)(i) and IV(B)(3). For instance, if Tipper tells Tippee the info because he wants Tippee to publicize the info to combat wrongdoing, neither test is satisfied, and Tippee has no liability (this was the situation in Dirks).

4. See Dirks v. SEC; III(G)(4)(c)(i) and IV(B)(3).

5. Notice that this chart covers only "insider trading," not other forms of 10b-5 liability. So Tippee can't be liable if he never buys or sells the issuer's stock. (By contrast, if Tippee makes a false statement about Issuer's stock, he can be liable under 10b-5 for the affirmative misstatement, but this isn't insider-trading. See III(E)(5).)

   Also, note that if Tippee is liable, Tipper will also be liable, even though Tipper never bought or sold. See III(G)(4) and IV(E).

6. For the requirement of scienter, see III(H)(5). Note that in contrast to the "Insider-as-Defendant" scenario, here the defendant (Tippee) must be shown to have known not only that the fact was material and non-public,

but also that it was disclosed to him in violation of Tipper's fiduciary duty. So even if Tipper knows he's breaching a confidence to Issuer, if Tippee's not aware of this fact Tippee isn't liable. See IV(B)(2); U.S. v. Chestman (discussed in IV(G)(2)). (But in that event, Tipper might still be liable.)

   If Tippee is a spouse, parent, child or sibling of Tipper, SEC Rule 10b-5-2 imposes a rebuttable presumption that Tippee knew he had a fiduciary duty to keep the info confidential and not to trade on it. So unless Tippee successfully rebuts the presumption, answer "yes" to part (iii) of the question in this box.

7. See III(D)(7).

8. For the requirement that P buy or sell, generally, see III(E), including Blue Chip Stamps. For the "contemporaneous trader" requirement imposed by ITSFEA, see III(L)(1)(b).

9. At least, P may not recover under the ITSFEA (Insider Trading and Securities Fraud Enforcement Act of 1988), which gives an express private right of action for contemporaneous traders victimized by 10b-5 violations. A court might still grant an implied private right of action to one who was hurt by insider trading but who did not trade contemporaneously (e.g., an acquirer of Issuer, who bought some shares before the insider traded and then had to pay more for shares acquired after the insider traded.) See IV(H)2)(e).

10. Even if Tippee is not liable, Tipper might still be. In particular, if Tipper has knowingly disclosed a confidence from Issuer to Tipper, and has intended to give Tippee a pecuniary benefit, Tipper will be liable even if Tippee doesn't know about the breach of confidence.

11. Tippee's conduct is almost certainly a criminal violation of the federal mail- and wire-fraud statutes. See IV(H)(1).

12. But P's recovery is probably the lesser of: (i) P's actual damages; and (ii) D's gains made (or losses avoided) by virtue of the insider-trading. See III(M)(2)(a).

Figure 8-3
Short-Swing Profits under §16(b)

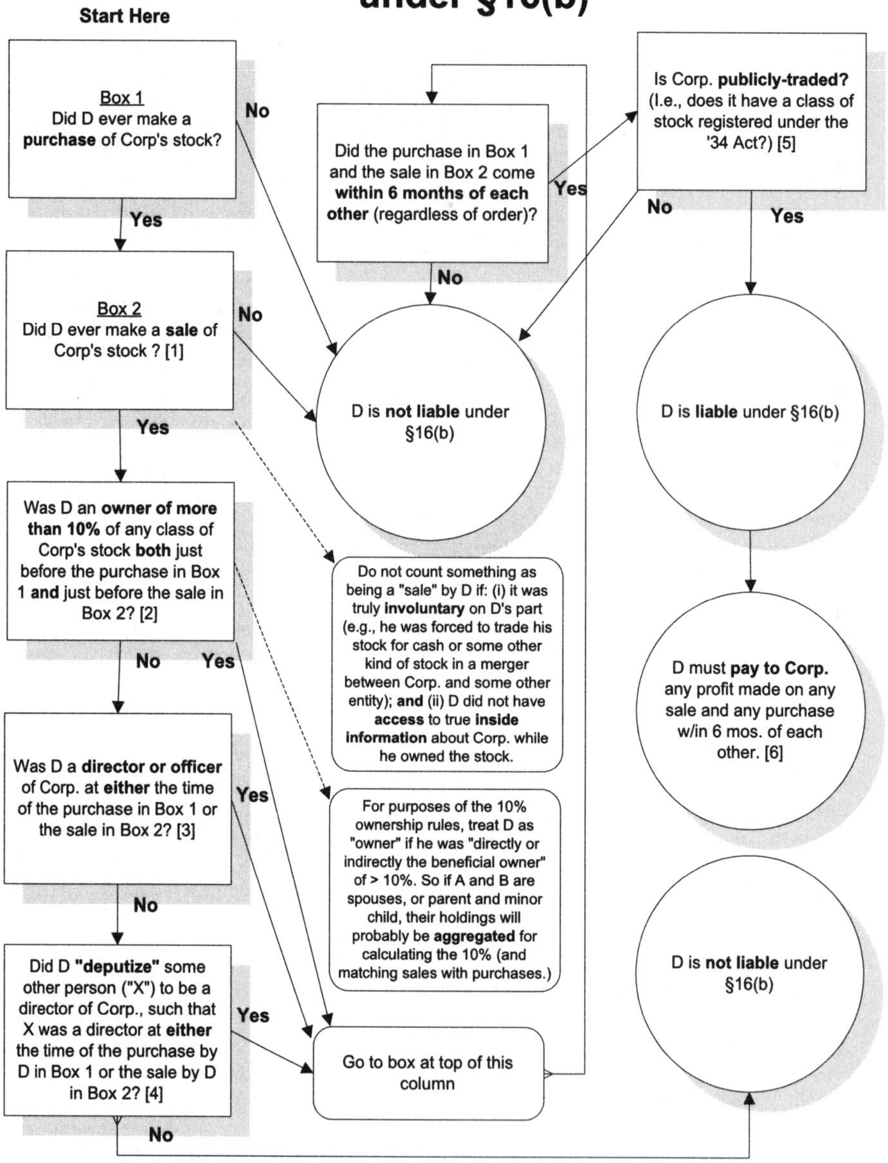

Start Here

Box 1
Did D ever make a **purchase** of Corp's stock?

→ **No**

Did the purchase in Box 1 and the sale in Box 2 come **within 6 months of each other** (regardless of order)?

→ **Yes** → Is Corp. **publicly-traded?** (I.e., does it have a class of stock registered under the '34 Act?) [5]

↓ **Yes**

Box 2
Did D ever make a **sale** of Corp's stock ? [1]

→ **No**

→ **No**

No → D is **not liable** under §16(b)

Yes → D is **liable** under §16(b)

↓ **Yes**

Was D an **owner of more than 10%** of any class of Corp's stock **both** just before the purchase in Box 1 **and** just before the sale in Box 2? [2]

Do not count something as being a "sale" by D if: (i) it was truly **involuntary** on D's part (e.g., he was forced to trade his stock for cash or some other kind of stock in a merger between Corp. and some other entity); **and** (ii) D did not have **access** to true **inside information** about Corp. while he owned the stock.

↓ **No** / **Yes**

D must **pay to Corp.** any profit made on any sale and any purchase w/in 6 mos. of each other. [6]

Was D a **director or officer** of Corp. at **either** the time of the purchase in Box 1 or the sale in Box 2? [3]

→ **Yes**

For purposes of the 10% ownership rules, treat D as "owner" if he was "directly or indirectly the beneficial owner" of > 10%. So if A and B are spouses, or parent and minor child, their holdings will probably be **aggregated** for calculating the 10% (and matching sales with purchases.)

↓ **No**

D is **not liable** under §16(b)

Did D **"deputize"** some other person ("X") to be a director of Corp., such that X was a director at **either** the time of the purchase by D in Box 1 or the sale by D in Box 2? [4]

→ **Yes** → Go to box at top of this column

↓ **No**

Footnotes:

1. On the issue of what is a "sale," see VI(E).

2. On the meaning of "owner," especially "beneficial owner," see VI(C)(2). On the requirement that D be an owner at both the buy time and the sell time, see VI(D)(2).

3. On the definition of "officer," see VI(C)(1). As to the fact that being an officer at either the buy time or sell time will suffice, see VI(D)(1).

4. See VI(C)(3).

5. On the requirement that Corp.'s stock be registered under the '34 Act, see VI(B)(2).

6. On the computation of profits, see VI(F). Note that the court will pair any buy and any sell that represent a net profit, and force D to disgorge the profit on that pairing, regardless of what D's overall profit/loss position was during the 6 mos.

Figure 9-1
Analyzing a Derivative Suit[1]

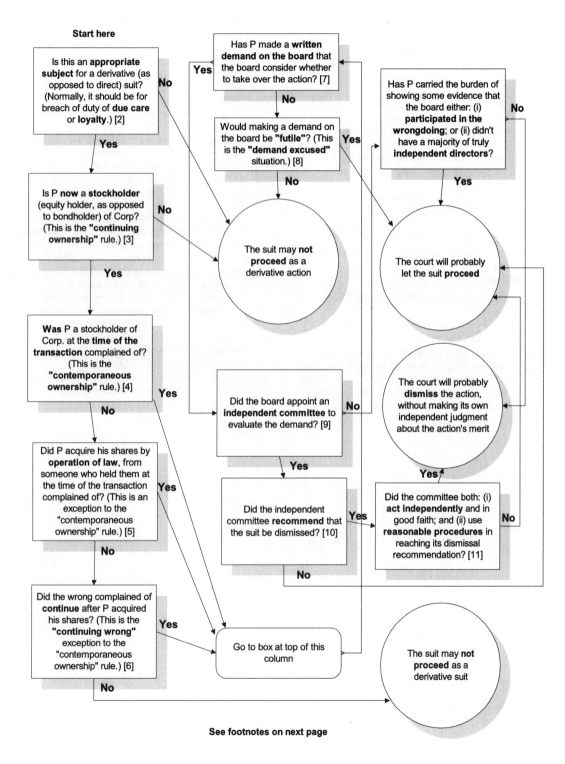

Start here

Is this an **appropriate subject** for a derivative (as opposed to direct) suit? (Normally, it should be for breach of duty of **due care** or **loyalty**.) [2]

Is P **now a stockholder** (equity holder, as opposed to bondholder) of Corp? (This is the **"continuing ownership"** rule.) [3]

Was P a stockholder of Corp. at the **time of the transaction** complained of? (This is the **"contemporaneous ownership"** rule.) [4]

Did P acquire his shares by **operation of law**, from someone who held them at the time of the transaction complained of? (This is an exception to the "contemporaneous ownership" rule.) [5]

Did the wrong complained of **continue** after P acquired his shares? (This is the **"continuing wrong"** exception to the "contemporaneous ownership" rule.) [6]

Has P made a **written demand on the board** that the board consider whether to take over the action? [7]

Would making a demand on the board be **"futile"**? (This is the **"demand excused"** situation.) [8]

The suit may **not proceed** as a derivative action

Did the board appoint an **independent committee** to evaluate the demand? [9]

Did the independent committee **recommend** that the suit be dismissed? [10]

Go to box at top of this column

Has P carried the burden of showing some evidence that the board either: (i) **participated in the wrongdoing**; or (ii) didn't have a majority of truly **independent directors**?

The court will probably let the suit **proceed**

The court will probably **dismiss** the action, without making its own independent judgment about the action's merit

Did the committee both: (i) **act independently** and in good faith; and (ii) use **reasonable procedures** in reaching its dismissal recommendation? [11]

The suit may **not proceed** as a derivative suit

See footnotes on next page

Notes to
Figure 9-1

Footnotes:

1. This flowchart analyzes derivative suits from a non-state-specific perspective, except that the law of Delaware is reflected on a number of points.

2. For instance, suits alleging that an insider failed to use due care, or engaged in self-dealing, or was paid excessive compensation, or usurped a corporate opportunity, will be derivative. Suits to compel dividends, to overturn improper anti-takeover devices, or to prevent oppression of minority s/h's, will generally be direct rather than derivative. See II(A)(2).

3. On the general requirement that P be a stockholder (as opposed to, say, a bondholder), see III(B). On the "continuing ownership" requirement, see III(D).

4. On the "contemporaneous ownership" rule, see III(C).

5. See II(C)(6).

6. On the "continuing wrong" exception, see III(C)(5).

7. On the demand-on-board requirement generally, see III(E).

8. In determining whether demand is excused because it's likely to be futile, see IV(B)(2) and (3). In determining whether demand would be "futile," courts (especially Del. courts) give weight to: (i) whether the board itself is charged with wrongdoing (favors a finding of futility); (ii) whether the board was disinterested and truly independent of the wrongdoer (favors non-futility); (iii) whether the board followed adequate procedures (favors non-futility); and (iv) whether the board's action was rational (favors non-futility). See IV(B)(3).

   If, despite the fact that demand on the board was excused, the board appoints an independent committee to consider the merits of the action, the court may consider the committee's recommendation (usually to dismiss the action) as if this were a "demand-required" case. However, the court is more likely to let the action go forward in this situation than in the demand-required/independent-committee situation. See IV(B)(1).

9. See IV(D). In considering whether the committee was "independent," many courts – especially those of Delaware – will take into account social ties between committee members and defendants. *Example:* Where committee members and defendants all have significant ties to Stanford University, the committee was not independent, and its dismissal recommendation was not entitled to judicial deference. [*In Re Oracle*]

10. Only rarely will the board not recommend that the action be dismissed. See IV(D)(1)(c).

11. See IV(D)(4)(b).

Figure 9-2
Indemnification of Directors and Officers[1]

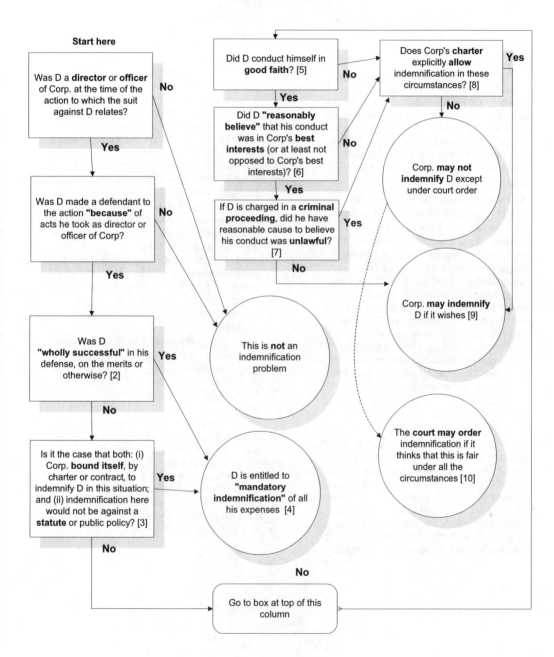

See footnotes on next page

Notes to
Figure 9-2

Footnotes:

1. This flowchart is not state-specific. It tries to give an overview of the way in which many states handle indemnification. It relies -- though not exclusively -- on the provisions of the MBCA.

2. On the "wholly successful" requirement for mandatory indemnification, see IX(C)(1). Notice that in most states, the suit does not have to be resolved through a judgment on the merits. Thus a dismissal on procedural grounds (e.g., statute of limitations), or even a settlement for a nominal sum, might be "wholly successful." See MBCA §8.52.

3. See IX(C)(2).

4. "Mandatory" indemnification essentially means that even if the corporation doesn't want to indemnify, it must do so.

   Where the case becomes "mandatory" because of a provision in Corp's charter (rather than because D was "wholly successful" in his defense), there are some exceptions to the mandatoriness. For instance, if the suit is a derivative one, Corp. won't be required to reimburse D for the judgment itself (just expenses) if D was significantly at fault; see MBCA §8.51(d)(1). (This avoids a circularity problem, in which D has to pay Corp., which pays him right back.) See n. 9 below for further info.

5. On the requirement of "good faith," see MBCA §8.51(a)(1)(i).

6. See MBCA §8.51(a)(1)(ii). In many states (and under the MBCA), the precise standard depends on whether D was acting in his official capacity. If D was acting in his official capacity as director or officer, he must have believed that his action was actually "in the corporation's best interests," but if he was acting in his private capacity (e.g., as the other party to a transaction with Corp., or as the taker of what was arguably a corporate opportunity), he must merely have believed that his action was "not opposed" to Corp's best interests. *Id.*

7. See MBCA §8.51(a)(1)(iii). If the case is not a criminal proceeding, treat the answer to this question as being "no" (so that Corp. may indemnify).

8. In other words, if Corp's charter explicitly allows or requires indemnification even in situations where most states wouldn't allow it (e.g., D's belief that his act was in Corp's best interests was not a reasonable one), most courts allow Corp. to indemnify. See MBCA §8.51(a)(2). (But there are exceptions -- see n. 9 below.)

9. If D meets the requirements of the three boxes at the top of the middle column (good faith, reasonable belief about best interests of Corp., and no reason to belief conduct unlawful), there are no exceptions to the general rule that Corp. may indemnify. But if D has flunked one of those requirements, and we get to the "may indemnify" circle only because Corp.'s charter allows or requires indemnification in this circumstance, there are two important exceptions:

   (a) in a derivative action, most states won't allow indemnification of D for any judgment for Corp. (just litigation expenses, and then only if D's conduct was in good faith) no matter what the charter says – see, e.g., MBCA §8.51(d)(1); and

   (b) some states won't allow indemnification if D received an inappropriate financial benefit (e.g., insider trading gains) from the transaction. (See MBCA §8.51(d)(2) (no indemnification allowed, even if charter allows, where D "received a financial benefit to which he was not entitled, whether or not involving action in his official capacity."))

10. See IX(G); MBCA §8.54(a)(3).

Figure 10-7
The Williams Act:
Analyzing an Acquirer's Compliance

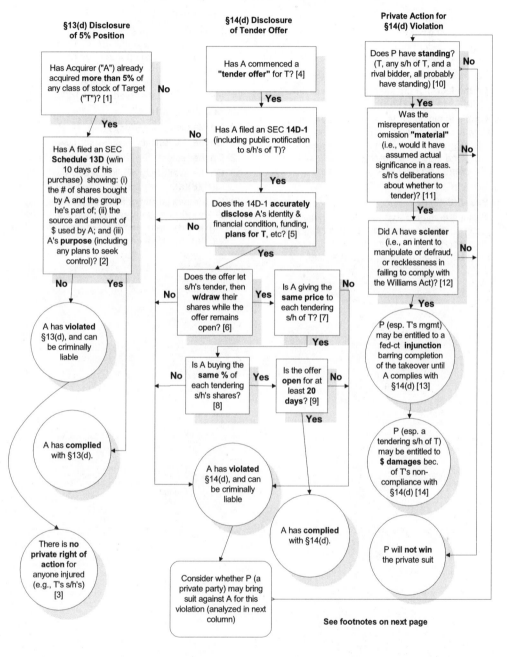

§13(d) Disclosure of 5% Position

Has Acquirer ("A") already acquired **more than 5%** of any class of stock of Target ("T")? [1]

No

Yes

Has A filed an SEC **Schedule 13D** (w/in 10 days of his purchase) showing: (i) the # of shares bought by A and the group he's part of; (ii) the source and amount of $ used by A; and (iii) A's **purpose** (including any plans to seek control)? [2]

No **Yes**

A has **violated** §13(d), and can be criminally liable

A has **complied** with §13(d).

There is **no private right of action** for anyone injured (e.g., T's s/h's) [3]

§14(d) Disclosure of Tender Offer

Has A commenced a **"tender offer"** for T? [4]

Yes

Has A filed an SEC **14D-1** (including public notification to s/h's of T)?

No

Yes

Does the 14D-1 **accurately disclose** A's identity & financial condition, funding, **plans for T**, etc? [5]

No

Yes

Does the offer let s/h's tender, then **w/draw** their shares while the offer remains open? [6]

No **Yes**

Is A giving the **same price** to each tendering s/h of T? [7]

No

Yes

Is A buying the **same %** of each tendering s/h's shares? [8]

No **Yes**

Is the offer **open** for at least **20 days**? [9]

No

Yes

A has **violated** §14(d), and can be criminally liable

A has **complied** with §14(d).

Consider whether P (a private party) may bring suit against A for this violation (analyzed in next column)

Private Action for §14(d) Violation

Does P have **standing**? (T, any s/h of T, and a rival bidder, all probably have standing) [10]

No

Yes

Was the misrepresentation or omission **"material"** (i.e., would it have assumed actual significance in a reas. s/h's deliberations about whether to tender)? [11]

No

Yes

Did A have **scienter** (i.e., an intent to manipulate or defraud, or recklessness in failing to comply with the Williams Act)? [12]

No

Yes

P (esp. T's mgmt) may be entitled to a fed-ct **injunction** barring completion of the takeover until A complies with §14(d) [13]

P (esp. a tendering s/h of T) may be entitled to **$ damages** bec. of T's non-compliance with §14(d) [14]

P will **not win** the private suit

See footnotes on next page

Notes to
Figure 10-7

Footnotes:

1. On the 5% threshold generally, see VI(B). On the issue of when acquirers are aggregated as a "group" for purposes of the 5% threshold, see VI(F)(1).

2. For what must be disclosed, see VI(B)(1).

3. On the lack of a private right of action under §13(d), see VI(F)(2)(b)(i).

4. On the meaning of "tender offer," see VI(G). Note that an acquirer's private offer to <u>one or a few s/h's</u> to buy their stake is not a tender offer, and thus does not trigger the §14(d) disclosure or "equal treatment" duties.

5. See VI(C)(1).

6. See VI(C)(2)(a).

7. This is the "<u>best price</u>" rule. In particular, it requires that if A offers one price initially and then increases it later, the increased price must be paid to those who have already

tendered. See VI(C)(2)(c).

8. This is the "<u>pro rata</u>" rule, which requires that if A is buying less than all the shares tendered, it must buy the same percentage of each tenderer's shares (so it can't, for instance, give an incentive for early tendering by saying, "First come, first served"). See VI(C)(2)(b).

9. See VI(C)(2)(d).

10. On standing, see VI(H)(4).

11. On the "materiality" requirement, see VI(H)(5).

12. On the "scienter" requirement, see VI(H)(6).

13. On the availability of injunctions, see VI(H)(8)(a).

14. On the availability of money damages, see VI(H)(4)(b) (no damages for competing bidder); VI(H)(4)(d) (damages for tendering s/h); VI(H)(8)(b) (damages generally).

Figure 10-8
Takeovers: The Judicial Response
to Defensive Measures[1]

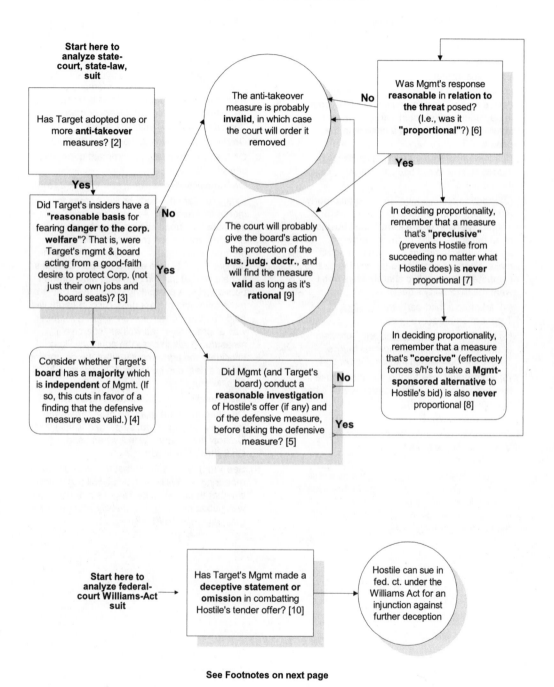

Start here to analyze state-court, state-law, suit

Has Target adopted one or more **anti-takeover** measures? [2]

Yes

Did Target's insiders have a **"reasonable basis** for fearing **danger to the corp. welfare"**? That is, were Target's mgmt & board acting from a good-faith desire to protect Corp. (not just their own jobs and board seats)? [3]

No

Yes

Consider whether Target's **board** has a **majority** which is **independent** of Mgmt. (If so, this cuts in favor of a finding that the defensive measure was valid.) [4]

The anti-takeover measure is probably **invalid**, in which case the court will order it removed

The court will probably give the board's action the protection of the **bus. judg. doctr.**, and will find the measure **valid** as long as it's **rational** [9]

Did Mgmt (and Target's board) conduct a **reasonable investigation** of Hostile's offer (if any) and of the defensive measure, before taking the defensive measure? [5]

No

Yes

Was Mgmt's response **reasonable** in **relation to the threat** posed? (I.e., was it **"proportional"**?) [6]

No

Yes

In deciding proportionality, remember that a measure that's **"preclusive"** (prevents Hostile from succeeding no matter what Hostile does) is **never** proportional [7]

In deciding proportionality, remember that a measure that's **"coercive"** (effectively forces s/h's to take a **Mgmt-sponsored alternative** to Hostile's bid) is also **never** proportional [8]

Start here to analyze federal-court Williams-Act suit

Has Target's Mgmt made a **deceptive statement or omission** in combatting Hostile's tender offer? [10]

Hostile can sue in fed. ct. under the Williams Act for an injunction against further deception

See Footnotes on next page

Notes to
Figure 10-8

Footnotes:

1. This chart relies mainly on Delaware law. Courts in other states follow more or less the same principles in scrutinizing anti-takeover measures.

2. Examples include:

   (1) adoption of a "<u>poison pill</u>" (typically, a device giving Target's present s/h's the option to buy additional stock in Target at a very favorable price if there is a change in the control of Target);

   (2) payment of "<u>greenmail</u>" to Hostile to induce Hostile to sell back its Target stock to Target;

   (3) granting of a "<u>lock up</u>" to some third party (such as: (a) an option to buy some asset of Target, often its "crown jewel" [best business], at an attractive price; or (b) a merger agreement with a third party on terms that make it hard or impossible for anyone else to compete, even if public shareholders don't want the third party's deal);

   (4) option to a third-party to <u>buy stock</u> in Target at an attractive price;

   (5) enactment of a "<u>supermajority</u>" provision (e.g., requiring 2/3's s/h approval before Target can be merged into another entity);

   (6) staggered terms for the board (to make it harder for Hostile to gain control even if it has a majority of the stock).

   See generally VIII(B).

3. On reasonable fear for corp. welfare, see VIII(G)(1). Some fears that may be considered:

   (1) that bidder will change Target's business practices in a harmful way (e.g., by breaking it up and selling off the pieces); (2) that Hostile's offer is coercive to s/h's; (3) that Hostile will overburden Target with debt.

4. On the significance of an <u>independent board</u>, see VIII(G)(4). Notice that having or not having an independent board (i.e., a board a majority of whose members are independent of management) is <u>never dispositive</u> in either direction -- what happens is merely that if the board is independent, the court is more likely to uphold any given anti-takeover measure than if the board isn't independent.

5. On reasonable investigation, see VIII(G)(3).

6. On the proportionality requirement generally, see VIII(G)(2).

7. On "preclusive" measures, see VIII(G)(2)(a)(i).

   <u>Example</u>: Target, nearly broke, agrees to merge into Acquirer. Acquirer demands an absolute lock-up, by which Target's controlling S/H's irrevocably promise to vote for the merger, and Target's board agrees to put the merger to a S/H vote even if the board comes to believe that this isn't the best deal for the public S/H's. A competing bidder then offers a more favorable merger deal. A court might well hold that the merger agreement with Acquirer was a "preclusive" (as well as "coercive") measure, in which case the court will likely invalidate the agreement so that the competing bidder's deal can be taken. [*Omnicare v. NCS Healthcare*]

8. On "coercive" measures, see VIII(G)(2)(a)(ii).

9. On when the court uses the pro-management "business judgment doctrine," see VIII(F)(2)(e). On how this doctrine works when used, see Ch.6-III(B)(1) and (5).

10. See VI(H), VIII(D). Note that the federal court rehearing the Williams Act suit will <u>not</u> review whether the conduct by Target's management was substantively <u>unfair</u>, merely whether it was <u>deceptive</u>; see VIII(D)(2).

Figure 10-9

Takeovers: Multi-Bidder Contests & Other Merger Scenarios, under Delaware Law[1]

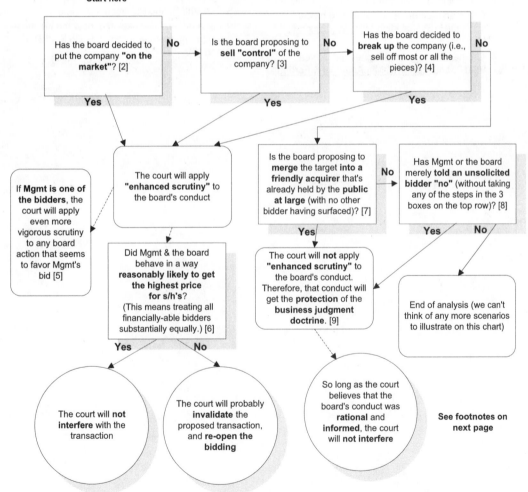

Use this chart to analyze any of these situations: (i) Target's management or board has **agreed** to be **taken over** by **one** bidder (perhaps while shunning the attentions of a second bidder); (2) management has decided to **sell the company** (or **control** of it), even though it hasn't yet made a deal; or (3) management has simply **"said no"** to an unsolicited proposal from a bidder (without taking any of the anti-takeover actions referred to in Fig. 10-2)

Start here

Has the board decided to put the company **"on the market"**? [2]   **No** →   Is the board proposing to **sell "control"** of the company? [3]   **No** →   Has the board decided to **break up** the company (i.e., sell off most or all the pieces)? [4]   **No**

Yes   **Yes**   **Yes**

If **Mgmt is one of the bidders**, the court will apply even more vigorous scrutiny to any board action that seems to favor Mgmt's bid [5]

The court will apply **"enhanced scrutiny"** to the board's conduct

Is the board proposing to **merge** the target **into a friendly acquirer** that's already held by the **public at large** (with no other bidder having surfaced)? [7]   **No** →   Has Mgmt or the board merely **told an unsolicited bidder "no"** (without taking any of the steps in the 3 boxes on the top row)? [8]

Yes   **Yes**   **No**

Did Mgmt & the board behave in a way **reasonably likely to get the highest price for s/h's**? (This means treating all financially-able bidders substantially equally.) [6]

The court will **not** apply **"enhanced scrutiny"** to the board's conduct. Therefore, that conduct will get the **protection** of the **business judgment doctrine**. [9]

End of analysis (we can't think of any more scenarios to illustrate on this chart)

Yes   **No**

The court will **not interfere** with the transaction

The court will probably **invalidate** the proposed transaction, and **re-open the bidding**

So long as the court believes that the board's conduct was **rational** and **informed**, the court will **not interfere**

See footnotes on next page

Notes to
Figure 10-9

Footnotes:

1. This chart reflects exclusively the law of Delaware, since that is where a large portion of publicly-held companies are incorporated.

2. This box refers to an anticipated sale of the target for cash (rather than a merger in which the target's s/h's get stock in the surviving corp). See VIII(H), especially the treatment of Revlon v. MacAndrews & Forbes.

3. This can include a merger for stock, if control will pass to a single person or small entity. See VIII(I), especially Paramount Comm. v. QVC. (In other words, this box is the opposite of the "merge into a friendly acquirer held by the public at large," treated in a later box.)

4. On "break up," see VIII(L)(1)(b).

5. On "management as a competing bidder," see VIII(H)(3), including Mills Acquisition v. MacMillan.

6. On the duty to get the highest price, see VIII(H), and Revlon v. MacAndrews & Forbes.

(But where one of the bidders is the controlling s/h, getting the "highest price" may mean taking a lower offer from that s/h instead of "accepting" a higher offer from an outside bidder that the controlling holder will veto. See VIII(H)(5), and Mendel v. Carroll.)

7. On merger into friendly publicly-controlled company, see VIII(I)(4), and Arnold v. Soc. for Savings. Notice that the key issue is whether the surviving company will be controlled by the "public at large" (in which case there's no enhanced scrutiny) or controlled by a single person or small entity not now in control of the target (in which case there is enhanced scrutiny.)

8. See VIII(J), and Paramount v. Time.

9. For a general discussion of how the business judgment doctrine works, see Ch.6-III(B)(1) and (5).

Figure 11-1
Was the Dividend Payment Proper?[1]

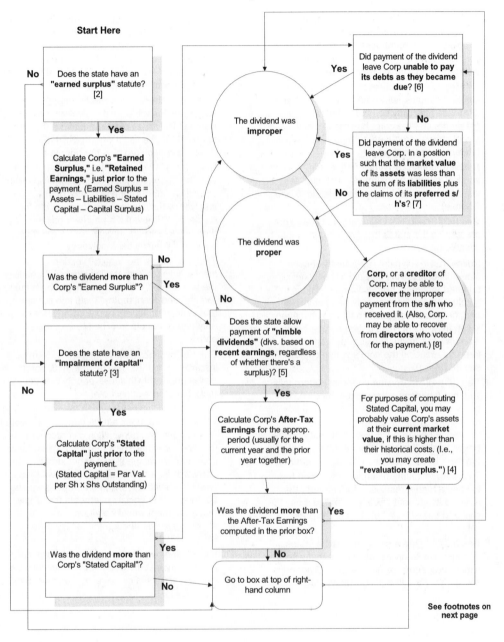

Start Here

No ← Does the state have an **"earned surplus"** statute? [2]

Yes ↓

Calculate Corp's **"Earned Surplus,"** i.e. **"Retained Earnings,"** just **prior** to the payment. (Earned Surplus = Assets – Liabilities – Stated Capital – Capital Surplus)

Was the dividend **more** than Corp's "Earned Surplus"? — **No**

Yes

Does the state have an **"impairment of capital"** statute? [3]

No

Yes ↓

Calculate Corp's **"Stated Capital"** just **prior** to the payment. (Stated Capital = Par Val. per Sh x Shs Outstanding)

Was the dividend **more** than Corp's "Stated Capital"? **Yes**

No

The dividend was **improper**

The dividend was **proper**

No → Does the state allow payment of **"nimble dividends"** (divs. based on **recent earnings**, regardless of whether there's a surplus)? [5]

Yes ↓

Calculate Corp's **After-Tax Earnings** for the approp. period (usually for the current year and the prior year together)

Was the dividend **more** than the After-Tax Earnings computed in the prior box? **Yes**

No ↓

Go to box at top of right-hand column

Yes ← Did payment of the dividend leave Corp **unable to pay its debts as they became due**? [6]

No ↓

Yes ← Did payment of the dividend leave Corp. in a position such that the **market value** of its **assets** was less than the sum of its **liabilities** plus the claims of its **preferred s/h's**? [7]

No

Corp, or a **creditor** of Corp. may be able to **recover** the improper payment from the **s/h** who received it. (Also, Corp. may be able to recover from **directors** who voted for the payment.) [8]

For purposes of computing Stated Capital, you may probably value Corp's assets at their **current market value**, if this is higher than their historical costs. (I.e., you may create **"revaluation surplus."**) [4]

See footnotes on next page

Notes to
Figure 11-1

Footnotes:

1. This is a "multi-state" chart: it tries to prepare you to analyze a dividend problem no matter what type of statute the state has. (Of course, you have to figure out what type of statute you're dealing with in order to use the chart.)

2. See I(C)(2). Most states still have "earned surplus" statutes, which effectively say that dividends may only be paid out of the overall net profits that the corp. has made since inception (i.e., "retained earnings," to use modern accounting jargon).

   Notice that the MBCA has neither the "earned surplus" nor the "impairment-of-capital" test, just a two-part insolvency test (see nn. 6 and 7 below).

3. See I(C)(3) and (4). Delaware and New York are among the states that have impairment-of-capital statutes.

   Notice that in a typical impairment-of-capital state, dividends may be paid not only out of retained earnings, but also out of "paid-in surplus" (the difference between par value and the amount originally paid by subscribers -- see I(C)(4)(a)), "revaluation surplus" (see n. 4 below) and "reduction surplus" (amounts freed by reducing the corp's stated capital -- see I(C)(4)(c)).

4. See I(C)(4)(b). Anytime your fact pattern tells you that a particular asset cost the corp. $x but is now worth more than $x, be on the lookout for "revaluation surplus" (the difference between the historical cost and the present value) as a source for the dividend payment in an impairment-of-capital state.

   To create revaluation surplus, the board has to pass a formal resolution to "write up" the asset to its present value -- it can't just pay the dividend based on a belief as to the present value.

5. See I(C)(5). Delaware is among the states allowing nimble dividends. Notice that where nimble dividends are allowed as a dividend source, they are in addition to the state's other source (e.g., earned surplus). So even if you see that, say, the dividend in an earned-surplus state is greater than the pre-dividend earned surplus, you can't say that the dividend was improper unless you first confirm that it wasn't allowed under a nimble provision.

   Be sure to check the correct number of years out of which nimble dividends can be paid. (Thus in Del., they can be paid from the after-tax profits in the fiscal year in which the dividend is declared plus the prior year.)

6. See I(6)(b). This box and the one below it deal with the "insolvency" standards for dividends -- virtually all states impose one or both insolvency tests as an additional hurdle for dividends. So even if a payment passes, say, the state's "earned surplus" test, it won't be allowed if it flunks the insolvency test.

   This box shows the "equity" version of the insolvency test (with the "bankruptcy" one in the box below). Although we've put both the "equity" and "bankruptcy" tests into the chart, and indicate that both apply, some states apply only one or the other. (The MBCA applies both.)

7. See I(6)(c). This is the "bankruptcy" form of insolvency test. As described in n. 6, some states apply only this test (or only the "equity" test), but others apply both.

8. See I(F) (s/h liability) and I(E) (director liability). When the corp. goes after a director who voted for the payment, generally it can recover only if the director either knew that the payment was improper or was negligent in not knowing. (In other words, a non-negligent approval by a director -- such as relying on proper-seeming but incorrect financial statements that show that a payment would be allowable -- will almost never be enough for liability. See I(E)(2).)

   It's not clear whether a creditor of Corp. can recover against the director in circumstances where Corp. itself could recover against him. See I(E)(4).

CAPSULE SUMMARY

TABLE OF CONTENTS
OF CAPSULE SUMMARY

CAPSULE SUMMARY

CHAPTER 1
INTRODUCTION

I. CHOOSING A FORM OF ORGANIZATION

A. Partnership vs. corporation: Choosing a form of organization usually comes down to choosing between a *partnership* and a *corporation*.

B. Nature of partnerships: There are two kinds of partnerships: "general" partnerships and "limited" partnerships.

1. **General partnership:** A "*general* partnership" is any association of two or more people who carry on a business as co-owners. A general partnership can come into existence by operation of law, with no formal papers signed or filed. Any partnership is a "general" one unless the special requirements for limited partnerships (see below) are complied with.

2. **Limited partnerships:** A "*limited*" partnership can only be created where: (1) there is a *written agreement* among the partners; and (2) a formal document is *filed* with state officials.

   a. **Two types of partners:** Limited partners have two types of partners: (1) one or more "*general*" partners, who are *each liable* for all the debts of the partnership; and (2) one or more "*limited*" partners, who are *not liable* for the debts of the partnership beyond the amount they have contributed.

C. Limited liability: Corporations and partnerships differ sharply with respect to *limited* liability.

1. **Corporation:** In the case of a corporation, a shareholder's liability is normally *limited to the amount he has invested.*

2. **Partnership:** The liability of partners in a partnership depends on whether the partnership is "general" or "limited."

   a. **General:** In a *general* partnership, *all partners are individually liable for the obligations of the partnership*.

   b. **Limited:** In a *limited* partnership, the general partners are personally liable but the limited partners are liable *only up to the amount of their capital contribution.* (But a limited partner will lose this limit on his liability if he *actively participates* in the management of the partnership.)

    c. Limited Liability Partnership (LLP): Most states now allow a third type of partnership, the *"limited liability partnership"* or *"LLP."* In an LLP, each partner may participate fully in the business' affairs without thereby becoming liable for the entity's debts.

D. Management:

1. **Corporation:** Corporations follow the principle of *centralized* management. The shareholders participate only by electing the board of directors. The board of directors supervises the corporation's affairs, with day-to-day control resting with the "officers" (i.e., high-level executives appointed by the board).

2. **Partnership:** In partnerships, management is usually *not* centralized. In a general partnership, all partners have an equal voice (unless they otherwise agree). In a limited partnership, all general partners have an equal voice unless they otherwise agree, but the limited partners may not participate in management.

E. Continuity of existence:
A corporation has "perpetual existence." In contrast, a general partnership *dissolved* by the *death* (or, usually, even the *withdrawal*) of a general partner. A limited partnership is dissolved by the withdrawal or death of a general partner, but not a limited partner.

F. Transferability:
Ownership interests in a corporation are readily transferable (the shareholder just sells stock). A partnership interest, by contrast, is not readily transferable (all partners must consent to the admission of a new partner).

G. Federal income tax:

1. **Corporations:** The corporation is *taxed as a separate entity.* It files its own tax return showing its profits and losses, and pays its own taxes independently of the tax position of the stockholders. This may lead to "double taxation" of dividends (a corporate-level tax on corporate profits, followed by a shareholder-level tax on the dividend).

2. **Partnership:** Partnerships, by contrast, are *not separately taxable entities*. The partnership files an information return, but the actual tax is paid by *each individual*. Therefore, double taxation is avoided. Also, a partner can use losses from the partnership to shelter from tax certain income from other sources.

3. **Subchapter S corporation:** If the owner/stockholders of a corporation would like to be taxed approximately as if they were partners in a partnership, they can often do this by having their corporation elect to be treated as a Subchapter S corporation. An "S" corporation does not get taxed at the corporate level, unlike a regular corporation; instead, each shareholder pays a tax on his portion of the corporation's profits.

H. Summary:

1. **Corporation superior:** The corporate form is superior: (1) where the owners want to limit their liability; (2) where free transferability of interests is important; (3) where centralized management is important (e.g., a large number of owners); and (4) where continuity of existence in the face of withdrawal or death of an owner is important.

2. **Partnership superior:** But the partnership form will be superior where: (1) simplicity and inexpensiveness of creating and operating the enterprise are important; or (2) the tax advantages are significant, such as avoiding double taxation and/or sheltering other income.

I. Limited Liability Companies (LLCs):

The fastest-growing form of organization since the 1990s has been the *limited liability company*, or *LLC*. All states have enacted special statutes recognizing and regulating LLCs. The LLC is neither a corporation nor a partnership, though it has aspects of each. Many people think that LLCs incorporate the best features of both corporations and partnerships.

1. **Advantages vs. standard partnership as to liability:** The biggest advantage of the LLC compared with either a general or limited partnership is that in the LLC, a "member" (analogous to a partner) is liable *only for the amount of his or her capital contribution*, even if the member actively participates in the business.

2. **Taxed as partnership:** The LLC's biggest advantage compared with a standard "C" corporation is that the LLC's members can elect whether to have the entity treated as a partnership or as a corporation. If they elect partnership treatment, the entity becomes a *"pass-through" entity,* and thus *avoids the double-taxation of dividends* that shareholders of a standard corporation suffer from.

3. **Operating agreement:** Owners of the LLC (called *"members"*) must agree among themselves how the business will operate (e.g., what kind of a vote is necessary to sell the LLC's assets, or whether the entity will be managed by its members or by a separate set of managers). The members do this by an *"operating agreement"* to which they are all party. Usually the operating agreement is in writing.

   a. **LLC is bound:** Most decisions hold that the LLC is itself *bound* by the operating agreement, even if only the members, and not the LLC itself, signed the agreement. This means that if one member sues the LLC, the operating agreement will control on matters with which it deals (e.g., the forum in which suits by or against the LLC may be brought).

4. **Piercing of veil:** Just as a *corporation's "veil"* may sometimes be *"pierced"* (see *infra*, p. 38), some decisions hold that the veil of the LLC

may sometimes be pierced, so as to make the members liable for the LLC's debts.

CHAPTER 2
THE CORPORATE FORM

I. WHERE AND HOW TO INCORPORATE

A. Delaware vs. headquarter state: The incorporators must choose between incorporating in their headquarter state, or incorporating somewhere else (probably Delaware).

  1. Closely held: For a *closely held* corporation, incorporation should usually take place in the state where the corporation's *principal place of business* is located.

  2. Publicly held: But for a *publicly held* corporation, incorporation in Delaware is usually very attractive (because of Delaware's well-defined, predictable, body of law, and its slight pro-management bias.)

B. Mechanics of incorporating:

  1. Articles of incorporation: To form a corporation, the incorporators file a document with the Secretary of State. This document is usually called the *"articles of incorporation"* or the "charter."

  a. Amending: The articles can be amended at any time after filing. However, any class of stockholders who would be adversely affected by the amendment must *approve* the amendment by majority vote. See, e.g., Model Business Corporation Act ("MBCA") § 10.04.

  2. Bylaws: After the corporation has been formed, it adopts *bylaws*. The corporation's bylaws are rules governing the corporation's internal affairs (e.g., date, time and place for annual meeting; number of directors; listing of officers; what constitutes quorum for directors' meetings, etc.). Bylaws are usually not filed with the Secretary of State, and may usually be amended by either the board or the shareholders.

II. ULTRA VIRES AND CORPORATE POWERS

A. *Ultra vires:*

  1. Classic doctrine: Traditionally, acts beyond the corporation's articles of incorporation were held to be *"ultra vires,"* and were unenforceable against the corporation or by it. (But there were numerous exceptions.)

  2. Modern abolition: Modern corporate statutes have generally *eliminated* the *ultra vires* doctrine. See, e.g, MBCA § 3.04(a).

B. Corporate powers today: Most modern corporations are formed with articles that allow the corporation to take *any lawful action*.

    1. Charitable contribution: Even if the articles of incorporation are silent on the subject, corporations are generally held to have an implied power to make *reasonable charitable contributions*. See, e.g., MBCA § 3.02(13).

    2. Other: Similarly, corporations can generally give bonuses, stock options, or other *fringe benefits* to their employees (even retired employees). See, e.g., MBCA § 3.02(12).

III. PRE-INCORPORATION TRANSACTIONS BY PROMOTERS

A. Liability of promoter: A *"promoter"* is one who takes initiative in founding and organizing a corporation. A promoter may occasionally be *liable* for debts he contracts on behalf of the to-be formed corporation.

    1. Promoter aware, other party not: If the promoter enters into a contract in the corporation's name, and the promoter *knows* that the corporation has not yet been formed (but the other party does *not* know this), the promoter will be *liable* under the contract. See MBCA § 2.04.

        a. Adoption: But if the corporation is later formed and *"adopts"* the contract, then the promoter may escape liability.

    2. Contract says corporation not formed: If the contract entered into by the promoter on behalf of the corporation *recites* that the corporation has not yet been formed, the liability of the promoter depends on what the court finds to be the parties' *intent*.

        a. Never formed, or immediately defaults: If the corporation is *never formed*, or is formed but then immediately *defaults*, the promoter will probably be *liable*.

        b. Formed and then adopts: But if the corporation is formed, and then shows its *intent to take over* the contract (i.e., *"adopts"* the contract), then the court may find that both parties intended that the promoter be released from liability (a *"novation"*).

B. Liability of corporation: If the corporation did not exist at the time the promoter signed a contract on its behalf, the corporation will not become liable unless it *"adopts"* the contract. Adoption may be *implied*.

Example: The corporation receives benefits under the contract, without objecting to them. The corporation will be deemed to have implicitly adopted the contract, making it liable and perhaps making the promoter no longer liable.

C. Promoter's fiduciary obligation: During the pre-incorporation period, the promoter has a *fiduciary obligation* to the to-be-formed corporation. He therefore may not pursue his own profit at the corporation's ultimate expense.

> **Example:** The promoter may not sell the corporation property at a grossly inflated price.

IV. DEFECTIVE INCORPORATION

A. Common law "de facto" doctrine: At common law, if a person made a "colorable" attempt to incorporate (e.g., he submitted articles to the Secretary of State, which were rejected), a "de facto" corporation would be found to have been formed. This would be enough to shelter the would-be incorporator from the personal liability that would otherwise result. This is the *"de facto corporation"* doctrine.

1. Modern view: But today, most states have *abolished* the de facto doctrine, and expressly impose personal liability on anyone who purports to do business as a corporation while knowing that incorporation has not occurred. See MBCA § 2.04.

B. Corporation by estoppel: The common law also applies the "corporation by *estoppel*" doctrine, whereby a creditor who deals with the business as a corporation, and who agrees to look to the "corporation's" assets rather than the "shareholders'|" assets will be estopped from denying the corporation's existence.

1. May survive: The "corporation by estoppel" doctrine probably survives in some states, as a judge-made doctrine.

V. PIERCING THE CORPORATE VEIL

A. Generally: In a few very extreme cases, courts may *"pierce the corporate veil,"* and hold some or all of the shareholders *personally liable* for the corporation's debts.

B. Individual shareholders: If the corporation's shares are held by *individuals*, here are some factors that courts look to in deciding whether to pierce the corporate veil:

1. Tort vs. contract ("voluntary creditor"): Courts are more likely to pierce the veil in a *tort* case (where the creditor is *"involuntary"*) than in a *contract* case (where the creditor is "voluntary").

2. Fraud: Veil piercing is more likely where there has been a grievous *fraud* or *wrongdoing* by the shareholders (e.g., the sole shareholder siphons out all profits, leaving the corporation without enough money to pay its claims).

3. **Inadequate capitalization:** Most important, veil piercing is most likely if the corporation has been *inadequately capitalized*. But most courts do not make inadequate capitalization *alone* enough for veil piercing.

   a. **Zero capital:** When the shareholder invests *no money whatsoever* in the corporation, courts are especially likely to pierce the veil, and may require less of a showing on the other factors than if the capitalization was inadequate but non-zero.

   b. **Siphoning:** Capitalization may be inadequate either because there is not enough *initial* capital, or because the corporation's profits are systematically *siphoned out* as earned. But if capitalization is adequate, and the corporation then has unexpected liabilities, the shareholders' failure to put in *additional* capital will generally *not* be inadequate capitalization.

4. **Failure of formalities:** Lastly, the court is more likely to pierce the veil if the shareholders have *failed to follow corporate formalities* in running the business.

   Example: Shares are never formally issued, directors' meetings are not held, shareholders co-mingle personal and company funds.

5. **Summary:** In nearly all cases at least *two* of the above four factors must be present for the court to pierce the veil; the most common combination is probably inadequate capitalization plus failure to follow corporate formalities.

C. **Parent/subsidiary:** If shares are held by a *parent corporation*, the court may pierce the veil and make the parent corporation liable for the *debts of the subsidiary*.

   1. **No liability generally:** Again, the *general* rule is that the corporate parent shareholder is *not liable* for the debts of the subsidiary (just as individual shareholders are not liable for the corporation's debts).

      a. **"Dominance" over subsidiary not enough:** The fact that the parent may in some sense *"dominate" the affairs* of the subsidiary will *not* by itself be enough to give rise to veil-piercing. Thus the fact that the parent *drains excess cash* from the subsidiary, *demands a veto power* over significant decisions by the subsidiary, or otherwise exercises some degree of *control* over the subsidiary's *operations*, will not suffice for piercing. So long as the degree of control by parent over subsidiary is within the bounds usually found in corporate America, creditors will probably not be able to attack the parent's assets.

   2. **Factors:** But as in the individual-shareholder case, certain acts by the parent may cause veil piercing to take place. Such factors include: (1) the parent and subsidiary fail to follow *separate corporate formalities* for the two corporations (e.g., both have the same board, and do not hold sepa-

rate directors' meetings); (2) the parent and subsidiary are operating pieces of the *same business*, and the subsidiary is undercapitalized; (3) the public is *misled* about which entity is operating which business; (4) assets are *intermingled* as between parent and subsidiary; or (5) the subsidiary is operated in an unfair manner (e.g., forced to sell at cost to parent).

    a. "Single economic entity" theory: As the Delaware courts summarize the idea, only if the two companies operate as a *"single economic entity"* will the veil generally be pierced, assuming that there is no fraud on creditors.

VI. INSIDER CLAIMS IN BANKRUPTCY (INCLUDING EQUITABLE SUBORDINATION)

A. Disallowance in bankruptcy: A bankruptcy court may *disallow* an insider's claim entirely if fairness requires.

    Example: The insider claims that his entire capital contribution is a "loan," but the court finds that some or all should be treated as non-repayable "equity" in the bankruptcy proceeding.

B. Equitable subordination: Alternatively, the bankruptcy court may recognize the insider's claims against the corporation, but will make these claims come *after* payment of all other creditors. Many of the same factors used for piercing the corporate veil (e.g., inadequate capitalization) will lead to this *"equitable subordination"* in bankruptcy.

CHAPTER 3

THE CORPORATE STRUCTURE

I. GENERAL ALLOCATION OF POWERS

A. Traditional scheme: A "traditional" scheme for allocating power in the corporation (reflected in most statutes) is as follows:

    1. Shareholders: The shareholders act principally by: (1) electing and removing *directors*; and (2) approving or disapproving *fundamental* or non-ordinary *changes* (e.g., mergers).

    2. Directors: The directors *"manage"* the corporation's business. That is, they formulate policy, and they *appoint officers* to carry out that policy.

    3. Officers: The corporation's officers administer the *day-to-day affairs* of the corporation, under the supervision of the board.

4. Modification: This traditional allocation of powers usually may be *modified* by the corporation where appropriate. This is often done in the case of closely held corporations.

B. Powers of shareholders: The main powers of the *shareholders* are as follows:

1. Directors: They have the power to *elect* and *remove directors*.

a. Election: Shareholders normally elect the directors at the *annual meeting* of shareholders. In other words, directors normally serve a one-year term. See Model Business Corporations Act (MBCA) § 8.05(b).

b. Vacancies: Shareholders usually have the right to elect directors to *fill vacancies* on the board, but the board of directors also usually has this power.

c. Removal: At common law, shareholders had little power to *remove* a director during his term of office. But today, most statutes allow the shareholders to remove directors *even without cause*. See MBCA § 8.08(a).

2. Articles and bylaws: The shareholders can amend the *articles* of incorporation or the *bylaws*.

3. Fundamental changes: The shareholders get to approve or disapprove of *fundamental changes* not in the ordinary course of business (e.g., mergers, sales of substantially all of the company's assets, or dissolution).

C. Power of directors: The *directors* "manage" the affairs of the corporation.

1. Shareholders can't give orders: Thus shareholders usually *cannot order the board of directors to take any particular action*.

2. Supervisory role: The board does not operate the corporation day to day. Instead, it *appoints officers*, and *supervises* the manner in which the officers conduct the day-to-day affairs.

D. Power of officers: The corporation's *officers* are appointed by the board, and can be removed by the board. The officers carry out the day-to-day affairs.

II. BOARD OF DIRECTORS

A. Election: As noted, members of the board of directors are always elected by the shareholders.

1. Straight vs. cumulative: The vote for directors may either be *"straight"* or *"cumulative."* (In most states, cumulative voting is allowed unless the articles of incorporation explicitly exclude it.)

a. **Cumulative:** In cumulative voting, a shareholder may ***aggregate his votes*** in favor of fewer candidates than there are slots available. (*Example:* H owns 100 shares. There are 3 board slots. H may cast all of his 300 votes for 1 candidate.) This makes it more likely that a minority shareholder will be able to obtain at least one seat on the board.

   i. **Removal of directors:** If cumulative voting is authorized, a director usually may not be ***removed*** if the number of votes that would have been sufficient to elect him under cumulative voting is voted against his removal.

B. **Number of directors:** The number of directors is usually fixed in either the articles of incorporation or in the bylaws. Most statutes require at least three directors. Most statutes also allow the articles or bylaws to set a variable (minimum and maximum) size for the board, rather than a fixed size. (If variable size is chosen, then the board gets to decide how many directors within the range there should be.)

C. **Filling vacancies:** Most statutes allow ***vacancies*** on the board to be filled ***either*** by the shareholders or by the board.

   1. **Term:** Statutes vary as to the term of a replacement director: some let him serve the full unexpired term of his predecessor, others make him stand for reelection at the next annual meeting. (This only matters if the predecessor's term was for more than one year).

   2. **Classes of stock:** The articles of incorporation may give each separate ***class of stock*** the power to elect one or more directors.

   3. **Holdover director:** A director holds office not only for the term for which he is elected, but ***until his successor is elected and qualified***. A director serving beyond the end of his term is called a ***"holdover"*** director.

D. **Removal of directors:** Most modern statutes provide that directors may be removed by a majority vote of ***shareholders***, either ***with or without cause***. Modern statutes also generally say that a ***court*** may order a shareholder removed, but only for ***cause***.

   1. **No removal by board:** But in most states a director may ***not*** be removed by his ***fellow directors***, even for cause.

E. **Directors' meetings:**

   1. **Regular vs. special:** There are two types of board meetings: ***regular*** and ***special***. A regular board meeting is one which occurs at a regular interval (e.g., monthly). All other meetings are "special." The frequency for regular meetings is usually specified in the bylaws.

2. **Notice:** No notice is necessary for a regular meeting. But prior notice (e.g., two days notice under the MBCA) is required for a special meeting.

3. **Quorum:** The board may only act if a *quorum* is present. Usually, the quorum is a *majority* of the total directors in office.

   Example: If there are nine directors, at least five must be present for there to be a meeting.

   a. **Lower number:** Some states allow the articles or bylaws to set a percentage for a quorum that is *less than a majority*.

   b. **Super majority:** Conversely, most statutes permit the articles or bylaws to make the quorum *more* than a majority (useful as a control device in closely-held corporations). See MBCA § 8.24(a).

   c. **Present at vote:** The quorum must be present *at the time the vote is taken* in order for the vote to constitute the act of the board. Thus even if a quorum is present at the start of the meeting, a director may leave and thereby remove the quorum.

F. **Act of board:** The board may normally take action only by a *vote of a majority* of the directors *present* at the meeting.

   1. **Higher number:** In most states, the articles of incorporation may set a *higher percentage* than a majority for all or certain board actions.

   2. **Requirement for meeting:** The board may normally take action *only at a meeting*, not by individual action of the directors.

      Example: A contract cannot be executed by the board merely by having a majority of the directors, acting at separate times and places, sign the contract document.

      But there are some exceptions to this general rule:

      a. **Unanimous written consent:** Nearly all states allow directors to act without a meeting if they give their *unanimous written consent* to the proposed corporate action. See MBCA § 8.21(a).

      b. **Telephone meetings:** Many states now permit the directors to act by means of a *telephone conference call*.

      c. **Ratification:** Also, if the board learns of an action taken by an officer, and the board does not object, the board may be deemed to have *"ratified"* this action, or the board may be *"estopped"* from dishonoring it. In either case, the result is as if the board had formally approved the action in advance.

   3. **Objection by director:** A director may *disassociate* herself from board action by filing a written dissent, or by making an oral dissent that is entered in the minutes of the meeting. This will shield the director from any possible liability for the corporate action.

G. Committees: The full board may appoint various **committees**. Generally, a committee may **take any action** which could be taken by the full board. (But there are exceptions. For instance, under the MBCA, committees may not fill board vacancies, amend the articles of incorporation or the bylaws, propose actions for shareholder approval, or authorize share repurchases. MBCA § 8.25(e).)

III. OFFICERS

A. Meaning of "officer": The term *"officer"* describes only the more important executives of the corporation, typically those **appointed directly by the board of directors.** Most states leave it up to the board or the bylaws to determine what officers there shall be.

B. Right to hire and fire: Officers can be both **hired** and **fired** by the board. Firing can be with or **without cause** (and can occur even if there is an employment contract, though the officer can then sue the corporation for breach).

C. Authority to act for corporation: The officer is an **agent** of the corporation, and his authority is therefore analyzed under agency principles. An officer does not have the **automatic right** to bind the corporation. Instead, one of four doctrines must usually be used to find that the officer could bind the corporation on particular facts:

1. **Express actual authority:** Express actual authority can be given to an officer either by the corporation's **bylaws**, or by a **resolution** adopted by the board.

   Example: A board resolution authorizes the Vice President to negotiate and sign a contract to dispose of a surplus plant.

2. **Implied actual authority:** "Implied actual authority" is authority that is *"inherent in the office."* Usually, it is authority that is inherent in the **particular post** occupied by the officer.

   a. **President:** The **president** is generally held to have implied actual authority, merely by virtue of his office, to engage in **ordinary** business transactions, such as hiring and firing non-officer-level employees and entering into ordinary-course contracts. But he does **not** usually have implied actual authority to bind the corporation to **non-ordinary-course** contracts such as contracts for the sale of real estate or for the sale of all of the corporation's assets.

   b. **Secretary:** The **secretary** has implied actual authority to **certify the records of the corporation**, including **resolutions** of the board of directors. Therefore, a secretary's certificate that a given resolution was duly adopted by the board is **binding** on the corporation in favor of a third party who relies on the certificate.

    c. Removal: The board may always explicitly **remove** implied actual authority that would otherwise exist (e.g., by notifying President that he may not hire anyone.)

3. Apparent authority: An officer has **"apparent authority"** if the corporation gives observers the **appearance** that the agent is authorized to act as he is acting. There are two requirements: (1) the corporation, by acts **other than those of the officer**, must **indicate to the world** that the officer has the authority to do the act in question; and (2) the plaintiff must be **aware** of those corporate indications and rely on them.

    a. President: In the case of a president, apparent authority will often flow merely from the fact that the corporation has given him that title — he will then have apparent authority to enter into ordinary course arrangements.

    Example: If Corp. gives X the title "President," this will signal to the world that X has authority to purchase office supplies. Therefore, if X does purchase office supplies from P, who knows that X has the title "President," X will bind Corp. even if the board of directors has explicitly resolved that X does *not* have authority to purchase such supplies.

4. Ratification: Under the doctrine of **"ratification,"** if a person with actual authority to enter into the transaction learns of a transaction by an officer, and either expressly affirms it or fails to disavow it, the corporation may be bound. Usually, P will have to show that the corporation either received benefits under the contract, or that P himself relied to his detriment on the existence of the contract.

IV. SHAREHOLDER ACTION

A. Meetings: Nearly all states require a corporation to hold an **annual meeting of shareholders**. See MBCA § 7.02(a).

1. Special meeting: Corporations may also hold a **"special"** shareholders' meeting. A special meeting is any meeting other than the regularly-scheduled annual meeting.

    a. Who may call: The board may call a special meeting. Also, anyone authorized by the bylaws to call a meeting (e.g., the president, under many bylaws) may do so. Finally, some statutes allow the holders of a certain percentage of the shares to call a special meeting.

    Example: MBCA § 7.02(a)(2) allows the holders of 10% of shares to call a special meeting. But in Delaware, shareholders may not call a special meeting.

B. Quorum: For a vote of a shareholders' meeting to be effective, there must be a **quorum** present. Usually, this must be a **majority of the outstanding**

shares. However, the percentage required for a quorum may be *reduced* if provided in the articles or bylaws.

    1. Minimum: Some states don't allow the percentage for a quorum to be reduced below a certain number (e.g., the number cannot be reduced below one-third in Delaware). But the MBCA sets no floor.

    2. Higher percentage: Conversely, nearly all states allow the articles or bylaws to set a *higher percentage* as the quorum.

C. Vote required: Once a quorum is present, the traditional rule is that the shareholders will be deemed to have approved of the proposed action only if a majority of the *shares actually present* vote in *favor* of the proposed action.

    1. Traditional rule: In other words, under this approach, an abstention is the equivalent of a vote against.

        a. MBCA: But the MBCA, in § 7.25(c), changes this by treating abstentions like votes that are not cast.

    2. Breaking quorum: Once a quorum is present, the quorum is deemed to exist for the rest of the meeting, even if shareholders *leave.*

    3. Written consent: Nearly all states allow shareholders to act by *unanimous written consent* without a meeting.

        a. Non-unanimous written consent: A minority of states allow shareholder action in the form of *non-unanimous* written consent.

        Example: Delaware § 228(a) allows shareholder action by the written consent of the same number of votes as would be needed to approve the action at a meeting.

    4. Meeting in cyberspace: Some states now allow shareholder meetings to occur on the *Internet*. See, e.g., Del. GCL § 211(a)(2) (allowing a meeting to occur electronically, so long as shareholders can hear the proceedings and vote by computer.)

CHAPTER 4

SHAREHOLDERS' INFORMATIONAL RIGHTS AND THE PROXY SYSTEM

I. SHAREHOLDER INSPECTION OF BOOKS AND RECORDS

A. Generally: State law generally gives shareholders the right to inspect the corporation's books and records.

    1. Common law: In most states, shareholders have a common-law right of inspection if they show a "proper purpose" for doing so.

2. Statute: Also, many states have enacted statutes codifying the shareholder's right of inspection.

B. Who may inspect: Usually "beneficial owners," as well as holders of record, may inspect.

1. Size or length of holding: Some statutes restrict the right of inspection to shareholders who either have held their shares for a certain time, or hold more than a certain percentage of total shares.

Example: New York BCL § 624 gives the statutory right of inspection only to one who: (1) has held for at least six months; or (2) holds at least 5% of a class of shares.

C. What records may be examined: Under most statutes, the holder has a right to inspect not merely specified records, but the corporate records *in general*.

1. More limited statutes: But other statutes are more limited.

Example: The MBCA does not give holders an automatic right to inspect sensitive materials like the minutes of board meetings, the accounting records, or the shareholder list. For these, he must make a demand "in good faith and for proper purpose," he must "describe with reasonable particularity" his purpose and the records he wants to inspect, and the records must be "directly connected with his purpose." See MBCA § 16.02(b).

D. Proper purpose: The shareholder generally may inspect records only if he does so for a *"proper purpose."*

1. Evaluation of investment: A shareholder's desire to *evaluate* his *investment* will usually be "proper."

Example: A holder will usually be allowed to examine accounting records to determine whether the stock's market price fairly reflects its true value.

2. Unrelated personal goal: Pursuit of unrelated *personal goals* will generally *not* be a proper purpose.

Example: A holder may not inspect if his purpose is to get access to trade secrets which he can sell to a competitor or use himself.

3. Deal with other shareholders: If the holder wants to get access to the shareholder's list to contact his *fellow shareholders* to take group action concerning the corporation, this will usually be proper.

Example: A holder will usually be given access to shareholder lists to solicit proxies in connection with an attempt to elect a rival slate of directors.

4. **Social/political goals:**   If the holder is pursuing only *social or political goals* that are not closely related to the corporation's business, this purpose will usually be improper.

    Example: P wants to stop D Corp from making munitions for the Vietnam War because he thinks the war is immoral; P's purpose is not "proper," so he cannot have D's shareholder list or its records of weapons manufacture.

5. **Multiple purposes of which one is proper:**   Suppose a shareholder has *multiple purposes* for requesting the inspection, of which one (or more) is appropriate and the other(s) not. Here, at least in Delaware inspection must be *allowed* — so long as there is *at least one proper purpose*, the presence of an *improper* purpose is *irrelevant*.

    a. **Court will look to the "real" purpose:**   Of course, the court will not blindly accept the shareholder's stated reason(s) for the inspection, and will instead normally try to ascertain the *"real"* reasons that are motivating her. If the court concludes that all of the real reasons are *illegitimate*, the fact that the holder has asserted a different reason that would be legitimate will be irrelevant.

E. **Financial reports:**   In most states, the corporation is *not* required to send an *annual report* or other annual financial information to the shareholder. (But federal law requires publicly held corporations to send a report, and some states require this for all corporations.)

F. **Director's right of inspection:**   A *director* in most states has a very *broad*, virtually automatic, right of inspection. (But most states deny him the right of inspection if he is acting with "manifestly improper motives.")

II. REPORTING REQUIREMENTS FOR PUBLICLY HELD COMPANIES

A. **What companies are "publicly held":**   Certain reporting requirements are imposed on "publicly held" companies. Basically, these are companies which either: (1) have stock that is traded on a national securities exchange; or (2) have assets of more than $10 million *and* a class of stock held of record by 500 or more people. These companies must make continuous disclosures to the SEC under § 12 of the Securities Exchange Act of 1934 (the "'34 Act"), and must comply with the proxy rules described below.

B. **Proxy rules generally:**   Any company covered by § 12 of the '34 Act (companies listed in the prior paragraph) fall within the SEC's *proxy solicitation* rules. If a company is covered, any proxy solicitation by either management or non-management (subject to some exemptions) must comply with detailed SEC rules. Basically, this means that whenever management or a third party wants to persuade a shareholder to *vote* in a certain way (whether the persuasion is written or oral, and whether it is by advertisement or one-on-one communication), the solicitation must comply with the SEC proxy rules.

C. Disclosure and filing requirements:

1. **Filing:** Any proxy solicitation documents that will be sent to shareholders must first be *filed with the SEC*.

2. **Proxy statement:** Every proxy solicitation must be accompanied or preceded by a written *"proxy statement."* This must disclose items like conflicts of interest, the compensation given to the five highest-paid officers, and details of any major change being voted upon.

3. **Annual report:** The proxy rules require than an *annual report* be sent to every shareholder.

4. **Anti-fraud:** Any *false* or *misleading* statements or omissions in a proxy statement are banned by SEC rules.

D. Requirements for proxy:
The proxy itself is a *card* which the shareholder signs, and on which he indicates how he wants to vote. SEC rules govern the format of this card.

1. **Function:** Most commonly, the proxy will be the method by which the shareholder indicates to management that he is voting for management's slate of *directors*. The proxy card will also be the shareholder's way of indicating how he votes on some major non-election issue, such as whether the company should merge with another corporation. The proxy is the method of casting shareholder votes in all situations except where the shareholder attends the shareholder's meeting.

2. **Broad discretion:** The proxy form may not confer unduly broad discretion on the recipient.

   Example: The card must list exactly what nominees management is proposing for election to the board; it may not confer on management the right to vote for unnamed candidates that management desires.

3. **Must be voted:** The recipient of the proxy (e.g., management or a group of insurgents waging a proxy contest) *must* vote the proxy as the shareholder has indicated, even if the shareholder has voted the opposite of the way the person who solicited the proxy would like.

E. Revocation of proxies:
Generally, a proxy is *revocable* by the shareholder, even if the proxy itself recites that it is irrevocable.

1. **Coupled with an interest:** However, if a proxy states that it is irrevocable *and* the proxy is *"coupled with an interest"* then it is *irrevocable*. A proxy is "coupled with an interest" when the recipient of the proxy has a property interest in the shares, or at least some other direct economic interest in how the vote is cast.

Example: A shareholder pledges his shares in return for a loan from Bank. The pledge is an interest, so the proxy will be irrevocable while the loan is outstanding.

III. IMPLIED PRIVATE ACTIONS UNDER THE PROXY RULES

A. Generally: The Supreme Court has recognized an *"implied private right of action"* on behalf of individuals who have been injured by a violation of proxy rules. [*J.I. Case Co. v. Borak*] There are three requirements which the plaintiff must satisfy:

1. **Materiality:** First, P must show that there was a *material* misstatement or omission in the proxy materials. In the case of an omission, the omitted fact is material if it would have "assumed actual significance in the deliberations of a reasonable shareholder."

2. **Causation:** Second, P must show a *causal link* between the misleading proxy materials and some damage to shareholders. However, P does not have to show that the falsehood or omission directly "caused" the damage to shareholders; he only has to show that the proxy solicitation itself (not the error or omission) was an essential part of the transaction.

   Example: If holders have to approve a merger, any material defect in the proxy materials will be deemed to have "caused" damage to the holders, since the entire proxy solicitation process was an essential part of carrying out the merger transaction.

   a. **Minority class whose votes are not needed:** If P is a member of a *minority class* whose votes were *not necessary* for the proposed transaction to go through, P may not recover no matter how material or how intentional the deception in the proxy statement was. [*Virginia Bankshares, Inc. v. Sandberg*].

      Example: FABI, a bank holding company, owns 80% of the shares of Bank. FABI wants to get rid of the 20% minority shareholders in Bank, so it proposes to buy out the minority holders at a price of $42. The minority holders are sent a proxy solicitation stating that the $42 price is "high" and "fair." Most of the minority holders approve the transaction. P, a minority holder who opposes the transaction, sues on the grounds that the proxy materials falsely stated that the price was "high" and "fair."

      Held, P has no claim here, even if the proxy materials were false. Because FABI could have voted its own shares in favor of the buyout, approval by the minority holders was not legally necessary. Therefore, no misstatements in the proxy materials sent to the minority holders could have "caused" the merger, or contributed to any damage suffered by P or the other minority holders. [*Virginia Bankshares, supra*].

3. **Standard of fault:** Third, P must show that D was *at fault* in some way. If the defendant is an "insider" (e.g., the corporation itself, its officers and its employee/directors), P only has to show that D was *negligent*. Some courts have also found *outside directors* and other outsiders liable for errors or omissions under the proxy rules, where the outsider was negligent.

4. **Remedies:** If P makes these three showings, he can get several possible types of relief: (1) he may be able to get an *injunction* against a proposed transaction (where the proxy solicitation was for the purpose of getting shareholder approval of the transaction, such as a merger); (2) he may very occasionally have an already-completed transaction *set aside*; and (3) he may obtain *damages* for himself and other holders, if he can prove actual monetary injury (e.g., he shows that due to lies in the proxy statement, shareholders approved the sale of the company at an unfairly low price).

IV. COMMUNICATIONS BY SHAREHOLDERS

A. **Two methods:** A *shareholder* may solicit her fellow shareholders to obtain their proxies in favor of her own proposed slate of directors or her own proposal. Depending on the circumstances, there are two methods for her to do so, in one of which the shareholder bears the expense and in the other of which the corporation bears the expense.

B. **Shareholder bears expense:** Under SEC Rule 14a-7, a shareholder who is willing to *bear the expense* of communicating with his fellow shareholders (e.g., printing and postage) has the right to do so. Management must either mail the shareholder's materials to the other stockholders, or give the soliciting shareholder a shareholder list so that he can do the mailing directly.

1. **Few restrictions:** There are very few restrictions on when and how this method is used. For instance, there is no length limit on the materials the shareholder may mail, and management has no right to censor or object to the contents.

C. **Corporation bears expense:** Alternatively, a shareholder may sometimes get a "shareholder proposal" submitted to fellow shareholders entirely at the *corporation's expense*. Under SEC Rule 14a-8, shareholder proposals may sometimes be required to be included in management's own proxy materials.

Example: An activist shareholder may be able to get management's proxy materials to include the activist's proposal that the company cease doing business with China.

1. **Exclusions:** Many kinds of proposals are *excluded* from 14a-8, so management can refuse to include them. Some of the important exclusions are:

    a. **Improper subject under state law:** A proposal may be excluded if "under the law of the [state where the corporation is incorporated, the proposal is] not a proper subject for action by security holders." This usually means that the proposal must be phrased as a *recommendation* by the shareholders that management consider doing something, rather than as an *order* by shareholders that the corporation do something (since under state law shareholders usually cannot order the corporation to do anything).

    b. **Not significantly related to corporation's business:** A proposal may be excluded if it is *not significantly related to the company's business* (i.e., if it counts for less than 5% of the corporation's total assets and less than 5% of its earnings and gross sales, and is "not otherwise significantly related to the [corporation's] business").

        Example: A proposal calls for Corp's widget division to be divested because it has a poor return on equity; if the widget division accounts for less than 5% of Corp's assets, earnings and sales, the proposal may be excluded.

        i. **Ethical/social issues:** But *ethical* or *social* issues may usually *not* be excluded for failure to meet these 5% tests, if the issues are otherwise related to the corporation's business.

            Example: The corporation's alleged force feeding of geese to produce pate de fois gras may not be excluded, even though it accounts for less than 5% of earnings, assets and sales.

    c. **Routine matters:** A proposal may be excluded if it relates to the *"conduct of the ordinary business operations"* of the company.

        Example: A proposal that the company charge 10% less for one of its many products would relate to ordinary business operations, and thus be excludible.

        i. **Compensation issues:** Proposals concerning *senior executive compensation* are *not* matters relating to the "ordinary business operations" of the company, and may therefore not be excluded.

            Example: A proposal suggesting that the board cancel any "golden parachute" contracts it has given to senior executives — i.e., contracts that give the executive a large payment if the company is taken over — must be included in the proxy materials.

    d. **Election of directors:** A proposal may be excluded if it relates to "a *nomination or election* to the company's *board of directors*[.]" Rule

14a-8(i)8). In other words, a holder who wants to propose his own slate of directors, or to oppose management's slate, must pay for the dissemination of his own materials, and may not require the corporation to disseminate for him.

i. **Change in procedures:** In fact, this exclusion applies also to any proposal that relates to a "***procedure*** for ... nomination or election [to the company's board." *Id*. This means that any proposal to change the ***general methods*** by which directors are to be elected may be excluded.

Example: A shareholder wants to propose that the company's bylaws be changed to require management to include in its own proxy materials the names of any slate of director candidates proposed by any shareholder owning more than 3% of the company's stock. That shareholder proposal to "change the election rules" can be excluded from the management proxy.

V. PROXY CONTESTS

A. **Definition:** A "proxy contest" is a competition between management and a group of outside ***"insurgents"*** to obtain shareholder votes on a proposal. Most proxy contests involve the election of directors, but there can be proxy contests over some non-election proposal as well.

Example: A proxy contest over whether the corporation should adopt a proposed "poison pill" takeover defense.

B. **Regulation:** Proxy contests are tightly regulated by the SEC.

1. **List access:** The SEC rules do not give the insurgent group access to the shareholder's list. (However, they may have this under state law, as described above.) But as noted, the SEC rules do allow the insurgents to force management to choose between mailing the insurgents' materials or giving the insurgents the list so that the insurgents can do this themselves. (Management will usually mail instead of giving up the list.)

2. **Disclosure required:** Both sides must comply with all disclosure regulations. Thus they must make sure that any "solicitation" (including oral solicitation) is preceded by a written proxy statement, and in the case of an election they must file special information about any "participant" in the solicitation.

C. **Costs:**

1. **Management's expenses:** The corporation may usually pay for any reasonable expense incurred by management in waging its side of the proxy contest.

2. Insurgents: If the insurgents are successful at getting control, they will usually be allowed to have the corporation reimburse them for their expenses (provided that the shareholders approve). If the insurgents are unsuccessful at getting control, they must bear their own expenses.

VI.　IMPROVED PUBLIC DISCLOSURE BY THE CORPORATION

A. Improvements to disclosure: As the result of turn-of-the-century corporate scandals, the federal government has made two major attempts to improve the disclosure obligations of public companies: *Regulation FD* and the *Sarbanes-Oxley Act*.

B. Regulation FD: Regulation FD, enacted by the SEC, stops a company from making *"selective disclosure."* Selective disclosure occurs when the company gives certain professional investors (e.g., security analysts for big Wall Street firms) information that the public isn't given til later. Now, under FD:

❏ If a public company *intends* to release material nonpublic information to certain professional investors (e.g., analysts), the company must *disclose* the information *simultaneously to the public*.

❏ And, if the public company realizes that it has *unintentionally* disclosed material nonpublic information to such a professional investor, it must cure the problem by then *"promptly"* disclosing that information to the public.

C. Sarbanes-Oxley Act: The *Sarbanes-Oxley Act,* passed by Congress in 2002, increases the responsibilities of people in charge of running the finances of public companies. Here are some of the major responsibilities that Sarbanes-Oxley imposes:

1. CEO/CFO certification: Most importantly, the company's *CEO* and *CFO* must each *certify the accuracy* of each quarterly and annual filing with the SEC.

2. Rules about Audit Committee: Each member of a company's *Audit Committee* must be *"independent"* of the company (e.g., not an employee, consultant, etc.)

3. Auditor independence: The company's *outside auditors* (the CPAs that perform the annual audit) must also be much more *independent* than previously. The auditors may no longer do other — potentially more lucrative — tasks for the company, such as bookkeeping, designing the computer system that does financial record-keeping for the company, etc.

4. **Whistleblower protections:** *"Whistleblowers"* get protection. More specifically, it's now a crime to take any action (including firing, demoting or harassing) against a person on account of that person's provision of truthful information to government or to the person's boss concerning the possible commission of a federal offense. Employees alleging a violation can bring a civil suit under some circumstances.

Example: Drone is a junior accountant for Corp. Drone learns that Boss, the head of Corp's accounting department, is giving false financial information to the company's auditors. Boss threatens Drone with being fired if Drone reports the violations to the CEO or to the SEC. Boss has committed a federal crime, punishable by up to 10 years imprisonment. And Drone may be able to sue Boss civilly under the whistleblower provision.

CHAPTER 5

CLOSE CORPORATIONS

I. INTRODUCTION

A. **What is close corporation:** A "close corporation" is one with the following traits: (1) a *small number* of stockholders; (2) the lack of any *ready market* for the corporation's stock; and (3) substantial participation by the *majority stockholder(s)* in the management, direction and operations of the corporation.

B. **Significance of close corporation status:** Close corporations present special problems relating to control. The various devices examined here are mainly ways of insuring that a minority stockholder will not be taken advantage of by the majority holder(s).

II. SHAREHOLDER VOTING AGREEMENTS, VOTING TRUSTS AND CLASSIFIED STOCK

A. **Voting agreements:** A *"shareholder voting agreement"* is an agreement in which two or more shareholders agree to *vote together* as a unit on certain or all matters. Some voting agreements expressly provide how votes will be cast. Other agreements merely commit the parties to vote together (without specifying how the vote is to go, so that the parties must reach future agreement).

1. **Generally valid:** Shareholder agreements are generally *valid* today.

2. **Enforcement:** There are two ways that a voting agreement may be *enforced:*

a. **Proxy:** First, the agreement may require each signatory to give to a third person an *irrevocable proxy* to vote the signer's shares in accordance with the agreement. Usually this irrevocable proxy arrangement will be enforced today.

b. **Specific performance:** Second, most courts today will grant *specific performance* of the terms of the voting agreement. See, e.g., MBCA § 7.31(b).

B. **Voting trust:** In a *voting trust*, the shareholders who are part of the arrangement *convey legal title* to their shares to one or more *voting trustees*, under the terms of a voting trust agreement. The shareholders become "beneficial owners" — they receive a "voting trust certificate" representing their beneficial interest, and get dividends and sale proceeds. But they no longer have voting power.

1. **Validity; requirements:** Most states enforce voting trusts, if they conform with statutory requirements. Usually, these requirements include the following:

   a. **Maximum term:** There is almost always a *maximum term* for the voting trust (usually ten years).

   b. **Disclosure:** Usually the trust's terms must be *publicly disclosed* (at least to the shareholders who are not part of the agreement).

   c. **Writing:** The trust must generally be *in writing*, and must be implemented by a *formal transfer* of the shares on the transfer records of the corporation.

2. **Strict compliance:** These requirements must be *strictly adhered to*. If not, the court is likely to hold the entire agreement unenforceable.

C. **Classified stock and weighted voting:** Shareholders may reallocate their voting power (and give minority holders a bigger voice) by using *classified stock*. The corporation sets up two or more classes of stock, and gives each class different voting rights or financial rights.

1. **General valid:** The use of different classes and weighting of voting is generally valid.

III. AGREEMENTS RESTRICTING THE BOARD'S DISCRETION

A. **Problem generally:** If the shareholders agree to restrict their discretion *as directors*, there is a risk that the agreement will violate the principle that the business shall be managed by the board of directors. If a court finds that the board's discretion has been unduly fettered, it may refuse to enforce the agreement.

B. Present law: However, this danger is not very great today. Most courts will probably uphold even a shareholder agreement that substantially curtails the board's discretion, so long as the agreement: (1) does not *injure* any *minority* shareholder; (2) does not injure *creditors* or the public; and (3) does not violate any express statutory provision.

IV. SUPER-MAJORITY VOTING AND QUORUM REQUIREMENTS

A. Modern view: Most statutes allow the shareholders to agree that a *"super-majority"* will be required for a vote or a quorum. In general, such super-majority quorum and voting requirements are upheld, even if they require unanimity.

> **Example:** Under the MBCA, the articles of incorporation may be amended to require some percentage greater than 50%, even unanimity, both for a quorum for a shareholders' meeting and for shareholder approval of proposed corporate action. Also, either the articles or the bylaws may impose a super-majority quorum or voting requirement for directors' meetings and directors' action.

1. Changing a requirement: If the charter is drafted to impose a super-majority voting or quorum requirement, some statutes allow the super-majority provision to be *removed* or *changed* only by the same super-majority percentage. (*Example*: Once the charter is amended to require two-thirds shareholder vote for any merger proposal, a two-thirds shareholder would be required to remove the super-majority provision.) In other states, the shareholders must expressly agree to this kind of "anti-amendment" scheme.

V. SHARE TRANSFER RESTRICTIONS

A. Why used: The shareholders of a close corporation will often agree to *limit the transferability* of shares in the corporation. This lets shareholders veto the admission of new "colleagues" and helps preserve the existing balance of control.

B. Enforcement: Today, share transfer restrictions will generally be *enforced*, so long as they are *reasonable*.

1. How imposed: Share restrictions may be imposed either by a formal agreement among the shareholders or, in some instances, by an amendment to the articles of incorporation or the bylaws.

C. Various techniques: Here are the five principal techniques for restricting share transfers:

1. **First refusal:**   Under a *right of first refusal*, a shareholder may not sell his shares to an outsider without first offering the corporation or the other shareholders (or both) a right to buy those shares at the same price and terms as those at which the outsider is proposing to buy. (Usually the corporation gets the first chance, and if it refuses, the other shareholders get the right to buy proportionally to their holdings.)

2. **First option:**   The *"first option"* is similar to the right of first refusal, except that the price is determined by the agreement creating the option.

3. **Consent:**   Stock transfers may be made subject to the *consent* of the board of directors or the other shareholders.

4. **Stock buy-back:**   A *buy-back right* is given to the corporation to enable it to buy back a holder's shares on the happening of certain events, whether the holder wants to sell or not. (*Example*: The corporation might be given the right to buy back shares of a holder/employee upon that person's retirement or termination of employment.) The corporation is *not obligated* to exercise a buy-back right.

5. **Buy-sell agreement:**   A buy-sell agreement is similar to a buy-back right, except that the corporation is *obligated* to go through with the purchase upon the happening of the specified event.

    Example: The corporation agrees in advance that it will repurchase the shares at a fixed price upon the death of a shareholder/employee.

D. **Notice and consent:**   Not everybody is necessarily bound by a share transfer restriction:

1. **Signor:**   Obviously if the shareholder signs an agreement, he will be bound.

2. **Subsequent purchaser without notice:**   A person who purchases shares *without actual knowledge* of pre-existing restrictions will generally *not be bound* by the restrictions. However, if the restriction is *conspicuously noted* on the share certificates, he will be bound.

3. **Non-consenting minority holder:**   Courts are split as to whether a person who is *already a shareholder* at the time the restrictions are imposed (and who does not consent) is bound. MBCA § 6.27(a) provides that a person who is already a holder at the time restrictions are imposed (e.g., by an amendment to the articles of incorporation or bylaws) will *not be bound* if he does not sign any agreement to that effect, and does not vote in favor of the restriction.

E. **Valuation:**   Most transfer restrictions require some *valuation* to be placed on the stock at some point. There are four common techniques:

1. **Book value:**   The value may be based upon the *"book value."* This is basically the corporation's assets minus its liabilities. (Sometimes adjust-

ments will be made to the corporation's historical balance-sheet figures to arrive at the book value used for valuation.)

2. **"Capitalized earnings" method:** If the *"capitalized earnings"* method is used, the parties use a formula that attempts to estimate the future earnings of the business, and they then discount these earnings to present value.

3. **"Mutual agreement" method:** If the *"mutual agreement"* method is used, the parties agree upon an initial fixed valuation and also agree that from time to time they will mutually agree upon an adjusted number to reflect changes in market value.

4. **Appraisal:** Last, if the *"appraisal"* method is used, the parties agree in advance on a procedure by which a neutral third-party appraiser will be selected; the appraiser then determines the value.

F. **Funding of buy-sell:** There are two main ways to *fund* a buy-sell agreement:

1. **Life insurance:** *Life insurance* can be purchased on each shareholder, in an amount sufficient to cover the estimated purchase price for that holder's shares.

2. **Installment payments:** Alternatively, the parties can agree that the shares will be purchased by the *installment method*. Usually, there will be a down payment, followed by quarterly or annual payments, usually paid out of the earnings of the business. (Often, life insurance is used to fund the down payment.)

G. **Requirement of "reasonableness":** Transfer restrictions will only be upheld if they are *"reasonable."*

1. **Outright prohibition and consent requirements:** Courts are especially likely to strike down an *outright prohibition* on the transfer of shares to third parties. Similarly, a provision that shares may not be sold to outsiders without the *consent* of the other shareholders is likely to be found unreasonable, if the others are permitted to withhold their consent *arbitrarily*.

2. **Options, first refusals and buy-sell agreements:** The other types of restrictions — first option, right of first refusal, buy-backs and buy-sell agreements — are more likely to be found "reasonable." In general, if the mechanism chosen by the parties is reasonable *at the time the method was agreed upon*, it will probably be found reasonable (and upheld) even though it turns out to produce a price that is much higher or lower than the market price at the time of sale.

VI. RESOLUTION OF DISPUTES, INCLUDING DISSOLUTION

A. Dissension and deadlock: The courts often have to deal with "dissension" and "deadlock" among the stockholders. "Dissension" refers to squabbles or disagreements among them. "Deadlock" refers to a situation where the corporation is paralyzed and prevented from acting (e.g., two factions each control the same number of directors, and the two factions cannot agree).

B. Dissolution: The major judicial remedy for dissension and deadlock is a court order that the corporation be *involuntarily dissolved*. Dissolution means that the corporation ceases to exist as a legal entity; the assets are sold off, the debts are paid, and any surplus is distributed to the shareholders.

1. **No general right:** *No state gives a shareholder an automatic right to a judicially-ordered dissolution.* Instead, each state has a statute setting forth *specific grounds* (strictly construed) on which dissolution may be granted.

2. **MBCA:** Thus under MBCA § 14.30(2), a shareholder must show one of these four things to get dissolution: (1) that the *directors* are *deadlocked*; (2) that those in control have acted in a manner that is "*illegal, oppressive*, or *fraudulent*"; (3) that the *shareholders* are *deadlocked* and have failed to elect new directors for at least two consecutive annual meetings; or (4) that the corporation's assets are being "*misapplied* or *wasted*."

3. **Judge's discretion:** Most states hold that even if the statutory criteria are met, the judge still has *discretion* to refuse to award dissolution (e.g., when it would be unfair to one or more shareholders).

4. **Remedy for oppression:** Most states allow dissolution to be granted as a remedy for *"oppression"* of a minority stockholder. (*Examples*: (1) Majority holder sells property to the corporation at inflated prices. (2) Majority holder tries to squeeze P out by refusing to pay him either a salary or dividends.)

5. **Buy-out in lieu of dissolution:** Under many statutes, the party opposing dissolution has the right to *buy-out* the shares of the party seeking dissolution at a judicially-supervised fair price.

6. **Dissolution of an LLC:** Most states allow for judicial dissolution of *LLCs*, just as for corporations.

    a. **Delaware:** For instance, the Delaware LLC Act says that on application by any member of the LLC, the court may "decree dissolution of [the LLC] whenever it is *not reasonably practicable* to *carry on the business* in conformity with [the LLC agreement]." §18-802.

        i. **Refusal to enforce operating agreement:** So, for instance, even if the LLC operating agreement has provisions for one member to buy out the other in case of deadlock, the court might instead decree a judicial dissolution of the LLC on account of deadlock, if the court believed that the operating-agreement buy-out provision would not be a "reasonably practical" method of continuing the business. [Cf. *Haley v. Talcott*]

C. **Alternatives to dissolution:** There are a number of alternatives to dissolution, including: (1) arbitration; (2) court appointment of a provisional director (to break a deadlock); (3) court appointment of a custodian (who will run the business); (4) appointment of a receiver (who will liquidate the business); and (5) a judicially-supervised buy-out in lieu of dissolution.

   1. **Fiduciary obligation of majority to minority:** A few states (especially Massachusetts) have formulated a theory of *fiduciary obligation*, under which a majority stockholder in a close corporation has a fiduciary obligation to *behave in good faith to a minority shareholder*.

      Example: P is a minority stockholder who has inherited her shares from her husband, an employee of Corporation. Corporation has previously bought back shares from its majority stockholder at a high price, but refuses to buy P's shares back at anything like the same price. *Held*, the controlling stockholder owed P a fiduciary duty, and was therefore required to cause Corporation to repurchase shares from P in the same portion, and at the same price, as it had purchased from the majority holder. [*Donahue v. Rodd Electrotype*].

      a. **Where applied:** The few courts that have recognized this "fiduciary obligation of majority to minority" tend to find it violated only where the majority holder causes the corporation to take action that has *no legitimate business purpose*.

         Example: Majority holders fire P, end his salary, drop him from the board, and refuse to pay dividends; *held*, these actions had no legitimate business purpose, and were used merely to deprive P of a reasonable return on his investment, so the majority holders violated their fiduciary obligations. [*Wilkes v. Springside Nursing Home, Inc.*].

   2. **Award of damages:** If the court does find that the majority has violated a fiduciary obligation to the minority, it can award *damages*.

CHAPTER 6

THE DUTY OF CARE AND THE BUSINESS JUDGMENT RULE

I. INTRODUCTION

A. **Duty generally:** The law imposes on a director or officer a *duty of care* with respect to the corporation's business. The director or officer must behave with that level of care which a *reasonable person* in *similar circumstances* would use.

1. **Damages vs. injunction:** If a director or officer violates this duty of care, and the corporation consequently loses money, the director/officer will be *personally liable* to pay *money damages* to the corporation. Separately, if the board of directors has approved a transaction without using due care (and the transaction has not yet been consummated), the court may grant an *injunction* against the transaction.

2. **Rare:** It is *very rare* for directors and officers to be found liable for breach of the duty of due care. (When this happens, it's usually because there is some taint of *self-dealing*, but not enough to cause the court to find a formal violation of the duty of loyalty.)

3. **Directors and officers:** The same duty of care is imposed on both *officers* and *directors*. However, what is "reasonable" conduct will often be different for an officer than for an outside director (since the officer normally has a better understanding of the corporation's affairs).

II. THE STANDARD OF CARE

A. **Basic standard:** The basic standard is that the director or officer must behave as a reasonably prudent person would behave in similar circumstances.

1. **No "accommodation" directors:** There is no such thing as an "accommodation" or "dummy" director. If a person sits on a board, he automatically (and non-waivably) bears the burden of acting with due care.

2. **Egregious cases:** However, liability for breach of the duty of due care is generally imposed only when the director or officer behaves *"recklessly"* or with *"gross negligence."*

   Example: D, a director, fails to attend board meetings, fails to read financial reports, fails to obtain the advice of a lawyer or accountant even though he is on notice that the corporation is being mismanaged — taken together, these acts amount to recklessness, and thus justify holding D liable for losses suffered by the corporation that could have been prevented by a director who exercised reasonable care. [*Francis v. United Jersey Bank*].

B. **Objective standard:** The standard of care is an *objective* one: the director is held to the conduct that would be exercised by a "reasonable person" in the director's position. So a director who is less smart, or less knowledgeable about business than an "ordinary" reasonable director nonetheless must meet this higher objective standard.

1. **Special skills:** On the other hand, if the director has *special skills* that go beyond what an ordinary director would have, he must *use* those skills. Thus a trained accountant, lawyer, banker, real estate professional, etc., if he learns of facts that would make a person in that profession suspicious, must follow through and investigate even though these facts would not make a non-professional suspicious.

C. **Reliance on experts and committees:** Directors are generally *entitled to rely* on *experts*, on reports prepared by insiders, and on action taken by a *committee* of the board. But all such reliance is allowed only if it is "reasonable" under the circumstances.

> **Example:** A director may rely on the financial statements prepared by the corporation's accountants; therefore, unless the director is on notice that the accountants are failing to uncover wrongdoing, the director will not be liable for, say, embezzlement that is not reflected in the financial statements.

D. **Passive negligence:** A director will not be liable merely for failing to *detect wrongdoing* by officers or employees.

1. **Director on notice:** However, if the director is on *notice* of facts suggesting wrongdoing, he cannot close his eyes to these facts.

2. **Monitoring mechanisms:** Also, in large corporations, it may constitute a violation of due care for the directors not to put into place *monitoring mechanisms* (e.g., stringent internal accounting controls, and/or an audit committee) to detect wrongdoing.

3. **Delaware law:** In Delaware, most corporations have exercised their statutory right to include a charter provision that directors will not be personally liable for lack of due care. But such an "exculpatory" provision can't block liability for breach of the duty of loyalty, or for lack of "good faith." So in Delaware, if the corporation has such an exculpatory clause, *directors will have liability for poor oversight only if:*

   [1] the directors "utterly *failed to implement any reporting or information system* or controls"; *or*

   [2] having implemented such a system or controls, the directors "*consciously failed to monitor or oversee [the system's] operations,* thus disabling themselves from being informed of risks or problems requiring their attention."

   [*Stone v. Ritter*]

   a. **Knowledge of shortcoming required:** To put it another way, directors who are protected by an exculpatory provision are still liable for lack of "good faith," but failure to supervise won't constitute lack of good faith unless the plaintiff shows that the directors *"knew that* *they were not discharging their fiduciary obligations*." [*Stone, supra*.]

    i. **Gross negligence not enough:** So what might be called *"oblivious gross negligence" won't be enough* for director-liability in Delaware where there's an exculpatory clause in the certificate of incorporation.

E. Causation: In many states, even if a director or officer has violated the duty of due care he is only liable for damages that are the *proximate result* of his conduct. (For instance, if the loss would have happened anyway, even had the directors all behaved with due care, there will be no liability in these courts.) However, other states, including Delaware, allow plaintiff to recover without a showing of causation against a director who violated his duty of care.

    1. **Joint and several:** If a board member violates his duty of due care, at least some courts hold him *jointly and severally liable* with all other directors who have violated that duty, so long as the board *collectively* was a proximate cause of the loss. (In other words, a director cannot say, "Even if I had been diligent, the other directors would still have ignored me and the loss would have happened anyway.")

III. THE BUSINESS JUDGMENT RULE

A. Function of rule: The "business judgment rule" saves many actions from being held to be violations of the duty of due care.

    1. **Relation to duty of due care:** Here is how the duty of due care and the business judgment rule fit together: (1) the duty of due care imposes a fairly stern set of *procedural* requirements for directors' actions; (2) once these procedural requirements are satisfied, the business judgment rule then supplies a much easier-to-satisfy standard with respect to the *substance* of the business decision.

B. Requirements: The business judgment rule basically provides that a *substantively-unwise decision* by a director or officer will *not by itself constitute a lack of due care*. However, there are three requirements (two of them procedural) which a decision by a director or officer must meet before it will be upheld by application of the business judgment rule:

    1. **No self-dealing:** First, the director or officer will not qualify for the protection of the business judgment rule if he has an *"interest"* in the transaction. In other words, any *self-dealing* by the director or officer will deprive him of the rule's protection.

    Example: X, an officer of Corp, has Corp buy supplies at inflated prices from another company of which X is secretly a major shareholder. X's decision to have Corp buy the supplies in this manner will not be protected by the business judgment rule, because the transaction in question amounted to self-dealing by X.

2. **Informed decision:** Second, the decision must have been an *"informed"* one. That is, the director or officer must have gathered at least a ***reasonable amount of information*** about the decision before he makes it.

   a. **Gross negligence standard:** Probably the *"gross negligence"* standard applies to the issue of whether the decision was an informed one. In other words, even if the director or officer is somewhat (but not grossly) negligent in failing to gather all reasonably available information, he will not lose the benefit of the rule. But if he was grossly negligent, he will lose the protection.

      Example: The Ds, directors of a publicly held corporation, approve a sale of the company without making any real attempt to learn the "intrinsic value" of the company, without having any written documentation about the proposed deal, without learning that no true bargaining took place with the buyer, and while spending only two hours on the decision even though there was no real emergency or time pressure. *Held*, the process used by the directors was so sloppy that their decision was not an "informed" one, so they do not have the protection of the business judgment rule and are in fact liable for the breach of the duty of due care. [*Smith v. Van Gorkom*].

3. **"Rational" decision:** Finally, the director or officer must have *"rationally believed"* that his business judgment was in the corporation's best interest. So the decision does not have to be substantively "reasonable," but it must be at least "rational" (i.e., not totally crazy). Note also that what must be rational is not the underlying *decision*, merely the *belief* that the decision is in the corporation's best interests.

   a. **No review of substance of underlying decision:** Because of this emphasis on the rationality of the "belief," not the rationality of the underlying decision, the court will generally focus on the directors' decision-making *process*, and will rarely consider the ***merits of the underlying decision.*** Or, as the idea is often put, the court will not use ***"20/20 hindsight"*** when it evaluates the board's decision — only if a transaction is "egregious on its face" will the court review the substance of the underlying decision.

C. **Exceptions:** Even where these three requirements for the business judgment rule are satisfied, there are one or two situations where the court may find the rule inapplicable:

1. **Illegal:** If the act taken or approved by the director or officer is a *violation of a criminal statute*, the defendant will lose the benefit of the business judgment rule.

   Example: The Ds, directors of a major corporation, approve the corporation's making of illegal political contributions. *Held*, the directors will not be protected by the business judgment rule, because the transaction in question violated a criminal statute. [*Miller v. American Telephone & Tele. Co.*].

2. **Pursuit of "social" goals:** Some courts may hold the business judgment rule inapplicable if the director is pursuing his own *social* or *political* goals (unrelated to the corporation's welfare). But other courts do not agree.

IV. RECENT STATUTORY CHANGES TO DIRECTOR LIABILITY

A. **Some approaches:** Some states have tried to restrict the liability of directors for breaches of the duty of due care. Here are some approaches:

   1. **Amendment:** Some states allow the shareholders to *amend the articles of incorporation* to eliminate or reduce directors' personal liability for violations of the duty of due care (e.g., Delaware § 102(b)(7));

   2. **Looser standard:** Some states have made the standard of care *looser*, so that only more outrageous conduct will be covered;

   3. **Limit on money damages:** Some states limit the *money damages* that may be recovered against the officer or director; and

   4. **Indemnification:** Most states now allow the corporation to *indemnify* directors and officers for liability for breach of the duty of due care.

CHAPTER 7

THE DUTY OF LOYALTY

I. SELF-DEALING TRANSACTIONS

A. **Definition:** A *"self-dealing transaction"* is one in which three conditions are met: (1) a Key Player (officer, director or controlling shareholder) and the corporation are on *opposite sides* of a transaction; (2) the Key Player has helped *influence* the corporation's decision to enter the transaction; and (3) the Key Player's personal financial interests are at least potentially *in conflict* with the financial interests of the corporation.

Example: A director/shareholder of Corp induces Corp to buy Blackacre from him at an inflated price.

B. Modern rule on self-dealing transactions: Courts will frequently intervene to strike down (or award damages for) a self-dealing transaction.

1. **General statement:** In most states, the approach to self-dealing transactions is as follows:

   a. **Fair:** If the transaction is found to be *fair* to the corporation, the court will *uphold* it. This is true regardless of whether the transaction was ever approved by disinterested directors or ratified by the shareholders.

   b. **Waste/fraud:** If the transaction is so unfair that it amounts to *"waste"* or *"fraud"* against the corporation, the court will usually void it at the request of a stockholder. This is true even though the transaction was approved by a majority of disinterested directors or ratified by the shareholders.

      i. **Standard for "waste":** The typical definition of "waste" is a very *restricted* one. Thus in Delaware, a transaction will not be invalidated as constituting waste unless it is "an exchange that is *so one sided that no business person of ordinary, sound judgment could conclude that the corporation has received adequate consideration."* Cf. *Brehm v. Eisner.* For instance, in the case of executive compensation, "If ... there is *any substantial consideration received* by the corporation, and if there is a *good faith judgment* [by the board] that in the circumstances the *transaction is worth while*, there should be no finding of waste, even if the fact finder would conclude ex post that the transaction was *unreasonably risky." Brehm, supra.*

   c. **Middle ground:** If the transaction does not fall into either of the two above categories — it's not clearly fair, but it's not so unfair as to amount to waste or fraud — the presence or absence of *director approval* and/or *shareholder ratification* will make the difference. If a majority of disinterested and knowledgeable directors have approved the transaction (or if the transaction has been ratified by the shareholders) the court will probably approve the transaction. If neither disinterested-director approval nor shareholder ratification has occurred, the court will probably invalidate the transaction.

2. **Three paths:** Thus there are three different ways that a proponent of a self-dealing transaction can probably avoid invalidation: (1) by showing approval by a majority of disinterested directors, after full disclosure; (2) by showing ratification by shareholders, after full disclosure; and (3) by

showing that the transaction was fair when made. We consider each of these "branches" below.

C. Disclosure plus board approval: A transaction may not be avoided by the corporation if it was *authorized* by a *majority of the disinterested directors*, after *full disclosure* of the nature of the conflict and the transaction.

    1. What must be disclosed: Two kinds of information must be disclosed to the board before it approves the transaction: (1) the material facts about the *conflict*; and (2) the material facts about the *transaction*.

    Example: If D, a director of XYZ Corp, wants to sell XYZ an office building he owns, he must disclose not only the fact that he owns the office building, but also any material facts about the deal, such as whether the price is a fair one in light of current market conditions.

        a. When disclosure must be made: Courts are split about *when* this disclosure must be made. Some courts require it to be made *before* the transaction. Others allow it to be *"ratified"* after the fact (e.g., by a resolution in which the board says that it has no objection to the transaction).

    2. Who is "disinterested" director: The approval must be by a majority of the *"disinterested"* directors. A director will be "interested" if either: (1) he or an *immediate member of his family* has a financial interest in the transaction; or (2) he or a family member has a *relationship* with the other party to the transaction that would reasonably be expected to *affect his judgment* about the transaction.

    Example: Prexy is president, director and controlling shareholder of XYZ. He wants to sell Blackacre, which he owns, to XYZ. Sidekick, who is an employee and director of XYZ, knows that he owes his job to Prexy. Sidekick will probably not be a "disinterested" director because his relationship with Prexy would be expected to affect his judgment about the transaction; therefore, Sidekick's vote to approve the transaction will not be counted.

    3. Quorum: A *quorum* for the vote by the disinterested directors merely has to consist of a majority of the disinterested directors, not a majority of the total directors. (Thus if there is a nine-member board, but only three disinterested directors, two of them will constitute a quorum, and both will have to vote in favor of the transaction to authorize it.)

    4. Immunization of unfairness: The fact that a majority of the disinterested directors (acting after full disclosure) have approved or ratified the transaction does not necessarily immunize it from attack, if the unfairness is *very great*. But the existence of such approval/ratification *shifts the burden of proof* to the person attacking the transaction, and the transaction will only be struck down if the unfairness is so great as to constitute *fraud* or *waste*.

D. Disclosure plus shareholder ratification: A self-dealing transaction will be validated if it is fully disclosed to the ***shareholders***, and then ***ratified*** by a ***majority*** of them.

    1. Disinterested shareholders: The courts are ***split*** about whether the ratification must be by a majority of ***disinterested*** shareholders, or merely by a majority of *all* shareholders (including, perhaps, the one who is doing the self-dealing).

        a. MBCA: Under MBCA § 8.63, a majority of the ***disinterested*** shareholders must approve the transaction.

E. Fairness as key criterion: Finally, a self-dealing transaction can be validated by a showing that it is, under all the circumstances, ***fair*** to the corporation. Such "overall fairness" will suffice even if the transaction was neither approved by the disinterested directors nor ratified by the shareholders. Fairness is generally determined by the facts as they were known ***at the time of the transaction***.

    1. No prior disclosure: In most courts, a fair transaction will be upheld ***even though it was never disclosed by the Key Player to his fellow executives, directors or shareholders.***

F. Indirect conflicts: A self-dealing transaction will be found not only where the Key Player is directly a party to the transaction, but also where he is ***indirectly*** a party, i.e., he owns an equity position in the other party to the transaction. The test is whether the Key Player's equity participation in the other party is big enough to expect his ***judgment*** to be ***affected***. See MBCA § 8.60(1)(i), (ii).

    Example: Prexy, in addition to being president, director and controlling shareholder of XYZ Corp, owns 20% of ABC Corp. A major transaction between ABC and XYZ will probably be a self-dealing transaction if Prexy influences the XYZ side of it, because Prexy's own 20% stake in ABC is probably large enough to affect his judgment about whether the transaction is good for XYZ.

    1. Interlocking directors: If the Key Player is merely a ***director*** (not a shareholder) of the other party to the transaction, this will usually ***not*** make the transaction a self-dealing one unless the transaction is a non-ordinary-course one requiring board approval. See MBCA § 8.60(1)(ii).

G. Remedies for violation: If there has been a violation of the rule against self-dealing, there are two possible remedies:

    1. Rescission: Normally, the court will ***rescind*** the transaction, where this is possible.

    Example: Prexy sells Blackacre to XYZ Corp, of which he is president and director. If the transaction is unfair, and was not ratified by directors or shareholders, the court will rescind it, giving title back to Prexy and the purchase price back to XYZ.

2. **Damages:** If because of passage of time or complexity of the transaction it cannot be rescinded, the court will award ***restitutionary damages***. That is, the Key Player will have to ***pay back*** to the corporation any benefit he received beyond what was fair.

II. EXECUTIVE COMPENSATION

A. **Business judgment rule:** If an officer or director influences a corporation's decision about his own compensation, this is technically a self-dealing transaction. However, courts are reluctant to strike down decisions about executive compensation. Such decisions receive the protection of the business judgment rule: the director's decision will be sustained so long as it is rational, informed, and made in good faith.

B. **Consideration:** In the case of ***deferred*** compensation plans, courts sometimes insist that the plan be set up in such a way that an executive will receive the deferred compensation only if he ***remains with the company.*** Thus a grant of stock options to all executives (regardless of whether they stay with the company) might be struck down as lacking in ***consideration***.

C. **Excessive compensation:** Even if a compensation scheme has been approved by a majority of the disinterested directors, or ratified by the shareholders, the court may still overturn it if the level of compensation is ***"excessive"*** or ***"unreasonable."*** That is, the compensation levels must be reasonably related to the ***value*** of the services performed by the executive.

1. **Few cases:** But courts very rarely strike down a compensation plan as excessive. One exception may be where a plan makes use of a ***formula*** which is not amended even though conditions change.

   Example: If XYZ enacts a formula paying its president 10% of pre-tax profits, and the corporation's profits increase so much that the president is earning $25 million a year, the court might strike the plan as excessive.

III. THE CORPORATE OPPORTUNITY DOCTRINE AND RELATED PROBLEMS

A. **Competition with corporation:** A director or senior executive ***may not compete*** with the corporation, where this competition is likely to ***harm*** the corporation.

   Example: Corp operates department stores in a particular city. A, B, and C, senior executives of Corp, secretly purchase a controlling interest in another department store in the same city. This is competition which is likely to harm Corp, so A, B, and C are violating their duty of loyalty to Corp.

1. **Approval or ratification:** Conduct that would otherwise be prohibited as disloyal competition may be validated by being *approved* by disinterested directors, or by being *ratified* by the shareholders. The Key Player must first make *full disclosure* about the conflict and the competition that he proposes to engage in.

2. **Preparation to compete:** Usually, courts will find that a Key Player has violated his duty of loyalty even if he just *prepares to compete* (rather than actually competing) while still in the corporation's employ. The court often will order the insider to *return all salary* he earned during the period of preparation.

3. **Competition after end of employment:** But if the executive first *leaves* the corporation, and only then begins preparations or actual competition, this does *not* constitute a violation of the duty of loyalty. (However, the insider may not use the corporation's *trade secrets.* Also, the insider will be barred from competing if he has signed a valid *non-competition agreement.*)

B. **Use of corporate assets:** A Key Player may not *use corporate assets* if this use either: (1) *harms* the corporation; or (2) gives the Key Player a *financial benefit*. "Corporate assets" include not only tangible goods, but also intangibles like information.

> **Example:** D, the president of XYZ, lives rent-free in a house owned by XYZ; this is a violation of the duty of loyalty to XYZ and to its other shareholders.

1. **Approval or payment:** Use of the corporate assets will not be a violation of the duty of loyalty if: (1) it is approved by disinterested directors (after full disclosure); (2) it is ratified by shareholders (after full disclosure); or (3) the Key Player pays the *fair value* for any benefit he has received.

C. **The "corporate opportunity" doctrine:** A director or senior executive may not usurp for himself a business opportunity that is found to "belong" to the corporation. Such an opportunity is said to be a *"corporate opportunity."*

1. **Effect:** If the Key Player is found to have taken a "corporate opportunity," the taking is *per se wrongful* to the corporation, and the corporation may recover *damages* equal to the loss it has suffered or even the *profits* it would have made had it been given the chance to pursue the opportunity.

2. **The Delaware multi-factor test:** Delaware law is especially influential in this area. Under Delaware law, a business opportunity presented to a

corporate officer or director will count as a "corporate opportunity" if it meets the following requirements:

❑ the corporation is "***financially able to exploit***" the opportunity;

❑ the opportunity is "within the corporation's ***line of business***";

❑ the corporation has an ***"interest or a reasonable expectancy"*** in the opportunity; and

❑ if the director or officer were to embrace the opportunity, he would thereby be placed in a ***conflict*** with his duties to the corporation.

[*Beam v. Stewart*]

    i.   **Either "line of business" or "interest or expectancy":** The language quoted above sounds as though the opportunity must satisfy *both* the "line of business" and "interest or expectancy" standards. But in practice, the Delaware courts seem to hold that the opportunity must merely satisfy *either* the "line of business" or "interest or expectancy" test, not both.

3. Other factors: Regardless of which main test is used, here are some additional factors that courts find important in determining whether an opportunity was a "corporate" one:

    a. whether the opportunity was offered to the insider as an ***individual*** or as a ***corporate manager***;

    b. whether the insider learned of the opportunity while acting in his role as the corporation's agent;

    c. whether the insider used ***corporate resources*** to take advantage of the opportunity;

    d. whether the opportunity was ***essential*** to the corporation's well being;

    e. whether the corporation is ***closely*** or ***publicly held*** (the case for finding a corporate opportunity is stronger in the case of a publicly held corporation); and

    f. whether the person taking the opportunity is an outside director or a ***full-time executive*** (more likely to be a corporate opportunity in the case of a full-time executive).

4. Who is bound: Generally, courts seem to apply the corporate opportunity doctrine only to ***directors***, ***full-time employees***, and ***controlling shareholders***. Thus a shareholder who has only a ***non-controlling interest*** (and who is not a director or employee) will generally ***not*** be subjected to the doctrine.

5. Rejection by corporation: If the insider offers the corporation the chance to pursue the opportunity, and the corporation *rejects* the opportunity by a majority vote of disinterested directors or disinterested share-holders, the insider may pursue the opportunity himself. The insider must make *full disclosure* about what he proposes to do. (Some but not all courts allow ratification *after the fact*.)

6. **Corporation's inability to take advantage:** Courts are split about whether it is a defense that a corporation would have been *unable* (for financial or other reasons) to take advantage of the opportunity. As noted above, in Delaware if the corporation could not have financially exploited the opportunity it won't be deemed to be a corporate opportunity.

7. **No need for pre-approval by corporation:** At least in Delaware, the Key Player does not need to *disclose* the opportunity to the board of the corporation *in advance*, so as to give the board the chance to argue that this is indeed a corporate opportunity that the corporation wishes to pursue. The Key Player is always free to disclose the opportunity and try to get the corporation to say that it's not interested (which would give the Key Player a sort of "safe harbor"), but the Key Player is *not required* to make advance disclosure. [*Broz v. Cellular Info. Systems, Inc.*]

8. **Corporation's inability to take advantage:** Courts are split about whether it is a defense that a corporation would have been *unable* (for financial or other reasons) to take advantage of the opportunity.

9. **Remedies:** The usual remedy for the taking of a corporate opportunity is for the court to order the imposition of a *constructive trust* — the property is treated as if it belonged to the corporation that owned the opportunity. Also, the Key Player may be ordered to account for *all profits* earned from the opportunity.

IV. THE SALE OF CONTROL

A. **Generally:** In some (but not most) situations, the court will prevent a "controlling shareholder" from selling that controlling interest at a *premium price*.

1. **"Control block" defined:** A person owns a "controlling interest" if he has the power to use the assets of the corporation however he chooses. A majority owner will always have a controlling interest. But the converse is not true: a less-than-majority interest will often be controlling (e.g., a 20-40% interest where the remaining ownership is highly dispersed and no other shareholder is as large).

2. **Generally allowed:** The general rule is that the controlling shareholder *may sell his control block for a premium, and may keep the premium for himself*.

   a. **Exceptions:** However, there are a number of exceptions (discussed below) to this general rule, including: (1) the "looting" exception; (2)

the "sale of vote" exception; and (3) the "diversion of collective opportunity" exception.

B. The "looting" exception: The controlling shareholder may not sell his control block if he knows or suspects that the buyer intends to *"loot"* the corporation by unlawfully diverting its assets.

> **Example:** ABC is an investment company with $6 per share of assets, but with nearly offsetting liabilities and a net asset value of six cents per share. Buyer offers to buy Seller's control block for $2 per share, a sum many times greater than market value. Because Seller knows or suspects that the only reason Buyer is willing to pay such a huge premium is because he intends to illegally transfer the liquid assets to himself, Seller may not sell his control block to Buyer at a premium price. If he does so, he will be liable to ABC and its other shareholders for damages.

1. Mental state: Clearly if the controlling shareholder either *knows* or *strongly suspects* that the buyer will loot, he may not sell to him. Also, if Seller *recklessly disregards* the possibility of looting, the same rule applies. Most, but probably not all, courts would also impose liability where the seller merely *"negligently"* disregards the likelihood that the buyer will loot.

2. Excessive price: In many courts, *excessive price alone* will *not* be enough to necessarily put the seller on notice that the buyer intends to loot. But an excessive price combined with other factors (e.g., the liquid and readily saleable nature of the company's assets) will be deemed to put the seller on notice.

C. The "sale of vote" exception: The controlling shareholder may not sell for a premium where the sale amounts to a *"sale of his vote."*

1. Majority stake: If the controlling shareholder owns a *majority* interest, the "sale of vote" exception will *not* apply. Thus even if the controlling shareholder specifically agrees that he will ensure that a majority of the board resigns so that the buyer is able to immediately elect his own majority of the board, this will not be deemed to be a sale of vote (since the buyer would eventually get control of the board anyway merely by owning the majority stake).

2. Small stake: If the seller has a very *small* stake (e.g., less than 20%) in the corporation, and promises to use his influence over the directors to induce them to resign so that the buyer can elect disproportionately many directors, then the "sale of vote" exception is likely to be applied.

3. "Working control": Where the seller has "working control," and promises to deliver the resignations of a majority of directors so that the buyer can receive that working control, courts are split about whether this constitutes a sale of vote.

4. **Separate payment:**   Also, if the contract of sale explicitly provides for a *separate payment* for the delivery of directors' resignations and election of the buyer's nominees to the board, this will be a sale of vote.

D. **Diversion of collective opportunity:**

1. **Business opportunity:**   A court may find that the corporation had a business opportunity, and that the controlling shareholder has constructed the sale of his control block in such a way as to *deprive the corporation of this business opportunity.* If so, the seller will not be allowed to keep the control premium.

    > **Example:** ABC Corp, due to scarce wartime conditions, is able to get interest-free loans from its customers. President sells his control block to a consortium of those customers, who then cancel the no-interest loan arrangements and who sell themselves much of ABC's production, although at standard prices. The president may be found to have diverted a business opportunity belonging to ABC, in which case he will not be allowed to keep the portion of the price he received for his shares that is above the fair market value of those shares. See *Perlman v. Feldmann.*

2. **Seller switches type of deal:**   If Buyer proposes to buy the entire company, but Seller instead *switches* the nature of the deal by talking Buyer into buying just Seller's control block (at a premium), a court may take away Seller's right to keep the premium, on the grounds that all shareholders deserve the right to participate.

E. **Remedies:**   If one of these exceptions applies (so that the seller is not entitled to keep the control premium) there are two remedies which the court may impose:

1. **Recovery by corporation:**   Sometimes, the court will allow the *corporation* to recover. (But this has the drawback that the purchaser who paid the control premium gets a windfall.)

2. **Pro rata recovery:**   Alternately, the court may award a *pro rata* recovery, under which the seller repays to the *minority shareholders* their pro rata part of the control premium (thus avoiding a windfall to the buyer).

V. OTHER DUTIES OF CONTROLLING SHAREHOLDERS

A. **Possible general fiduciary duty:**   Almost no courts have held that a controlling shareholder owes any kind of *general fiduciary duty* to the minority shareholders. (A few courts have recognized such a fiduciary duty limited to the case of a ***close*** corporation. See, e.g., *Donahue v. Rodd Electrotype*, discussed at the end of the chapter, "Close Corporations," *supra*, p. C-61).

B. Duty of complete disclosure: When a controlling shareholder or group deals with the non-controlling shareholders, it owes the latter a ***duty of complete disclosure*** with respect to the transaction, as a matter of state common law.

> **Example:** Controlling shareholders in ABC give notice of the proposed redemption of a minority block, without telling the minority holders that due to secret developments the minority holders would benefit by exercising certain conversion rights. *Held*, this failure to give complete disclosure violated the majority's common law obligation to the minority. See *Zahn v. Transamerica Corp.*; *Speed v. Transamerica Corp.*

C. Parent/subsidiary relations: When the controlling shareholder is another corporation (the ***parent/subsidiary*** context), essentially the same rules apply.

   1. Dividends: When the parent corporation controls the parent's ***dividend*** policy, this is in theory self-dealing. But so long as dividends are paid pro rata to all shareholders (including the parent), courts will rarely overturn the subsidiary's dividend policy even though this was dictated by the needs of the parent.

   2. Other types of self-dealing: Other types of self-dealing transactions between parent and subsidiary will be struck down if they are ***unfair*** to the minority shareholders of the subsidiary, and were entered into on the subsidiary's side by a board ***dominated by directors appointed by the parent***.

   Example: Subsidiary and Parent agree to a price and terms under which Subsidiary will sell to Parent the oil it produces. If Subsidiary's board is dominated by directors appointed by Parent, Parent will have to bear the burden of proving that the transaction is fair to Subsidiary and to the minority holders of Subsidiary.

   3. Corporate opportunities: If the parent takes for itself an opportunity that should belong to the subsidiary, the court will apply the ***"corporate opportunity"*** doctrine, and void the transaction.

   4. Disinterested directors: The parent can avoid liability both for self-dealing transactions and for the taking of corporate opportunities by having the truly ***disinterested directors*** of the subsidiary form a ***special committee*** which negotiates at arm's length with the parent on behalf of the subsidiary.

CHAPTER 8

INSIDER TRADING

I.   INTRODUCTION TO INSIDER TRADING

A. Generally: The term "insider trading" has no precise definition, but basically refers to the buying or selling of stock in a publicly traded company based on material, non-public information about that company.

1. **Not all illegal:**   Not all insider trading (as defined above) is illegal. In general, only insider trading that occurs as a result of someone's *willful breach* of a *fiduciary duty* will be illegal (at least under the federal securities laws, which are the main source of insider trading law).

2. **Illustrations:**   Either *buying on undisclosed good news*, or *selling on undisclosed bad news*, can be insider trading (and will often be illegal).

   a. **Buying before disclosure of good news:**   Thus if an insider at Oil Corp buys stock at a time when he knows, and the market doesn't, that Oil Corp has just struck a huge gusher, this is illegal insider trading.

   b. **Sale before disclosure of bad news:**   Similarly, if an insider at Oil Corp sells his stock at a time when he knows (and the market does not) that Oil Corp is just about to report an unexpected large loss, this too is illegal insider trading.

3. **Harms:**   The possible harms from insider trading include: (1) harm to the *reputation* of the corporation whose stock is being insider-traded; (2) harm to *market efficiency*, because insiders will delay disclosing their information and prices will be "wrong"; (3) harm to the *capital markets*, because investors will stay away from what they think is a "rigged" market; and (4) harm to *company efficiency*, because managers may be induced to run their companies in an inefficient manner (but one that produces large insider trading profits).

4. **Bodies of law:**   There are three bodies of law which may be violated by a particular act of insider trading:

   a. **State common law:**   A few states impose *common-law* restrictions on insider trading.

   b. **10b-5:**   The federal *SEC Rule 10b-5* prohibits any "fraudulent or manipulative device" in connection with the purchase or sale of security; this has been interpreted to bar most types of insider trading.

   c. **Short-swing profits:**   Section 16(b) of the federal Securities Exchange Act makes insiders liable to repay to the corporation all profits they make from "*short swing* trading profits" (whether based on insider information or not).

Note: Of these three bodies of law, SEC Rule 10b-5 is by far and away the most important limit on insider trading.

II. STATE COMMON-LAW APPROACHES

A. **Suit by shareholder:** A shareholder can in theory bring a state common law action against an insider trader for "*deceit*."

   1. **Face-to-face:** If the insider buys from the outsider in a *face-to-face* transaction, the rule is that the insider has *no duty to disclose* material facts (e.g., good news) known to him. So usually, even in this face-to-face situation, the plaintiff outsider will not be able to recover in deceit even though he would not have sold at the price he did had he known the undisclosed good news. But there are some exceptions:

      a. **Fraud:** If the insider knowingly *lies* or tells a *half truth*, he will be liable under ordinary deceit principles.

      b. **Special facts:** Many states recognize a *"special facts"* exception to the general rule that silence cannot constitute deceit.

        Example: If the insider *seeks out* the other party, or makes elaborate attempts to *conceal* his own identity, the "special facts" doctrine may be employed.

      c. **Minority rule:** A minority of states impose a more general rule that in face-to-face transactions, the insider has an affirmative obligation to disclose material facts known to him.

   2. **Garden variety impersonal insider trading:** If the insider trading takes place in an *impersonal* rather than a face-to-face way (i.e., it occurs by means of *open-market purchases* on the stock market), virtually no states allow the outsider to recover on common-law principles.

B. **Suit by corporation:** A very few states have allowed the *corporation* to recover against an insider who buys or sells based on undisclosed material information.

   1. ***Diamond* case:** The best known example is *Diamond v. Oreamuno*, where the corporation was permitted to recover against the insiders who sold before disclosing bad news; recovery was allowed even though there was no direct tangible harm to the corporation.

   2. **ALI:** The ALI follows the approach of *Diamond*, by making it an actionable breach of loyalty for the insider to use "material non-public information concerning the corporation" to either cause harm to the corporation, or to secure a pecuniary benefit not available to other shareholders.

III. SEC RULE 10b-5 AND INSIDER TRADING

A. **Summary:** The principal proscription against insider trading is SEC's *Rule 10b-5*, enacted pursuant to the Securities Exchange Act of 1934.

1. **Text:** SEC Rule 10b-5 makes it unlawful: (1) to "employ any device, scheme, or artifice to *defraud*"; (2) to make any "untrue statement of a material fact or to *omit to state* a material fact. . . ."; or (3) to engage in any "act, practice, or course of business which operates or would operate as a *fraud or deceit* upon any person." All three of these types of conduct are forbidden only if they occur "in connection with the purchase or sale of any security."

2. **Disclose-or-abstain:** The insider does not have an affirmative obligation to *disclose* the material, non-public information. Rather, he must *choose* between disclosure and abstaining from trading.

3. **Misrepresentation:** If an insider makes an affirmative *misrepresentation* (as opposed to merely omitting to disclose information), he can be liable under 10b-5 even if he does not buy or sell the stock.

4. **Nature of violation:** Violation of 10b-5 is a *crime*. Also, the SEC can get an *injunction* against the conduct. Finally, a private party who has been injured will, if he meets certain procedural requirements, have a *private right of action* for damages against the insider trader.

5. **Private companies:** Rule 10b-5 applies to fraud in the purchase or sale of securities in *privately-held* companies, not just publicly held ones.

B. **Requirements for private right of action:** An outsider injured by insider trading has a right of action for damages under Rule 10b-5, if he can meet certain procedural requirements:

1. **Purchaser or seller:** P must have been a *purchaser* or *seller* of the company's stock during the time of non-disclosure.

2. **Traded on material, non-public info:** D must have misstated or omitted a *material* fact.

3. **Special relationship:** If the claim is based on insider trading, D must be shown to have had a *special relationship* with the issuer, based on some kind of *fiduciary duty* to the issuer.

4. **Scienter:** D must be shown to have acted with *scienter*, i.e., he must be shown to have had an intent to deceive, manipulate or defraud.

5. **Reliance and causation:** P must show that he relied on D's misstatement or omission, and that that misstatement or omission was the proximate cause of his loss. (In cases of silent insider trading rather than misrepresentation, these requirements usually don't have much effect.)

6. Jurisdiction: There is a federal jurisdictional requirement: D must be shown to have done the fraud or manipulation "by the use of any means or instrumentality of *interstate commerce* or of the *mails*, or of any *facility of any national securities exchange*." In the case of any *publicly-traded security*, this requirement will readily be *met*. But where the fraud consists of deceit in a *face-to-face sale of shares*, especially shares in a *private company*, then the jurisdictional requisites may well be *lacking*.

Note: The first five of these requirements are discussed below.

C. P as purchaser or seller: P in a private 10b-5 action must have been either a *purchaser* or *seller* of stock in the company to which the misrepresentation or insider trading relates. [*Blue Chip Stamps v. Manor Drug Stores*].

1. Non-sellers: Thus one who already owned shares in the issuer and who *decides not to sell* because the corporation or its insiders makes an unduly optimistic representation, or fails to disclose negative material, may not sue.

2. Options: Some courts hold that this "purchaser or seller" requirement also means that a plaintiff who buys or sells *options* on a company's stock has no standing to sue an insider who trades on the company's stock.

D. "Material" non-public fact: D must be shown to have made a *misstatement* or *omission* of a *"material"* fact.

1. "Material": A fact is "material" if there is a "substantial likelihood that a reasonable shareholder would consider it important" in deciding whether to buy, hold, or sell the stock.

a. Mergers: The fact that the company is engaged in "merger" discussions is *not* necessarily "material." This is a fact-based question that depends on how far along the negotiations are, whether a specific price is on the table, whether the investment bankers have been brought in, etc.

b. Fact need not be outcome-determinative: To be "material," a fact does *not* have to be one that, if known to the investor, would have *changed the investor's decision*. The "total mix" test means that "a material fact is one that would *affect* a reasonable investor's *deliberations* without necessarily changing her ultimate investment decision." [*Folger Adam Co. v. PMI Industries, Inc.*].

2. Non-public: If the claim is that D traded silently rather than made a misrepresentation, the omission must be of a *non-public* fact. But "non-public" is interpreted broadly: even if a fact has been disclosed, say, to a few reporters, it is still non-public (and trading is not allowed) until the investors as a *whole* have learned of it.

E. Defendant as insider, knowing tippee or misappropriator: In the case of silent insider trading, D will not be liable unless he was either an *insider*, a *"tippee,"* or a *"misappropriator."* In other words, mere trading while in possession of material non-public information is *not by itself enough* to make D civilly liable under 10b-5.

> **Example:** D is sitting in a taxi, and finds handwritten notes left by the prior occupant. The notes indicate that ABC Corp. is about to launch a tender offer for XYZ Corp. D buys XYZ stock. D won't be liable under 10b-5, because he was not an insider of XYZ, nor a "tippee" of one who was an insider of XYZ, nor a "misappropriator" who "stole" the information from anyone.

1. **Insiders:** An *"insider"* is one who obtains information by virtue of his *employment* with the company whose stock he trades in. One can be an insider even if one is a *low-level employee* (e.g., a secretary). Also, people who do work on a contract basis for the issuing company (e.g., professionals like accountants and lawyers) can be a "constructive" insider. See *infra*, p. C-85.

2. **Knowing tippee:** A person will be a *"tippee,"* and will be liable for insider trading, if he *knows that the source of his tip has violated a fiduciary obligation to the issuer.* Conversely, if the tippee does not know this (or if the insider has not breached any fiduciary obligation), the tippee is not liable.

> **Example:** X, a former employee of ABC Corp, tells D that XYZ is engaging in massive financial fraud. X is not acting for any pecuniary benefit, but instead just wants to expose the fraud. D tells his clients to sell their ABC stock. *Held*, D did not violate 10b-5, because X was not violating any fiduciary duty, so D was not a knowing "tippee." *Dirks v. SEC*.

3. **Misappropriator:** A *"misappropriator"* is one who takes information from anyone — especially from a person who is *not the issuer* — in violation of an express or implied *obligation of confidentiality*.

> **Example:** Lawfirm represents Behemoth, a big company that is secretly planning a takeover of Smallco. D, a partner at Lawfirm, learns from Behemoth about these plans, and buys Smallco stock. *Held*, D has violated 10b-5, because he misappropriated the information from Behemoth, in violation of an implied promise of confidentiality. This is true even though neither D nor Lawfirm was an insider of Smallco, the issuer. [*U.S. v. O'Hagan*].

F. Scienter: A defendant is liable under 10b-5 only if he acted with *scienter*, i.e., with intent to *deceive*, manipulate or defraud. Probably this is met if D makes a misstatement *recklessly*. (In silent insider trading cases, the scienter requirement means that the defendant must have known that the information to which he had access was material and non-public.)

G. Trading "while in possession" of info, vs. trading "on the basis of" info: Is it enough for liability that D was merely ***"in possession"*** of the inside information at the time of the trade, even if the government cannot prove that D in some sense ***"used"*** the information in making his decision to trade? The answer is essentially ***"yes,"*** as a result of the SEC's adoption of an important rule, ***Rule 10b-5-1.***

    1. "Awareness" test: 10b-5 (the basic anti-fraud rule) prohibits trading "on the basis of" material nonpublic information. But 10b-5-1 now defines "on the basis of" to *mean **"was aware of"** the information"* at the time of the purchase or sale. In other words (except for a "safe harbor" which we'll discuss below), the government or private plaintiff merely has to show that D was ***"aware"*** of the inside information at the time he traded, *not* that the inside information in any sense ***caused or even affected*** D's decision to trade. (So D can't defend by saying, "Sure I sold the stock at a time when I knew that bad news was coming, but my *real* reason for selling was something else.")

        a. Safe harbor for preplanned trading: But Rule 10b-5-1 also gives the insider an important ***"safe harbor"***: if before becoming aware of the inside information, the insider adopts a ***"written plan for trading securities"*** that ***locks the insider into making particular types of purchases or sales at particular times*** or under particular circumstances, sales that are made according to this preplanned trading arrangement won't be deemed to be "on the basis of" the inside information, even if the insider knows the information at the time the trade actually occurs.

        Example: Prexy, the head of XYZ Corp., owns $100 million of XYZ stock, and would like to gradually diminish the proportion that XYZ stock constitutes of his net worth. In late 2004, therefore, Prexy adopts an irrevocable written contract with Broker, under which Prexy instructs Broker to sell $5 million of Prexy's XYZ stock during the first week of each calendar quarter for the next three years. On June 25, 2005, Prexy learns that XYZ will soon need to announce poor quarterly earnings, which will likely lead to a decline in the stock. On July 2, before the poor earnings are reported, Broker sells $5 million of stock for Prexy.

        Even though the sale took place at a time when Prexy was in possession of material nonpublic information, Prexy has not committed insider trading, because he has successfully used the preplanned-trading-arrangement safe harbor of Rule 10b-5-1. The idea is that because in late 2004 Prexy irrevocably made the decision to sell shares in the first week of July, 2005 — a decision that would bind him no matter what happened to the market price or status of XYZ — he won't be deemed to have sold "on the basis of" information that he didn't acquire until after making that irrevocable decision.

H. Causation; reliance:

1. **Misrepresentation:** If the case involves affirmative misrepresentation (not just silent insider trading), P will be given the benefit of a ***presumption*** that P ***relied*** on the misrepresentation and that it ***caused*** P's injury. In other words, because of the fact that the stock market is usually "efficient," D's misstatement will be presumed to have ***affected the price*** at which the plaintiff bought or sold.

   Example: D, an insider at XYZ, falsely says, "Profits will be up this quarter." P buys for $20 per share. Profits go down, and the stock drops to $10. The misstatement will be presumed to have affected the market price, and P will be presumed to have relied on the fairness of that price.

   a. **Rebuttable:** But this presumption of reliance may be *rebutted*.

2. **Silent insider trading:** If the case involves silent insider trading, the requirements of reliance and causation are not very important (and probably are ignored by the courts) so you can safely ignore them.

I. "Contemporaneous trader's" right to sue: In 1988, Congress specifically allowed any insider-trader to be sued civilly by any *"contemporaneous trader"* who traded in the *other direction*. The plaintiff can recover his own losses up to the amount of gain achieved, or loss avoided, by the defendant. P does not have to prove that the insider trading "caused" P's loss. (The statutory provision creating this right of action doesn't define "insider trading"; that's left to the courts, as it has always been.)

   Example: D, Senior Vice President of XYZ Corp., learns from his job that XYZ will soon be acquired by ABC Corp. at a price of $40 per share. D buys 1000 shares of XYZ on March 1 at a price of $20 per share. On March 2, P sells 2000 shares of XYZ at $20 each. The merger is announced on March 3, and the price goes to $40 immediately. D sells at $40, and thus makes a $20,000 profit. P may sue D civilly, and may recover $20,000. That is, P gets the lesser of: (1) P's lost profits (which are probably $40,000, since that's the profit he would have made on his shares if the market had been aware of the inside information at the time P made his sale); and (2) D's gains ($20,000).

1. **Information not from issuer:** This express private right of action applies even though the inside information does not derive from the issuer, but rather, from some third party. However, under court rulings that still apply — like *Dirks, supra*, p. 81 — the trade is not "insider trad-

ing" unless the trader knew that the information was obtained by the trader or his tipper in violation of some *fiduciary responsibility*.

> **Example:** On the facts of the above example, P could recover even if D learned the information while working at ABC, the acquirer, rather than while working at XYZ, the issuer. But if D had learned the information by overhearing a conversation on a park bench — or in any other way not involving a breach of fiduciary responsibility by D or D's source — then this would not be "insider trading" at all, and P could not recover under the express private right of action now given to "contemporaneous traders" injured by insider trading.

J. Damages: If P meets all of these requirements for a private 10b-5 action, there are various ways that the *measure of damages* might be calculated.

1. Misrepresentation: If D has made a *misrepresentation*, P generally receives damages that would be needed to put him in the position he would have been in had his trade been delayed until after the misrepresentation was corrected.

2. Silent trading; P is "contemporaneous trader": If D is a silent insider-trader, and P is a *"contemporaneous trader,"* P may recover the lesser of: (1) P's own losses (probably measured by how much gain P would have made, or how much loss he would have avoided, had the inside information been disclosed before P traded); and (2) D's gains made, or losses avoided, from the transaction. See the example to Par. (H) above.

3. P is acquirer who has to pay more: If P is an *acquirer* who as the result of D's insider trading or tipping in the target's stock is forced to *pay more* to acquire the target, P's liability is probably *not limited* to the gains made by D.

> **Example:** Suitor is planning to acquire Target. Target's stock is now $20 per share, and Suitor plans to offer the public $30. Dennis, a managing director at InvestCo., Suitor's investment banker, buys 1000 shares in Target at $20, and tells his friends so they can buy too. As a result of this trading and tipping, the price of Target jumps immediately to $30. Suitor finally has to pay $40, rather than $30, to buy all Target's 1 million shares. Probably Suitor can recover $10 million — the amount it had to pay extra — from Dennis, even though Dennis only made $20,000.

4. SEC civil penalties: Also, the *SEC* may recover *civil penalties* against an insider trader. The SEC may recover a civil penalty of up to *three times* the profit gained or loss avoided by the insider trader. See '34 Act, § 21A(a)(3) and 21A(b).

a. **"Controlling person's" liability:** Furthermore, as the result of changes made by Congress in 1988 to the Securities Exchange Act, a person or organization who *"controls"* an insider trader, and carelessly fails to take steps to prevent foreseeable insider trading, may be liable for the same three-fold SEC civil penalties as the insider.

Example: D insider-trades based on information he learned while working as an associate in the mergers and acquisitions department of Law Firm. Law Firm can be liable for three-fold civil penalties if the SEC shows that Law Firm recklessly disregarded the risk that D might insider trade and failed to take reasonable steps to limit this risk of such trading.

IV. WHO IS AN "INSIDER" OR "TIPPEE"?

A. Recap: Remember that only a person who is either an "insider" or a "tippee" is covered by 10b-5.

1. Who is "insider": A person is an "insider" only if he has some sort of *fiduciary relationship* with the issuer that requires him to keep the non-public information confidential.

2. Who is "tippee": A person is a *"tippee"* only if: (1) he receives information given to him in **breach** of the insider's fiduciary responsibility; (2) he **knows** that (or, perhaps, **should know** that) the breach has occurred; and (3) the insider/tipper has received some **benefit** from the breach (or intended to make a pecuniary gift to the tippee).

B. Acquired by chance: Thus if an outsider acquires information *totally by chance*, without anyone violating any fiduciary obligation of confidentiality, the outsider may trade with impunity.

Example: The outsider randomly overhears inside information in a restaurant without any fiduciary violation by the speaker or by the outsider. The outsider may trade with impunity.

C. Acquired by diligence: Similarly, if an outsider acquires non-public information through his *own diligence*, he may trade upon it.

Example: A security analyst ferrets out non-public information by interviewing former employees and others who when they speak to the analyst are not receiving or intending to confer any pecuniary benefit. The analyst may trade upon the information.

D. Intent to make a gift: If an insider gives an outsider information with the *intent to make a gift* of *pecuniary value* to the outsider, the outsider will be a "tippee," and both *insider and outsider* will be liable.

Example: *A* gives an inside stock tip to his mistress, *B*, with the intent that *B* be able to make some money by buying the stock. Even though *A* doesn't expect or get any profit himself, *A* and *B* are both liable under 10b-5.

E. **"Constructive" insider:**   A person who is given confidential information by the issuer so that he can *perform services* for the issuer will be a "temporary" or *"constructive"* insider. Thus an investment banker, accountant, lawyer, or consultant will be a constructive insider (and thus may not trade, or tip others to trade).

F. **Disclosure between family members:** If the tipper learns information from a *close relative*, this relationship is *not* by itself enough to give the tipper a fiduciary responsibility. This is true even if the relative or the relative's family control the issuer, the information "belongs" to the issuer, and the tipper knows all this.

> **Example:** The Waldbaum family, which controls publicly-held Waldbaum Corp., agrees to sell Waldbaum Corp. to another company, for a price higher than the current market price. Ira Waldbaum, President of Waldbaum, tells his sister; she tells her daughter, Susan. Susan tells her husband, Keith, and then tells him to keep the information secret. Keith tells D, his stockbroker, who secretly buys Waldbaum stock for himself. D is charged with the crime of violating 10b-5.
>
> *Held*, D is not guilty of violating 10b-5. The mere family relationship between Susan and Keith was not enough to make Keith a "fiduciary" regarding the merger information; this is true even though Keith knew the information came from the issuer (Waldbaum Corp.) and knew that the information derived from Susan's family's control of the issuer. (But if Keith had promised confidentiality to Susan as a condition of hearing the news, then he would have been a fiduciary.) Because Keith was not a fiduciary, his tippee, D, has no 10b-5 liability. (But D *is* guilty of violating SEC Rule 14e-3, which prohibits trading on non-public information about a tender offer.) [*U.S. v. Chestman*].

G. **Confidential information from other than issuer (the "misappropriation" problem):** Where an outsider receives confidential information but *not from the issuer*, the situation is trickier.

1. **Criminal liability under other provisions:** Often, trading by the outsider in this situation will constitute *mail* or *wire fraud*. This will be the case if the outsider has "misappropriated" the information.

> **Example:** D is a reporter for the *Wall Street Journal*. He learns that company XYZ will be the subject of a favorable news story in the *Journal*. He buys XYZ stock. *Held*, even though D's information did not come from the issuer (XYZ) he has "misappropriated" it from his

employer, so he will be criminally liable under federal wire and/or mail fraud statutes. [*Carpenter v. U.S.*].

2. 10b-5: There is confusion about whether *Rule 10b-5* is violated when the outsider trades based on confidential information from someone other than the issuer.

    a. SEC action: Courts are split on whether the *SEC* may bring a civil or criminal action in this situation, but most courts would probably allow such an action.

    b. Civil liability to investors: Even if one who trades on confidential information not derived from the issuer is civilly or criminally liable in an SEC enforcement action, this does not necessarily mean that investors may successfully bring a private damage action against him (in the absence of any statute on point).

    c. Suit by acquiring corporation: If the outsider learns the information in breach of his fiduciary obligation to the *would-be acquirer* of a target, and then trades in the target's stock, there is a good chance that the *acquirer* will be able to recover damages against the outsider under 10b-5.

3. Rule 14e-3: SEC Rule *14e-3* prohibits trading on non-public information *about a tender offer*, even if the information comes from the *acquirer* rather than the target, and even if the information is *not obtained in violation of any fiduciary duty.* There may be (this is not yet certain) an implied private right of action on behalf of the offeror and/or other investors in the target for a 14e-3 violation.

H. One's own trading plans: It is *not* a violation of 10b-5 for one who is about to launch *his own tender offer* to buy shares on the open market without disclosing his plans.

    Example: Raider secretly buys 4% of Target Corp stock on the New York Stock Exchange, without announcing that he plans to institute a tender offer. He then institutes a tender offer at a much higher price. Raider has not violated 10b-5 by his open-market purchases, even though he was concealing the material fact that he would soon be taking an action which would raise the price.

V. RULE 10b-5: MISREPRESENTATIONS OR OMISSIONS NOT INVOLVING INSIDER TRADING

A. Breach of fiduciary duty: The fact that an insider has breached his *state-law fiduciary duties* may occasionally (but rarely) constitute a violation of 10b-5.

1. **Lie to directors:** For instance, if an insider lies to the board of directors and thereby induces them to *sell him stock* on favorable terms, this would be a 10b-5 violation.

   Example: The chief scientist of XYZ Corp falsely tells the board of directors that there have been no new developments, when there has in fact been a major scientific breakthrough that will improve the company's prospects. The board then issues stock options to the scientist. The scientist will be held to have violated 10b-5, because he violated his state-law duty of disclosure to his corporate employer.

2. **Breach of duty without misrepresentation:** But if an insider violates his fiduciary duties to the corporation or its shareholders *without making a misrepresentation*, this will *not* constitute a 10b-5 violation. In other words, there is no doctrine of "constructive fraud" to trigger a 10b-5 violation.

   Example: The controlling shareholder of XYZ Corp carries out a short-form merger on terms that are substantively unfair to the minority stockholders. Even though this violates a controlling shareholder's fiduciary obligations to the minority shareholder, there will be no 10b-5 violation because there has been no fraud or deception. See *Santa Fe Industries v. Green.*

B. **Misrepresentation without trading:** If a corporation or one of its insiders makes a *misrepresentation*, it/he will be liable *even though it/he does not trade in the company's stock.*

   Example: D, the president of XYZ, falsely tells the public, "Our profits will be up this quarter." D can be liable under 10b-5 even though he has never bought any XYZ stock.

   1. **Scienter:** However, remember that D will not be liable for misrepresentation in a 10b-5 suit unless he acted with *scienter*, i.e., he knew his statement was false or recklessly disregarded the chance that it might be false. That is, D will not be liable for mere *negligent* misstatement.

   2. **Merger discussions:** If a company is a company is engaged in *merger* discussions, and its insiders knowingly and falsely deny that the discussions are taking place, this may make them liable under 10b-5. (Therefore, they should say, "No comment," instead of falsely denying.)

   3. **Fraud by one not associated with issuer:** Even a person *not associated with the issuer* can commit fraud by knowingly or recklessly *making a false statement* about the issuer or the issuer's stock.

C. **Omission by non-trader:** Where the company or an insider simply *fails to disclose* material inside information that it possesses, it/he will *not* be liable as long as it/he does not buy or sell company stock.

Example: D Corp signs a huge contract which improves its prospects enormously. It keeps the deal quiet for 10 days. So long as neither the company nor its insiders buys or sells any D Corp stock during this period, no violation of 10b-5 has occurred.

1. **Exceptions:** But there are two exceptions to this general rule that there is no duty to disclose:

   a. **Leaks:** If rumors are the result of *leaks* by the company or its agents, the company probably has an obligation under 10b-5 to correct the misapprehension.

   b. **Involvement:** If the company heavily *involves itself* with outsiders' statements about the company, it may thereby assume a duty to correct errors in those outsider's statements.

   Example: X, a securities analyst, submits his estimates of ABC Corp's next quarterly earnings to ABC's investor relations director, W. W knows that these estimates are wrong but says nothing. X releases the estimates to the public. ABC and/or W may have violated 10b-5.

VI. SHORT-SWING TRADING PROFITS AND § 16(b)

A. **Generally:** Section 16(b) of the Securities Exchange Act of 1934 contains a "bright line" rule by which all *"short-swing"* trading profits received by insiders must be returned to the company.

   1. **Gist:** The gist of § 16(b) is that if a statutorily-defined insider buys stock in his company and then *resells within six months,* or sells and then *repurchases within six months*, any profits he makes must be *returned to the corporate treasury.* This rule applies even if the person in fact had no material non-public information.

   2. **Who is covered:** Section 16(b) applies to any *"officer," "director,"* or *beneficial owner of more than 10%* of any class of the company's stock.

   3. **Public companies:** Section 16(b) applies only to the insiders of companies which have a class of stock registered with the SEC under § 12 of the '34 Act. Thus a company's insiders are covered only if the company either: (1) is listed on a national securities exchange; or (2) has assets greater than $5 million and a class of stock held of record by 500 or more people.

   4. **Who may sue:** Suit may be brought by the corporation or by *any shareholder.* But any recovery goes into the corporate treasury. (The incentive is to the plaintiff's lawyer, who gets attorney's fees out of the recovery.)

      a. **P must continue to be stockholder:** P must not only be a stockholder in the corporation at the time she files suit under 16(b), but she must also *continue* to be a stockholder as the suit progresses. However, if P is forced to exchange her shares for shares in a different corporation as the result of the target corporation's *merger*, P may continue her suit as long as she keeps the shares in the surviving corporation. *Gollust v. Mendell.*

5. Public filings: To aid enforcement, any officer, director, or 10%-owner must file with the SEC (under 16(a)) a statement showing any change in his ownership of the company's stock. This must be filed within 10 days after any calendar month in which the level of ownership changes.

B. Who is insider:

1. "Officer": Two groups of people may be *"officers"* for § 16(b) purposes: (1) anyone who holds the title of "President," "Vice President," "Secretary," "Treasurer" (or "Principal Financial Officer"), or "Comptroller" (or "Principal Accounting Officer"); (2) anyone (regardless of title) who performs *functions* that correspond to the functions typically performed by these named persons in other corporations.

2. "Beneficial owner": A person is a beneficial owner covered by § 16(b) if he is "directly or indirectly" the beneficial owner of more than 10% of *any class* of the company's stock (he need not own 10% of the overall equity).

    a. Attribution: Stock listed in A's name may be *attributed* to B. A person will generally be regarded as the beneficial owner of securities held in the name of his or her *spouse* and their *minor children* (but usually not *grown children*). Thus a sale by Husband might be matched against a purchase by Wife; similarly, a sale and purchase by Wife might be attributed to Husband if Husband is a director or officer.

3. Deputization as director: A corporation may be treated as a "director" of another corporation if the former appoints one of its employees to serve on the latter's board.

Example: ABC Corp owns a significant minority interest in XYZ Corp. ABC appoints E, its employee, to serve on the board of XYZ. ABC will be deemed to have "deputized" E to serve as director, so ABC will be treated as a constructive director of XYZ, and any short-swing trading profits reaped by ABC in XYZ stock will have to be returned to XYZ.

C. When insider status required:

1. Director or officer at only one end of the swing: If D is a director or officer at the time of *either* his sale or his purchase of stock, § 16(b) applies to him even though he does not have the status at the other end of the trade.

2. 10% owner: But the same rule does not apply to a 10% owner. A person is caught by the "10% owner" prong only if he has the more-than-10% status at **both** ends of the swing.

    a. Purchase that puts one over: The **purchase** that puts a person **over 10%** does not count for § 16(b) purposes.

    Example: D has owned 5% of XYZ for a long time. On January 1, he buys another 10%. On February 1, he sells 4%. There are no short-swing profits that must be returned to the company.

    b. Sale that puts one below 10%: In the case of a **sale** that puts a person **below 10%** ownership, probably we measure the insider status **before** the sale.

    Example: D already owns 15% of XYZ. He then buys another 10% on January 1. On February 1, he sells 16%. On March 1, he sells the remaining 9%. Probably D has short-swing liability for 16% sale, but not for the second 9%, since we probably measure his insider status as of the moment just before the sale.

D. What is a "sale," in the case of a merger: If the corporation merges into another company (and thus disappears), the insiders will not necessarily be deemed to have made a "sale." D will escape short-swing liability for a merger or other unorthodox transaction if he shows that: (1) the transaction was essentially **involuntary**; *and* (2) the transaction was of a type such that D almost certainly did **not have access** to inside information.

    Example: Raider launches a hostile tender offer for Target. On Feb. 1, Raider buys 15% of Target pursuant to the tender offer. Target then arranges a defensive merger into White Knight, whereby each share of Target will be exchanged for one share of White Knight. The merger closes on May 1, at which time Raider (like all other Target shareholder) receives White Knight shares in exchange for his Target stock. On June 1, Raider sells his White Knight stock on the open market for a total greater than he originally paid for the Target stock. Raider does not have any § 16(b) problem, because the overall transaction was essentially involuntary, and was of a type in which Raider almost certainly did not have access to inside information about White Knight's affairs.

E. "Profit" computed: If there is a covered purchase/sale or sale/purchase, the courts will compute the profit in a way that produces the **maximum possible number**. In other words, the court takes the shares having the lowest purchase price and matches them against the shares having the highest sale price, ignoring any losses.

CHAPTER 9
SHAREHOLDERS' SUITS

I.   INTRODUCTION

A. What is a derivative suit: When a person who owes the corporation a fiduciary duty breaches the duty, the main remedy is the ***shareholder's derivative suit***. In a derivative suit, an individual shareholder (typically an outsider) brings suit ***in the name of the corporation***, against the individual wrongdoer.

  1. Against insider: A derivative suit may in theory be brought against some outside third party who has wronged the corporation, but is usually brought against an ***insider***, such as a director, officer or major shareholder.

B. Distinguish derivative from direct suit: Not all suits by shareholders are derivative; in some situations, a shareholder (or class of shareholders) may sue the corporation, or insiders, ***directly***.

  1. Illustration of derivative suits: Most cases brought against insiders for breach of the fiduciary duties of ***care*** or ***loyalty*** are ***derivative***. Examples include: (1) suits against board members for failing to use due care; (2) suits against an officer for ***self-dealing***; (3) suits to recover ***excessive compensation*** paid to an officer; and (4) suits to reacquire a ***corporate opportunity*** usurped by an officer.

  2. Illustration of direct actions: Here are some of the types of suits generally held to be ***direct***: (1) an action to enforce the holder's ***voting rights***; (2) an action to compel the ***payment of dividends***; (3) an action to prevent management from improperly ***entrenching*** itself (e.g., to enjoin the enactment of a "poison pill" as an anti-takeover device); (4) a suit to prevent ***oppression*** of minority shareholders; and (5) a suit to compel ***inspection*** of the company's books and records.

  3. Delaware law on the distinction: Delaware has a simple ***two-part test*** for distinguishing between direct and derivative actions. In Delaware, the distinction turns solely on the two following questions:

   [1] who ***suffered the alleged harm*** (the corporation, or the suing stockholders individually)? and

   [2] who would ***receive the benefit*** of any recovery or other remedy (the corporation, or the stockholders individually)?

   a. Summary: So if the shareholders have suffered the harm (in a way that doesn't derive from harm to the corporation), and they would get the benefit of any recovery, the action is "direct."

    b. No need for "special injury": Delaware now *rejects* its former "special injury" test, by which an action was derivative, not direct, unless the plaintiff shareholder(s) had an injury that was qualitatively different from that suffered by other shareholders. Now, as long as the injury is suffered by the shareholders alone — and does not derive from an injury to the corporation — the fact that *all* shareholders have been injured in the same way *doesn't prevent* the injury from being a direct one. [*Tooley v. Donaldson, Lufkin & Jenrette Inc.*]

C. Consequence of distinction: Usually, the plaintiff will want his action to proceed as a *direct* rather than derivative suit. If the suit is direct, P gets the following benefits: (1) the procedural requirements are much simpler (e.g., he doesn't have to have owned stock at the time the wrong occurred); (2) he does not have to make a demand on the board of directors, or face having the action terminated early because the corporation does not want to pursue it; and (3) he can probably keep all or part of the recovery.

II. REQUIREMENTS FOR A DERIVATIVE SUIT

A. Summary: There are three main requirements that P must generally meet for a derivative suit: (1) he must have been a shareholder at the time the acts complained of occurred (the *"contemporaneous ownership"* rule); (2) he must *still* be a shareholder at the time of the suit; and (3) he must make a *demand* (unless excused) upon the board, requesting that the board attempt to obtain redress for the corporation.

B. "Contemporaneous ownership": P must have owned his shares *at the time of the transaction* of which he complains. This is the *"contemporaneous ownership"* rule.

    1. "Continuing wrong" exception: An important exception is for "continuing wrongs" — P can sue to challenge a wrong that began before he bought his shares, but that continued after the purchase.

    2. Who is a "shareholder": P must have been a "shareholder" at the time of the wrong. It will be sufficient if he was a preferred shareholder, or held a convertible bond (convertible into the company's equity). Also, it will be enough that P is a "beneficial" owner even if he is not the owner of record. But a *bond holder* or other ordinary creditor may *not* bring a derivative suit.

C. Continuing ownership: P must *continue* to own the shares not only until the time of suit, but until the moment of judgment. (But if P has lost his shareholder status because the corporation has engaged in a merger in which P was compelled to give up his shares, some courts excuse the continuing ownership requirement.)

D. Demand on board: P must make a ***written demand*** on the board of directors before commencing the derivative suit. The demand asks the board to bring a suit or take other corrective action. Only if the board refuses to act may P then commence suit. (But often the demand is "excused," as is discussed below.)

E. Demand on shareholders: Many states require P to also make a demand on the ***shareholders*** before instituting the derivative suit. But many other states do not impose this requirement, and even those states that do impose it often excuse it where it would be impractical.

III. DEMAND ON BOARD; EARLY TERMINATION BASED ON BOARD OR COMMITTEE RECOMMENDATION

A. Demand excused: Demand on the board is ***excused*** where it would be ***"futile."*** In general, demand will be deemed to be futile (and thus excused) if the board is accused of having ***participated*** in the wrongdoing.

    1. Delaware view: In Delaware, demand will not be excused unless P carries the burden of showing a ***reasonable doubt*** about whether the board either: (1) was ***disinterested*** and ***independent***; or (2) was entitled to the protections of the ***business judgment*** rule (i.e., acted rationally after reasonable investigation and without self-dealing).

        a. Difficult to get: But Delaware makes it very difficult for P to make either of these showings. For instance, he must plead facts showing either (1) or (2) with ***great specificity***. Also, it is usually not sufficient that P is charging the board with a violation of the duty of ***due care*** for approving the transaction; usually, a breach of the duty of ***loyalty*** by the board must be alleged with specificity.

    2. New York: New York follows roughly the same rules as Delaware about when demand will be excused. In New York, demand will be excused if (and only if) the complaint alleges "with particularity" ***any*** of the following:

        [1] "that a ***majority of the board*** is ***interested*** in the challenged transaction." (A director can be "interested" either because she has a direct self-interest in the transaction, or because, although she has no direct self-interest in the transaction, she has lost her independence by being "controlled" by a self-interested director.)

        [2] that the board "***did not fully inform themselves*** about the challenged transaction to the extent reasonably appropriate under the circumstances." In other words, a director who merely "passively ***rubber-stamp[s]*** the decisions of the active managers" does ***not*** thereby exempt herself from liability.

[3] that "the challenged transaction was so *egregious on its face* that it *could not have been the product of sound business judgment* of the directors."

[*Marx v Akers*]

B. Demand required and refused: If demand is required, and the board rejects the demand, the result depends in part on who the defendant is.

   1. Unaffiliated third party: If the suit is against a *third party* who is not a corporate insider, P will almost never be permitted to continue his suit after the board has rejected it.

   2. Suit against insider: Where (as is usually the case) the suit is against a corporate *insider*, P has a better chance of having the board's refusal to pursue the suit be overridden by a court. But P will still have to show either that: (1) the board somehow *participated* in the alleged wrong; or (2) the directors who voted to reject the suit were *dominated or controlled* by the primary wrongdoer. (These requirements are similar to those needed to establish that demand is "excused," but it is usually somewhat easier to get the court to rule that the demand would be futile and therefore should be excused than to get the court to overturn the board's rejection of a required demand.)

C. Independent committee: Today, the corporation usually responds to P's demand by appointing an *independent committee* of directors to study whether the suit should be pursued. Usually, the committee will conclude that the suit should *not* be pursued. Often, but not always, the court will give this committee recommendation the *protection of the business judgment rule*, and will therefore *terminate the action before trial*.

   1. New York view: In New York, it is difficult for P to overcome the independent committee's recommendation that the suit be terminated. The court will reject the recommendation if P shows that the committee members were not in fact independent, or that they did not use reasonable procedures. But if the court is satisfied with the committee's independence and procedures, the court will *not review the substantive merits* of the committee's recommendation that the suit be dismissed.

   2. Delaware: It is somewhat easier to get the court to disregard the committee's termination recommendation in Delaware. Delaware courts take two steps: (1) First, the court asks whether the committee acted independently, in good faith, and with reasonable procedures. If the answer to any of these questions is "no," the court will allow the suit to proceed. (2) Even if the answer to all of these questions is "yes," the court may (but need not) apply its *own independent business judgment* about whether the suit should be permitted to proceed. (This second step will only be applied in "demand excused" cases.)

a. **Tough standard for independence in Delaware:** Concern about whether the members of independent committees are really psychologically independent has led the Delaware courts to impose a ***heavy burden*** on the committee to demonstrate its members' independence. In Delaware, the committee "has the burden of establishing its own independence by a yardstick that must be 'like Caesar's wife' — ***'above reproach.'"*** *Beam ex rel. Martha Stewart Living Omnimedia, Inc. v. Stewart.*

   i. **Social ties considered:** Furthermore, the Delaware courts now ***consider social ties*** — not just direct financial ties — in deciding whether the committee members have carried their burden of showing that they are really independent of the persons whose conduct they are investigating. [*In Re Oracle Corp. Derivative Litigation*]

   Example: A derivative suit is brought against several insiders of Oracle Corp., charging them with insider trading. Oracle appoints a Special Litigation Committee, consisting solely of two directors that Oracle says are independent. The SLC investigates, and finds that the suit is meritless and should be discontinued. But the plaintiff point out that both SLC members have jobs at Stanford (as professors), which two of the defendants attended. The SLC members and the defendants have other social ties as well (e.g., one SLC member supervised one defendant as a graduate student decades previously). Oracle asserts that (1) unless the SLC members were under the "domination and control" of a defendant or of the corporation, the members are automatically independent; and (2) because the SLC members were independent under this test, the SLC's conclusion that the action was meritless and should be discontinued must be followed by the court.

   Held, for the plaintiffs. The court rejects the defendants' "domination and control" test, and will consider social ties between the SLC members and the defendants in deciding whether the SLC members are independent of the defendants. Here, those social ties were so extensive that the SLC members were not independent, so the SLC's dismissal recommendation won't be accorded any deference by the court, and the suit will go forward. [*In Re Oracle Corp., supra.*]

3. **More liberal view:** A few courts are even more willing than the Delaware courts to ignore the committee's recommendation of termination. Such courts believe that even a committee of ostensibly "independent" directors will for structural reasons rarely recommend a suit against insiders, so that the committee should be viewed as biased. In a few states, the

solution is a ***court-appointed committee*** of non-directors, whose recommendation the court will accept.

4. **MBCA:** Under the MBCA, the court must dismiss the action if the committee of independent directors votes to discontinue the action "in ***good faith*** after conducting a ***reasonable inquiry*** upon which [the committee's] conclusions are based." MBCA § 7.44(a). So the court under the MBCA will almost never review the substantive merits of the suit if the independent directors vote to discontinue.

IV. SECURITY-FOR-EXPENSES STATUTES

A. **Generally:** About 14 states have so-called ***"security-for-expenses"*** statutes, by which P must post a ***bond*** to guarantee repayment of the corporation's expenses in the event that P's claim turns out to be without merit.

B. **Not substantial impediment:** But such statutes do not usually serve as much of an impediment to the bringing of suits, mostly because the corporation often doesn't take advantage of them for various tactical reasons.

V. SETTLEMENT OF DERIVATIVE SUITS

A. **Judicial approval:** Most states require that any ***settlement*** of a derivative suit be ***approved by the court***. The court must be convinced that the settlement is in the best interests of the corporation and its shareholders.

1. **Factors:** When the court decides whether to approve the settlement, the most important factor is usually the relation between the size of the net financial benefit to the corporation under the settlement and the probable net benefit if the case were tried.

B. **Notice:** In the federal courts and in many states, shareholders must be given ***notice*** of any proposed settlement of a derivative action, as well as the opportunity to ***intervene*** in the action to oppose the settlement.

C. **Corporate recovery:** All payments made in connection with the derivative action must be ***received by the corporation***, not by the plaintiff.

VI. PLAINTIFF'S ATTORNEY'S FEES

A. **"Common fund" theory:** Courts usually award the plaintiff's attorneys a reasonable *fee* for bringing a successful derivative action. Under the ***"common fund"*** theory, the fee is paid out of the amount recovered on behalf of the corporation.

B. **Calculation of fee:** There are two main approaches to calculating the amount of the fee:

1. **"Lodestar" method:**   Under the *"lodestar"* method, the key component is the *reasonable value of the time* expended by the plaintiff's attorney. This is computed by taking the actual number of hours expended, and multiplying by a reasonable hourly fee. Often, the award is then adjusted upward to reflect the fact that there was a substantial contingency aspect to the case.

2. **"Salvage value" approach:**   The other approach is the *"salvage value"* approach. Here, the court calculates fees by awarding a percentage of the total recovery (usually in the range of 20-30%).

3. **Combination method:**   Some courts combine the two techniques: they begin with the lodestar computation, but set a particular percentage of the recovery as a *ceiling* on the fee.

VII. WHO GETS TO RECOVER

A. Pro rata recovery: Usually, the corporation will make the recovery. But occasionally this will be unjust, so the court may order that some or all of the recovery be distributed to *individual shareholders* on a *pro rata basis* (i.e., proportionally to their shareholdings). Here are two situations where this might be done:

1. **Wrongdoers in control:**   Where the alleged wrongdoers remain in substantial *control* of the corporation (so that if a recovery were paid to the corporation, it might be diverted once again by the same wrongdoers).

2. **Aiding and abetting:**   Where most of the shares are in the hands of people who in some sense *aided and abetted* the wrongdoing.

VIII. INDEMNIFICATION AND D&O INSURANCE

A. Indemnification: All states have statutes dealing with when the corporation may (and/or must) *indemnify* a director or officer against losses he incurs by virtue of his corporate duties.

1. **Mandatory:**   Under most statutes, in two situations the corporation is *required* to indemnify an officer or director: (1) when the director/officer is completely *successful* in defending himself against the charges; and (2) when the corporation has previously bound itself by charter, law or *contract* to indemnify.

2. **Permissive:**   Nearly all states, in addition to this mandatory indemnification, allow for *"permissive"* indemnification. In other words, in a large range of circumstances the corporation *may*, but need not, indemnify the director or officer.

   a. **Third party suits:**   In suits brought by a *third party* (in other words, suits not brought by the corporation or by a shareholder suing derivatively), the corporation is permitted to indemnify the director or officer if the latter: (1) acted in *good faith*; (2) was pursuing what he reasonably believed to be the *best interests of the corporation*; and (3) had no reason to believe that his conduct was *unlawful*. See MBCA § 8.51(a).

Example: D, a director of XYZ, acts grossly negligently, but not dishonestly, when he approves a particular corporate transaction. XYZ may, but need not, indemnify D for his expenses in defending a suit brought by an unaffiliated third person against D, and for any judgment or settlement D may pay.

  b. **Derivative suit:** If the suit is brought by or on behalf of the corporation (e.g., a *derivative* suit), the indemnification rules are *stricter*. The corporation may *not* indemnify the director or officer for a *judgment* on behalf of the corporation, or for a *settlement* payment. But indemnification for litigation *expenses* (including attorney's fees) is allowed, if D is not found liable on the underlying claim by a court.

  c. **Fines and penalties:** D may be indemnified for a *fine* or *penalty* he has to pay, unless: (1) he knew or had reason to believe that his conduct was *unlawful*; or (2) the deterrent function of the statute would be frustrated by indemnification.

3. **Who decides:** Typically, the decision on whether D should be indemnified is made by *independent members* of the board of directors. Also, this decision is sometimes made by independent legal counsel.

4. **Advancing of expenses:** Most states allow the corporation to *advance* to the director or officer money for counsel fees and other expenses as the action proceeds. The director or officer must generally promise to *repay* the advances if he is ultimately found not entitled to indemnification (but usually need not make a showing of financial ability to make the repayment).

5. **Court-ordered:** Most states allow D to *petition the court* for indemnification, even under circumstances where the corporation is not permitted, or not willing, to make the payment voluntarily.

B. **Insurance:** Nearly all large companies today carry directors' and officers' (D&O) *liability insurance*. Most states explicitly allow the corporation to purchase such insurance. Furthermore, D&O insurance may cover certain director's or officer's expenses even where those expenses *could not be indemnified*.

  1. **Typical policy:** The typical policy *excludes* many types of claims (e.g., a claim that the director or officer acted dishonestly, received illegal compensation, engaged in self-dealing, etc.).

2. **Practical effect:** Insurance will often cover an expense that could not be indemnified by the corporation. For instance, money paid to the corporation as a judgment or settlement in a *derivative* action can usually be reimbursed to the director or officer under the D&O policy.

CHAPTER 10

STRUCTURAL CHANGES, INCLUDING MERGERS AND ACQUISITIONS

I. CORPORATE COMBINATIONS GENERALLY

Note: For the entire following discussion, the business that is being acquired is referred to as "Little Corp" and the acquirer is "Big Corp."

A. **Merger-type deals:** A "merger-type" transaction is one in which the shareholders of Little Corp will end up mainly with *stock in Big Corp* as their payment for surrendering control of Little Corp and its assets. There are four main structures for a merger-type deal:

1. **Statutory:** First is the traditional *"statutory merger."* By following procedures set out in the state corporation statute, one corporation can merge into another, with the former (the *"disappearing"* corporation) ceasing to have any legal identity, and the latter (the *"surviving"* corporation) continuing in existence.

   a. **Consequence:** After the merger, Big Corp owns all of Little Corp's assets, and is *responsible for all of Little Corp's liabilities.* All contracts that Little Corp had with third parties now become contracts between the third party and Big Corp. The shareholders of Little Corp now (at least in the usual case) own stock in Big Corp. (Alternatively, under many statutory merger provisions, Little Corp holders may receive some or all of their payment in the form of *cash* or Big Corp debt, rather than Big Corp stock.)

2. **Stock-for-stock exchange ("stock swap"):** The second method is the *"stock-for-stock exchange"* or *"stock swap."* Here, Big Corp makes a separate deal with each Little Corp holder, giving the holder Big Corp stock in return for his Little Corp stock.

   a. **Plan of exchange:** Under the standard stock swap, a Little Corp holder need not participate, in which case he continues to own a stake in Little Corp. However, some states allow Little Corp to enact (by approval of directors and a majority of shareholders) a *"plan of exchange,"* under which all Little Corp shareholders are *required* to exchange their shares for Big Corp shares. When this happens, the net result is like a statutory merger.

3. **Stock-for-assets exchange:** The third form is the *"stock-for-assets" exchange*. In step one, Big Corp gives stock to Little Corp, and Little Corp transfers substantially all of its assets to Big Corp. In step two (which usually but not necessarily follows), Little Corp dissolves, and distributes the Big Corp stock to its own shareholders. After the second step, the net result is virtually the same as with a statutory merger. [406] (However, approval by Big Corp shareholders might not be necessary, as it probably would for a statutory merger.)

4. **Triangular or subsidiary mergers:** Finally, we have the *"triangular"* or *"subsidiary"* merger.

   a. **Forward triangular merger:** In the "conventional" or *"forward"* triangular merger, the acquirer creates a subsidiary for the purpose of the transaction. Usually, this subsidiary has no assets except shares of stock in the parent. *The target is then merged into the acquirer's subsidiary.*

      Example: Big Corp creates a subsidiary called Big-Sub. Big transfers 1,000 of its own shares to Big-Sub, in return for all the shares of Big-Sub. Little Corp now merges into Big-Sub. Little Corp shareholders receive the shares in Big Corp.

      i. **Rationale:** This is very similar to the stock-for-stock exchange, except that all minority interests in Little Corp is automatically eliminated. (Also, the deal *does not have to be approved by Big Corp's shareholders,* unlike a direct merger of Little Corp into Big Corp.)

   b. **Reverse merger:** The other type of triangular merger is the *"reverse"* triangular merger. This is the same as the forward triangular merger, except that the acquirer's subsidiary *merges into the target*, rather than having the target merge into the subsidiary.

      Example: Same facts as above example, except Big-Sub merges into Little Corp, so that Little Corp is now a surviving corporation that is itself a subsidiary of Big Corp.

      i. **Advantages:** This reverse triangular form is better than a stock-for-stock swap because it automatically eliminates all Little Corp shareholders, which the stock-for-stock swap does not. It is better than a simple merger of Little Corp into Big Corp because: (1) Big Corp does not assume all of Little Corp's liabilities; and (2) Big Corp's shareholders do not have to approve. It is better than the forward triangular merger because Little Corp survives as an entity, thus possibly preserving contract rights and tax advantages better than if Little Corp were to disappear.

B. Sale-type transactions: A *"sale-type"* transaction is one in which the Little Corp shareholders receive cash or bonds, rather than Big Corp stock, in return for their interest in Little Corp. There are two main sale-type structures:

1. **Asset-sale-and-liquidation:** First, there is the *"asset-sale-and-liquidation."* Here, Little Corp's board approves a sale of all or substantially all of Little Corp's assets to Big Corp, and the proposed sale is approved by a majority of Little Corp's shareholders. Little Corp conveys its assets to Big Corp, and Little Corp receives cash (or perhaps Big Corp debt) from Big Corp. Usually, Little Corp will then dissolve, and pay the cash or debt to its shareholders in proportion to their shareholdings, in a *liquidating distribution*.

2. **Stock sale:** Second is the *"stock sale."* Here, no corporate level transaction takes place on the Little Corp side. Instead, Big Corp buys stock from each Little Corp shareholder, for cash or debt. (After Big Corp controls all or a majority of Little Corp's stock, it may but need not cause Little Corp to be: (1) dissolved, with its assets distributed to the various stockholders or (2) merged into Big Corp, with the remaining Little holders receiving Big Corp stock, cash or debt.)

   a. **Tender offer:** One common form of stock sale is the *tender offer*, in which Big Corp publicly announces that it will buy all or a majority of shares offered to it by Little Corp shareholders. (Alternatively, Big Corp might *privately negotiate* purchases from some or all of Little Corp's shareholders.)

3. **Differences:** Here are the big differences between the asset-sale and the stock-sale techniques:

   a. **Corporate action by target:** The asset sale requires *corporate action* by Little Corp, and the stock sale does not. Thus Little Corp's *board must approve* an asset sale but need not approve a stock sale.

   b. **Shareholder vote:** Similarly, the asset sale will have to be formally approved by a majority vote of Little Corp's *shareholders*, whereas the stock sale will not be subjected to a shareholder vote (each Little Corp shareholder simply decides whether to tender his stock).

   c. **Elimination of minority stockholders:** In an asset-sale deal, Big Corp is guaranteed to get Little Corp's business without any remaining interest on the part of Little Corp shareholders. In the stock sale, Big Corp may be left with some Little Corp holders holding a *minority interest* in Little Corp (though if the state allows for a "plan of exchange," this minority may be eliminated).

   d. **Liabilities:** In an asset sale, Big Corp has a good chance of escaping Little Corp's *liabilities* (subject, however, to the law of fraudulent transfers, the bulk sales provisions of the UCC, and the possible use of the "de facto merger" doctrine). In a stock sale, Big Corp will effectively take Little Corp's liabilities along with its assets, whether it wants to or not.

e. **Tax treatment:** There are important tax differences between the two forms. In general, the tax treatment of an asset sale is much less favorable for the seller than is a stock sale. See below.

C. Approvals for sale-type deals:

1. **Asset sale:** In the case of an *asset sale*, here is how the approvals work:

   a. **Target side:** On the Little Corp side: (1) Little's board of directors must approve; and (2) (in most states) Little's shareholders must approve by a *majority* of all votes that *could be* cast, not just a majority of the votes actually cast. (But the MBCA requires just a majority of the shares actually voting, assuming a quorum is present.)

      i. **The "substantially all assets" test:** Not every sale of assets triggers this obligation. Under most statutes, the shareholder approval is required only if all or *"substantially all"* of Little's assets are being sold. (Under the MBCA, approval is required if Little would be left "without a significant continuing business activity.")

   b. **Acquirer side:** On the Big Corp side of the asset-sale transaction: (1) the Big Corp board must approve; but (2) the Big Corp *shareholders* need *not* approve.

2. **Stock sale:** In the case of a *stock sale*, each Little Corp stockholder would decide whether to sell his stock to Big Corp, and no approval by Little's board (or any formal vote of Little's stockholders) is necessary for some or all of Little's stockholders to do this.

   a. **Back-end merger:** On the other hand, once Big got control of Little by having acquired most of Little's shares, it might want to conduct a *back-end merger* of Little into Big (or into a subsidiary of Bid), and this would normally require a vote by Little's board and shareholders. But each of these votes would probably be a formality, due to Big's majority ownership and board control of Little.

D. Approval for merger-type deals: Here is how approvals work for *merger-type* deals:

1. **Statutory merger:** In a traditional *statutory* merger:

   a. **Board approval:** The boards of directors of both Big (the survivor) and Little (the disappearing corporation) must approve.

   b. **Holders of target:** The shareholders of Little Corp must approve by majority vote of the shares permitted to vote (except in a short-form merger, as discussed below).

   c. **Holders of survivor:**   The shareholders of Big Corp also must approve by majority vote (except in the case of a "whale/minnow" merger, see below).

   d. **Classes:**   Under many statutes, if there are *different classes* of stock on either the Big Corp or Little Corp side, each class must *separately approve* the merger.

   e. **Small-scale ("whale/minnow") mergers:**   If a corporation is being merged into a *much larger* corporation, the shareholders of the surviving corporation usually *need not approve*. Under Delaware law and under the MBCA, any merger that does not increase the outstanding shares of the surviving corporation by *more than 20%* need not be approved by the survivor's shareholders. (But this assumes that there are enough *authorized but unissued* shares to fund the merger; if the number of authorized shares must be increased, this will usually require a shareholder vote to amend the articles of incorporation.)

   f. **Short-form mergers:**   Under most statutes, including Delaware and the MBCA, if one corporation owns *90% or more* of the stock of another, the latter may be merged into the former *without approval* by the shareholders of *either* corporation.

   Example: Big Corp owns 92% of Little Corp shares. Under the Delaware or MBCA short-form merger statute, Little Corp may be merged into Big Corp, and the 8% minority shareholders of Little Corp given stock in Big Corp, or cash, without any shareholder approval by either the Big or Little shareholders. But Little Corp shareholders will have appraisal rights, described below.

2. **Hybrids:**   Here is how approvals work for "hybrid" transactions, i.e., those that are *"merger-type"* but not pure statutory mergers:

   a. **Stock-for-stock exchange:**   In a *stock-for-stock exchange*, the proposal: (1) must be approved by the Big Corp board but *not* by its shareholders; and (2) need not be formally approved by either Little Corp's board or its shareholders (though in a sense each shareholder "votes" by deciding whether to tender his shares).

   b. **Stock-for-assets deal:**   In the case of a stock-for-assets deal: (1) on the Big Corp side, board approval is necessary but shareholder approval is not (as long as there are enough authorized but unissued shares to fund the transaction); and (2) on the Little Corp side, this is like any other asset sale, so Little's board must approve the transaction, and a majority of shareholders must then approve it.

   c. **Triangular mergers:**

      i. **Forward merger:**   In a *forward* triangular (or "subsidiary") merger: (1) Big-Sub's board and shareholders must approve (but this is a formality, since Big Corp will cast both of these votes, and Big Corp's board (but not its shareholders) must also approve; and (2) on the Little Corp side, both the board and shareholders will have to approve the merger, just as with any other merger.

ii. **Reverse merger:** In the case of a *reverse* triangular merger, essentially the same board and shareholder approvals are needed as for the forward merger.

E. **Taxation:** Merger-type transactions are *taxed* quite differently from sale-type transactions.

1. **Reorganizations:** What we have called *"merger-type"* transactions are called *"reorganizations"* by the tax law. In general, in a reorganization the target's shareholders *pay no tax* at the time of the merger.

    Example: Little Corp is merged into Big Corp, with each Little Corp shareholder receiving one Big Corp share for each Little Corp share. The Little Corp shareholders will not pay any tax until they eventually sell their Big Corp shares, at which time they will pay tax on the difference between what they receive for the Big Corp shares and what they originally paid for the Little Corp shares.

    There are three different types of tax-free reorganizations:

    a. **"Type A" reorganization:** A "type A" reorganization is one carried out according to state *statutory merger* provisions. The principal requirement is that the Little Corp shareholders have a *"continuity of interest,"* i.e., that most of the compensation they receive be in the form of Big Corp stock.

    b. **"Type B" reorganization:** A "type B" reorganization is a *stock-for-stock exchange.* To qualify as a type B deal, Big Corp must end up with *at least 80%* of the voting power in Little Corp, and must not give Little Corp shareholders anything other than its own stock (e.g., it may not give any cash).

    c. **"Type C" reorganization:** A "type C" reorganization is basically a stock-for-assets exchange. Big Corp must acquire *substantially all* of Little Corp's assets, in return for Big Corp stock. (But Big Corp may make part of the payment in *cash* or bonds, so long as *at least 80% of the acquisition price* is in the form of Big Corp stock.)

2. **Sale-type transactions:** If the transaction is a *sale-type* one (i.e., it is not a "reorganization"), here is how it is taxed:

    a. **Asset sale:** In an *asset sale*, the target pays a corporate-level tax; then, if it dissolves and pays out the cash received in the sale to its own shareholders as a liquidating distribution, the target share holders each must pay a tax on the distribution.

Example: Big Corp buys all of Little Corp's assets for $1 million cash. Little Corp will pay a tax on the amount by which this $1 million exceeds the original cost of Little Corp's assets. If the remainder is paid out in the form of a liquidating distribution to Little Corp shareholders, each shareholder will pay a tax based on the difference between what he receives and what he originally paid for his Little Corp shares.

   b. **Sale of stock:** In a *stock* sale, there is only *one level* of taxation, at the shareholder level. (*Example*: Some or all Little Corp shareholders sell their stock to Big Corp. Each shareholder pays a tax on the difference between what he receives per share and what he originally paid per share.) This tax is less, typically, than the combined two levels of tax in the case of an asset sale.

   i. **Buyer dislikes:** But the tax consequences on the *buyer's* side are less attractive than in the asset-sale situation. Thus *the buyer will always want an asset sale and the seller will always want a stock sale*.

F. **Federal securities law:** Here are the federal *securities-law* implications of the various types of combinations:

   1. **Sale-type transactions:**

   a. **Asset sales:** If Big Corp is acquiring Little Corp's assets for cash, and Little Corp is publicly held, the only federal securities laws that are relevant are the *proxy* rules. Little Corp will have to send its holders a proxy statement describing the proposed transaction, so that the holders may intelligently decide whether to approve.

   b. **Stock sale:** If there will be a sale of stock by each Little Corp shareholder to Big Corp, Big Corp will usually proceed by a tender offer. If so, it will have to send special tender offer documents to each Little Corp shareholder.

   2. **Merger-type deals:**

   a. **Stock-for-stock exchange:** If the deal will be a *stock-for-stock exchange*, for securities-law purposes this is the equivalent of public issue of stock by the acquirer. Thus if Big Corp will be acquiring each Little Corp share in exchange for a share of Big Corp, Big will have to file a *registration statement* and supply each Little Corp shareholder with a prospectus. Also, the tender offer requirements will generally have to be complied with.

   b. **Statutory merger; stock-for-assets deal:** If the deal will be a *statutory merger* or a *stock-for-assets exchange*: (1) Little Corp will have to send each shareholder a proxy statement to get the shareholder's approval; and (2) Big Corp must file a registration statement and supply a prospectus, as if it were issuing new stock to Little Corp's shareholders.

II. CORPORATE COMBINATIONS — PROTECTING SHAREHOLDERS

A. **Appraisal rights:** *Appraisal rights* give a dissatisfied shareholder in certain circumstances a way to be "cashed out" of his investment at a price ***determined by a court*** to be fair.

1. **Mergers:** In nearly every state, a shareholder of either company involved in a ***merger*** has appraisal rights if he had the right to ***vote*** on the merger.

   Example: Little Corp merges into Big Corp. Any shareholder of either Big Corp or Little Corp who had the right to vote on the merger will in most states have appraisal rights.

   a. **Whale-minnow:** In the ***"whale-minnow"*** situation — that is, a merger in which a corporation is merged into a much larger one, so that the increase in outstanding shares of the larger company is small — the surviving corporation's shareholders do ***not*** get appraisal rights (since they would not get to vote).

   b. **Short-form merger:** But shareholders of the ***subsidiary*** in a ***short-form merger*** get appraisal rights even though they would not get to vote on the merger.

2. **Asset sales:** In most states shareholders of a corporation that is ***selling substantially all of its assets*** also get appraisal rights.

   a. **Sale for cash, followed by quick dissolution:** But if the selling corporation liquidates soon after the sale, and ***distributes the cash*** to the shareholders, usually there are no appraisal rights. See, e.g., MBCA § 13.02(a)(3) (no appraisal rights where liquidation and distribution of cash proceeds occurs within one year after the sale).

   b. **Delaware:** Delaware does ***not*** give appraisal rights to the stockholders of a corporation that sells its assets.

3. **Publicly-traded exception:** Many states deny the appraisal remedy to shareholders of a company whose stock is ***publicly traded***. (So does the MBCA, in most situations.)

4. **Triangular mergers:**

   a. **Forward:** In the case of a ***forward*** triangular merger: (1) on the acquirer's side, Big Corp's shareholders will not get appraisal rights;

and (2) on the target's side, Little Corp's shareholders generally *will* get appraisal rights.

b. **Reverse:** In the case of a *reverse* triangular merger: (1) Big Corp shareholders do not get appraisal rights; and (2) Little Corp holders will get appraisal rights if Big-Sub is statutorily merging into Little Corp, but not if Little Corp is issuing its own stock in return for Big-Sub's stock in Big Corp.

5. **Procedures:** Here are the usual procedures for appraisal:

   a. **Notice:** At the time the merger or sale transaction is announced, the corporation must notify the shareholder that he has appraisal rights.

   b. **Notice of payment demand by holder:** The holder must then give *notice* to the corporation, *before the shareholder vote*, that he demands payment of the fair value of his shares. Also, the holder must *not vote* his shares in favor of the transaction.

   c. **Deposit of shares:** Early in the process (in some states, before the vote is even held), the holder must *deposit his shares* with the company.

   d. **Payment:** Then, the company's obligations vary from state to state. In some states, the corporation does not have to pay anything until the court finally determines what is due. But under the MBCA, the corporation must at least pay the amount that *it* concedes is the fair value of the shares (with the rest due only after a court decision as to fair value).

6. **Valuation:** The court then determines the *"fair value"* of the dissenter's shares, and the corporation must pay this value.

   a. **Don't consider the transaction itself:** Fair value must be determined *without reference* to the transaction that triggers the appraisal rights.

   Example: Little Corp is worth $10 per share in the absence of any takeover attempt. Big Corp, recognizing possible synergies with its own business, acquires Little Corp for $15 per share. For appraisal purposes, the fair value of Little Corp stock will be $10, not the higher $15 price that reflects the benefits of the acquisition.

   b. **No "minority" or "nonmarketability" discount:** Most courts do not reduce the value of P's shares to reflect that P held a minority or non-controlling interest. Instead, the court usually takes the value of the whole company, and then divides by the number of shares (so P, even though she is a minority holder, gets the same per-share price as the insiders would have gotten.) See, e.g., *In Re Valuation of Common Stock of McLoon Oil Co.*

    c. **"Delaware block" method:** Most courts use the "Delaware block" valuation method. Under this, the court considers three factors: (1) the *market price* just prior to the transaction; (2) the *net asset value* of the company; and (3) the *earnings valuation* of the company. These three factors can be weighted however the court chooses.

        i. **Abandoned in Delaware:** Delaware itself no longer requires use of the Delaware block approach. Delaware courts will now accept additional evidence of valuation, such as valuation studies prepared by the corporation, and expert testimony about what "takeover premium" would be paid.

7. Exclusivity: Appraisal rights are the *exclusive* remedy available to an unhappy shareholder in some, but not all, circumstances.

    a. **Illegality:** If the transaction is *illegal*, or *procedural requirements* have not been observed, the shareholder can generally get the transaction *enjoined*, instead of having to be content with his appraisal rights.

    b. **Deception:** Similarly, if the company *deceives* its shareholders and thereby procures their approval of the transaction, a shareholder can attack the transaction instead of having to use his appraisal rights.

    c. **Unfair:** On the other hand, if the shareholder is merely contending that the proposed transaction is a *bad deal* for the shareholders, or is in a sense *"unfair,"* appraisal normally *is* the exclusive remedy (and the shareholder cannot get an injunction). But if unfairness is due to *self-dealing* by corporate insiders, the court may grant an injunction.

B. "De facto merger" doctrine: Under the *"de facto merger"* doctrine, the court treats a transaction which is not literally a merger, but which is the functional equivalent of a merger, as if it were one. The most common result of the doctrine is that selling stockholders get *appraisal rights*. Also, selling stockholders may get the right to vote on a transaction, and the seller's creditors may get a claim against the buyer.

1. Only occasionally accepted: Only a few courts have accepted the de facto merger theory, and they have done so only in specialized circumstances. They are most likely to do so when the target has transferred all of its assets and then dissolves, and when the target's shareholders receive most of their consideration as shares in the acquirer rather than cash and/or bonds.

    Example: Glen Alden Corp. agrees to acquire all of the assets of List Corp. (a much larger company). Glen Alden plans to pay for these assets by issuing a large amount of its own stock to List (so that List will end up owning over three-quarters of Glen Alden). Glen Alden will assume all of List's liabilities, and will change its name to List

Alden Corp. List will then be dissolved, and its assets (stock representing a majority interest in List Alden) will be distributed to the original List shareholders. (The purpose of this bizarre structure is to deny the shareholders of Glen Alden appraisal rights, which they would have if Glen Alden was selling all of its assets to List, but will not have if Glen Alden "bought" List.)

Held, this transaction was a de facto merger, so Glen Alden's shareholders have appraisal rights. See *Farris v. Glen Alden Corp.*

2. **Usually rejected:** Most courts, including most notably Delaware, *reject* the de facto doctrine.

3. **Successor liability:** But even courts that normally reject the de facto merger doctrine may apply it (or something like it) to deal with problems of *"successor liability."*

    Example: Big Corp acquires the assets of Little Corp, and carries on Little Corp's business. Normally, Little Corp's liabilities will not pass to Big Corp unless Big Corp has explicitly assumed them in the purchase contract. But a tort claimant who is injured by a product manufactured by Little Corp before the sale might be permitted to recover against Big Corp, on the theory that Big Corp should be treated as if Little Corp had merged into it.

C. **Judicial review of substantive fairness:** Courts will sometimes review the *substantive fairness* of a proposed acquisition or merger. This is much more likely when there is a strong self-dealing aspect to the transaction.

    1. **Arm's length combination:** If the buyer and the seller do *not have a close pre-existing relationship* at the time they negotiate the deal, courts will rarely overturn the transaction as being substantively unfair. For instance, under Delaware law a person who attacks the transaction for substantive fairness must: (1) bear the *burden of proof* on the fairness issue; and (2) show that the price was so *grossly inadequate* as to amount to *"constructive fraud."* P will rarely be able to satisfy this double-barreled test.

    2. **Self-dealing:** But if the transaction involves *self-dealing* (i.e., one or more insiders influence both sides of the transaction), the court will give much stricter scrutiny. For instance, in Delaware, the proponents of the transaction must demonstrate its *"entire fairness."*

        a. **Two-step acquisition:** This test is applied in *two-step acquisitions*.

            Example: Big Corp attempts to acquire Little Corp by means of a two-step hostile tender offer. Big Corp first buys 51% of Little Corp stock for $35 per share. As the second step, it then seeks to merge Little Corp into Big Corp, with the remaining Little Corp shareholders receiving $25 per share. (In the original tender offer, it announces that it plans to take the second step if the first step succeeds.) An unhappy Little Corp shareholder might (but probably would not) succeed in getting a court to enjoin this second-step "back end merger" on the grounds that it is substantively unfair. (The court would probably scrutinize the transaction fairly closely, but uphold it on the grounds that all shareholders were treated equally and knew what they were getting into.)

    b. Parent-subsidiary: Similarly, the court will take a close look for possible self-dealing where the transaction is a ***parent-subsidiary merger.***

       Example: ABC Corp owns 80% of XYZ Corp (with the rest owned by a variety of small public shareholders). Most XYZ directors have been appointed by ABC. ABC proposes to have XYZ merge into it, with each XYZ share being exchanged for one share of ABC. Nearly all of the public XYZ minority holders oppose the merger, but ABC's 80% ownership allows the merger to be approved by a majority of all XYZ holders. A court would be likely to closely scrutinize this merger, because ABC's dominance of XYZ (and its ability to persuade the XYZ board to approve the transaction) amounted to self-dealing. Therefore, ABC will bear the burden of demonstrating that the merger terms are "entirely fair" to the minority holders of XYZ, and the court will enjoin the transaction if this showing is not made. (ABC could guard against this problem by having XYZ negotiate its side of the merger by the use of only "independent" directors, i.e., those not dominated by ABC.)

III. RECAPITALIZATIONS — HURTING THE PREFERRED SHAREHOLDERS

  A. Problem: A board of directors dominated by common shareholders (as is usually the case) may try to help the common shareholders at the expense of the ***preferred*** shareholders. Typically, the common shareholders try to cancel an arrearage in preferred dividends, so that the common holders can receive a dividend.

  B. Two methods: There are two basic recapitalization methods by which the common shareholders can attempt to eliminate the accrued preferred dividends:

    1. Amending articles: First, they can cause the articles of incorporation to be ***amended*** to eliminate the accrued dividends as a corporate obligation. (But in most states, the preferred shareholders will have to agree ***as a separate class*** that this amendment should take place. See MBCA § 10.04(a)(9).

2. Merger: Second, the corporation can be *merged* into another corporation, with the survivor's articles not providing for payment of any accrued preferred dividends. (Again, in most states the preferred get to vote on the merger as a separate class. But under Delaware law, the preferred would not have this right.)

C. Courts don't interfere: Courts are generally very *reluctant* to interfere with such anti-preferred recapitalizations, even where the plans seems to be objectively unfair to the preferred holders. But in addition to possible veto rights, the preferred holders will also generally get *appraisal rights*.

IV. FREEZEOUTS

A. Meaning of "freezeout": A "freezeout" is a transaction in which those in control of a corporation *eliminate the equity ownership* of the non-controlling shareholders.

1. Distinguished from "squeezeout": Generally, "freezeout" describes those techniques whereby the controlling shareholders *legally compel* the non-controlling holders to give up their common stock ownership. The related term "squeezeout" describes methods that do not legally compel the outsiders to give up their shares, but in a practical sense coerce them into doing so. Squeezeouts are especially common in the close-corporation context, and are discussed briefly below.

2. Three contexts: There are three common *contexts* in which a freezeout is likely to occur: (1) as the second step of a *two-step acquisition* transaction (Big Corp buys, say, 51% of Little Corp stock, and then eliminates the remaining 49% holders through some sort of merger); (2) where two *long-term affiliates merge* (the controlling parent eliminates the publicly-held minority interest in the subsidiary); and (3) where the company *"goes private"* (the insiders cause the corporation or its underlying business to no longer to be registered with the SEC, listed on a stock exchange and/or actively traded over the counter).

3. General rule: In evaluating a freezeout, the court will usually: (1) try to verify that the transaction is basically *fair*; and (2) scrutinize the transaction especially closely in view of the fact that the minority holders are being cashed out (as opposed to being given stock in a different entity, such as the acquirer).

B. Techniques for carrying out a freezeout:

1. Cash-out merger: The leading freezeout technique today is the simple *"cash-out" merger*. The insider causes the corporation to merge into a well-funded shell, and the minority holders are paid cash in exchange for their shares, in an amount determined by the insiders.

Example: Shark owns 70% of Public Corp. He wants to freeze out the minority holders. He creates Private Corp, of which he is the sole shareholder, and funds it with $1 million. He now causes both Public Corp and Private Corp to agree to a plan of merger under which each of Public's 1,000,000 shares will be exchanged in the merger for $1 in cash. The 30% minority holders in Public are completely eliminated by the $300,000 cash payments, and Shark receives $700,000 with which to pay down the bank debt that funded Private Corp in the first place. Such a "cash out" merger is allowed by most modern merger statutes, including MBCA § 11.01(b)(3).)

2. **Short-form merger:** A freezeout may also be done via the *short-form* merger statute. If ABC Corp owns 90% or more of XYZ Corp, then in most states at ABC's request, XYZ can be merged into ABC with all XYZ holders paid off in cash (rather than ABC stock).

3. **Reverse stock split:** Finally, a freezeout may be carried out by means of a *reverse stock split*. Using, say, a 600:1 reverse stock split, nearly all outsiders may end up with a fractional share. Then, the corporation can compel the owners of the fractional shares to exchange their shares for cash.

C. **Federal law on freezeouts:**

1. **10b-5:** A minority shareholder may be able to attack a freezeout on the grounds that it violates SEC Rule 10b-5. If there has been *full disclosure*, then P is unlikely to convince the court that 10b-5 has been violated, no matter how "unfair" the freezeout may seem to the court. But if the insiders have concealed or *misrepresented* material facts about the transaction, then a court may find a 10b-5 violation.

2. **SEC Rule 13e-3:** Also, SEC Rule 13e-3 requires extensive disclosure by the insiders in the case of any *going-private* transaction. If the insiders do not comply with 13e-3, they may be liable for damages or an injunction.

D. **State law:** A successful attack on a freezeout transaction is more likely to derive from *state* rather than federal law. Since a freezeout transaction will usually involve self-dealing by the insiders, state courts will *closely scrutinize* the *fairness* of the transaction.

1. **General test:** In most states, the freezeout must meet at least the first, and possibly the second, of the following tests: (1) the transaction must be *basically fair*, taken in its entirety, to the outsider/minority shareholders; and (2) the transaction must be undertaken for some *valid business purpose*.

2. **Basic fairness:** For the transaction to be "basically fair," most courts require: (1) a fair *price*; (2) fair *procedures* by which the board decided to

approve the transaction; and (3) adequate ***disclosure*** to the outside shareholders about the transaction.

> **Example:** Signal owns slightly more than half of UOP Corp., with the balance owned by the public. Four key directors of UOP are also directors of Signal (and owe Signal their primary loyalty). Two of these directors prepare a feasibility study, which concludes that $24 is a fair price for Signal to pay for the balance of UOP. Signal then offers $21 per UOP share. There is no negotiation between UOP and Signal on this price, and the non-Signal-affiliated UOP directors are never told about the $24 feasibility study. The deal goes through.
>
> *Held*, this acquisition did not meet the test of basic fairness to UOP's minority shareholders. The price was not fair (since Signal's own directors admitted that $24 was a fair price); the procedures were not fair (since there were no real negotiations between the two companies); and the disclosure was not fair (e.g., the public was never told about the feasibility study showing $24 as a fair price). See *Weinberger v. UOP, Inc.*

    a. Independent committee: A parent-subsidiary merger is much more likely to be found fair if the public minority stockholders of the subsidiary are represented by a ***special committee of independent directors*** who are not affiliated with the parent (e.g., if UOP had been represented by non-Signal-affiliated directors in a true bargaining session with Signal, the transaction in *Weinberger* might have been upheld).

3. "Business purpose" test: Apart from the requirement that the transaction be basically fair, some but not all courts will strike down the freezeout unless it serves a ***"valid business purpose."*** In other words, in some courts the insiders, even if they pay a fair price, cannot put through a transaction whose sole purpose is to eliminate the minority (public) stockholders.

    a. Going private: This business purpose test is especially likely to be flunked when the transaction is a ***going-private*** one (as opposed to a two-step acquisition or a merger of long-term affiliates).

    b. Delaware abandons: Delaware has abandoned the business purpose requirement, so in Delaware only the test of "basic fairness" has to be met.

4. Closely-held corporations: If the freezeout takes place in the context of a ***close corporation***, most courts will probably scrutinize it more closely than in the public-corporation context. This is especially true of ***"squeezeouts."***

Example: Shark, who owns 70% of Close Corp, tries to coerce Pitiful, his long-time assistant, to sell his 30% stake. Shark fires Pitiful, cuts off his salary, and refuses to pay dividends, then offers to buy Pitiful's stake for a fraction of its true value. A court is likely to strike this transaction on the grounds that it is unfair, since it leaves Pitiful with no way to make a reasonable return on his investment.

V. TENDER OFFERS, ESPECIALLY HOSTILE TAKEOVERS

A. Definition of tender offer: A tender offer is an offer to stockholders of a publicly-held corporation to *exchange their shares* for cash or securities at a price higher than the previous market price.

   1. Used in hostile takeovers: A cash tender offer is the most common way of carrying out a *"hostile takeover."* A hostile takeover is the acquisition of a publicly held company (the *"target"*) by a buyer (the *"bidder"*) over the *opposition of the target's management*.

   2. Williams Act: Tender offers are principally regulated by the *Williams Act*, part of the federal Securities Exchange Act of 1934.

B. Disclosure by 5% owner: Any person who *"directly or indirectly"* acquires *more than 5%* of *any class* of stock in a publicly held corporation must disclose that fact on a statement filed with the SEC (a "Schedule 13D" statement).

   1. Information disclosed: The investor must disclose a variety of information on his 13D, including the source of the funds used to make the purchase, and the investor's *purpose* in buying the shares (including whether he intends to *seek control*).

   2. "Beneficial owner": A 13D must be filed by a "beneficial owner" of the 5% stake, even if he is not the record owner.

   3. When due: The filing must be made *within 10 days* following the acquisition. (Thus an investor has 10 days beyond when he crosses the 5% threshold, in which he can make further purchases without informing the world.)

   4. Additional acquisitions: Someone who is already a 5%-or-more owner must refile his 13D anytime he acquires *additional* stock (though not for small additions which, over a 12-month period, amount to less than 2% of the company's total stock).

   5. Groups: A *"group"* must file a 13D. Thus if A and B each buy 4% of XYZ acting in concert, they must file a 13D together as a "group" even though each acting alone would not be required to file. (A group can be formed even in the absence of a written agreement.)

6. **No tender offer intended:**   The requirement of filing a Schedule 13D applies *no matter what the purchaser's intent is*. Thus even if an investor has no intent to seek control or make a tender offer, he must still file.

C. **Rules on tender offers:**   Here are the main rules imposed by the Williams Act upon tender offers:

1. **Disclosure:**   Any tender offeror (at least one who, if his tender offer were successful, would own 5% or more of a company's stock) must make extensive *disclosures*. He must disclose his identity, funding, and purpose. Also, if the bidder proposes to pay part of the purchase price in the form of securities (e.g., preferred or common stock in the bidder, junk bonds, etc.) the bidder's financial condition must be disclosed.

2. **Withdrawal rights:**   Any shareholder who tenders to a bidder has the right to *withdraw* his stock from the tender offer *at any time while the offer remains open*. If the tender offer is extended for any reason, the withdrawal rights are similarly extended until the new offer-expiration date.

3. **"Pro rata" rule:**   If a bidder offers to buy only a *portion* of the outstanding shares of the target, and the holders tender more than the number than the bidder has offered to buy, the bidder must buy *in the same proportion from each shareholder*. This is the so-called *"pro rata"* rule.

4. **"Best price" rule:**   If the bidder *increases* his price before the offer has expired, he must pay this increased price to *each* stockholder whose shares are tendered and bought up. In other words, he may not give the increased price only to those who tender after the price increase. This is the *"best price"* rule.

5. **20-day minimum:**   A tender offer *must be kept open for at least 20 business days*. Also, if the bidder changes the price or number of shares he is seeking, he must hold the offer open for *another 10 days* after the announcement of the change.

D. **Hart-Scott-Rodino Act:**   The Hart-Scott-Rodino Antitrust Improvements Act (H-S-R) requires a bidder to give notice to the government of certain proposed deals, and imposes a waiting period before the deal can be consummated. H-S-R applies only where one party has sales or assets of more than $100 million and the other has sales or assets of more than $10 million.

E. **Definition of "tender offer":**   There is no official definition of "tender offer."

1. **Eight factors:**   Courts and the SEC often take into account eight possible factors which make it more likely that a tender offer is being conducted: (1) *active and widespread solicitation* of the target's public shareholders; (2) a solicitation for a *substantial percentage* of the target's stock; (3) an offer to purchase at a *premium* over the prevailing price; (4)

firm rather than negotiable terms; (5) an offer *contingent* on receipt of a *fixed minimum number* of shares; (6) a *limited time period* for which the offer applies; (7) the *pressuring* of offerees to sell their stock; and (8) a *public announcement* by the buyer that he will be acquiring the stock.

2. **Vast quantities not sufficient:** Mere purchases of large quantities of stock, without at least some of these eight factors, do *not* constitute a tender offer.

3. **Privately-negotiated purchases:** A *privately-negotiated purchase*, even of large amounts of stock, usually will *not* constitute a tender offer. This is true even if the acquirer conducts simultaneous negotiations with a number of large stockholders, and buys from each at an above market price.

4. **Open-market purchases:** Usually there will not be a tender offer where the acquirer makes *open-market purchases* (e.g., purchases made on the New York Stock Exchange), even if a large percentage of the target's stock is bought.

F. **Private actions under § 14(e):** Section 14(e) of the '34 Act (part of the Williams Act) makes it unlawful to make an "untrue statement of a material fact," to "omit to state" any material fact, or to engage in any "fraudulent, deceptive, or manipulative act," in connection with a tender offer.

1. **Substantive unfairness:** This section does *not* prohibit conduct by a bidder that is *substantively unfair*, but that does not involve misrepresentation or nondisclosure.

   Example: Bidder withdraws an attractive and over-subscribed tender offer, and replaces it with a much less attractive one. *Held*, even though this may be substantively unfair conduct, it is not deceptive, and therefore does not violate § 14(e) of the Williams Act. See *Schreiber v. Burlington Northern*.

2. **Standing:** Several types of people can bring a suit for a violation of § 14(e), including: (1) the target (which can seek an injunction against deceptive conduct by the bidder); (2) a *bidder* (which can get an injunction against the target's management or against another bidder, but which *cannot* get *damages* against anyone); (3) a *non-tendering shareholder* (who can get either damages or an injunction); and (4) a person who *buys* or *sells* shares in reliance on information disclosed or not disclosed in tender offer documents.

3. **Materiality:** Plaintiff must show that the misrepresentation or omission was *"material."* That is, he must show that the omitted or misstated fact would have assumed actual significance in a reasonable shareholder's deliberations about whether to tender.

4. **Scienter:** Plaintiff probably must show *scienter* (i.e., an *intent* to deceive, manipulate or defraud) on the part of the defendant in a private § 14(e) action.

5. **Reliance:** D must normally show that he *relied* on D's misrepresentation (e.g., that he read D's tender offer materials). But there is no reliance requirement if P is complaining about the *omission* of a material fact.

6. **Remedies:** A private party may generally get either an *injunction* against consummation of the tender offer or *damages*.

G. **State regulation of hostile takeovers:** Many states have statutes which attempt to discourage hostile takeovers and protect incumbent management.

1. **Modern statutes:** Most modern anti-takeover statutes operate not by preventing the bidder from buying the shares, but instead depriving him of the *benefit* of his share acquisition, by: (1) preventing the bidder from *voting the shares* he has bought unless certain conditions are satisfied; (2) preventing the bidder from conducting a *back-end merger* of the target into the bidder's shell, or vice versa; or (3) requiring the bidder to pay a specified *"fair price"* in any back-end merger.

2. **Delaware Act:** The most important modern statute is the *Delaware* anti-takeover statute, Del. GCL § 203. Section 203 prohibits any "business combination" (including any *back-end merger*) between the corporation and an "interested stockholder" for *three years* after the stockholder buys his shares. Anyone who buys more than 15% of a company's stock is covered. The net effect of the Delaware statute is that anyone who buys less than 85% of a Delaware corporation cannot for three years conduct a back-end merger between the shell he uses to carry out the acquisition and the target, and therefore: (1) cannot use the target's assets as security for a loan to finance the share acquisition; and (2) cannot use the target's earnings and cash flow to pay off the acquisition debt.

H. **Defensive maneuvers:** Here are some of the defensive maneuvers that a target's incumbent management may use to defeat a hostile bidder.

1. **Pre-offer techniques:** Techniques that can be used before a concrete takeover attempt emerges are usually called *"shark repellants."* These generally must be approved by a majority of the target's *shareholders*. Here are some of the more common ones:

a. **Super-majority provision:** The target may amend its articles of incorporation to require that *more than a simple majority* of the target's shareholders approve any merger or major sale of assets. (Alternatively, the target can provide that such a merger or asset sale be approved by a majority of the *disinterested* shareholders.) There are called *"super-majority"* provisions.

b. Staggered board: A target might put in place a *staggered* board of directors (i.e., only a minority of the board stands for election in a given year, so that a hostile bidder cannot gain control immediately even if he owns a majority of the shares.)

c. Anti-greenmail amendment: The target might amend its charter to prohibit the paying of *"greenmail"*, so as to discourage any hostile bidder bent on receiving greenmail.

d. New class of stock: The target might create a *second class* of common stock, and require that any merger or asset sale be approved by each class; then, the new class can be placed with persons friendly to management (e.g., the founding family, or an Employee Stock Ownership Plan).

e. Poison pill: *"Poison pill"* plans try to make bad things happen to the bidder if it obtains control of the target, thereby making the target less attractive to the bidder.

    i. "Call" plans: A *"call"* plan gives stockholders the right to buy cheap stock in certain circumstances. Most contain a "flipover" provision which is triggered when an outsiders buys, say, 20% of the target's stock. When the flipover is triggered, the holder of the right (the stockholder) has an option to *acquire shares of the bidder* at a cheap price.

    ii. "Put" plans: Other poison pills are *"put"* plans. If a bidder buys some but not all of the target's shares, the put gives each target shareholder the right to sell back his remaining shares in the target at a pre-determined *"fair"* price.

    iii. No approval required: Shareholder approval is *not* generally required for a poison pill plan. Also, such plans may sometimes be implemented *after* a hostile bid has emerged.

2. Post-offer techniques: Here are some techniques that can be used *after* a hostile bid has surfaced:

a. Defensive lawsuits: The target's management can institute *defensive lawsuits* (e.g., a state suit alleging breach of state-law fiduciary principles, or a federal court suit based on the federal securities laws). Usually, lawsuits just buy time.

b. White knight defense: The target may find itself a *"white knight,"* who will acquire the target instead of letting the hostile bidder do so. Often, the white knight is given a *"lockup,"* that is, some special inducement to enter the bidding process, such as a *"crown jewel" option* (i.e., an option to buy one of the target's best businesses at a below-market price).

c. Defensive acquisition: The target might make itself less attractive by arranging a *defensive acquisition* (e.g., one that causes the target to take on a lot of debt).

d. Corporate restructuring: The target may *restructure* itself in a way that raises short-term stockholder value.

   Example: Target borrows heavily from banks and then pays holders a large one-time dividend, possibly followed by large asset sales to pay down the debt.

e. Greenmail: The target may pay *"greenmail"* to the bidder (i.e., it buys the bidder's stake back at an above-market price, usually in return for a "standstill" agreement under which the bidder agrees not to attempt to re-acquire the target for some specified number of years).

f. Sale to friendly party: The target may sell a less-than-controlling block to a *friendly party*, i.e., one who can be trusted not to tender to the hostile bidder. Thus the target might sell new shares to its employees' pension plan, to an ESOP (employee stock ownership plan), or to a "white squire." In Delaware, if a friendly party owns 16%, the Delaware anti-takeover statute, GCL § 203, will be triggered, thus preventing a bidder from arranging a back-end merger or asset sale for three years.

g. Share repurchase: The target might *repurchase* a significant portion of its shares from the public, if insiders hold a substantial but not controlling stake (thus raising the insiders' stake).

I. Federal securities law response: A bidder who wants to *overturn* the target's defensive measures probably will *not* be able to do so using the federal securities laws. If the bidder can show the target's management has actually deceived the target's shareholders, it may be able to get an injunction under § 14(e) of the '34 Act. But if incoming management has merely behaved in a way that is arguably "unfair" to the target's shareholders (by depriving them of the opportunity to tender into the bidder's high offer), there will generally be no federal securities-law violation.

J. State response: The bidder has a much better chance of showing that the target's defensive maneuvers violate *state law*.

   1. Summary of Delaware law: Most case law concerning what defensive maneuvers a target may employ comes from Delaware.

   a. Business judgment rule: In Delaware, the target and its management will get the protection of the *business judgment rule* (and thus their defensive measures will be upheld) under the following circumstances (summarized in *Unocal Corp. v. Mesa Petroleum Co.*):

i. **Reasonable grounds:** First, the board and management must show that they had ***reasonable grounds*** for believing that there was a ***danger to the corporation's welfare*** from the takeover attempt. In other words, the insiders may not use anti-takeover measures ***merely to entrench themselves in power*** — they must reasonably believe that they are protecting the stockholders' interests, not their own interests. (Some dangers that will justify anti-takeover measures are: (1) a reasonable belief that the bidder would ***change the business practices*** of the corporation in a way that would be harmful to the company's ongoing business and existence; (2) a reasonable fear that the particular takeover attempt is ***unfair and coercive***, such as a two-tier front-loaded offer; and (3) a reasonable fear that the offer will leave the target with unreasonably high levels of debt.)

ii. **Proportional response:** Second, the directors and management must show that the defensive measures they actually used were "reasonable in relation to the threat posed." This is the ***"proportionality"*** requirement.

(1) **Can't be "preclusive" or "coerecive":** To meet the proportionality requirement, a defensive measure must ***not*** be either ***"preclusive"*** or ***"coercive."*** A "preclusive" action is one that has the effect of foreclosing virtually ***all*** takeovers (e.g., a poison pill plan whose terms would dissuade any bidder, or the granting of a "crown jewels option" to a white knight on way-below-market terms). A "coercive" measure is one which "crams down" on the target's shareholders a management-sponsored alternative (e.g., a lower competing bid by management, if management has enough votes to veto the hostile bid and makes it clear that it will use this power to block the hostile bid).

iii. **Reasonable investigation:** Third, the target's board must act upon ***reasonable investigation*** when it responds to the takeover measure.

b. **Independent directors:** Court approval of the anti-takeover devices is much more likely if the board that approved the measure has a majority composed of ***"independent"*** directors (i.e., those who are not full-time employees and who are not closely affiliated with management).

c. **Consequences if requirements not met:** If one or more of the three requirements summarized in (a) above are not met, the court will refuse to give the takeover device the protection of the business rule.

But it will not automatically strike the measure; instead, it will treat it like any other type of self-dealing, and will put management to the burden of showing that the transaction is "entirely fair" to the target's shareholders.

K. Decision to sell the company (the "Level Playing Field" rule): Once the target's management decides that it is *willing* to sell the company, then the courts give *"enhanced scrutiny"* to the steps that the target's board and managers take. Most importantly, management and the board must make every effort to obtain the *highest price* for the shareholders. Thus the target's insiders must create a *level playing field*: all *would-be bidders must be treated equally*.

> **Example:** Target is sought by Raider and White Knight. Target's board favors White Knight. Target's board gives White Knight a "crown jewels option" to buy two key Target subsidiaries for a much-below-market price.
>
> *Held*, Target's board violated its obligation to get the best price, and it was not entitled to favor one bidder over another, such as by the use of a lockup to prematurely end the auction. [*Revlon, Inc. v. MacAndrews & Forbes Holdings, Inc.*].

1. Management interested: If the target's *management* is one of the competing bidders, the target's board must be especially careful not to favor management (e.g., it must not give management better access to information). Normally, the target's *independent directors* should form a special committee to conduct negotiations on the target's behalf.

L. Sale of control: Similarly, *"enhanced scrutiny"* will now be give to transactions in which the board *"sells control"* of the company to a single individual or group.

> **Example:** Target's shares are widely dispersed, with no controlling shareholder. Acquirer, although it's a public company, has a controlling shareholder, Boss, who owns 30% of its shares. Target negotiates a merger agreement with Acquirer, under which each holder of Target will get a share of the combined Target-plus-Acquirer company. Because Target's board is proposing to sell "control" of Target to a single individual (Boss), the court will carefully scrutinize the deal, and make extra sure that all other possible buyers or merger partners are treated equally.

1. Friendly merger into non-controlled public company: It is only where the target is merging into a friendly *"controlled"* acquirer that enhanced scrutiny will be triggered — if the target is merged into a friendly acquirer that's *already held by the public at large* with no single controlling shareholder or group, there will be *no enhanced scrutiny*. [*Arnold v. Soc. for Savings Bancorp, Inc.*].

M. Board may "just say no": If the target's board has *not* previously decided to put the company up for sale or dramatically restructure it, then the board basically has a right to *reject unwanted takeover offers*, even all-cash, high-priced offers that the board has reason to think most shareholders would welcome. In other words, the board may *"just say no,"* at least in Delaware.

1. **Illustrations:** Thus the target's board may, as a general rule, refuse to *redeem* a previously-enacted *poison pill*, refuse to *recommend a merger* or put the proposed merger to a *shareholder vote*, or otherwise *refuse to cooperate*. [*Paramount Communic. v. Time*].

N. Particular anti-takeover devices: Here is how the courts respond to some of the particular anti-takeover devices:

1. **Greenmail:** Most courts seem to *allow greenmail*.

   Example: If the target's board is worried that a particular bidder will damage the corporation's existence or its business policies, it may buy the bidder's shares back at a premium.

2. **Exclusionary repurchase:** If the target *repurchases* some of its shares at a price higher than the bidder is offering, it *may* refuse to buy back any of the bidder's shares as part of the arrangement (at least in Delaware). [*Unocal v. Mesa Petroleum*].

3. **Poison pill plans:** Most *poison pill* plans have been *upheld*. Only where the poison pill plan has the effect of foreclosing virtually all hostile take-overs is it likely to be struck down. [*Moran v. Household International, Inc.*].

4. **Lock-ups:** *Lock-ups* are the type of anti-takeover device that is most likely to be *invalidated*. This is especially true of *crown jewel* options. Lock-ups, including crown jewel options, are not *per se* illegal; for instance, they can be used to produce an auction where none would otherwise exist. But if a crown jewel option or other lock-up is used to end an auction prematurely rather than to create one, it may well be struck down.

   a. **Conditions making approval a "mathematical certainty":** A bidder will sometimes demand some sort of lock-up as a condition of entering a bid that binds that bidder — the bidder will often refuse to run the risk of being a *"stalking horse"* for some later, higher bidder who will end up taking the company. In Delaware, at least some combinations of *deal-protection measures* given to satisfy the first bidder's "I won't be a stalking horse" demand (and thus to lock up the deal for that bidder) will be found to *violate* the Level Playing Field rule. If the deal-protection measures constitute, in the court's opinion, *an "absolute lock up"* that makes approval of the merger a *mathematical certainty,* the combination will be *invalid*, even if the bidder is the only or highest bidder in the picture, and will walk away if not given the lock up.

Example: NCS is on the verge of bankruptcy. Finally, Genesis offers to buy it in a stock-for-stock merger. But Genesis makes it clear that it won't risk being a stalking horse bidder whose bid might be used to extract a better bid from someone else. Genesis demands, and NCS gives, a package of protections, including a voting agreement in which NCS stockholders controlling more than half the stock irrevocably bind themselves to vote for the merger, and a "force the vote" clause in which NCS' board promises to submit the merger to a shareholder vote even if the board no longer believes the merger is a good deal. NCS insists that there be no "fiduciary out" clause by which the board can refuse to submit the merger for shareholder approval if the board later concludes that its fiduciary obligation to stockholders is to try to avoid the merger. Hours after the NCS-Genesis merger agreement is signed, Omnicare makes a better merger proposal. NCS' board wants to take the better proposal, but the prior NCS-Genesis merger agreement, with its lock up concessions, make that deal's completion a virtual certainty. Therefore, Omnicare sues for an injunction to block the NCS-Genesis deal.

Held, for Omnicare. A target's board can't give a bidder "coercive" or "preclusive" lock up provisions. Where the concessions to the first bidder make it "mathematically impossible" for the target's shareholders to vote down the first merger in favor of a better one, the concessions amount to an "absolute lock up," and will be invalidated. [*Omnicare, Inc. v. NCS Healthcare, Inc.*]

i. **Narrow interpretation:** But *Omnicare, supra*, will apparently be *narrowly construed* in Delaware. For instance, the target's board and controlling shareholders *can* agree that they won't vote for any competing transaction for a substantial period of time, if they also give the target's minority holders the right to kill the first merger by voting it down. In other words, as long as the target's concessions *still leave a mathematical chance* that the outside shareholders can disapprove the first deal, the concessions won't be deemed "coercive" or "preclusive."

5. **Stock option:** An option to the acquirer to *buy stock in the target* will likely be struck down if it is for so many shares, or for so low a price, or on such burdensome terms, that its mere existence has a materially *chilling effect on whether other bidders will emerge*.

6. **Termination fee:** A fee payable to the acquirer if the merger should be terminated by the target may be upheld or struck down, depending on the amount and other circumstances.

CHAPTER 11
DIVIDENDS AND SHARE REPURCHASES

I. DIVIDENDS — PROTECTION OF CREDITORS

A. Terminology:

1. **Dividend:** A *"dividend"* is a cash payment made by a corporation to its common shareholders pro rata. It is usually paid out of the current earnings of the corporation, and thus represents a partial distribution of profits.

2. **Stated capital:** *"Stated capital"* is the stockholder's ***permanent investment*** in the corporation.

   a. **Par stock:** If the stock has *"par value,"* stated capital is equal to the number of shares outstanding times the par value of each share.

   b. **No-par:** If the stock is *"no-par"* stock (now permitted in most states), stated capital is an arbitrary amount that the board assigns to the stated capital account. (This amount is never more than the shareholders paid for their stock when they originally bought it, but is otherwise whatever the directors decide it should be when the stock is issued.)

3. **"Earned surplus":** *"Earned surplus"* is equal to the ***profits*** earned by the corporation during its existence, less any dividends it ever paid out. ("Retained earnings" is a more modern synonym.)

4. **"Capital surplus":** *"Capital surplus"* is everything in the corporation's "capital" account other than "stated capital." "Paid in" surplus, "revaluation" surplus, and "reduction" surplus are the main types of capital surplus.

B. Dividends generally:

1. **Authorized by board:** The decision to pay a dividend must always be made by the ***board of directors***.

2. **Two tests:** All states place certain ***legal limits*** (mostly financial ones) on the board's right to pay dividends, and directors who disregard these limits may be liable. In most states, a dividend may be paid only if ***both*** of the following general kinds of requirements are satisfied: (1) payment of the dividend will not impair the corporation's ***stated capital***; and (2) payment will not render the corporation ***insolvent***.

C. Capital tests:

1. **"Earned surplus" statutes:** In most states, there are *"earned surplus"* restrictions: dividends may be paid ***only out of the profits which the corporation has accumulated*** since its inception.

2. **"Impairment of capital" statutes:** A substantial minority of states merely prohibit dividends that would *"impair the capital"* of the corporation. These states are less strict than the "earned surplus" states: they allow the payment of dividends from *either* earned surplus or *unearned surplus*.

   a. **Paid-in surplus:** Thus an "impairment of capital" statute allows a corporation with no earned surplus to pay its entire *"paid-in surplus"* out again as dividends. "Paid-in surplus" is the difference between what the shareholders paid for their shares when they were originally issued, and the "stated capital" represented by those shares.

   b. **Revaluation surplus:** Many "impairment of capital" states also allow the board to create, and then pay out, "revaluation" surplus. This is the surplus produced by "writing up" the corporation's assets to their current market value (rather than using the historical prices normally reflected on a balance sheet).

   c. **Reduction surplus:** Finally, a "impairment of capital" statute usually allows the *"reduction surplus"* to be paid out. "Reduction surplus" is caused by reducing the corporation's stated capital (which in the case of stock having a par value requires a shareholder-approved amendment to the articles of incorporation).

3. **Nimble dividends:** Some states allow payment of *"nimble* dividends." These are dividends paid out of the *current earnings* of the corporation, even though the corporation otherwise would not be entitled to pay the dividends (because it has no earned surplus in an earned-surplus state, or because payment would impair its stated capital in an impairment-of-capital state).

   a. **Delaware:** Delaware GCL § 170(a) allows payment of nimble dividends: even if there is no earned surplus (normally required for a dividend in Delaware), the dividend may be paid out of the corporation's net profits for the current or preceding fiscal year.

D. **Insolvency test:** Even if a dividend payment would not violate the applicable capital test (earned-surplus or impairment-of-capital, depending on the state), in nearly all states payment of a dividend is prohibited if it would *leave the corporation insolvent*.

   1. **UFCA:** In half the states, this ban is imposed by the Uniform Fraudulent Conveyance Act (UFCA), which has the effect of prohibiting dividends by an insolvent corporation.

   2. **"Equity" meaning:** In most states, a corporation is insolvent if it is *unable to pay its debts as they become due* (the *"equity"* meaning of "insolvent"). A minority of states define a corporation as insolvent if the

market value of its assets is less than its liabilities (the *"bankruptcy"* meaning).

E. MBCA: The MBCA imposes *only* an insolvency test, not a capital-related test. Under MBCA § 6.40(c), no dividend may be paid if it would leave the corporation insolvent under *either* the "equity" or the "bankruptcy" definition of insolvent.

    1. Popular: The MCBA's approach to dividends has been *popular*: about 37 states have adopted it either wholly or with minor variations.

F. Liability of directors: If the directors approve a dividend at a time when the statute prohibits it, they may be *personally liable*:

    1. Bad faith: If the directors *know* that the dividend is forbidden at the time they pay it, they are personally liable in nearly all states.

    2. Negligence: If they act in good faith but are *negligent* in failing to notice that the dividend is forbidden, they are liable in some but probably not most states.

    3. Creditor suit: Usually, the suit to recover an improperly-paid dividend must be brought by the corporation (perhaps by means of a shareholder derivative suit, or by a trustee for the corporation once it declares bankruptcy). But some states allow suit to be brought by a *creditor* against the director(s) who approve an improper dividend.

    4. MBCA: Under the MBCA, the corporation may hold liable any director who negligently approves an improper dividend.

G. Liability of shareholders: A *shareholder* who receives an improper dividend may also be liable.

    1. Common law: At common law, the shareholder will be liable and required to return the improper dividend if *either*: (1) the corporation was insolvent at the time of, or as the result of the payment of, the dividend; or (2) the shareholder *knew*, at the time he received the dividend, that it was *improper*. But if the corporation is solvent and the shareholder takes the dividend without notice that it violates the statute, the shareholder does *not* have to return it at common law.

    2. Statute: Some corporation statutes make the shareholder liable to return the improper dividend, even if he would not be liable at common law. Apart from the basic corporation statute, the statute dealing with fraudulent conveyances (e.g., the Uniform Fraudulent Conveyance Act) may permit a creditor or bankruptcy trustee to recover against a shareholder.

II. DIVIDENDS — PROTECTION OF SHAREHOLDERS; JUDICIAL REVIEW OF DIVIDEND POLICY

A. Generally: A disgruntled shareholder will sometimes try to persuade the court to order the corporation to pay a *higher* dividend than it is already paying.

   1. General rule: This is left to case law by most states. Usually, P will only get the court to order a higher dividend if he shows that: (1) the low-dividend policy is *not justified by any reasonable business objective*; and (2) the policy results from *improper motives* that harm the corporation or some of its shareholders.

   2. Plaintiff rarely succeeds: Plaintiffs very rarely succeed in making these showings. Therefore, courts rarely order a corporation to change its dividend policies for the benefit of some group of shareholders.

   3. Closely-held: Courts are more likely to order an increase in dividend payments when the corporation is *closely held* rather than publicly held. Some courts now hold that minority stockholders who are not employed by the corporation are entitled to a *return on their investment* in the form of a dividend, even in the face of an otherwise valid corporate objective (e.g., expanding the business). Courts sometimes say that the insiders have a *fiduciary duty* to grant a reasonable dividend to the outside minority investors.

III. STOCK REPURCHASES

A. Repurchases generally: A *"stock repurchase"* occurs when a corporation *buys back* its own stock from stockholders. This may happen by open market repurchases, by a "self-tender" (i.e., a tender offer by a public company offering to buy some number of shares pro rata from all shareholders), or by face-to-face selective purchases.

B. Protection of shareholders: One shareholder may object to the corporation's repurchase of another shareholder's shares (e.g., on the grounds that the corporation has paid too high a price, or has refused to give all shareholders an equal opportunity to have their shares repurchased).

   1. General rule: Generally the court will not overturn a corporation's repurchase arrangements at the urging of a shareholder, so long as the board of directors: (1) behaves with reasonable care (i.e., makes reasonable inquiries into the corporation's financial health and the value of its shares before authorizing the repurchase); and (2) does not violate the duty of loyalty (e.g., the directors are not buying from themselves at an above-market price).

2. **Self-dealing by insiders:** The court will look extra closely at a repurchase that appears to *benefit the insiders* unduly.

Example: Ian, 40% owner of XYZ, induces the board to have XYZ repurchase his holdings for 50% more than the current stock market price. The court will look upon this as self-dealing, and will strike down the transaction unless Ian bears the burden of proving that the transaction is "entirely fair" to the corporation and its remaining shareholders.

C. **Protection of creditors; financial limits:** In general, share repurchases are subject to the same *financial limits* for the protection of creditors as are *dividends*.

CHAPTER 12

ISSUANCE OF SECURITIES

I. STATE-LAW RULES ON SHARE ISSUANCE

A. **Par value:** If shares have a *par value*, the corporation *may not sell the shares for less than this par value*. This rule protects both the corporation's creditors, and also other shareholders.

1. **"Watered stock" liability:** If shares are issued for less than their par value, *creditors* will sometimes be allowed to recover against the stockholder who received the cheap stock (usually called *"watered stock"*).

   a. **"Misrepresentation" theory:** Most courts apply the *"misrepresentation"* theory, under which only a creditor who has *relied* on the corporation's false assertion that the shares were issued for at least par value, may recover. Under this theory, one who becomes a creditor *before* the wrongful issuance, and one who becomes a creditor after the wrongful issuance but with *knowledge of it*, may not recover since he has not "relied."

2. **Kind of consideration:** In most states, shares may be paid for not only in cash, but also by the contribution of *property*, or by the performance of *past services*. States vary as to whether shares may be purchased and returned for *promises* to perform services or donate property (e.g., Delaware does not allow payment in the form of a promise to perform future services).

   a. **MBCA:** But the MBCA is more liberal: any kind of consideration is valid, so long as the board acts in good faith and with reasonable care. Thus promissory notes and promises to perform future services are both valid consideration under the MBCA.

3. **Valuation:** If the board of directors sells stock to a stockholder in return for past or future services or property, the board's good faith computation

of the value that should be attributed to those services or property will usually ***not be overturned*** by a court. See, e.g., Delaware § 152 ("in the absence of actual fraud in the transaction, the judgment of the directors as to the value of such consideration shall be conclusive").

4. **Use of no-par or low-par stock:** Observe that all of these problems of "watered stock" are less likely to arise today, because of the extensive use of no-par or low-par stock.

B. **Preemptive rights:** A *"preemptive right"* is a right sometimes given to a corporation's existing shareholders permitting them to ***maintain their percentage of ownership*** in the corporation, by enabling them to buy a portion of any newly-issued shares.

> **Example:** Inventor holds 49% of stock in Mousetrap Corp. If preemptive rights exist, then before Mousetrap's 51% holder can induce the board to issue new shares to himself or to the public, Inventor must first be given the right to buy as many new shares as will be needed to maintain Inventor's 49% ownership, on the same terms as offered to the 51% holder or to the public.

1. **Statutes:** Today, every state governs preemptive rights by statute. All modern statutes allow the corporation to ***dispense*** entirely with preemptive rights if it chooses. This choice by the corporation is embodied in the articles of incorporation.

  a. **Opt-in provisions:** Under most statutes, the preemptive rights scheme is an *"opt-in"* scheme. In other words, the corporation does not have preemptive rights unless it expressly elects, in the articles of incorporation, to have such rights. The MBCA follows this "opt-in" pattern; see § 6.30(a).

  b. **Opt-out:** A minority of states give the corporation an *"opt-out"* election — the corporation has preemptive rights unless it expressly specifies, in the articles of incorporation, that it does not want such rights.

2. **Exceptions:** Even where preemptive rights would otherwise apply, there are some important ***exceptions*** under most statutes:

  a. **Initially-authorized shares:** Preemptive rights usually do not apply to shares that are part of the amount that is ***initially authorized*** at the time the corporation is first formed. (However, initially-authorized-but-unissued shares *do* become covered by the preemptive scheme if a certain time period — e.g., six months under the MBCA — elapses following the date of incorporation.)

  b. **Treasury shares:** Under most statutes, ***treasury shares*** (that is, shares that were once outstanding, but that have been repurchased by the corporation) are not covered. (But the MBCA does not exclude treasury shares.)

    c. Property or services: Shares that are issued in exchange for ***property*** or ***services*** are generally not covered. Similarly, shares issued to allow the exercise of employee ***stock options*** are usually not covered.

3. "Fiduciary duty" concerning dilution: Even in situations where there are no preemptive rights (either because they have been waived by the corporation, or because the case falls into an exception where preemptive rights do not apply), courts may protect minority stockholders against dilution by a ***"fiduciary obligation"*** theory. According to some courts, a majority stockholder has a fiduciary duty not to cause the issuance of new shares where the purpose is to ***enhance his own control at the expense of the minority***.

    a. Unfair price: The court is most likely to impose this fiduciary duty where the new shares are issued at a ***bargain price*** to those who are already in control.

    b. Bona fide business purpose required: Even if the price is fair, the court will frequently strike down the sale of new stock by the corporation to its controlling shareholders if there is ***no valid business purpose*** behind the sale. For instance, if the court becomes convinced that the controlling shareholder has caused the sale to take place solely for the purpose of ***enhancing his own control***, the court is likely to strike the transaction even though the price was fair.

    c. Preemptive rights as a defense: If preemptive rights *do* apply, but the plaintiff ***declines to participate*** (perhaps because he doesn't have the money), courts are split about whether P may attack the sale of new shares to other existing shareholders on the grounds that the price is unfairly low. Some courts treat the fact that P declined to exercise his preemptive rights as a ***complete defense*** (so the court will not inquire into whether the shares were sold at an unfairly low price). Other courts hold that the existence of preemptive rights is ***not*** a defense, and that the board must bear the burden of showing that the price of the sale to insiders was at least within the range of fairness.

II. PUBLIC OFFERINGS — INTRODUCTION

A. Generally: Public offerings of securities are extensively regulated by the Securities Act of 1933 (the "'33 Act").

1. Section 5: The key provision of the '33 Act is § 5. Section 5 makes it unlawful (subject to exemptions) to ***sell any security*** by the use of the mails or other facilities of interstate commerce, ***unless a registration statement is in effect for that security***. This "registration statement" must contain a large amount of information about the security being offered, and about the company that is offering it (the "issuer"). Additionally, § 5 prohibits the sale of any security unless there is delivered to the buyer, before or at the same time as the security, a *"prospectus"* which contains the most important parts of the registration statement.

2. **Disclosure:** The entire scheme for regulating public offerings works by compelling *extensive disclosure*. The SEC does *not* review the *substantive merits* of the offering, and cannot bar an offering merely because it is too risky, overpriced, or valueless.

B. **"Security":** The '33 Act applies to sales of "securities." "Security" is defined very broadly. It includes not only ordinary "stocks," but "bonds," "investment contracts," and many other devices.

1. **Stock in closely held business:** Even where the owners of a closely held business sell *all* of the stock in the company to a single buyer who will operate the business himself, this is still the sale of a "security," so it must comply with the public-offering requirements (unless an exemption applies).

2. **Debt instruments:** *Debt instruments* will often be "securities." For instance, a widely-traded *bond* will typically be a security. But a single "note" issued by a small business to a bank will typically not be a security. In general, the more a debt instrument looks like an "investment," and the more widely traded it is, the more likely the court will be to find it a "security." [*Reves v. Ernst & Young*].

III. PUBLIC OFFERINGS — MECHANICS

A. **Filing process:** Here is how the process of going public works:

1. **Filing of registration statement:** The process begins when a registration statement is *filed* with the SEC.

2. **20-day waiting period:** The issuer must now wait for the registration statement to become *"effective."* This normally happens *20 days* after it is filed.

3. **Price amendment:** The registration statement is usually filed *without a price*. Then, the statement is *amended* to include the price term just before the end of the 20-day waiting period.

B. **Rules during the three periods:**

1. **Pre-filing:** During the *pre-filing* period (before the registration statement has been filed with the SEC), no one (including underwriters or issuers) may sell or even *offer to sell* the stock. (This means that press releases touting the issue, and oral offers, are forbidden, with narrow exceptions.)

2. **Waiting period:** During the *"waiting period"* (after filing but before the effective date), most offers to sell and offers to buy are allowed, but sales and binding *contracts* to sell are not allowed.

   a. **Red herring:** The underwriters may (and typically do) distribute during the waiting period a *"red herring,"* i.e., a *preliminary prospectus* which is identical to the final prospectus except that it typically omits the price.

   b. **No binding offers to buy:** During the waiting period, no offer to buy or "acceptance" will be deemed binding. Thus even if Customer says, "Yes, I'll buy 1,000 shares," he is not bound and can renege after the effective date.

3. **Post-effective period:** Once the registration statement becomes effective, underwriters and dealers may make offers to sell, and actual sales, to anyone. However, the final *prospectus* (complete with the final price) must be sent to any purchaser *before or at the same time* he receives the securities.

IV. PUBLIC OFFERINGS — EXEMPTIONS

A. **Generally:** There are two key *exemptions* to the general rule that securities can only be issued if a registration statement is in force:

   1. **Sales by other than issuer, underwriter or dealer:** First, § 4(1) of the '33 Act gives an exemption for "transactions by any person other than an issuer, underwriter, or dealer." Because of an exemption for most sales by dealers, registration will generally be required only where the transaction is being carried out by a person who is an *"issuer"* or *"underwriter."* (But these terms are defined in a broad and complex way.)

   2. **Non-public offerings:** Second, under § 4(2), there is an exemption for "transactions by an issuer *not involving any public offering*." So if an issuer can show that its sale was "non-public" rather than "public," it need not comply with the registration requirements.

B. **Private offerings:** There are two different bodies of law by which an issuer may have its offering treated as *"private"* rather than "public":

   1. **Statutory exemption:** First, the issuer may show that the broad *statutory* language of § 4(2) (exempting transactions "not involving any public offering") applies.

      a. **Sales to institutions:** For instance, a sale by a corporation of a large block of stock or bonds to one or a few large and sophisticated *institutions* (e.g., insurance companies or pension funds) will be a private offering based on this statutory exemption.

    b. Sales to key employees: Similarly, stock sales to key employees will usually qualify under this statutory exemption.

    c. General test: In general, an offering will not be "private" unless: (1) there are not very many offerees (though there is no fixed limit); and (2) the offerees have a significant level of *sophistication* and a significant degree of *knowledge* about the company's affairs.

    Example: XYZ Corp offers shares to 10 secretarial-level employees at the company, without giving them any special disclosure. Since the secretaries' knowledge of the company's financial affairs is probably limited, this is a "public" rather than "private" offering, even though the number of offerees is small. Therefore, a registration statement must be used.

2. SEC Rule 506: Separately, SEC has enacted *Rule 506*. If Rule 506's conditions are met, the offering will be deemed "private" regardless of whether it would be private under the cases decided under the general § 4(2) statutory exemption.

    a. Gist: The gist of Rule 506 is that an issuer may sell an unlimited amount of securities to: (1) any number of *"accredited"* investors; and (2) up to *35 non-accredited* investors. (An "accredited" investor is essentially one who is worth more than $1 million, or has an income of more than $200,000 per year.)

    b. Sophisticated: Although an "accredited" investor can be very unsophisticated without ruining the Rule 506 exemption, a non-accredited investor must be *sophisticated.* (More precisely, the issuer must *"reasonably believe"* that the non-accredited investor, either alone or with his "purchaser representative," has such *knowledge and experience* in financial and business matters that he is capable of evaluating the merits of the investment.)

    c. No advertising: The issuer may not make any general *solicitation* or *advertising*, for a Rule 506 offer.

    d. Disclosure: If the offering is solely to accredited investors, there are no disclosure requirements. But if even one investor is non-accredited, then *all* purchasers (accredited or not) must receive specific disclosures about the issuer and the offering.

C. Small offerings: Two other SEC rules give an exemption for offerings that are *"small"* (as opposed to "private"):

1. Rule 504: Rule *504* allows an issuer to sell up to a total of *$1 million* of securities. (All sales in any 12-month period are added together.)

    a. Unlimited number: There is no limit on the *number* of investors in a purchase.

    b. Disclosure: No particular disclosure is required.

    c. Advertising: Generally, the offering may not be publicly advertised or accomplished by widespread solicitation.

2. **Rule 505:** Under Rule *505*, the issuer can sell up to *$5 million* of securities in any 12-month period.

    a. Number: The number of investors is limited to 35 non-accredited and any number of accredited investors (like Rule 506).

    b. Disclosure: The same *disclosure* to all investors as would be required under 506 is required under 505, if there is even a single non-accredited investor.

    c. Type of investor: But 505 (in contrast to 506) imposes no requirements concerning the *type of investor*: the investor need not be either accredited or sophisticated.

D. Sales by non-issuer:

1. **Sales by or for controlling persons:** If a *controlling stockholder* sells a large number of shares by soliciting a large number of potential buyers, this may be held to be a "public offering." If so, the shareholder will have to register the shares, or else he (as well as his broker) will face liability for the crime of distributing unregistered stock. The key concept is *"distribution"*: if a broker sells for a controlling shareholder in what is found to be a "distribution," a registration statement is required. (The larger the number of shares sold, and the larger the number of potential buyers contacted, the more likely a "distribution" is to be found.)

    a. Rule 144: But SEC Rule *144* provides a safe harbor: if the terms of the rule are complied with, sales by or for a controlling shareholder will not need to be registered. The key requirements for 144, in the case of a sale by a controlling shareholder, are:

        i. Limit on amount of sales: The sales must be made *gradually:* In any three-month period, the controlling shareholder may not sell more than the greater of: (1) 1% of the total shares outstanding; or (2) the average weekly trading volume for the prior four weeks.

        ii. Holding period: The controlling shareholder must normally have held the securities *for at least two years* before reselling them. (But this does not apply if he bought the shares in a public offering.)

        iii. Disclosure: The issuing company must be a *"public"* company (one which files periodic reports with the SEC), or must make equivalent information about itself publicly available. So Rule

144 is not usually usable by the controlling shareholder of a private company.

    iv. Ordinary brokerage transactions: The stock must be sold in ordinary brokerage transactions. The controlling shareholder's broker may not *solicit* orders to buy the stock.

    v. Notice: A *notice* of each sale must be filed with the SEC at the time the order to sell is placed with the broker.

2. Non-controlling shareholder: *Non-controlling* persons may also sometimes have to register their shares before selling them. A person who has previously bought stock from the issuer in a private transaction, and who now wishes to resell that stock, could be liable for making an unregistered public offering if a court finds that he *bought with an intent to resell* rather than for investment.

    a. Rule 144: But Rule 144 may help in this situation, too.

        i. Held less than three years: If the non-controlling shareholder has held his restricted stock for *less than three years*, then he may only use Rule 144 if all the requirements listed above for controlling-shareholder sales are met.

        ii. Held for more than three years: But if a non-controlling shareholder has held his restricted stock for *more than three years*, most limitations are removed: a non-controlling shareholder who buys stock in a private offering and then holds that stock for three years may sell *to whomever he wishes*, and whatever amounts he wishes, by whatever type of transaction he wishes, without reference to whether the company files SEC reports, and without any need to file any notice with the SEC. (But, of course, the resale must not itself constitute a brand new public offering.)

E. Other exemptions: There are two other significant exemptions:

  1. Intrastate offerings: Section 3(a)(11) of the '33 Act exempts "*intrastate* offerings." However, this exception is very hard to qualify for, and is rarely used except in isolated areas that are very far from any state border.

  2. Regulation A: Regulation A is a set of SEC Rules that gives an exemption for certain issues of up to $5 million. Its main use is for offerings made under employee stock option or stock purchase plans.

V. PUBLIC OFFERINGS — CIVIL LIABILITIES

A. Generally: There are four liability provisions under the '33 Act, at least three of which impose civil liability in favor of an injured investor.

B. Section 11: Section 11 imposes liability for any material errors or omissions *in a registration statement*.

    1. Who may sue: A Section 11 suit may be brought by *anyone* who buys the stock covered by the registration statement (even if he did not buy at the initial public offering).

    2. Reliance: P does not have to show that he *relied* on the registration statement. (However, D can raise the affirmative defense of showing that P knew of the untruth or omission at the time he purchased it.)

    3. Who may be sued: A wide range of people may be sued under § 11, including: (1) everyone who signed the registration statement (which always includes at least the issuer and the principal officers); (2) everyone who is a *director* at the time the registration statement was filed; (3) every *expert* who consented to being named as having prepared part of the registration statement; and (4) every *underwriter*.

    4. Standard of conduct: The issuer's liability is *absolute*; even if the misstatement or omission was inadvertent and in fact non-negligent, the issuer is strictly liable. But all other defendants may raise the *"due diligence"* defense.

        a. Expertised portions: With respect to any part of the registration statement prepared by an *expert*: (1) the expert can establish the due diligence defense only by affirmatively showing that he conducted a *reasonable investigation* that left him with reasonable ground to believe, and the actual belief, that the part he prepared was accurate; but (2) all other persons (the *non-experts*) merely have to prove the negative proposition that they "had *no reasonable ground to believe and did not believe*" that there was any material misstatement or omission. (Thus an ordinary director can entrust to the issuer's accounting firm the preparation of the audited financial statements, as long as he is not on notice of inaccuracies.)

        b. Non-expertised portions: With respect to parts of the registration not prepared by experts, D must show that: (1) he made a *reasonable investigation*; and (2) after that investigation, he was left with reasonable ground to believe, and did in fact believe, that there was no material misstatement or omission. (Inside directors will usually find this harder to show than will outside directors.)

C. Section 12(1): Section *12(1)* imposes liability on anyone who sells a security that *should have been registered but was not*. Liability here is imposed even for an honest and in fact non-negligent mistake. However, a buyer may only sue his immediate seller, not someone further back in the chain of distribution.

D. Section 12(2):   Section *12(2)* imposes liability for untrue statements of material fact and for omission of material fact. Unlike § 11, it is ***not limited to misstatements made in the registration statement***. (For instance, misstatements made ***orally***, or in a writing other than the registration statement, are covered.) Not only the seller but anyone who is a "substantial factor" in making the sale (e.g., a ***broker*** or public relations consultant for the seller) may be sued. A ***negligence*** standard is used.

E. Section 17(a):   Section 17(a) imposes a general ***anti-fraud*** provision. Unlike the three sections discussed above, most courts have held that 17(a) does not support a private right of action by investors (merely a right on the part of the government to prevent or punish violations).

VI. PUBLIC OFFERINGS — STATE REGULATION

A. State "Blue Sky" laws generally: Every state regulates some aspects of securities transactions through regulations collectively known as ***"blue sky"*** laws.

    1. '96 Act changes rules: However, Congress took away a large portion of the states' Blue Sky Powers, in the ***National Securities Improvement Act of 1996.*** State regulation of securities ***issuance*** is now largely ***preempted*** by federal regulation.

EXAM TIPS

TABLE OF CONTENTS
of EXAM TIPS

EXAM TIPS

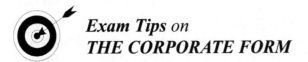

Exam Tips on
THE CORPORATE FORM

Here are the main things to watch for in connection with the corporate form:

Ultra Vires

☛ ***Ultra vires* generally:** If your fact pattern indicates that the corporation is doing something which *violates a statute* or a provision of the corp's *charter*, consider whether the corporate action is unenforceable because of the *ultra vires* doctrine.

   ☞ **Party tries to escape contract:** Be especially alert for the ultra vires issue when the pattern involves a *contract* between the corp. and a third party, and one of the parties is trying to *wriggle out* of the contract on the grounds that the charter doesn't allow the contract. In this situation, discuss the fact that at common law, this might have furnished a defense to whichever party (the corp. or the third party) didn't want to comply, but that under modern statutes ultra vires usually *won't be a defense* in this situation.

   ☞ **Shareholder sues to block:** But where a *shareholder sues to block the transaction*, indicate that ultra vires may still be grounds for an injunction under many modern statutes.

> *Example:* Corp's charter limits debt to $75,000. The board (which includes all but one shareholder) unanimously decides to borrow $100,000. S, the absent shareholder, sues to block the loan. The court might well issue an injunction on grounds of ultra vires. (But if all shareholders agreed to the loan, and it was the bank that was trying to wriggle out of the contract on ultra vires grounds, then a court would probably *decline* to apply ultra vires.)

Pre-incorporation contracts

☛ **Pre-incorporation contracts generally:** When your fact pattern involves a *pre-incorporation contract*, here are the two main issues to watch out for:

   ☞ **Promoter liability:** First, is the *promoter* (the founder/organizer) liable?

☞ **Assurances by promoter:** The most common exam situation is that the other party to the contract *knows* that the corporation hasn't been formed yet, but the promoter *assures him* that it will be. If the corporation is *never formed*, the promoter will generally be found *personally liable*.

Example: A, a promoter, induces X to make a contract with "Z Corp., a corporation to be formed." (A tells X that he, A, will be one of the stockholders of Z Corp. when it's formed). Z Corp. is never formed. X sues A. X will probably win, because A has induced X to believe that the corp. will be formed, so A should bear responsibility if it never is.

☞ **Corporation defaults:** Another frequently-tested situation is that the promoter tells the other party the corp. will be formed, and the corp. *is formed*, but it defaults. Here, too, the promoter will usually be *held liable* (though it's always a question of what the promoter and the other party originally intended).

☞ **Liability of corporation:** Second, is the *corporation* liable?

☞ General rule: Here, remember that the general rule is that the corp. will generally *not* be liable under the pre-incorporation agreement, unless the corp. *expressly or impliedly adopts* the agreement.

Example: If the corp. *receives benefits* under the agreement, this is likely to be found to be an implied adoption of the agreement.

Defective incorporation

☛ **Defective incorporation generally:** Professors often test the situation in which investors *attempt* to form a corp., but *no corp. is actually formed* due to some *procedural defect* (e.g., failure to pay filing fees). Here, the issue becomes, are the investors liable?

☞ **"De facto corporation" doctrine:** Refer to the possibility that the *"de facto corporation"* doctrine will apply, in which case the individual defendants won't be liable. But you should conclude that the doctrine probably *won't apply*, because most states (and the RMBCA) have abolished it. Best odds for the doctrine's applying: where the defendants are purely passive investors, who didn't conduct the business's operations but merely supplied $.

☞ **"Corporation by estoppel" doctrine:** Also, discuss the possibility that the *"corporation by estoppel"* doctrine may apply. This has a better chance of working than the "de facto corp." doctrine: if P (the creditor) *thought the business was a corp.*, and indicated his willingness to *deal with it as a corp.*, the court may estop him from pursuing the individual would-be "shareholders."

Piercing the corporate veil

☛ **Piercing the veil, generally:** Professors also often give you the issue of whether the *"corporate veil"* should be *"pierced."* Look for this issue wherever the corporation ends up *insolvent* and can't perform its obligations — always consider the possibility that the creditor can sue the individual shareholders (even if the facts don't indicate that the creditor is in fact suing the shareholders).

☞ **Inadequate capitalization:** In veil-piercing questions, keep in mind that the most important factor is whether the corp. was *inadequately capitalized* — if it was, P is much more likely to achieve piercing.

☞ **Some other factor:** But also, keep in mind that in addition to inadequate capital, piercing usually requires *some other factor*, of which the most common are:

❑ *misrepresentation* (e.g., "My corp. has all the capital it will need to perform the contract with you"); and

❑ failure to *follow corporate formalities* (e.g., no board of directors is elected, or shareholder loans are taken from the corp. without repayment or without promissory notes).

☞ **Liability of shareholders:** Where the issue is whether individual human (as opposed to corporate) shareholders should be held liable, remember that an *active* shareholder who *controls the company's management and policies* is *more likely* to be held liable than a *passive* investor who hardly participates in corporate decision-making.

Example: Trucker is owned in equal shares by Able, Baker and Charlie. Able works in the business full-time as head of sales and finance, and Baker works there full-time as head of operations. Charlie has a job outside the business, and is uninvolved in Trucker's operations. At a time when Trucker has let its liability policy lapse, a truck belonging to the company kills P, a pedestrian. All other factors being equal, Able's and Baker's daily involvement in the business makes it much more likely that they'll be held personally liable to P than that Charlie will be.

☞ **Parent-subsidiary:** In the case of a *parent-subsidiary relationship*, the subsidiary's veil will probably be pierced (so the parent is held liable) if it can be said that the parent and subsidiary operated as a *"single economic entity."* But the mere fact that the parent *"dominated"* the subsidiary (e.g., by appointing directors, or exercising veto power over major decisions) *won't* be enough.

☛ **Preferring parent's interests:** If the parent consistently uses its influence over the subsidiary to implement policies that *favor the parent's interests* over the subsidiary's interests, the subsidiary's veil is likely to be pierced.

Example: Transport, a trucking company, incorporates a wholly-owned subsidiary, HotTrucks. HotTrucks engages in the high-risk business of transporting hazardous waste (which Transport does not do, because of the risks). HotTrucks has no cash or liquid assets; its sole asset is the right to use trucks owned by Transport. HotTrucks pays all of its net profits to Transport each quarter. Transport, through its control of HotTrucks' board, causes HotTrucks not to buy business liability insurance in order to save money. A truck used by HotTrucks is, due to driver negligence, involved in an accident that kills P. Can P pierce the corporate veil to hold Transport liable?

Yes. That's because, apart from HotTrucks' lack of sufficient assets, HotTrucks has been run in a way that better serves the interests of Transport (pursuit of high-risk business which Transport wouldn't do on its own because of the risks, plus upstreaming of all net profit to Transport) than the interests of HotTrucks.

☞ **LLC:** If the case involves an *LLC* (as opposed to a corporation), consider whether the veil can nonetheless be pierced. But failure to follow *formalities* probably *won't* be a reason for piercing (since LLCs have virtually no formalities that they're required to follow.) On the other hand, *inadequate capitalization* may well be a reason for piercing the LLC's veil.

Exam Tips *on*
THE CORPORATE STRUCTURE

Here are the main things to watch for in connection with the corporate structure:

Removal of directors

☛ **Removal generally:** Whenever your fact pattern describes an attempt to *remove a director*, here's what you should keep in mind:

    ☞ **Removal by shareholders for cause:** The *shareholders*, by majority vote, can always remove a director for *cause* (e.g., fraud, gross incompetence, or a breach of the duty of loyalty).

    ☞ **Removal by shareholders w/o cause:** Also, most modern statutes (including the MBCA) let a *majority of the shareholders* remove a director *even without cause*, unless the corp's charter provides differently.

☞ **No removal by directors:** *Directors*, even by majority vote, *cannot* remove a fellow director even for cause, unless the charter or bylaws specifically say they can.

☞ **Removal by court:** The *court* may (under most modern statutes) remove a director for *cause* (e.g., fraudulent or dishonest conduct, or gross abuse of power).

Removal of officers

☛ **Removal of officer, generally:** If your fact pattern involves the *removal of an officer* (e.g., the president), here's what you should remember:

☞ **Removal by board:** The *board* has the power to remove an officer, *with or without cause*. That's true even if the officer has an employment contract — the board has power to remove the officer anyway (and the officer's only recourse is a suit for damages, not a suit to enjoin the dismissal or to compel reinstatement).

☞ **Removal by shareholders:** *Shareholders*, even by majority vote, do *not* have the power to remove an officer.

Election of directors

☛ **Director elections, generally:** *Election of directors* is often tested.

☞ **Vote to fill vacancy:** The most common issue about election of directors involves *filling board vacancies*. Here, the usual rule (and the RMBCA approach) is that the vacancy can be filled *either by shareholder vote* or *board vote*.

☞ **Effect of cumulative voting:** Don't overlook the possibility that a corp. may have *cumulative voting*. In cumulative voting, a shareholder may *aggregate his votes* in favor of fewer candidates than there are slots available.

> *Example:* A, B and C each own 100 of G Corp's 300 shares outstanding, and are its 3 directors under annual terms. C dies, and D inherits her shares. The bylaws say that a 90% majority is required for election of new directors. You have to say whether, at the next holders' meeting, D can elect herself as a director, against the wishes of A and B. If G Corp. has cumulative voting, D can do so — she can cast all 300 of her votes in favor of herself, and thus come up with a "100% vote" (i.e., 1 vote for each share outstanding) for herself, even if A and B don't vote for her.

Special shareholders' meeting

☞ **When s/h's can compel meeting:** You'll sometimes be asked about when share-holders can *compel the calling of a special shareholders' meeting*. In general, the board is *not obligated* to call such a meeting (even if a majority of holders requests it) unless the particular action sought to be accomplished must be approved by shareholders.

> *Example:* P, majority holder of X Corp., wants to remove Pres., the corp's president. P calls for a special meeting of shareholders to consider his motion to fire Pres. The board refuses. P can't compel the board to hold the special meeting, because shareholders don't have the power to fire officers, and therefore don't have the right to call a special meeting to consider the firing of officers.

Corporate structure

☞ **Charter and bylaw terms:** Issues involving the *corporate structure* are often hidden in fact patterns that tell you about the provisions of the corp's *charter* and *bylaws*. *Be certain to read these charter and bylaws terms carefully*, because they're likely to be implicated in events that you're told about later in the question.

☞ **Alteration of charter:** If the facts indicate that the board has taken an action which *conflicts* with the corp's *charter*, remember that the charter can *only be altered by the shareholders*, not the board — so the board's action is probably illegal.

> *Example:* X Corp's charter says that the board consists of 5 members, who will be elected annually. The board unilaterally votes to expand its size to 9, and to stagger terms. This action will be illegal, because only a majority of shareholders, not a board majority, may vary the charter.

Notice, quorum and meeting requirements

☞ **Notice, quorum and meeting requirements, generally:** Whenever you have to decide the validity of a particular board action, check for failure to comply with *notice*, *quorum* and *meeting* requirements. In particular:

☞ **Notice to board:** A special meeting of the board must normally be preceded by *notice* to the board members. The notice must specify the subject(s) (and no unlisted subject may be discussed).

☞ **Waiver:** However, the notice requirement will be deemed *waived* as to any director who *attends the meeting* and does not object at the start of the meeting to the lack of notice.

☞ **Quorum requirement:** The board may act only if a *quorum* is present.

☞ **Fixed-size board:** If the board has a *fixed size*, a quorum is a majority of *that size* (even if there are now vacancies).

☞ **Variable-size board:** If the board has a *variable size*, a quorum is a majority of the directors *in office* at the start of the meeting.

☞ **Supermajority requirements:** Most states let a corporation's charter or bylaws establish a *supermajority* requirement for a quorum.

Example: Corp's bylaws say that a quorum will consist of 5 out of its 7 directors. This provision will be given effect, so a meeting at which only 4 of 7 are present will be of no effect.

☞ **Presence at meeting required:** Normally, the board may take action *only at a meeting*. Directors must be *present to vote* (i.e., they *may not vote by proxy*).

Example: Paul, one of Corp's directors, can't come to the board meeting, so he gives his proxy to Steve, and has Steve vote for him at the meeting. Paul won't be deemed present, and his vote won't count.

☞ **Telephone meeting:** Look out for the possibility of a *telephone meeting*: in most states (and under the RMBCA), if the director is present for a conference call in which a quorum participates, the director is deemed to be in attendance at the meeting, and his vote counts.

☞ **Majority of those present:** The board may take action only upon a vote of a *majority* of the directors *present at the meeting*. (So the action doesn't have to be supported by a majority of directors in *office*, only a majority of those *present*, assuming that a quorum is present.)

☞ **Later ratification:** If the facts indicate that the meeting/quorum/majority-vote requirements *weren't met*, consider the possibility that the board action is valid anyway, because the directors subsequently *ratified* it by affirming it or failing to disavow it.

Example: No quorum is present when the board purports to approve a contract with a third party. A year later, at a regular meeting, attended by a quorum, a majority of those present vote to approve the transaction. This is a ratification, so the contract is binding as if it had been properly approved the first time. (Same result if the board *tacitly* ratifies, as by *accepting benefits* under the contract.)

Authority to bind corporation

☞ **Authority, generally:** Whenever the fact pattern states that an officer acted on behalf of the corp., consider whether the officer had ***authority*** to bind the corp. under any of these 4 doctrines:

>   **[1]** *express actual authority*;
>
>   **[2]** *implied actual authority*;
>
>   **[3]** *apparent authority*; and
>
>   **[4]** *ratification*.

☞ **Express authority:** Look for indications as to whether the officer was *expressly* authorized to make the contract. An explicit grant of authority usually comes from either the corp's bylaws, or from a resolution adopted by the board.

> ☞ **Delegation:** Sometimes the board may expressly ***delegate*** to an officer the power to decide whether to take a particular action. If the board has the authority to take that action, it also has the right to delegate to the officer the power to decide whether to take that action, and to then take it.
>
> *Example:* Corp. is in the business of selling office furniture at retail. Corp's board (acting with a quorum) passes a resolution empowering Prexy, Corp's president, to study possible opportunities and to decide whether to change Corp's principal business. Prexy makes such a study, and decides (without further consultation with the board) to change Corp's business from furniture to computer sales. Prexy can properly make the change — since the Board had the authority (without a shareholder vote) to change the corporation's business, it had the authority to delegate to Prexy the power to change the business.
>
> > ☞ **Need for shareholder approval:** But keep in mind the converse as well — if the board *doesn't* have the power to take an action by itself, it *can't* delegate to an officer the power to take that action. This is true, for instance, of a ***sale of substantially all the corporation's assets***, or any other decision that would require ***shareholder approval***.
> >
> > *Example:* Same facts as above example. Corp also authorizes Prexy to sell all of Corp's assets (all of which relate to the furniture business) if he decides that Corp's future would be brighter in some other line of business. Prexy decides to hold an auction of all of the assets. The auction is without proper authority — since shareholder approval is required virtually everywhere for a sale of substantially all of a corporation's assets outside the ordinary course of business (see, e.g., MBCA §§ 12.01 and 12.02), the Board could neither approve such a

sale by itself nor delegate to anyone else the power to do so.

☞ **Implied actual authority:** If the officer had a *title* within the corp. that would typically include the power to make the deal in question, then the officer had *"implied actual authority"* (i.e., authority that's "inherent in the office.")

> *Example:* Pete, who is actually the Pres. of Corp., signs a deal to buy office furniture "Corp, by Pete, its President." Pete has implied actual authority, because the president of a corporation would typically have authority to make a deal for furniture.

☞ **Extraordinary action without board approval:** Look for situations in which *extraordinary* action is taken by the corp.'s president, without board approval. Such action is probably *invalid*, since it doesn't fall within any form of authority.

> *Example:* X Corp. is a 10-employee business with $1 million in annual revenues. Pres., the president of X Corp., signs an agreement to pay a $100,000-per-year lifetime pension to a retiring vice-president. The board isn't told of the agreement, and thus doesn't authorize it. The contract is probably not enforceable against X Corp., because it was an extraordinary contract, that did not fall within any theory of authority. (For instance, the authority isn't "implied actual," because such a deal is too large and unusual to come within the usual powers of the president of a corp. this size.)

Exam Tips on
SHAREHOLDERS' INFORMATIONAL RIGHTS & THE PROXY SYSTEM

There are three basic fact patterns that are most likely to be tested in connection with this chapter:

❏ A s/h's request to *inspect corporate records* has been denied;

❏ Management has refused to *include a s/h's proposal* in its proxy materials; and

❏ A s/h is attempting to *revoke a proxy.*

S/h's right to inspect records

☛ **Right of inspection:** In fact patterns where a s/h has asked to *inspect corp. records*, the most testable issue is whether the s/h has stated a proper purpose for the inspection.

☞ **"Reasonable relation" standard:** Remember that a purpose is proper (so that the corp. must allow the inspection) so long as it is *reasonably related to the requester's interest as a stockholder*, and not likely to *damage* the corp.

> ☞ **Return on investment:** Anything that relates to evaluating the investor's *return on his investment* is likely to be found proper.
>
> *Example:* P, a s/h in D Corp., wants to inspect D's records to see how much profit D is making, and how much could be distributed as dividends. This is a proper purpose.
>
> ☞ **Proxy solicitation:** If the s/h wants a lists of other s/h's so he can *solicit proxies* to unseat incumbent management, this is generally a *proper* purpose.
>
> ☞ **Pursuit of personal goals:** On the other hand, a purpose is improper where the s/h requests the info in order to pursue *personal goals* unrelated to ownership of stock in the corp.
>
> *Example:* P is a s/h of D Corp., but also is the controlling s/h of a competitor of D, X Corp. P wants to review D's detailed product-by-product revenues and costs. If the court believes that P will use this info. to have X Corp. compete more effectively with D, the court will find the purpose improper.

Shareholder proposals

☞ **Shareholder proposals, generally:** Whenever a fact pattern involves a *shareholder proposal*, consider whether any of the exclusions set forth in SEC Rule 14a-8(i) apply (in which case management may refuse to include the proposal in its proxy materials).

> ☞ **State-law limits:** Remember that a proposal doesn't have to be included if it concerns a matter that is *"not a proper subject for action by security holders."* Thus make sure that that the s/h isn't proposing to *order management to do something*, if holders don't have the right to make such an order under state law. (Since s/h's don't normally have the right to order the company to do anything, a lot of proposals are excludible under this ground.)
>
> > *Example:* X Corp. is a nuclear-based utility. An anti-nuke s/h group asks for inclusion of a proposal "ordering the corporation to cease building or operating new nuclear power plants." Because under the law of virtually all states s/h's can't tell the corp. how to conduct its operations, this proposal advocates a step that is "not a proper subject for action by shareholders," and is thus non-includible.

☞ **Recommendation:** But if the proposal is couched as a *recommendation* to management or the board, rather than an order, it's *not* excludible on this ground.

> *Example:* In the above example, if the s/h proposal seeks s/h approval of a *recommendation* to the board that it commission no new nuclear plants, it's probably includible.

☞ **Ordinary business operations:** If the proposal relates solely to the corporation's *"ordinary business operations,"* it's *excludible* as too routine. (But if the proposal involves a *controversial* problem or issue, it won't fall within the "ordinary business operations" exclusion even if it also relates to the company's routine business operations.)

☞ **Election of directors:** If the proposal relates to the *election of directors*, it's *excludible* (so that the s/h group that wants to electioneer has to pay for its own proxy materials).

> *Example:* A s/h group opposes management's slate of directors for the upcoming election. The group's statement of reasons for its opposition is excludible, because it relates to the election of directors.

☞ **General causes:** If the proposal relates to *general economic, political, racial, social* or other similar causes, it will nonetheless be *includible* if it has some *tangible link* to the corp's affairs.

> *Example:* An anti-nuke group tenders a "no new nuclear power plants" recommendation to a power company that currently uses nuke plants. The proposal will be *includible* even though it relates to a general social/political cause, because it relates to the company's business. But if a general proposal opposing "all uses of nuclear energy" is tendered to a company that neither uses nor proposes to use nuclear energy in any way, it's probably *excludible* as "not significantly related to the company's business."

Proxies, including revocation

☛ **Revocation of proxies:** If the fact pattern relates to a *proxy*, you're most likely to be tested on whether the s/h may *revoke* the proxy.

☞ **"Coupled with an interest" rule:** Here, remember that the rule is that even if the proxy purports to be irrevocable, it's *revocable unless* it's *"coupled with an interest."*

> ☛ **Illustrations:** Only if the recipient is a person who has a legal interest in the stock, or in the corporation, does the proxy meet the "coupled with an interest" requirement. So if the recipient has a *contract to buy the stock*, or has lent money with the stock as

pledge, the proxy can be irrevocable. But an ordinary proxy given, say, to management, is *revocable even if it says it's irrevocable*.

Exam Tips *on*
CLOSE CORPORATIONS

S/h voting agreements

Validity of agreements: The most frequently-tested issue regarding close corporations is the *validity of s/h voting agreements.*

☛ **Limitations on board's discretion:** Be on the lookout for agreements that *limit the discretion of the board of directors*. Although s/h agreements are generally *valid*, an agreement which substantially restricts the authority of the board will be *struck down* if it either: (i) violates a statutory provision; (ii) *injures a minority s/h*; or (iii) injures the corp's creditors or the public.

    ☞ **Particular person in key job:** You're most likely to see a s/h agreement in which a majority of the holders agree to *put and keep a particular person* (perhaps one of the majority) into a *key job*, and a minority-holder objects. Here, "injury to the minority-holder plaintiff" should be the focus of your answer.

> *Example:* A, B and C together control 75% of the stock of D Corp, and they are its sole directors. They sign a s/h agreement that says that unless all vote to cancel the agreement, all will cast their board votes so as to put and keep A in the President's position. P, a 10% holder, does not have a board seat, and now sues A, B and C (and the corp.) to have the voting agreement stuck down. If P can show that A is not doing an appropriate job running the business (or is otherwise injuring P by the way he's running it), the court may strike down the agreement. But if P doesn't show this, the court will probably uphold the agreement even though it substantially restricts the directors' freedom of action.

    ☞ **Agreements to elect board members:** Agreements under which each of the signers agrees to vote so as to *elect all of the signers to the board* are generally *valid*.

        ☞ **Binding of later stockholders:** A closer question is whether a person who then *buys (or gets a gift of) stock from one of the original signers* is bound by, or will get the benefit of, such an "all s/hs agree to elect all s/hs to the board" agreement. The answer is probably "yes," at least where the shares are conspicuously *marked* with the fact that there is a voting agreement that governs.

Example: A, B and C are the only s/hs in D Corp. All agree that all will vote so as to put all 3 on the board. C (who has too few shares to be able to vote herself to the board if no one else votes for her) dies, and bequeaths her shares to E. A and B refuse to vote E to the board. E sues to enforce the agreement. You should say that there's a good chance that a court will hold that the original signers intended that both the benefit and burden would "run" with the stock, in which case the court will require A and B to vote E onto the board (but E must vote for them as well). You should also point out that this result is more likely if the shares were marked with notice of the agreement than if they're not.

☞ **Share-transfer restrictions:** Look for s/h agreements which contain *share transfer restrictions.*

☛ **Lack of knowledge:** Remember that a person who purchases shares *without actual knowledge* of pre-existing restrictions will *not* be bound unless the restrictions were *conspicuously noted* on the share certificates.

☛ **Right of first refusal:** If the fact pattern involves a right of *first refusal* (by the corporation or by the other shareholders), the restriction normally applies only if the shares are *sold*, not if they are to be transferred by a *gift* or *bequest*.

☛ **"Manifestly unreasonable" standard for consent:** Remember that if the restriction requires *consent* of the corporation or of other shareholders, it will be upheld if (and only if) it's not an *unreasonable restraint* on alienation. (The MBCA makes the consent requirement enforceable if *"not manifestly unreasonable,"* making such restrictions usually enforceable. § 6.27(d)(3).)

Example: Corp's 10 shareholders sign an agreement in which all agree that no one may sell any shares without the *unanimous* consent of all the other holders (and with no requirement that this consent not be unreasonably withheld). Even under the MBCA's tough-to-violate "manifestly unreasonable" standard, a court might hold that this requirement of unanimous consent is a "manifestly unreasonable" restraint, at least where one holder refuses to consent just to be obstinate, or in order to extort a "consent fee" from the one who wants to sell.

Dissolution of corporation

☛ **Compulsory dissolution:** Fact patterns on close corps sometimes pose the issue of whether one party can compel *dissolution* of the corp.

    ☞ **When allowed:** Keep in mind that most statutes (e.g., the RMBCA) allow the court to order dissolution at the request of one s/h, if certain conditions occur. Most states allow dissolution if:

        ❏ The *s/h's* or the *directors* are *deadlocked* in a way that prevents the corp. from operating; or

        ❏ The directors (or controlling s/h's) are *oppressing* or *defrauding* a minority holder; or

        ❏ The corp's *assets* are being *wasted*.

    ☞ **Dissolution of LLC:** If the fact pattern involves an *LLC* rather than a corporation, remember that the jurisdiction probably allows judicial dissolution on factors similar to those for corporations. If it's a Delaware LLC, cite to the Del. LLC Act, allowing the court to decree dissolution of the LLC "whenever it is not reasonably practicable to carry on the business in conformity with the [LLC agreement.]"

Exam Tips on
THE DUTY OF CARE AND THE
BUSINESS JUDGMENT RULE

The duty of care — and its sibling, the business judgment rule — are two of the most frequently-tested subjects. Be alert to these issues whenever a fact pattern involves a decision by an officer or the board which could be characterized as *unwise*.

The Business Judgment Rule

☛ **Duty of care and the Business Judgment rule:** Never consider "duty of care" in the abstract — always discuss it in *conjunction* with the *business judgment rule*. In other words, phrase the initial issue as "did the directors exercise due care?" but then say something like, "If the conditions for the business judgment rule are met, the court will find that the board satisfied its duty of care even though the transaction turned out badly or seems to the court to have been substantively unwise."

    ☞ **Requirements for:** Remember the *three things* a director must do to *qualify* for the business judgment rule:

        ❏ she must *not* be *"interested"* (i.e., have a *financial stake* apart from the corp's own interest) in the subject matter of the action;

- ❏ she must be *reasonably informed* about the decision she's making; and

- ❏ she must *rationally believe* that the judgment she's making is in the *best interests* of the corp.

☞ **Absent directors:** Remember that *absent directors* are held to the same standard as directors who attended the meeting during which the board approved of a particular action. Thus if the board as a whole violated the duty of due care (i.e., didn't qualify for the business judgment rule), the absent directors will also be liable.

☞ **Investigation:** Most frequently-tested aspect of the bus. judg. rule: the directors don't make an *adequate investigation* before they *commit large sums of money* to a project.

> *Example:* Pres., the head of Corp., wants to sell Corp. to Acquirer. Pres. is worried that the present demand for Corp.'s products will be transitory, and believes that the most favorable sale would be one that is accomplished rapidly. Therefore, Pres. urges the Corp. board to approve the sale without debate, and does not fully brief the board on the reasons why Acquirer's offer is the best one that can be gotten. Nor does Pres. or the board have an outsider review the price or other sale terms. The board probably does not qualify for the bus. judg. rule, because it was not adequately informed. If so, the board will be liable for failure to satisfy its duty of care, if its carelessness caused a disadvantageous sale to be made.

> ☞ **Lack of reading:** A variant is that a report describing the proposed transaction is prepared, but some directors *don't read it* — these directors don't get the protection of the bus. judg. rule, because they haven't taken the available steps to make themselves "reasonably informed."

> ☞ **Reliance on others' opinions:** Questions sometimes involve board *reliance* on the *opinions of others*. Here, the rule is that the board is entitled to rely on others where it is *reasonable* to do so. For instance, the board can typically rely on the opinion of the corp's CPAs, if the latter say that a proposed acquisition is a profitable business that is being sold for a standard multiple of earnings.

> ☞

☞ **Good faith:** Also, check whether the directors have acted in *good faith.* The requirement of good faith has two main components:

☞ First, the directors must have acted in a ***non-self-interested manner***. If they are acting so as to further their own business interests, at the expense of, say, a minority holder, the directors will not qualify for the bus. judg. rule.

> *Example:* The board refuses to pay out any of $5 million of accumulated earnings as dividends. P, a minority holder, sues to overturn this refusal, and the majority directors defend on the grounds that their dividend policies are protected by the bus. judg. rule. If P can show that the directors' purpose was to "freeze out" P — by depriving him of income so that he'd sell his shares back to the majority at a low price — the directors won't receive the protection of the bus. judg. rule.

☞ Second, the directors ***must not have been aware that they were not discharging their fiduciary obligations.*** (Cite to *Stone v. Ritter* on this point.) At least in Delaware, this means that the directors must have put in some sort of reporting or information system, and must have believed that they were doing some sort of monitoring of data from that system.

☞ **"Rational belief" standard:** A fact pattern will ***rarely fail*** to meet the ***"rational belief"*** requirement for the bus. judg. rule. Remember that so long as the directors' belief that the action was in the corp's interest is not ***wholly irrational***, this prong will be deemed satisfied. And this is true even if the action results in ***financial loss*** to the corp.

> *Example:* To prevent a minority s/h from acquiring control, Corp. buys shares from 3 other s/h's at the asking price of $80/share, a price in excess of both book value and market value. As long as the decision was "plausible," the fact that the judge disagrees about the decision's wisdom — or the fact that later events showed that the shares were not worth the price paid — won't prevent the bus. judg. rule from applying.

Exam Tips on
THE DUTY OF LOYALTY

The duty of loyalty is the single most frequently-tested subject on exams. Duty of loyalty issues often appear in the same fact patterns as duty of care issues. Watch particularly for ***self-dealing transactions*** (transactions in which a director has a ***financial*** *interest*) and situations in which a director or senior exec. takes personal advantage of an *opportunity* which might *belong to the corporation.*

Self-dealing transactions

☛ **The problem generally:** *Self-dealing transactions* are usually easy to spot. Look for situations in which the corp. has *conducted business* with a director or senior exec. ("Key Player"), or with a member of a Key Player's family.

Once you spot a self-dealing transaction, remember that you have to do a *multi-step analysis* to determine whether it's a breach of the duty of loyalty:

> *Step 1:* Did the Key Player *disclose* the conflict and the nature of the transaction *in advance* to either senior management or the entire board (whichever would normally be expected to make the decision for the corp. on whether to do the transaction)? If "yes," go to Step 2. If "no," go to Step 3.

> *Step 2:* [For advance disclosure situations]: Did a majority of the *"disinterested directors"* (or a *"disinterested superior"* if the Key Player is not a director) *approve* the transaction? If "yes," there was *no breach* of the duty of loyalty. If "no," go to Step 3.

> *Step 3:* [For situations where there was no advance-disclosure-plus-approval]: Did the Key Player *disclose* the conflict and nature of the transaction *after* it was entered into (either before suit or within a reasonable time after suit was filed), to either senior management or the board (as appropriate — see Step 1)? If "yes," go to Step 4. If "no," go to Step 5.

> *Step 4:* [For after-the-fact disclosure situations]: Did a majority of the *"disinterested directors"* (or a "disinterested superior" if the Key Player is not a director) *ratify* the transaction? If "yes," there was no breach of the duty of loyalty. If "no," go to Step 5.

> *Step 5:* [For situations where the board never gave proper approval or ratification]: Did a majority of *disinterested shareholders*, following disclosure of the conflict and the transaction, either *approve it* in advance or *ratify it* afterwards? If "yes," go to Step 6. If "no," go to Step 7.

> *Step 6:* [For situations where the disinterested s/h's approved]: Was the transaction a *"waste"* of corporate assets, viewed as of the time of s/h approval or ratification? If "no," there was *no breach* of duty of loyalty. If "yes," it *is a breach* of the duty of loyalty.

> *Step 7:* [For sits. where there is neither board nor s/h approval or ratif.]: Was the transaction *"fair"* to the corp. when entered into? If "yes," there is no breach of duty of loyalty. If "no," there is a *breach* of loyalty.

Example: Pres, the president of A Corp., negotiates an agreement for A Corp. to buy all of Y Corp's outstanding shares. Only one of A's 6 other directors is told by Pres. that Pres's immediate family holds all of Y Corp's shares. The board approves the transaction. Y Corp. proves to have little value. A minority s/h brings a derivative action against Pres. for damages from the purchase. You should say that since there was never disclosure of the conflict to all the independent directors [Steps 1 and 3 above], and since there was no shareholder approval [Step 5], the court will strike down the transaction unless it believes that the transaction was "fair" to the corporation [Step 7].

Other examples of self-dealing: (1) Pres. negotiates to have all of Corp's properties cleaned by X Co., and doesn't disclose that he has a large ownership interest in X Co. (2) B, a director of Corp., conveys equipment worth $50K to Corp. in return for $100K of stock, without disclosing that the equipment is only worth $50K (and while knowing that most directors think it's worth $100K).

☞ **Immunization by pre-approval:** Always remember that *pre-approval* (after disclosure) by a majority of the *disinterested directors* or a majority of *disinterested shareholders* will *immunize* the transaction, and a court will not even consider whether the transaction is "fair." (See Steps 2 and 5.)

☞ **Ratification after the fact:** Also, post-transaction *disinterested-shareholder ratification* of the transaction, made after disclosure and before suit, will always *immunize* the transaction (Step 5), and post-transaction disinterested-*director* ratification will usually immunize it (Steps 3-4).

☞ **Fairness is dispositive:** Remember that if the facts suggest to you that the transaction was *"fair"* (i.e., not disadvantageous) to the corp., *viewed as of the time it was made*, it won't be set aside or serve as the basis for damages, even if there was no disclosure, no independent-director approval and no shareholder approval. That is, fairness puts a *complete end* to the inquiry.

Corporate opportunity doctrine

☛ **Corporate opportunity, generally:** Whenever a fact pattern indicates that a Key Player has taken personal advantage of an opportunity, consider whether the doctrine of *corporate opportunity* applies. Remember that this doctrine prohibits a Key Player from taking advantage of an opportunity which belongs to the corp., unless he first *discloses* the offer to the other directors or to senior management.

☞ **Factors:** Here are some factors which strengthen the inference that an opportunity is a corporate one:

- ❏ The Key Player *learned* of the opportunity while acting in his role as the *corp's agent* rather than as an individual;

- ❏ The opportunity is *closely related* to the corp's *existing or prospective activities*;

- ❏ The opportunity is *essential* to the corp's *well-being*; or

- ❏ The corp. had (and the Key Player knew that the corp. had) a *reasonable expectation* that the opportunity would be regarded as a corporate one.

> *Example:* At a board meeting of A Corp., B, a director of the corp., learns that the corp. is planning on expanding, and that it's examining 3 parcels adjacent to one of its existing plants. B pays $3,000 for an option to buy one of those parcels for $120,000, and does not tell his fellow directors before doing this. B has probably usurped a corp. opportunity, since he learned of the parcel's availability from his work for the corp., the parcel is closely related to the corp's prospective activities (expansion), and the corp. reasonably expected that any parcels considered during the board meeting would be viewed as corporate opportunities. Therefore, B can probably be required to turn over the option to the corp.

☞ **Full-time employee vs. director:** It generally takes less of a conflict for the corp. opportunity doctr. to apply when the Key Player is a *full-time employee* than where she is an *outside director*.

☞ **Where corp. can't use opportunity:** If the corp. opport. doctr. otherwise seems to apply, check whether the fact pattern contains signs that the corp. *wouldn't have been able to take advantage* of the opportunity even had it known of the opportunity. Say that courts are *split* about whether corporate inability (e.g., *lack of financial resources*) can be a defense.

Executive compensation

☛ **Executive compensation as "waste":** Be alert for duty-of-loyalty issues where the fact pattern involves *executive compensation*. Make sure that the corp. is receiving some benefit as a result of the compensation scheme — if it's not, it's likely to be invalid as a *"waste"* of corporate assets.

☞ **Advance approval:** If a compensation arrangement is *approved in advance* by *disinterested directors or disinterested s/h's*, this pretty much *immunizes* it from s/h attack, even if a court might otherwise believe the compensation is *"excessive."* (Courts are split as to whether this is true even where the person receiving the compensation is a *senior executive* who has *participated in the*

process by which the compensation was set.)

☞ **Stock options:** *Stock options* are ordinarily acceptable, provided they do not result in clearly excessive compensation.

☞ **Retirement benefits:** *Retirement benefits* may pose a problem, especially if they are awarded at the *moment of retirement,* without being part of a general or pre-existing plan. Here, a s/h could claim that this is waste (or without consideration), because the corp. isn't getting anything in return.

> *Example:* At the moment when Bill, a senior manager at A Corp., says he's retiring, Prexy [pres. of A Corp.] makes a written promise to pay Bill a $4,000/mo. pension for life. A Corp. does not have any general pension plan. A s/h might successfully attack this promise as being waste and without consideration, in which case the court may order the promise not to be enforced.

Interlocking directors

☛ **Interlocking directors, generally:** Sometimes you'll have a problem of *interlocking directors* (X is a director of two corps who do business with each other). Here, say that the duty-of-loyalty problems are typically *not as severe* as where a director deals for himself: unless the director's *own financial interest is substantially at stake*, the fact that he sits on both boards won't create a conflict when the two corps do a transaction together (as long as there's disclosure of the fact that the director sits on both boards).

> *Example:* X is a director of both A Corp. and B Corp., and each corp. knows this. At a B Corp. meeting, X votes to have B Corp. buy certain property from A Corp. Unless X's financial stake in A Corp. (and the size of the transaction) are enough to give X a significant financial incentive to have B Corp buy the property, X's voting for the transaction is *not* a breach of his duty of loyalty to B.

Obligations of controlling s/hs

☛ **Freeze-outs:** Keep in mind that a *controlling s/h* may (it's not clear) have an obligation to behave in a *fiduciary manner* towards minority holders. This principle is most likely to be applied if the majority tries to *"freeze out"* the minority. Be especially alert to freeze-out and other mistreatment-of-minority problems if the corp. is a *closely-held* one.

> *Example:* A, B, C, and D each own 25% of Corp. Corp. has always paid generous dividends to each s/h, since Corp's own operations don't need much capital. A, B, and C learn that D is desperately in need of cash, and is counting on continuation of the dividend stream. The 3 vote to suspend dividends for the sole reason of pressuring D, so that they can induce him to

sell his stock back to Corp. cheaply. This is probably a violation of the duty of loyalty, since A, B and C have served their own interests rather than the interests of all holders.

☞ **Actual loss required:** Even if you conclude that there's been a breach of the duty of loyalty, be sure to check that the corp. has suffered an *actual loss* — if there's no actual loss, then there can't be any recovery.

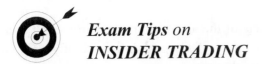

Exam Tips on
INSIDER TRADING

Be alert to insider trading whenever a fact pattern involves the purchase or sale of stock based on *information which was not available to the general public*.

Insider trading generally

☞ **Consequences of insider-trading:** First, check for the core insider-trading scenario: a corporate insider has learned something non-public that will affect the price of the stock, and he then *either buys or sells before the info becomes public.* The insider has violated *SEC Rule 10b-5.* In that even, the insider faces two consequences:

❏ First, he can be sued civilly by the *SEC.*

❏ Second, *any private person* who has traded in the stock at a less favorable price during the time the insider was trading has an *"implied private right of action"* under federal law, and can therefore recover civil damages from the insider.

Example: D is a director of J Corp, a public company. He learns that J has developed a major new invention which it's about to patent, that will make the corp. more valuable. At a time when the public doesn't know about the invention, D buys J Corp. stock on the stock exchange, at $25/share. When J announces the deal, the stock goes to $50/share, and D sells. Both the SEC, and anyone who sold stock during the approximate time when D was buying, can bring a civil action against D. (Also, D has committed a crime.)

☞ **Purchase or sale:** Check to make sure that the private plaintiff *bought or sold* while the insider was trading the inside info. If not, P can't recover.

Example: Prexy says that Corp.'s earnings will be down next quarter. Prexy knows that in fact the earnings will be sharply up, and Prexy is in fact buying secretly for his own account. Joe shows that he would have bought had Prexy remained silent, but he declined to buy because of Prexy's false statement. Joe can't recover against Prexy under 10b-5, because only those who sell or buy while the insider is trading can recover.

☞ **No recovery by corporation:** Remember that this "buy or sell" requirement means that the ***corporation itself cannot recover*** for insider trading under 10b-5, unless it was itself a purchaser or seller of shares at the same time as the insider trading was going on.

Example: On the facts of the above example, Corp. can't recover under 10b-5 against Prexy, if Corp. didn't issue any of its own shares while Prexy was buying.

"Material" inside information

☛ **Materiality requirement:** Remember that the inside info must be *"material."*

☞ **Merger negotiations:** You're most likely to have a materiality issue when the inside info is that ***merger negotiations have begun,*** but are very ***preliminary.*** If all that's happened is that another company has approached, say, the target's CEO but the CEO has told them he's probably not interested, that may not yet be "material" inside info. (But once the CEO has decided to try to make a deal, and certainly once the CEO has gotten the board of directors involved in whether to sell, the info *is* now material.)

"Non-public" information

☛ **Non-public requirement:** Also, remember that the info must be truly *"non-public."* It's not enough that the other party to the transaction doesn't know of it — if a substantial number of members of the public do know of it, there can't be 10b-5 liability.

Example: Corp., a privately-held company, has just announced its new quarterly earnings, which are good. Prexy, Corp's president, buys stock from Pete in a face-to-face transaction. Pete hasn't heard the earnings report yet, but Corp. has already sent a press release to several local newspapers containing the info. The info isn't "non-public," so Prexy hasn't violated 10b-5.

Private sales of non-publicly-traded stock

☛ **Private sales:** Keep in mind that 10b-5 also applies to *private sales* of *non-publicly-traded stock* based on insider info.

☞ **Interstate commerce hook required:** But a *facility of interstate commerce* (phone, mail or a national securities exchange) must be used for any 10b-5 violation. This jurisdictional requirement is sometimes missing in private-sale fact patterns.

> *Example:* Prexy buys stock directly from Dupe in a face-to-face transaction. Even if Prexy had insider info, there's no 10b-5 violation.

Tipper/tippee liability

☞ **Tipper/tippee liability generally:** A large portion of 10b-5 questions turn on whether and when there's *tipper liability* and *tippee liability*.

   ☞ **Intent to make a pecuniary gift:** The tipp*er* can be liable, *even if he doesn't personally benefit,* if he *intends to make a pecuniary gift to the tippee.*

> *Example:* Prexy, head of Oilco, tells Fred, his friend, "We just struck a large well, so you might want to buy some stock quickly." Fred buys lots of stock, which rises after Oilco releases the news. Prexy is liable even though he did not buy or sell, and didn't get — or desire — any personal financial gain from tipping Fred; it's enough that he desired to confer a financial benefit on Fred.

   ☞ **Tipper must be "insider":** Most importantly of all, the tipper is generally *not liable unless he is an "insider" of the issuer.* Normally, an insider is one who *works for, or is a director of,* the issuer (the company whose shares are bought or sold).

      ☞ **Constructive insider:** But *non-employees* can be *constructive insiders.* Thus *lawyers*, investment bankers, accountants, etc., can be insiders if they've been given the info by issuer, to enable them to perform tasks on the issuer's behalf.

      ☞ **One who stumbles upon info:** Someone who *stumbles upon* the inside info *without having a fiduciary duty regarding that info* is *not* an insider, and can't be liable as a tipper (or as a tippee).

> *Example:* While sitting on a commuter train, D overhears Prexy, who he knows to be head of Oilco, tell Friend, "We just brought in a huge gusher today." If D tells E to buy Oilco stock, and E does so, neither D nor E is liable under 10b-5, because D didn't have any fiduciary duty regarding the info and thus isn't an "insider."

      ☞ **Bidder's own info:** When the inside info is news of an impending takeover, a person who works for or controls the *bidder* is *not an "insider" of the target.*

> *Example:* Prexy, head of Bigco, is planning to have Bigco make a tender offer for Smallco. If Prexy personally buys shares in Smallco before announcing the tender offer, there's no 10b-5 vio-

lation, because Prexy is not an insider of Smallco, the issuer. Same result if Prexy tips Friend and Friend buys. But make sure Prexy is not a "misappropriator," as explained in the next paragraph.

☞ **Misappropriation theory:** But remember that under the *"misappropriation"* theory, one who is an *"outsider"* (vis a vis the issuer) can still be a tipper, if he steals the information and trades on it or passes it on.

Example: Veep is a Vice President at Bigco, which is planning to make a tender offer for Smallco. Veep knows or should know that this information is secret and proprietary to Bigco. If Veep buys Smallco shares, he's liable under 10b-5 as a "misappropriator." If Veep passes on the info to his friend Leonard, who buys, Veep and Leonard are probably both liable, as tipper and tippee respectively.

☞ **Tippee's liability is derivative:** The tipp*ee*'s liability is *derivative from the liability of the tipper* — if the conditions for tipper liability aren't satisfied, the tippee can't be liable no matter what the state of his knowledge or intent.

Example: On the earlier Prexy-Friend example, this principle is why Friend isn't liable under 10b-5 if Friend buys after being tipped by Prexy.

☞ **Knows of breach of fiduciary obligation:** Even if the tipper is liable, the *tippee won't* be liable unless he *knew or should have known* that the tipper was *breaching a fiduciary obligation* to the corp. whose shares were traded.

Example: Joe is a carpet installer. While installing carpet at the house of Prexy, head of Oilco, he sees an Oilco memo on Prexy's desk saying, "We just struck a huge gusher." Joe tells Fred, his friend, "You should buy Oilco stock right away, because I heard they just struck oil," but doesn't tell Fred how he learned the info. *Joe* is liable as a tipper [he knew he was breaching a fiduciary duty to Oilco and Prexy by stealing the info, and he intended to confer a benefit on Fred]. But *Fred won't* be liable as a tippee, since he didn't know, and had no reason to know, that Joe got his info as a result of a fiduciary breach.

State-law causes of action

☛ **State-law actions, generally:** Next, consider the possibility that there may be a *state-law* cause of action for the insider trading.

☞ **Silent/impersonal transaction on exchange:** If all the insider did was to silently, and impersonally, buy or sell *on a stock exchange* while in possession of the information, there's probably no state-law (just federal law) liability.

☞ **Face-to-face:** But if the insider buys *face to face* with someone (call him X), X may be able to recover against the insider under state common-law principles if either:

  ☞ **Affirmative misrepresentation:** The insider made an *affirmative misrepresentation.*

  Example: Insider says to P, "I'll sell you my stock at $15/share; the company will be reporting a good quarter soon and the stock will go up." In fact Insider knows that the quarter will be bad, and the stock goes down. P will probably be able to have the transaction rescinded and/or get damages.

  or

  ☞ **Unfair methods:** The insider remains silent, but *uses unfair methods* to seek out a buyer or to *conceal his own identity.* This is the *"special facts"* doctrine.

  Example: Pres. has inside info that Corp's earnings will go up. Pres. has a broker locate X, a stockholder in Corp., and has the broker buy shares from X without disclosing that he's acting for Pres. A state recognizing the "special facts" doctrine will probably let X rescind the transaction or get damages.

☞ **Corporation's own action:** Consider the possibility that the *corp. itself* may be able to bring its own state-law action against the insider-trader, to recover on behalf of all s/h's the profits the trader made. Say that the NY case of *Diamond v. Oreamuno* would allow corp. recovery here, but that most states do not.

  Example: On above example, Corp. could recover from Pres the profits Pres made on the trade with X, under *Diamond.* This is true even though Corp. itself didn't suffer any direct loss — only X had direct losses, from selling his shares at a low price.

Short-swing profits (§ 16(b))

☛ **Short-swing rules, generally:** Finally, be on the lookout for situations in which an insider may be liable for *short-swing profits.* Remember that under § 16(b) of the Exchange Act, a corp. which is traded on a *national stock exchange* can recover *profits made by a director, officer or more-than-10% s/h* from the *purchase-and-sale,* or the *sale-and-purchase,* of that corp's securities *within any 6-month period.*

  ☞ **6-month period:** Remember that there's no § 16(b) cause of action unless there's been *both a purchase and sale within the same 6-month period.*

Example: On Feb. 1, Prexy, head of Corp., sells 1,000 shares of Corp. stock at $25. On March 1, Corp. discloses poor earnings, and the stock immediately falls to $10. If Prexy doesn't buy any stock back until Dec. 1, there's no 16(b) violation. But if he buys back 500 shares on July 1 at $10, he's automatically liable to Corp. for $15 x 500, regardless of whether he had any insider knowledge on either Feb. 1 or July 1.

☞ **10% holders:** If D is a *s/h* (but *not* an officer or director), be sure that she was a ***more-than-10%*** s/h when she acquired the stock. § 16(b) won't apply to a s/h unless she owned more than 10% of the corp's stock at both the time of purchase and the time of sale. ***The purchase that lifts the buyer over 10% does not count*** for § 16(b) purposes.

> *Example:* Prior to Dec. 1, Acquirer Corp. owned 50,000 shares (5%) of Target Corp. On Dec. 1, Acquirer buys an additional 140,000 shares (14%) of Target for $10/share, thereby becoming a 19% s/h in Target. On Feb. 1, Acquirer sells all its shares in Target for $20/share. Acquirer has no §16(b) liability, because there never was a time when it made a purchase while already — before the purchase — a 10% holder. (As to the sale, it's not clear whether we evaluate the 10% status before or after the sale, but there's a good chance that we measure that status *before* the sale.)

☞ **Directors:** However, where D is a ***director***, § 16(b) applies as long as he occupied that position on ***either*** the purchase date *or* sale date. Therefore, be alert for situations where the director ***resigned or was removed*** from the board before selling the stock, since these are ***covered***.

> *Example:* D is a director of X Corp, a publicly-traded corp. with 100,000 shares outstanding. On March 1, D (who owns no X stock) buys 1,000 shares at $10. On July 1, D is removed from his seat for cause, on account of unauthorized expenses he charges to the company. On July 15, D sells his 1,000 shares at $15. X can recover $5,000 from D under §16(b), because D was a director at the time of the purchase, and it doesn't matter that D was no longer a director at the time of sale.

☞ **Matching of purchases and sales:** When you calculate profits for §16(b), remember that the ***lowest purchase price is matched against the highest sale price,*** so as to ***maximize*** the corp's recovery. (Stock certificate numbers are not matched up, in other words.)

> *Example:* D, a director of X Corp., buys 4,000 shares of X at $25 on Feb. 1. On March 1, D exercises an option to buy 1,000 shares at $15. On June 1, D sells 1,000 shares (whose certificates show that

they were part of the 4,000-share lot), for $20 per share. X can recover $5,000 from D ($5 x 1,000), because we ignore the actual share certificates and match the lowest purchase price against the highest sale price.

Exam Tips *on*
SHAREHOLDERS' SUITS

Choosing between direct and derivative actions

☛ **Making the distinction:** Whenever the facts involve a shareholder suit, first determine whether the suit should be characterized as a *direct action* or a *derivative action*.

    ☞ **Direct suits:** Remember that if the injury is primarily to some or all s/hs "personally," the suit to redress it is a *direct* action. Here are kinds of suits that are usually "direct":

        ❏ suits to enforce the s/hs' *voting rights*;

        ❏ suits to *compel payments of dividends*;

        ❏ suits to *prevent oppression of or fraud* on minority s/hs;

        ❏ suits to *compel inspection* of the corp's books and records.

    ☞ **Derivative suits:** Conversely, a *derivative* action is the exclusive remedy where the alleged harm is done primarily to the *corporation*, rather than to an individual s/h. Examples of suits that are generally derivative:

        ❏ suits claiming breach of the *duty of care*;

        ❏ suits claiming breach of the *duty of loyalty* (e.g., suits claiming self-dealing, usurpation of a corp. opportunity, or excessive compensation).

Derivative actions

☛ **Requirements for derivation action:** If the action is derivative, confirm that the requirements for a derivative action have been met. In particular:

    ☞ **Contemporaneous ownership:** Verify that either the *"contemporaneous ownership"* rule is satisfied, or that some exception applies. Thus P must normally have *already owned his shares at the time of the transaction of which he complains*. But there are two exceptions:

❏ where the wrong began before P brought his shares, but ***continued after*** P bought (the ***"continuing wrong"*** exception); or

❏ where P acquired his shares by ***"operation of law,"*** and his ***predecessor owned*** the shares before the wrongdoing (the "operation of law" exception). Shares which P acquired by ***inheritance*** are often part of the exam fact pattern, and fall within this exception.

☞ **Demand on directors:** Check to see whether P has made a ***demand*** on the directors to redress the improper action. If not, determine whether demand is ***excused*** because it's ***likely to be futile*** (though not all states excuse demand even when futile).

    ☞ **Demand excused for futility:** Keep in mind that in many states, demand is excused as futile where ***all or a majority*** of the ***board*** is ***charged*** with breach of the duty of ***due care*** or of the duty of ***loyalty***.

    Example: Trucking Corp. runs a trucking business. Its board has 15 members. Management has a consultant prepare a report that says that if the corp. doesn't buy $1 million worth of new trucks within the next year, the company will lose business and probably become insolvent. The report is given to every member of the board, but only 5 read it. The board unanimously votes not to buy new trucks, and to spend the $1 million available to buy another business. Trucking Corp. becomes insolvent shortly thereafter for lack of new trucks. S, a s/h throughout the relevant period, brings a derivative action against those board members who didn't read the report, for breach of the duty of care in not buying the trucks. In many states, demand on the board will be excused, because this demand would likely be futile since a majority of the board members are being accused of a breach of the duty of care.

☞ **Business judgment rule:** If P has made a demand on the board, and the board ***rejects*** the demand, the board's decision will generally receive the ***protection of the business judgment rule*** (so that as long as the decision not to bring the litigation is ***rational***, P will not be allowed to continue with his derivative action).

    ☞ **Suit allowed to go forward:** But the court will allow P's suit to ***go forward*** despite the board's rejection of the demand, if either:

    [1] the ***board significantly participated*** in the alleged wrong; or

    [2] the directors who voted to reject the suit were ***dominated or controlled by the alleged wrongdoers***.

☞ **Special committee:** Look for situations in which the board has appointed a special *committee* to evaluate the derivative action, and the committee has recommended dismissal. Confirm that the members of the committee are ***truly independent*** of the directors accused of wrongdoing — if they're not, the derivative action should be allowed to proceed despite the committee's recommendation.

> *Example:* The 5 directors of Corp. (most of whom are part of management) are fearful of a hostile takeover attempt. These 5 directors therefore vote to sell off valuable corporate assets at below-market prices, solely to make Corp. a less attractive target. The board then votes to expand to 9 members, and to stagger the terms so that only 3 directors can be replaced each year. The 4 new directors are all close friends of the existing directors. P brings a derivative action against Corp for damages from the asset sales. The board votes to create a litigation committee consisting of the 4 new directors. The committee votes to recommend dismissal of P's suit. You should say that the court should let the suit proceed, because the committee was not truly independent — its members were all close friends of the original directors accused of the wrongdoing.

Indemnification of officers and directors

☛ **Indemnification problems, generally:** Look out for questions that require you to say whether a corp's ***indemnification*** of its officers or directors was proper.

  ☞ **Where defendant wins in litigation:** Recall that nearly all states ***permit*** the corp to indemnify any director or officer whose position is ***upheld*** in litigation, so questions on this fact pattern are easy. (In fact, most states ***require*** the corp. to indemnify in this "successful defendant" situation.)

  ☞ **When person loses in litigation:** Conversely, remember that most states do ***not permit*** an agreement to indemnify a director or officer whose position is ***not upheld*** (e.g., a dir. or off. who's found liable to the corp. in a derivative action).

  ☞ **Settlement:** Where the action is ***settled*** by means of a payment by the dir/off to the corp., usually state statutes say that the dir/off ***can*** be indemnified for his ***litigation expenses***, but ***can't*** be indemnified for the ***settlement payment***.

> *Example:* Veep, a v.p. of Corp., is sued in a derivative action in which P says that Veep entered into an unfairly favorable contract to buy property from Corp. Veep spends $30,000 on legal fees, then settles by paying $20,000 to Corp. Corp. can probably indemnify

Veep for the $30,000 legal fees, but not the $20,000 settlement.

☞ **Decision-maker must be independent:** Make sure that the *decision* about whether to indemnify is made by a *sufficiently independent party.* Thus directors closely affiliated with the defendant(s) can't decide to allow the indemnification payment — a *committee* of independent directors (i.e., directors not charged with wrongdoing and independent of those who are so charged), should make this decision.

> *Example:* P brings a derivative suit charging all members of Corp's board with selling Corp's assets at an unfairly low price to avoid a hostile takeover. The suit is settled with each board member paying $10,000. The entire board votes to pay the litigation expenses, including legal fees, of each board member. Probably this indemnification is invalid — since every board member was charged with wrongdoing, they couldn't make an arms' length decision to indemnify themselves.

Exam Tips *on*
MERGERS AND ACQUISITIONS

When you're analyzing an exam question on Mergers & Acquisitions, focus first on whether the transaction is "friendly" or "hostile." The issues that get tested are generally quite different depending on which category the transaction falls into.

Friendly acquisitions — generally

Self-dealing rules: When you're analyzing a "friendly" acquisition (with no other, hostile, bidder in the picture), the main thing to check is whether the transaction violates the rules on *self-dealing*.

☛ **Where self-dealing analysis is required:** If the Target's board or management receives some "goodies" for themselves (not being given to other shareholders), and then recommend the acquisition, refer in your answer to the fact that the transaction is somewhat self-interested.

☞ **Overall fairness is dispositive:** However, indicate that as long as the court believes that the transaction was, overall, *"fair"* to the stockholders, the presence of some element of self-interest by Target's board or management won't cause the court to enjoin the transaction or award damages.

For instance, a large *side-payment* to Target's *board or management* won't usually result in the deal's being enjoined, if the price paid to shareholders is "fair."

> *Example:* Target's stock is trading at $30/share. Acquirer offers to buy all shares at $60/share. Acquirer also promises to keep as officers the President and Treasurer of Target, at four times their current salaries, and to pay each other board member of Target a bonus equal to 4 times their annual directors' fees. All board members vote to recommend the acquisition to Target's shareholders. While the lucrative deals given to board members may make the transaction slightly self-interested, the court will let the transaction go through, and not award damages against the board, if the court thinks the transaction is "fair." Since the offering price is much higher than the prior market price, the court will probably conclude that the transaction is fair.

☞ **Independent committee:** Check to see if Target's board appoints an *"independent committee"* to approve the merger. The committee is probably "independent" so long as it's composed of board members who aren't on the Acquirer's side of the transaction — the fact that some committee members might get some benefit from the sale (as in the above example) won't be enough to make them non-independent.

> ☞ **Approval of committee is dispositive:** If an independent committee approves the deal, after *reasonable investigation* and *deliberation*, the court usually *won't even examine the "fairness"* of the transaction. Instead, the court will probably hold that the transaction is *protected by the business-judgment rule*, so long as the price and other terms aren't *irrational*. (This assumes that the court believes the board has behaved in a way likely to get the highest available price. See the discussion of the "level playing field" rule, below.)
>
> So where an independent committee has investigated and approved the deal, even a pretty low price won't be enough to cause the court to enjoin the transaction or award damages for the board's failure to exercise due care (but a price so low as to be completely irrational might be).

Friendly acquisitions — procedural formalities

☛ **Procedural formalities:** Make sure that there was compliance with *procedural formalities.* In particular, if the friendly transaction is a merger or asset-sale (as opposed to a tender offer), make sure that *stockholders have approved it*, by the requisite majority.

☞ **Majority of share outstanding:** Unless the charter says otherwise, only a *simple majority* of shares must approve. But this must be a majority of *all shares outstanding*, not just a majority of shares voting. So abstentions hurt.

☞ **Holders must have notice and opportunity to vote:** Don't forget that the formalities must be observed even where failure to meet them didn't change the outcome. That is, there's *no doctrine of "harmless error"* when formalities surrounding a sale — such as the requirement of shareholder approval — are not observed.

> *Example: A* owns 60% of Corp's single class of shares, *B* 20% and *C* 20%. *A* controls a majority of the Board. The Board unanimously approves a sale of substantially all of Corp's assets to *X*. No notice of a shareholders meeting to approve the sale is ever sent to *B* and *C*, nor is such a meeting held. Corp's board then signs a bill of sale purporting to convey title to the assets. The sale is not valid, because the required notice to shareholders and shareholders' approval never occurred — the fact that *A* could have voted his shares in favor and thus ensured a majority vote in favor is irrelevant.

☞ **Insiders count:** The majority for approval can include *insiders*, even insiders who will be on the other side of the transaction (e.g., management in a management-led buyout).

☞ **Disclosure required:** Make sure that the shareholders received *proper disclosure* about the transaction before the vote. For instance, if it's a stock merger, and holders weren't given accurate info about the acquirer's finances or business prospects, the court may enjoin the transaction or award damages against the board.

Friendly acquisitions — S/hs' right of appraisal

☞ **Right of appraisal generally:** If shareholders have a right to vote on the transaction, keep in mind that an unsatisfied shareholder may have the right of *appraisal*, i.e., the right to have the corporation *buy his shares* for a "fair price." In other words, in a stock merger, or in a sale of substantially all of the Target's assets for cash that won't be promptly re-distributed to the holders, the right of appraisal probably exists.

> *Example: A* owns 60% of Corp's single class of shares, *B* 20% and *C* 20%. *A* controls a majority of the Board. The Board unanimously approves a sale of substantially all of Corp's assets to *X* for $100,000, which Corp plans to reinvest in a different line of business. In the shareholder vote that follows, *A* votes for the sale (ensuring a majority in favor, as required) but *B* and *C* vote against it, because they think the change-of-business plan is foolhardy. After the sale goes through, *B* and *C* have a right of appraisal in nearly all states — that is, they can force Corp. to buy their shares for their fair market value.

☞ **Holder who votes "yes" loses right:** But remember that a holder who *votes for the transaction* (or doesn't comply with other procedural requirements, like giving prompt notice of a demand for appraisal) *forfeits* her appraisal rights.

☞ **Exclusive remedy:** Also, remember that where a holder has appraisal rights, these are usually her *exclusive remedy.* So a holder who has appraisal rights usually can't sue to block the transaction as unfair, even if the circumstances are ones that would otherwise support an injunction (e.g., an excessively low price).

Hostile takeovers — generally

Exams often focus on hostile takeovers and the defensive tactics used by the Target to repel the hostile bid. When you've got a question involving a hostile bid, here's what to look for:

Hostile takeovers — the Williams Act

☛ **Williams Act requirements:** First, check whether all parties have complied with the *Williams Act.*

☞ **Disclosure by 5% holder:** A party needs to comply with § 13(d)'s *disclosure requirements* if she directly or indirectly *acquires more than 5% of any class* of Target's publicly-held stock. A person needs to comply even if she has not made (and doesn't intend to make) a tender offer, and doesn't intend to purchase more stock.

☛ **Two or more act in concert:** The disclosure requirement also applies when two or more people agree to *act in concert* in acquiring new stock, or even in voting stock they already own (as long as, together, they own at least 5% of a class of stock).

Example: Sam and Harold are officers of Target, and together own 47% of Target's stock. Raider makes a tender offer for all Target shares. Sam and Harold agree to try to block Raider's offer. In particular, they agree that they will vote together to oppose the offer, and will work together to persuade other holders to do the same.

Sam and Harold are required to file a Schedule 13D disclosure form (showing that they have agreed to work together) even though they are not intending to acquire any new shares. That's because their combination has increased their effective voting power, and is a transaction by a more-than-5% holder.

☞ **Disclosure by tender-offeror:** If a person makes a *"tender offer,"* the person has to comply with *additional disclosure* rules under §14(e). But an offer to buy a large percentage of a corporation's stock doesn't automatically make the offer a "tender offer" — widespread solicitation, a firm price, and a time limit, will usually all have to be present for a tender offer. Open-market purchases usually won't suffice.

☞ **No injunction:** But even if you spot a §13(d) or §14(e) disclosure-rule violation, don't assume that the court will **block** the transaction. Usually, the court will **let the acquirer acquire and vote the shares**, even though he got them while failing to make dislosure. (A holder will have to be content with a civil-damages action).

☞ **Implied right of action for disclosure errors:** Any time you have a shareholder solicitation in connection with a takeover attempt, check whether the **solicitation materials** were **accurate**. If they're not, any holder has an **implied private right of action** against the soliciter under §14(e) of the '34 Act. But P has to prove that:

❑ the misrepresentation or nondisclosure by D was **material**;

❑ D acted with **"scienter"** (recklessness or intent to mislead); and

❑ P **relied** on the incorrect materials (if D's error was a misrepresentation, rather than an omission).

Example: Acquirer makes a tender offer for all of Target's shares, at $65/share. Acquirer tells Prexy, the head of Target, that Acquirer will keep all product lines. Acquirer promises Prexy that Prexy will still have a job after the acquisition. Spoiler comes along and tells Prexy that he'll bid $70/share for a controlling interest in Target; Spoiler says he'll liquidate the company, and fire Prexy. Prexy tells these facts to Target's board. The board approves solicitation materials that recommend that each holder tender to Acquirer's offer. The materials don't mention the offer from Spoiler. Holder, a shareholder in Target, receives these materials, votes for the merger, then finds out the materials didn't mention the higher offer from Spoiler.

Holder can recover civil damages from Prexy and the rest of Target's board, because: (1) the omission about Spoiler's offer was "material" (existence of a higher offer would almost always be important to a holder who's deciding whether to tender); (2) the board knew about the other offer, so the omission was probably at least "reckless," and thus constituted "scienter"; and (3) Holder probably doesn't need to show he read the materials and relied, because you can't really rely on an omission (as opposed to an affirmative misrepresentation).

Hostile takeovers — defensive measures

☞ **Defensive measures generally:** Analyze any *defensive measures* employed by Target. Unless the facts tell you that some other body of law applies, you'll usually do well to apply the Delaware approach, which is well-developed and specific. (We'll apply Delaware rules here.) The court will probably invalidate the defensive measure unless four requirements are met:

❏ **Reasonable fear of danger:** First, Target's board and management must have *reasonable grounds* for believing that there's a *danger to Target's own welfare* (as opposed to the welfare of management). Management and the board *can't act merely to perpetuate themselves* in power.

> *Example 1:* Target is faced with a hostile takeover. Target's board adopts a plan stating that all employees of Target will receive a severance payment of one year's salary for every five years with the company. The payments are to be made only if the employee is fired after a change of control in Target. A court might well hold that this provision was intended mainly to perpetuate Target's management in power and defeat the takeover, not to benefit shareholders. In that case, the court will probably invalidate the measure.

> *Example 2:* Target is faced with a hostile takeover from Raider. Target's stock is trading at $10/share, after having been $20 just six months previously. Raider is offering $13. Target's board reasonably believes that the 50% selloff is due to general stock-market conditions, not long-term problems with Target's business operations (which the board believes to be sound and improving). The board therefore recommends that holders not tender. The board also votes to have Target issue new shares representing a 15% stake, which Target sells at $11/share to White Knight, a buyer who has indicated that he will support incumbent management in any takeover battle.
>
> Probably these measures satisfy the "reasonable grounds for fearing threat to corporate welfare" test (and will be upheld if they meet the other tests, which they probably do).

❏ **Proportionality:** Second, the anti-takeover defense must be *reasonable in relation to the threat posed*. The response can't be *"preclusive"* (one that makes it almost impossible for the hostile bid to succeed) or *"coercive"* (one that forces holders to accept management's own alternative to the hostile bid).

> *Example 1:* Target is faced with a hostile bid from Raider. Target's

board announces a contract to sell Target's most profitable subsidiary at a below-market price to Newcorp, a new company set up by Target's management; the contract will only take effect if Raider's bid is successful. If Raider (or a stockholder in Target) challenges this contract, it will probably be invalidated as being a waste of Target's assets and thus coercive.

Example 2: Raider announces a hostile bid for Target at $200/share. Target has 152,000 shares outstanding. In response to Raider's offer, Target: (1) sells to White Knight 48,000 shares of Target at $150/share in return for White Knight's agreemen that he won't acquire any further shares without management's consent for 5 years; (2) buys back 100,000 shares from other holders. Simultaneously, Prexy, the head of Target, promises White Knight that Prexy won't sell Prexy's 3,000 shares in Target to anyone but White Knight, in return for White Knight's promise that if White Knight gets control of Target, White Knight will employ Prexy.

A court would almost certainly hold that this package of defensive measures is "preclusive," in that it prevents anyone but White Knight from getting control of Target no matter what they do. Therefore, the court will invalidate the measures.

❏ **Investigation:** Third, the board must take the defensive measure not only in good faith, but only after *reasonable investigation*.

❏ **Disinterested board:** Finally, in a close case the court is more likely to approve the defensive measure if it was adopted by a board a *majority* of whose members were *disinterested* (i.e., *outside*) members.

Hostile takeovers — board's duty to get the highest price

☛ **"Get highest price" duty:** If Target's board indicates a *willingness to sell the company* (or control of the company), then remember that the board's main duty is to *obtain the highest price* for shareholders.

☞ **Level playing field:** This means that Target's board must create a *"level playing field"* — the board *can't favor a white knight over a hostile bidder*.

Example: Target has just learned that Raider, a notorious hostile bidder who often liquidates his prey, has acquired 6% of Target and may be about to acquire more. With board approval, Target's management approaches Friendly Corp. about the possibility of Friendly's acquiring all of Target's assets. Target then gives Friendly nonpublic financial data about Target and declines to give the same data to Raider. Since Target's board (by approaching Friendly) has indicated that the company is for sale, Target had an obligation to obtain the highest price, and to treat all bidders more-or-less equally in order to obtain that highest price. By favoring Friendly in disclosure, Target violated these duties. The court will order Target to give the same data to Raider, and will probably enjoin any deal made with Friendly in the absence of the required "level playing field."

☞ **Sale of control:** The "level playing field" rule applies not only where Target's management is selling the entire company, but also where management or the board has decided to sell *control* to a single individual or entity.

> *Example:* On the facts of the above example, suppose that Target offered to sell Friendly not Target's assets, but, instead, stock representing a 30% interest in Target. Assuming that 30% would be a controlling stake in Target (which would be the case if no one else had, say, more than a 15% stake), the offer to sell "control" to Friendly would be enough to trigger Target's "level playing field" obligations. So Friendly would have to give the same financial data to Raider (and would not be allowed to consummate the 30%-deal with Friendly if this would be less favorable for Target's shareholders than the bid from Raider).

☞ **"Just say no" defense:** Finally, remember that Target's board always has the right to *"just say no"* when it receives an unsolicited offer. In other words, the board may refuse to approve the transaction or recommend it to shareholders, even if this has the effect of blocking the deal. (But if the board tries to make an alternative deal — like selling to a white knight — then the board isn't just "saying no," and it must comply with the "level playing field" rule.)

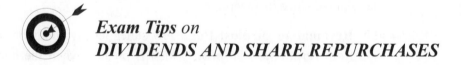

Exam Tips on
DIVIDENDS AND SHARE REPURCHASES

Issues regarding dividends and share repurchases are easy to spot — just look for fact patterns in which a corp. has declared (or failed to declare) a cash dividend, or repurchased shares.

Dividends and the Business Judgment Rule

☛ **Protection of the business judgment rule:** Remember that a board's decision to pay (or not pay) dividends is generally protected by the *business judgment rule*.

So either way it goes, the decision won't be reversed so long as it's rational, unless there's fraud, illegality or self-dealing.

☞ **Rationality is dispositive:** Therefore, first check to see whether the dividend policy is *rational* — if there's some *plausible business purpose* behind it, the court normally won't second-guess.

> *Example:* For the past 5 years, Corp. has racked up pre-tax earnings equal to 50% of its sales. Yet Corp. has not paid a dividend during this time. The board has done this so that Corp. will have substantial retained earnings, and will thus be more attractive to an acquirer. P, a minority s/h, sues to compel payment of a dividend. P's suit will probably fail, since the board's action is rational (and there's no allegation of fraud, illegality or self-dealing by the directors).

☞ **Fraud or illegality:** Second, check to make sure that the directors' decision on dividends wasn't *fraudulent*, *illegal*, or in *bad faith*.

> ☞ **Squeeze-out:** A common scenario is that the majority directors *refuse to declare* a dividend from available cash, because they want to *squeeze out a minority s/h* (e.g., by coercing her into selling out cheaply). If the court thinks that this is what happened, the court will order a dividend to be declared.

☞ **Wrongful declaring of dividend:** Conversely, check for situations where the directors *declare a dividend* that they *shouldn't*.

> ☞ **Insolvency:** Of course, a dividend isn't legal if its payment would result in the corp's becoming *insolvent*.

> ☞ **Earned surplus requirement:** Also, check the source out of which the dividend is being paid — in most states, dividends may be paid only out of *earned surplus*, i.e., historical profits the corp. has earned since its inception.

> > ☞ **Revaluation surplus:** But a few states let dividends be paid from *revaluation surplus*, which is created when the corp's assets are revalued upward to reflect their current fair market value rather than their historical cost.

> > *Example:* Corp. is founded in 2004, and has a $50,000 total operating loss in 2004-06. In 2006, it buys property from S for $60,000, but the board later in the year concludes that the property is now worth $120,000. Now, Corp. pays a $10,000 dividend to s/h's. If the state doesn't allow revaluation surplus as a source for dividends, then this dividend payment is illegal (since there's no operating surplus, only a $50,000 lifetime

operating deficit). But if revaluation surplus *is* allowed as a dividend source, then the dividend is ok (since there's $60K worth of reval. surplus less $50K of operating deficit) — but anything more than a $10K dividend would still be illegal.

☞ **Nimble dividends:** Also, recall that some states allow payment of *"nimble dividends"* — dividends from the corp's *current earnings* (or its earnings from the last two years), even if the corp. does not have a "lifetime" surplus.

Share repurchases

☛ **Same conditions apply:** If the facts describe a *share repurchase*, remember that a corp's decision to repurchase outstanding shares is generally subject to the *same conditions as the declaration of dividends* (i.e., there must be adequate funds available). So check whether the same amount could be spent on dividends. Also, check whether the *price paid* by the corp. is *reasonable*.

☞ **No self-dealing:** Also, check to make sure there's no *self-dealing* in the repurchase.

☞ **Purchase of controlling s/h's shares:** For instance, if a *controlling s/h* causes the corp to buy his shares, that s/h will probably have to show either that: (i) the price was *"entirely fair"*; or (ii) a majority of *disinterested directors* or disinterested s/h's *approved* or *ratified* it. (But remember that there's *no blanket rule* that requires that the corp. buy back the minority holders' shares just because it's buying the controlling s/h's shares.)

Exam Tips on
ISSUANCE OF SECURITIES

The most common exam topics from this chapter are: (1) subscription agreements; (2) preemptive rights; and (3) watered stock.

Subscription agreements

☛ **Revocation of agreement:** Concerning *subscription agreements*, the most frequently-tested issue is whether a subscriber may *revoke* a pre-incorporation subscription. Here, recall that there are two principles applicable in most states:

☞ **6-month irrevocability:** First, most states say that the subscription is *irrevo-*

cable for some period, usually 6 months.

> *Example:* G, and A and B agree to pay $3,000 each for all of the stock of Corp., a corp. to be formed by G. One week later, before anything further has happened, A and B write to G, stating "We hereby revoke any agreement to buy stock in Corp." In most states (incl. Del. & under the RMBCA), G can form the corp. and have it sue A and B for the purchase price, because the subscription acts like an offer to the corp. that is irrevocable for some time, probably 6 mos.

☞ **All s/h's act together to rescind:** Second, even states making the subscription irrevocable for some time allow *all s/h's, acting together, to rescind* the agreement. (But if even one subscriber insists, the subscription remains in force.)

> *Example:* On the facts of the above example, G, A and B could get together and all agree to rescind, but A and B by themselves can't.

Preemptive rights

☛ **Preemptive rights generally:** Questions on *preemptive rights* are surprisingly common. A preemptive-rights issue can pop up even where the question does not use the phrase "preemptive rights" — you should look for such an issue whenever s/h *A* buys shares, then shares are offered to s/h *B* without *A*'s getting a chance to avoid dilution by buying additional shares.

☞ **Opt-in:** Don't forget that under most statutes, pre-emptive rights work on an *"opt in"* basis: unless the corp. in its charter specifically provides that there will be pre-emptive rights, such rights won't exist.

☞ **Where rights don't apply:** Actually, most preemptive-rights issues involve the four main situations in which such rights *don't apply*:

> ❏ *Previously-authorized, but unissued, shares.* (However, under some statutes the unauthorized-but-unissued shares become covered by the pre-emptive rights scheme after passage of a certain amount of time, e.g. 6 mos., following formation.)

> ❏ *Treasury stock* (i.e., shares that were once outstanding, but that have been repurchased by the corp.).

> ❏ Issuance of new shares that are *preferred shares rather than common shares* and are *not convertible* into common shares.

> > *Example:* Corp elects to have its common shareholders have pre-emptive rights. Paul owns 30% of the common. Corp issues a new class of stock, preferred stock, and sells $50 million worth to

Investor. Assuming that the preferred stock is not convertible into common, the issuance of the preferred does not trigger Paul's pre-emptive rights, so he has no right to buy any of the preferred. (If the preferred *was* convertible to common, then the issuance of the preferred *would* trigger Paul's preemptive rights.) See MBCA § 6.30(b)(5).

❏ Most often-tested of all, shares *exchanged for services or assets.*

Example: Corp. was incorporated 2 years ago with initial autho-rized capital of 10,000 shares of $100 par value stock. Corp. then issues 5,000 shares, 2,500 each to A and B. Later, Corp. issues 1,000 shares to C in return for C's transfer of title to Blueacre, which Corp. wants for a future plant site. Even if Corp. has pre-emptive rights, A can't exercise any rights as the result of the deal with C, because C got his shares as the result of an exchange for assets. (Also, since C's shares were part of the originally-autho-rized amount, this fact, too, may prevent pre-emptive rights from arising in A, though the passage of 2 years might be enough under the statute to cause pre-emptive rights to re-attach to the 5,000 authorized-but-originally-unissued shares.)

Payment for stock

☛ **Form and amount of payment:** Issues relating to the *form* and *amount* of con-*sideration* paid for stock are also common on exams.

☞ **Past vs. future payment:** The principal issue relating to the *"form"* of consid-eration is the distinction between *past* services or property given in exchange for stock, and promises of *future* services or property:

　　☞ **Past payment:** If the consideration is *past services* to the corp., or *existing property* already transferred to the corp., this is clearly *valid* consideration (at least if it's got a value that's *no less than the par value* of the stock).

　　☞ **Promise of future payment:** But if the consideration is a *promise* of *future* services, or a promise to *transfer property in the future*, some statutes make this *invalid* consideration. (But most modern statutes, including the RMBCA, allow such promises to be consid-eration.)

☞ **Watered stock:** As to the "amount" of consideration, you mainly have to worry about the problem of *"watered stock."* That is, if the shares are exchanged for money, property or services whose *value is less than the stated par value of the shares*, in many states the transaction is an illegal issuance of watered stock.

Example 1: Corp. issues 100 shares, each with par value of $100, to A in exchange for A's promissory note for $7,500. This presents a watered-stock issue, because the value of the thing received by the corp. (the note) is less than the $10,000 aggregate par value of the stock.

Example 2: Corp. issues 100 shares, again each with par value of $100, to A in exchange for A's promise to work for Corp. for one year at a salary of $100,000. If the market value (and value to Corp.) of A's services for a year is less than $110,000, the issue may be invalid as watered stock.

But again, it's the *exceptions* that are usually tested. Most important:

❏ **"Good-faith" exception:** There's a *"good faith"* (or *"business judgment"*) exception to the "no watered stock" rule: as long as the board in its good faith business judgment *believes* that the funds, property or services to be received in exchange are worth at least the par value, the court won't second-guess. Thus in Example 2 above, if the board honestly and plausibly believes that A's services for a year are worth $110K, the court won't find the stock to have been watered, even though the court might not agree with the board's assessment of A's value.

❏ **Value at time of stock issuance:** Also, when stock is exchanged for property, don't be tricked into thinking that the stock is watered just because the recipient *obtained* the property for less than the par value of the stock. What's relevant is the value of the property at *the time the stock is issued*, not how much the recipient originally paid for the property.

Example: Corp. issues 100 shares of $100 par value stock to A in return for office equipment currently appraised at $11,000. A had bought the equipment 6 months earlier at an auction, for $8,000. The stock isn't watered, because the present value (measured by the appraisal) is greater than the par value of the stock; it doesn't matter how much A originally paid for the equipment.

❏ **Estoppel:** Finally, remember that if the corp. has placed the legend *"fully paid"* on shares that were sold at a discount, in some states the corp. is *"estopped"* from later claiming otherwise — so the corp. or another s/h cannot later have the transaction rescinded, or recover the discounted amount from the issuee.

☞ **Creditor complaints:** Sometimes you'll see a question in which the person complaining about watered stock is not another s/h (as in the above examples), but a ***creditor***. This will generally happen only if the corp. is now ***insolvent***.

☞ **Misrepresentation theory:** The most common theory for letting the creditor recover against the s/h who received the watered stock is the ***"holding out"*** or ***"misrepresentation"*** theory. Under this theory, the creditor can recover from a s/h the amount of the "water" (the difference between par value and value of what the s/h paid) if the creditor shows that he extended credit in ***reliance*** on the corp's assertion that all stock previously issued was for par value. (Because of the reliance requirement, creditors usually can't use the holding-out theory where they lent ***before*** the watered-stock issue, or lent after but with ***knowledge*** of the watering.)

SHORT-ANSWER QUESTIONS

Note: These questions are selected from among the "Quiz Yourself" questions in the full-length *Emanuel Law Outline* on Corporations *(EOC)*, which were in turn adapted from the *Law in a Flash on Corporations* flash-card set. We've kept the same question numbering here as in *EOC*. Since some questions have been omitted here, there are gaps in the numbering.

CHAPTER 1

INTRODUCTION

1. Scrooge and Marley own a catering business, the Roast of Christmas Present, Inc. They each own 50% of the shares. Marley dies in a freak accident when one of the corporation's employees, Bob Cratchit, drops a haunch of venison on him. Since Marley was a 50% owner of the corporation, does the corporation terminate along with him? _____

2. Curly owns part of the Nyuck-Nyuck Wise Guys, a major league baseball team. Curly becomes disgusted with the whole business of baseball when the team makes a $50-million, five-year deal with a free agent, Mr. Potatohead. Without telling the other owners, Curly purports to transfer his interest in the team to Shemp. (Curly is one of several hundred owners.) On the issue of whether Curly's interest is in fact transferable, does it matter whether the team is a partnership or a corporation? _____

4. Tarzan and Jane each is a 50% owner of the Me Tarzan, You Jane Charm School, Inc., a standard "C" corporation. Last year, the charm school earned a $10,000 profit, which was spent on new etiquette videos. Do Tarzan and Jane each owe tax personally on their respective (50%) shares of the company's profit? _____

CHAPTER 2

THE CORPORATE FORM

6. Scrooge McDuck is the majority shareholder of the Huey Dewey Louie Real Estate Development Corp. The company makes a $19,000,000 profit one year. McDuck donates $500,000 of it to a nonprofit charity he controls, the McDuck Foundation for the Preservation of Wetlands. Assume that a fairly typical statute (e.g., the MBCA) applies. If a minority shareholder challenges the donation as improper, what result? _____

7. Marie Antoinette, a promoter for the as-yet-unformed Let 'Em Eat Cake Baked Goods Company, signs a requirements contract on the company's behalf (and in the company's name) with the Wilted Flour Company, covering all the company's flour needs for the next three years.

(a) Suppose that after Let 'Em is formed, and before it takes any action with reference to the contract, its board sends Wilted a letter saying, "We don't want the flour, so don't send it." Can Wilted recover against Let 'Em for breach of contract? _____

(b) Suppose the letter in (a) was never sent. What action by Let 'Em, if any, would cause Let 'Em to be bound by the contract? _____

8. Oliver Wendell Douglas, a promoter for the yet-to-be-formed Hooterville Produce Company, contracts to buy a 160-acre farm on Hooterville Produce's behalf from Mr. Haney. Douglas signs the land sale contract in Hooterville's name, without making it clear to Haney that Hooterville (as Douglas knows) doesn't exist yet. The closing is set for August 1st. Hooterville Produce is formed one month before that. The board, consisting of Hank Kimball, Fred Ziffel, and Sam Drucker, passes a resolution ratifying the land sale contract. Shortly thereafter, Hooterville Produce becomes insolvent, and the closing never takes place.

(a) Can Haney hold Douglas personally liable on the land sale contract? _____

(b) Suppose that before the contract was signed, Haney knew that Hooterville Produce didn't yet exist, and said to Douglas, "Why don't you sign the contract in the corporation's name anyway." Can Haney hold Douglas personally liable? _____

9. Benjamin Disraeli intends to form a corporation, Sceptered Isle Tableware, to manufacture salt and pepper shakers in the shape of British kings and queens. Disraeli fills out the articles of incorporation, and has his lawyer file them with the Secretary of State for the state of Thames on October 1. On October 10, Disraeli, signing as "Sceptered Isle Corp by Ben Disraeli, President," enters into a lease on some manufacturing space owned by Victoria Regina. On December 1, Sceptered Isle runs out of money, and defaults on the lease. On December 15, Disraeli gets a letter from the Secretary of State saying that the articles of incorporation are not valid because they were not signed by the incorporator(s) (a fact that Disraeli didn't realize until he got the letter). Disraeli signs the articles and sends them back promptly, whereupon the Secretary of State accepts them for filing on Jan. 2. Victoria Regina, discovering that Sceptered Isle has no assets, sues Disraeli personally. Ignore any issue of whether the corporation was adequately capitalized.

(a) Under the common law, what doctrine(s) should Disraeli assert as a defense? Will the defense(s) work? _____

(b) Under the MBCA, will Disraeli be liable under the lease? _____

10. Snow White wants to incorporate her business as The Poison Apple Produce Company. There are eight shareholders: Snow White, Dopey, Grumpy, Sleepy, Doc, Bashful, Sneezy, and Happy. Each owns an equal number of shares in the company. Bashful and Happy are passive investors, with no involvement in the company except the cash they invested; the rest are actively involved in management. The company becomes insolvent, primarily due to Dopey's mismanagement, which, perhaps, is predictable with a name like that. Evil Stepmother Trucking Company has an outstanding invoice for $20,000 due from Poison Apple. There was a defect in formation that all the Poison Apple shareholders knew about and ignored. Can Evil Stepmother go after all of them personally? Answer both under common law and under the modern approach. _____

11. The Three Little Pigs are each one-third owners of the Huff 'N Puff Construction Company, Inc. Huff N' Puff has a board of directors (at least on paper), but none of the Pigs are on it. The board never meets or signs any documents. The Pigs don't set regular salaries for themselves; instead, any time any of them needs money for living expenses, he takes it from the safe, without keeping a record of how much he took. Cumulatively over the last two years, the Pigs have taken out $100,000 more for "living expenses" than the company earned. The real estate market suffers a sharp downturn, and Huff N' Puff is unable to pay one of its largest suppliers, Big Bad Wolf Masonry Supplies. Big Bad Wolf seeks payment from the Pigs personally. What result? _____

13. Larry, Curly, and Moe have for several years conducted their house-painting business as a partnership. During that time, they have each kept $50,000 in cash invested as capital in the partnership. They then decide that it would be better to operate as a corporation. Consequently, they incorporate as O-A Wizeguy House Painting Corp. They liquidate the partnership, and each contributes $10,000 to the corporation's stock. At the same time, each lends the corporation $40,000. Shortly thereafter, the corporation becomes insolvent. At that point, it has $200,000 in unpaid debts, of which $120,000 is due to Larry, Curly and Moe ($40,000 each), and the balance of $80,000 is owed to Shemp, a supplier who has no affiliation with the three owners. There is $40,000 in cash available for distribution.

(a) If you represent Shemp, what doctrine will you assert as the basis for getting as much of the cash for your client as you can? _____

(b) How is the court most likely to divide the cash? _____

CHAPTER 3
THE CORPORATE STRUCTURE

14. Alfred Pennyworth is a 51% owner of Metropolis Crimefighters, Inc. Metropolis has two officers who serve as its directors and employees, Batman and Robin. Alfred is not a director or officer of the corporation. Alfred is out shopping one day when he sees a nice, sedate station wagon, the Travel Queen Family Truckster, which he thinks would make a far more sensible company car than the Batmobile. He signs a lease for the Travel Queen on behalf of Metropolis. When Batman and Robin see the Travel Queen, Robin exclaims, "Holy Corporations, Batman! Is Metropolis Crimefighters bound by this lease?" Well — is it? _____

15. Brady Strippers, Inc., a furniture refinishing company, has two shareholders, Mike Brady and Carol Brady, and three directors, who are elected annually. Mike owns 60 shares of Brady Strippers stock, with Carol owning the other 40 shares. All shares can vote. Mike wants to elect Greg, Peter, and Bobby as directors; Carol wants to elect Marcia, Jan, and Cindy.

(a) You represent Carol. What advice should you give her about what she should do to maximize the number of directors she can elect (and is there any special procedural advice you have for her about how to implement your substantive advice)?

_____

(b) If Carol follows your advice in part (a), how many directors is she likely to end up with? _____

(c) If Carol doesn't follow your advice, what's likely to happen?

_____

16. The Heavenly Choir Musical Instrument Company has a board of directors whose number is fixed in the charter at 5. Three of these members are Richie Valens, Janis Joplin and the Big Bopper. The three are killed in a plane crash, leaving just two members (less than a majority of board seats, and thus less than a quorum.) Can the two remaining directors fill the vacancies anyway? _____

17. The Acme Electrical Company — "Let us fix your shorts" — has bylaws providing for regular, quarterly board of directors meetings, which are to take place at the company headquarters on the first Wednesday of each calendar quarter, unless a different time or place is set by prior board resolution. A quorum is three of the five directors. One of the directors is Wile E. Coyote. At the most recent quarterly meeting Coyote was not present, but the other four directors were. At that meeting, the board (by unanimous vote of all present) approved an acquisition. As soon as he found out about the acquisition (2 days after the meeting approving it), Coyote challenged it, stating (accurately) that he did not receive constructive or actual notice of the time and place set for the meeting.

(a) Does the lack of notice to Coyote make the board's action invalid? _____

(b) What difference, if any, would it make if the meeting had been a special rather than regular quarterly meeting? _____

19. Jack is president of the Fee Fi Fo Produce Company. Undertaking a new crop line is considered major enough to require approval of the board of directors. Nonetheless, Jack is at the Cow Tavern one day when Butcher, another patron, proposes to sell him some "magic beans," which Butcher claims will produce giant beanstalks. Fee Fi Fo doesn't plant beans currently. Jack says, "I can't buy the company unless my board of directors approves." Several members of the five-person board are out-of-town. So Jack telephones each board member, one at a time, and asks them to approve the transaction. Four say "yes," but the fifth, Giant, says "no." Is Jack authorized to enter the purchase contract? _____

20. Same facts as the previous question. Now, however, assume that all five directors say "yes."

(a) What procedural step can Jack take to implement the action without a formal board meeting at which a quorum is present? _____

(b) Would your answer to part (a) work if Giant persisted in saying "no" to the proposed acquisition, while the other four directors said "yes"? _____

21. Benedict Arnold is a member of the Libber Tea Company board of directors. He has two years left on his board term. The company does not have cumulative voting. George III, Libber Tea's majority shareholder, sells his interest to George Washington. At the next annual shareholders' meeting, Washington says (to everyone's surprise), "I now move to remove Arnold from the board of directors." Washington does not give any reason in support of his desire to remove Arnold. The motion is duly seconded. All shareholders but Washington vote against the motion (i.e., vote to keep Arnold), but since Washington owns a majority of the shares the motion passes. The jurisdiction has enacted the MBCA. Libber's articles of incorporation are silent on the issue of removal of directors.

(a) Putting aside any issues of notice, was Arnold validly removed from the board?

_____

(b) Now, focusing solely on the issue of notice, was Arnold's removal handled properly? _____

(c) Would your answer to part (a) be different in a jurisdiction that follows the traditional common-law approach to removal of directors? _____

23. Frontier Foods, Inc., appoints Betty Crockett treasurer of the corporation, with the express authority to handle corporate funds, and no express authority to do anything else. However, whenever the other officers and employees have their hands full, Betty steps in and helps out by purchasing inventory on the corporation's behalf. She's purchased hardtack for Frontier Foods from the Tuffas Leather Company several times before, and Frontier has always paid the invoices. Betty now makes out a new purchase order for fifty cases of hardtack, and Tuffas manufactures her order. Before it's delivered, some board members find out that they can get a much better deal on hardtack from a competitor. They try to cancel Betty's hardtack purchase order, claiming that it was unauthorized. Is the purchase order a valid corporate obligation? Cite the doctrines you use in arriving at your answer.

_____

25. Ferdinand de Gama is the chairman of the board of the Cheap & Good Boat Company. Cheap & Good's articles of incorporation have a purposes clause, limiting the company's boat production to pleasure boats no longer than twenty feet. De Gama believes that there is much money to be made in larger, ocean-going vessels. He gets the board to call for a special meeting of the shareholders, to discuss amending the purposes clause in the articles to encompass larger vessels. That's the agenda that's included in the notice to shareholders announcing the special meeting. The corporate president, Marco Polo, convenes the meeting. After the shareholders vote in favor of the amendment, de Gama figures that, since everyone's all together anyway, it would be an ideal place to discuss a merger with the Chinese Junk Company, which specializes in ocean-going vessels. The combined company would be known as the Cheap Junk Company. Discussion takes place, and the shareholders then present approve the merger. Has the merger received proper shareholder approval? _____

26. Popeye tires of life at sea and decides to open a chain of massage parlors, "Sweet Pea Parlors, Inc." There are 100 shares outstanding. Popeye owns 51 shares, Olive Oyl 30 and Bluto 19. Each shareholder is elected to the 3-person board of directors. At a time when each of the three stockholder/board-members has 2 1/2 years to go on his board term, Popeye sells his shares to Sea Hag. (Assume that there are no share-transfer restrictions preventing this.) The corporation's charter is silent on the issue of cumulative voting. Sea Hag wants to join the board of directors immediately (and in fact would prefer to replace all directors with ones beholden to her.) Because of bad lawyering by Sea Hag's lawyer, the share-purchase agreement did not require Popeye to resign from the board, and he refuses to do so now. The state has enacted the MBCA. What procedural step would you advise Sea Hag to take right away (and how will things work out if she takes that step)?

_____

27. Same basic facts as the prior question. Now, assume that, at a duly-noticed shareholders meeting, Olive Oil and Bluto show up, but Sea Hag doesn't. (Nor does Sea Hag give anyone else her proxy). At the meeting, Olive Oil introduces a motion to change the company's accountant. (Assume that this is a proper subject for shareholder action. Also, assume that the charter and bylaws are silent about all issues relevant to this question.)

    (a) Assume that both Olive Oil and Bluto vote their shares in favor of the motion. Is the corporation now authorized to change accountants? _____

    (b) Assume that Olive Oil votes her shares for the motion, and Bluto votes his shares against it. Putting aside any issue of procedural irregularity with respect to the holding of the meeting, has the motion passed? _____

CHAPTER 4

SHAREHOLDERS' INFORMATIONAL RIGHTS AND THE PROXY SYSTEM

28. Hannibal Lechter Foods, Inc., a privately-held company, makes a popular meal extender for cannibals, "Manburger Helper" (". . . when you need a helping hand."). Robinson Crusoe, a 1% shareholder, believes that the directors are cooking the books; however, they refuse to allow him to see the corporation's books to find out if he's right. Under the prevailing approach, does Crusoe have a right to examine the corporation's accounting records for this purpose? _____

29. The Botch Ewlism Food Company has assets of $15 million. It has 350 shareholders of preferred stock and 350 shareholders of common stock. Botch Ewlism's shares are traded over-the-counter.

    (a) Does Botch have to file annual and/or quarterly financial reports with the SEC?

_____

    (b) Is Botch subject to the SEC's proxy-solicitation rules? _____

30. Nyuck-Nyuck Corp. is a huge public company, with its shares traded on the NYSE. The management of Nyuck-Nyuck, consisting of Larry, Curly, and Moe, owns a majority of the stock. Therefore, management doesn't need proxies from anyone else in order to arrange a quorum at the annual meeting, or to cause any properly-noticed shareholder action to be approved at that meeting. Consequently, management would like to be able to skip the cumbersome step of sending anything to outside shareholders before the annual meeting. Is there anything that, according to federal proxy rules, management must send to shareholders before the meeting despite the absence of a proxy solicitation (and if so, what)? _____

32. Clampett Oil Company's stock is traded on the NYSE. Clampett's board of directors wants to merge Clampett with the Drysdale Corporation. Clampett's board has to get shareholder approval for the merger, so it sends out proxy materials soliciting proxy appointments to vote on the merger. The proxy solicitation contains the board's recommendation that the merger be approved. However, the proxy materials don't mention that, because Drysdale owns 54% of Clampett, all of Clampett's directors were named by Drysdale. (Clampett's charter does not allow cumulative voting). The merger is approved by Clampett's shareholders. Ellie May Clampett, a minority shareholder of Clampett Oil, files suit for an injunction against the transaction, on the grounds that the proxy materials omitted a material issue of fact (Drysdale's domination of Clampett's board).

(a) For this part, assume that according to Clampett's charter, the merger needed to be approved by a two-thirds majority of Clampett's shareholders. Will Ellie May get the injunction she seeks? _____

(b) For this part, assume that only a simple majority needed to approve the merger. Assume also that Ellie May wasn't initially aware of the omission about board domination, voted to approve the transaction, and then found out (after the merger went through) about the domination. She now sues in federal court for monetary damages. (Assume that state law does not allow appraisal rights in this situation, whether or not the holder votes in favor of the transaction.) Will Ellie May get damages? _____

33. Pongo has owned 10% of the voting stock of the Cruella De Vil Clothing Company for several years. Cruella De Vil stock is traded on the NYSE. Pongo hears that management intends to expand its line of furs to include dalmatian pelts, and he's furious. Pongo wants to submit a proposal under the shareholder proposal rule, 14a-8, to be included in management's proxy materials for the upcoming annual meeting. Pongo's proposal asks management to consider not manufacturing clothing made from furs, which currently account for 10% of the company's product line. Management isn't submitting a proposal on the same subject for the annual meeting. Must management include Pongo's proposal in its proxy materials? _____

34. WorldCon, a public company, issues a quarterly report to the SEC reporting that the company made $100 million that quarter. The quarterly report is accompanied by all required certifications about the accuracy of the report, signed by, among others, Bernie Fibbers, CEO and controlling shareholder of the company. Bernie knows that the $100 million of profit was obtained by improperly treating $200 million of expenses as if they had been capital expenditures (thus changing what would have been an $80 million loss into the reported $100 million profit). You are a federal prosecutor, and you have learned the above facts.

(a) What, if any, juicy federal securities-law charge can you bring against Bernie to put him away for a long time? _____

(b) What will you have to prove to win a conviction on that charge? _____

CHAPTER 5
CLOSE CORPORATIONS

35. The Three Musketeers Toy Company, a close corporation, makes war toys — "My First Uzi," "Baby's Teething Grenade," "Battlin' Scuds 'N' Patriots," etc. Aramis owns 60% of Three Musketeers' voting stock; Athos and Porthos each own 20%. Three Musketeers's board of directors has three members, who are elected via cumulative voting. Athos and Porthos agree in writing that before voting for directors they will confer and agree upon a mutually-acceptable candidate, so that they will be sure that between them they elect at least one director to the board. The agreement is to last three years. Before the very next annual meeting, Athos changes his mind and votes his shares in favor of Aramis's nominees.

(a) Is the voting agreement valid? _____

(b) Assume that the court finds the agreement valid. What relief will the court most likely award? _____

36. March Hare and Mad Hatter are minority shareholders of Alice's Wonderland Travel Adventures, Inc., a close corporation. Hare and Hatter sign a document under which both agree that Hare will have the power to vote both his own and Hatter's shares on any issue put to a shareholder vote. At the same time, Hatter also transfers physical possession of his shares to Hare. The agreement has a duration of eight years. No one knows about the agreement except the two signatories, and Hatter's shares remain listed on the corporation's books as belonging to Hatter. At the next shareholder meeting, Hatter purports to vote his shares, but Hare says that he has the power to vote them (and shows the document to the corporate secretary). The secretary goes to court for a ruling as to who may vote the shares. Assume that the MBCA is in force.

(a) If you are representing Hatter, what argument will you make to the judge? _____

(b) If you are representing Hare, what argument will you make to the judge? _____

(c) What is the most likely result? _____

37. The I-Say-Boy Dairy Company, a close corporation, has four shareholders, with Foghorn Leghorn and Miss Prissy between them owning 60% of the voting stock. The two minority shareholders are Dawg and Weasel. Foghorn and Prissy agree between themselves to elect themselves as two of the three members of the board of directors and to appoint themselves officers at a combined annual salary of $400,000, regardless of the company's level of sales and profits. Two years later (while the agreement is still in force), Foghorn and Miss Prissy stick to the agreement. The combined $400,000 in salaries is somewhat excessive in light of the company's modest sales and profits, but there's enough cash in the company till to pay the salaries for now. The agreement complies with applicable procedural statutes. Dawg sues to have the agreement declared invalid. Will he succeed? _____

39. The Jekyll & Hyde Cosmetics Company, a close corporation, has, and has always had, bylaws providing that, before a shareholder may sell his shares to a third party, the corporation has a 60-day option period during which the corporation can purchase the shares at the "book" (i.e. net asset) value as stated on the company's most recent balance sheet. This valuation method was agreed upon by the shareholders 20 years ago, at a time when book value was the most common method for valuing a business such as this one. Dr. Jekyll owns 10% of Jekyll & Hyde's shares. He wants to sell, and so notifies Jekyll & Hyde. Jekyll & Hyde's chairman, Shelley, writes back, offering the current book value, $25 a share. Jekyll balks, since the market value of the shares is now around $100 a share. (Cosmetics businesses now typically sell for a substantial multiple of book value, due to a change over the last 20 years in how the market values successful companies in this industry.) Jekyll tries to sell to Walton at $100 a share. The company refuses to issue a new certificate in Walton's name. The company seeks to rescind the sale and to compel Jekyll to accept the company's price. What result? _____

40. Ricky Ricardo is founder, chairman of the board, and president of the Ricky Ricardo Babaloo Club, Inc., a close corporation. He owns 60% of Babaloo's voting stock. When he retires, Babaloo buys some of his shares for $1,000 a share. Lucy Ricardo, a minority shareholder, immediately thereafter offers her shares to the corporation at $1,000 each. Babaloo claims it can't afford to pay that much, offering instead $400 a share. (In reality, the corporation could easily afford to pay the $1,000.)

    (a) If you represent Lucy, what argument will you make with respect to the company's obligation to Lucy? _____

    (b) Will you succeed with the argument you made in part (a)? _____

CHAPTER 6

THE DUTY OF CARE AND THE BUSINESS JUDGMENT RULE

41. Teddy Roosevelt is chairman of the board of a Delaware-chartered linen supply company, Bully Sheet, Inc. The board of directors is thinking of paying a dividend to the shareholders. (The directors are aware that the jurisdiction, like most, prohibits dividends when the effect would be to leave the corporation unable to pay its bill.) The directors therefore call in the company's chief financial officer, Ben Counter, who tells them that paying the dividend would not affect Bully Sheet's ability to meet its financial obligations. The directors

are somewhat surprised by this, since they know that the company hasn't met its payroll recently. Nonetheless, relying on Counter's report, they go ahead and declare a dividend.

(a) A shareholder subsequently brings a derivative action against the directors, trying to hold them liable for improperly paying the dividend at a time when the corporation could not in fact afford to pay it. The directors defend by claiming that they satisfied their duty of care by relying on the opinion of an expert, Counter. Who's correct? _____

(b) What could the board and shareholders of Bully Sheet do to make sure that future claims like the derivative claim in (a) could not possibly succeed? _____

42. Carlo Bonaparte is majority shareholder of the Elba Real Estate Development Corporation. His two sons, Napoleon and Joseph, are minority shareholders, as well as officers and directors of the corporation. When Carlo dies, he leaves his interest in Elba to his widow, Letizia, who also becomes a director. Napoleon, as President, asks for board approval of the use of $1 million of corporate funds to attempt to acquire the island of Sardinia from an unaffiliated third party. In a 3-hour board meeting to consider the acquisition, Letizia and Joseph ask a number of questions, to which Napoleon gives answers that seem at least superficially reasonable. The board also reads a report on the proposed acquisition prepared by the company's accountants; the report concludes that the acquisition will probably be profitable, and that the price, though high, is within a reasonable range. At the conclusion of the meeting, Letizia says, "Well, I'd prefer that we stockpile our cash rather than going into this somewhat risky venture, but Nappy, if you really think it'll work out ok, I'll support you despite my doubts, because you've got a good feel for these real-estate purchase deals and I trust you to make money for the company."

Joseph votes against the acquisition, but between Letizia and Napoleon the proposal has enough votes to pass. A typical reasonably-able real estate investor would probably have voted against the transaction, because the price was about 25% above prevailing prices for such property, and the financial risks were clearly visible. The acquisition proves disastrously unprofitable, and causes the company to go broke. Joseph sues Letizia, alleging that she violated her duty of due care in voting for the acquisition.

(a) If you represent Letizia, what doctrine would you assert as a reason for holding Letizia not liable? _____

(b) If you make the argument referred to in part (a), what will be the likely result of the suit? _____

44. Frank N. Stein wants to incorporate in Delaware his business, Frankie's Body Shop, which sells cadavers to be used in medical research. In order to lure qualified directors to his board, he agrees to put a clause in the articles of incorporation attempting to insulate the directors from breaches of the duty of care.

(a) Assume that the clause says, "No director shall be liable for money damages of any sort, arising from the violation of the duty of due care, regardless of the nature of the act or omission giving rise to the violation." Will the clause be enforceable as written? _____

(b) Assume that the clause says, "No director shall be liable for money damages arising from the violation of the duty of due care, so long as the director acted in good faith, without knowingly violating any statute or other law, and without obtaining any improper personal benefit." Will clause be enforceable as written? _____

CHAPTER 7
THE DUTY OF LOYALTY

46. The Addams Shroud Company provides funeral supplies. It has seven directors — Gomez, Morticia, Puggsley, Wednesday, Fester, Lurch, and Cousin Itt. Of the seven, four of them — Gomez, Morticia, Wednesday, and Puggsley — are also major shareholders of the Arsenic and Old Lace Fabric Company, which makes, among other things, black fabric. The Addams Shroud Company uses a lot of black fabric that it buys from various suppliers. Gomez negotiates a requirements contract on Addams Shroud's behalf with Arsenic and Old Lace. When it comes time for the Addams's board to approve the contract, the four "interested" directors abstain (after making sure that the others know the full details of the conflict and of the contract). The three remaining directors vote, 2-1, to approve the contract. The dissenter argues that the contract has not been properly approved, because a quorum of the board did not participate in the decision. Has the Addams's board properly approved the contract, in a manner that will immunize the contract from attack on conflict grounds? _____

47. The Enterprise Tribble Company makes funny toys called, predictably enough, tribbles. James Kirk is one of the five directors of Enterprise. He is also majority shareholder of Romulan Card Stores, a chain of greeting card and novelty toy stores. Kirk believes that Romulan can sell Enterprise's entire tribble output. Romulan and Enterprise negotiate a contract, whereby Romulan agrees to pay $5 per tribble (a fair price based on what the parties know at the time), for two years, for 1,000,000 tribbles per year (which is likely to be most of Enterprise's output). Kirk fully discloses his conflict and the material elements of the contract to the other, disinterested members of the Enterprise board, who unanimously approve the contract. It comes as a surprise to everyone when tribbles feature prominently in a Star Trek episode shortly after the contract goes into effect, such that the demand for tribbles — and the price Romulan can charge for them — skyrockets. A minority shareholder of Enterprise, Scotty, can't take it any longer, and files a derivative lawsuit against Kirk, citing the unfairness of the deal and seeking to void it on grounds of conflict of interest. What result? _____

48. Mr. Bill is president of Sluggo Storage Systems, Inc. He earns $150,000 per year in that post. The company has no provision for a pension or death benefit for Mr. Bill (or for any other worker). Mr. Bill is killed in a freak accident when he is run over by a steamroller. At the next board meeting, the board unanimously votes to pay Mrs. Bill, Mr. Bill's widow, an annual pension of $75,000.

(a) You represent Spot, a minority shareholder of Sluggo. Spot is not too happy about the pension, but can't think of any grounds upon which to object. What grounds would you recommend? _____

(b) Will the grounds for objection that you recommended in part (a) be successful?

_____

49. Mona Lisa Burgers, Inc. — "the burgers with the mysterious sauce" — is an enormous (and rapidly expanding) fast-food chain. Mike Angelo owns 5% of Mona Lisa's outstanding shares, which are publicly traded. Mike is not an officer or director of Mona Lisa, however. Mike knows (as anyone who reads the local business press would know) that Mona Lisa is considering putting a restaurant into the fast-growing suburb of David. Through friends on the David Township planning and zoning board, Mike learns the location of a new freeway that is about to be built through David. He snaps up nearby real estate, knowing that traffic will skyrocket, as will the value of the property. Mike never offers the property to Mona Lisa. Instead, he opens a fast-food restaurant of his own, Sistine Chicken & Ribs.

   (a) Mona Lisa sues Mike for usurpation of a corporate opportunity, claiming (quite accurately) that the land would be ideal for a Mona Lisa burger joint. Is Mike likely to be liable? _____

   (b) Would Mike be liable if, in addition to the above facts, Mike were an outside (i.e., non-employee) director of Mona Lisa? _____

   (c) Would Mike be liable if he was not a director or stockholder at all, but was Mona Lisa's Senior Vice President in charge of sales and marketing? _____

51. Peter Pan is a senior executive, and one of seven board members, of the huge, public Darling Pharmaceuticals Company. Darling's area of focus is cancer treatment and prevention. Peter Pan learns about research at Hook University concerning "fairy dust," whose main value is that it makes people fly, but whose secondary value is that people who take it and fly are less likely to get cancer. Peter thinks that fairy dust represents a great commercial opportunity. He calls the chairman and 5% owner of Darling Pharmaceuticals, Wendy Darling, and discusses the opportunity with her at length (making full disclosure of what he thinks the benefits will be). Peter finally says, "So, whaddya think? Shouldn't Darling Pharmaceuticals be in on a deal like this?" Wendy pauses and says, "Naaaah. You take it." Peter buys the rights to fairy dust for himself, and it quickly becomes wildly successful. The corporation sues Peter on grounds of usurping a corporate opportunity.

   (a) If you represent Peter, what defense will you raise? _____

   (b) Will this defense be successful? _____

   (c) Suppose fairy dust merely helps people fly, but doesn't prevent cancer. Assuming that the defense you raised in part (a) is unavailable, has Peter usurped a corporate opportunity? _____

52. Peter Minuit is vice president of the New England Potato Company, which owns vast tracts of land in New York on which it grows potatoes. He learns through friends that Chief Firewater is willing to sell Manhattan Island, prime potato-growing land in New York, for $24. Peter knows that New England Potato is hard-pressed financially, doesn't have $24 on hand, and probably couldn't borrow it from a bank. He therefore doesn't mention the opportunity to New England Potato's board or president, and instead buys

Manhattan with his own funds, with an eye toward putting a big apple orchard there. New England Potato sues Peter for usurpation of a corporate opportunity.

   (a) If you represent Peter, what's the main defense that you should raise. _____

   (b) Is this defense likely to be successful? _____

53. Abner Doubleday is a 55% shareholder of the NASDAQ-listed Splendid Splinter Baseball Bat Company, Inc. The fair market value of Splendid Splinter's stock on NASDAQ is $20. Doubleday decides he wants to give up the bat business and go into something really lucrative — forging sports memorabilia. Scuff Spitballer, a reputable businessman, offers to buy Doubleday's shares for $30 each, if he's willing to sell all of them. Doubleday accepts the offer. Splendid Splinter's minority shareholders sue Doubleday on behalf of Splendid Splinter, seeking the $10 premium he received for his shares over fair market value. Who wins? _____

54. Ali Baba Art Galleries, Inc., buys and sells fabulously expensive works of art. Ali Baba, controlling shareholder of the galleries, sells his shares to Scheherezade, at a price $20 a share above market value. Scheherezade immediately begins to sell to herself the Galleries's inventory of art works at grossly understated prices. By the time minority shareholders wake up and sue Scheherezade, she has secreted the works (apparently in the vaults of an unidentified Swiss bank), and is thus effectively judgment-proof.

   (a) You represent one of the minority holders. On what theory might you sue Ali Baba for the difference between the true value of the artworks sold by Scheherezade to herself and the price she paid? _____

   (b) State the factors (not necessarily ones presented explicitly in the above statement of facts) that, if proved at trial, would support your theory of recovery. _____

55. The Sleeping Beauty Sewing Machine Company has seven directors. Its shares are publicly traded, with a price hovering around $10 a share. Evil Stepmother decides she wants to acquire control of the company. Evil Stepmother approaches five of the directors — Grumpy, Dopey, Sleepy, Bashful, and Doc — and asks them to sign a document in which they agree that they will (1) immediately resign and (2) as a final act on the board, vote for Evil's nominees as their successors as directors. The document also states that Evil will pay each director $20 a share for his shares. The five directors together own about 7% of the company's stock. (The President owns about 25% of the stock, and the rest is held by the public at large.) The directors sign the agreement, then resign and vote as they've agreed to do.

   (a) What is the best theory under which a minority holder in the company could sue the 5 resigning directors? _____

   (b) Will that theory succeed? _____

CHAPTER 8
INSIDER TRADING

56. Aquaman is president of a marine research company, Wet Dreams, Inc. On April 1, the research director of Wet Dreams tells Aquaman they've come up with "Oxygum," a means of breathing underwater by chewing a special kind of gum. Aquaman knows a great product when he hears it. He delays announcing the invention to the public, so he can buy up all the Wet Dreams stock he can get his hands on. Sure enough, when Aquaman makes the announcement, the price of Wet Dreams stock immediately rises from $1 to $50 a share.

    (a) What SEC rule, if any, is Aquaman likely to have violated? _____

    (b) Has Aquaman in fact violated that rule? _____

57. Choo Choo Charlie is president of Good, Inc., a manufacturer of black licorice candy, whose common stock is traded on the NYSE. He negotiates an acquisition of Plenty, Inc., a company that makes hard candy coatings. After the acquisition, the company will be known as Good & Plenty, Inc. Once the main terms of the acquisition are finalized, Choo Choo Charlie waits a week before announcing it in a press release, so that Plenty can notify one of its vacationing directors. During that week, a Good shareholder, Olive Oyl, sells 1,000 shares of her Good stock at the market price, $10 a share. When Choo Choo Charlie finally announces the acquisition, Good stock rockets to $15 a share. Olive brings a private action against Charlie for violating SEC Rule 10b-5. Will Olive recover?

_____

58. Richard Squishy, CEO of HealthNorth Corp., has just learned from his CFO that the company has earned lower-than-expected profits for the just-completed quarter. He sells 100,000 shares of stock for gross proceeds of $2 million before the lower profits are announced to the public. When sued by the SEC for insider trading, he argues, "I concede that I knew about the lower earnings. However, I made the sale not for that reason, but because I needed the $2 million for a new house that I was contractually obligated to pay $3 million for the next week." Assuming that the trier of fact believes that Squishy is telling the truth about his motivation, is he liable for insider trading? _____

59. Santa Claus is president of publicly traded Hohoho, Inc., a company that makes wooden toys and delivers them to children all over the world on Christmas Eve, charging parents. Hohoho's marketing VP, Rudolph Reindeer, convinces Santa that there are big "bucks" to be made in buying toys from other manufacturers and passing them on to parents at a higher price. On July 1, Santa negotiates a huge contract with Skintendo Computer Games. Santa then waits until July 15 before he announces the contract in a press release. During the period from July 2 through July 14, Santa buys 10,000 shares of Hohoho at $10. After the announcement, the shares quickly rise in price to $15. Then, over the next 2 months, they rise to $25. Cindy Lou Hoo, who dabbles in stock as a hobby, files a private 10b-5 claim against Santa. Cindy Loo alleges that: (1) she already owned 2,000 shares of Hohoho as of July 1; and (2) she would have bought an additional 1,000 shares of Hohoho stock on July 3, had Santa disclosed the Skintendo contract promptly. She therefore claims that Santa's failing to promptly disclose the contract, while trading in the stock, has cost Cindy Lou profits she would have made. Assuming that the court believes Cindy Lou's factual assertions, will Cindy Lou recover (and if so, how much)? _____

60. The Nat King Coal Mining Company is always drilling at new test sites. One such site, on Nomansan Island, is quite positive. Nat King's chief geologist tells company insiders that in his judgment, there's a 30% chance that the Nomansan site has commercial quantities of coal; he also tells them that if the site is in fact commercially viable at all, it's probably a huge find, which will at least double the company's proven reserves. Immediately (and before anything is said to the public), the corporation's vice president of operations, Cole Dust, buys up all the Nat King Coal stock he can afford. Sure enough, the find turns out to be commercially viable, the stock price skyrockets, and Cole's a rich man. The SEC sues him for insider-trading in violation of 10b-5.

   (a) If you represent Cole, what defense would you offer? _____

   (b) Will the defense you raise in (a) succeed? _____

61. James Bond is sitting at a bar drinking a vodka martini, shaken not stirred. He overhears a man nearby telling a friend about how his company has secretly been buying up gold bullion on the world market, to such an extent that it now controls the market. Bond looks up and recognizes the man as Auric Goldfinger, chairman of the publicly traded Twenty-Four Carat Corp. Bond checks out the financial papers and finds out that this information hasn't been made public. He buys up all the Twenty-Four Carat Corporation stock he can, and, sure enough, when the information becomes public, the stock price skyrockets. Has Bond insider-traded in violation of Rule 10b-5? _____

62. D.B. Cooper is president of Cooper Printing, Inc., a publicly traded company. He goes out for drinks one night at the Parachute Inn. He meets a woman, Brenda Starr, and they share a few cocktails. D.B. doesn't hold his alcohol too well, and he blabs to Starr that the reason Cooper Printing is doing so well is that, when the presses aren't busy, they print counterfeit money. He adds that the FBI is hot on their tracks, and will probably discover the counterfeiting operation soon. It never occurs to D.B. that he's conveying commercially-valuable information. However, Brenda drinks in this hot tip and, the next day, sells short as much Cooper Printing stock as she can. (That is, she sells borrowed shares, hoping the price will fall and she can buy them back at a lower price, pocketing the difference.) The SEC discovers all of the above facts, and charges Brenda with insider trading in violation of Rule 10b-5. Is Brenda liable? _____

63. "King" Lear is director of research at the Bard of Avon Company, which produces men's cosmetics. A researcher at Bard of Avon, Dorian Gray, comes up with a treatment that stops aging. Lear knows a gold mine when he sees one, and, before the breakthrough is announced, he buys all the Bard of Avon shares he can afford — 10,000 shares at $5 a share — on the NYSE. That same day, Lady Macbeth sells 50,000 Bard of Avon shares at $5 a share. The following day, Gray's treatment is announced by Bard of Avon's president, Shakespeare, and the stock price shoots up to $10 a share. Lady Macbeth brings a claim against Lear for insider trading, under the federal statute giving an express private right of action in these circumstances. Assuming that Lady M. proves all elements of her

claim, how much will she recover? _____

66. McSpeedy Gonzales is a corporation that runs a chain of very fast food restaurants. Mary McCheese, a stockbroker for the firm of Merrily Lynchem, tells Sylvester Katt in a phone conversation that McSpeedy Gonzales has just reported profits of $2 a share for the most recent quarter, and that in McCheese's opinion the stock is an excellent buy. McCheese knows that in fact the company has made only a $1 per share profit (down from the prior year), and that the $2 figure is due to a computational error by Merrily's fast-food analyst. Sylvester relies on his conversation with McCheese, and buys 1,000 shares of McSpeedy. The truth about McSpeedy's earnings comes out a week later, and the stock tanks. Sylvester sues McCheese for a 10b-5 violation. McCheese defends on two grounds: (1) that she neither bought nor sold McSpeedy stock at any time; and (2) that she was not a McSpeedy corporate insider, nor did she learn her information by means of a breach by anyone of a fiduciary duty to McSpeedy. Therefore, she says, she can't have violated 10b-5. If McCheese's two factual assertions are correct, which, if either, of McCheese's defenses is valid? _____

67. Joker is the president of the Metropolis By-Products Company, whose shares are publicly traded. Joker buys 11,000 Metropolis shares at $10 each on March 15. The by-products business is booming, and the shares are trading at $15 by June 1. On that fateful day, Joker trips on a catwalk at the factory and falls into a vat of chemicals. His ensuing medical bills are enormous, compelling him to sell 1,000 of the shares for $15 each on June 15. At the moment he sells the shares, Joker doesn't know anything about the company's operations that the general public doesn't know.

> **(a)** You represent Robin, who owns a small number of Metropolis shares. What federal securities claim might you make against Joker? _____
>
> **(b)** Will your claim succeed? _____
>
> **(c)** Assuming the claim succeeds, how much will you recover, and to whom will it go?

_____

68. Fairy Godmother decides she's a real bozo for making wishes come true for nothing. As a result, she incorporates under the name Magic Wand, Inc., and begins taking on Fairy Godmother trainees, whom she teaches to perform miracles. The company grows by leaps and bounds, until it has sales of $100 million annually and has shares traded on the NYSE. Fairy Godmother owns 15% of Magic Wand's common stock. On March 1, she buys another 5,000 shares of the common stock at $10, and sells 1,000 shares at $15 on April 1. On May 1, Rex Judicata, a lawyer, reads about these transactions. On June 1, he buys 50 shares of Magic Wand stock, and immediately pursues a derivative claim on Magic Wand's behalf, seeking Fairy Godmother's profit under §16(b). Does Judicata have standing to pursue the claim? _____

70. Calvin buys 1,000 shares of Hobbes Fantasy Vacations, Inc. stock at $10 a share on May 1. On June 1, Calvin is elected to Hobbes's board of directors. On July 1, he sells his 1,000 shares for $15 apiece. A 16(b) claim is filed against him. Will Calvin be liable under §16(b)? _____

71. Albert Einstein is president of the Gone Fission Toy Company, which makes nuclear-powered toys. Gone Fission's stock is traded on the NYSE. On April 1, Einstein buys 500 shares of Gone Fission at $11 each. On May 1, he sells 500 shares at $8 each. On June 1, he buys 1,000 shares at $5 each. On July 1, he sells 1,000 shares at $6 each. If Einstein is sued under §16(b), how much, if anything, will he owe to Gone Fission? _____

CHAPTER 9

SHAREHOLDERS' SUITS

72. Chateau Marmoset, Inc., is a winery. Its board of directors wants to reduce the market price of Chateau Marmoset's shares (so insiders can buy the shares up more cheaply). Therefore, the board refuses to declare a dividend. This does, in fact, drive down the price of Chateau Marmoset stock. A Chateau Marmoset minority shareholder, Cher Donnay, brings suit against the directors to force them to pay a dividend.

　　(a) If you represent Cher, would you prefer that the court characterize your suit as a derivative suit, or a direct suit? _____

　　(b) How will the court in fact characterize your suit? _____

73. The Peter Minuit Real Estate Development Corp. has seven directors. One of them, Chief Floating Zone, owns an island he wants the company to buy from him for $24 and some subway tokens. (All directors are aware that Floating Zone owns the island.) There is some evidence before the board that the price is perhaps 20-30% above market rates. Five of the seven directors (one of whom is Floating Zone himself) vote to approve the transaction; the other two dissent. The transaction goes through. Manny Hattan, a Peter Minuit shareholder, bring a derivative claim against Floating Zone for self-dealing, and against the other four board members for breaching their duty of care in approving the high-priced transaction. (Hatten has not first made a demand on the board that they bring the suit instead of him.) The company files a motion to dismiss for failure to make a demand on directors. Assume that Delaware law is to be followed.

　　(a) What argument should Hatten make about why demand on the board should be excused? _____

　　(b) Will this argument succeed? _____

74. Snow White is a shareholder of Seven Dwarfs Microcomputers, Inc., which has seven directors. The Munchkinsoft Computer Co. makes a secret offer to the board of Seven Dwarfs to buy Seven Dwarfs at $25 a share. The directors instead collectively ask Munchkinsoft to give each director a consulting contract; in return, the directors promise to recommend to the shareholders that they accept *$20* a share for the Seven Dwarfs stock. The sale is approved at the $20 figure in part due to the directors' recommendation (which doesn't mention the $25 offer or the consulting contracts). The true facts about the recommendation later emerge. Snow White brings a derivative suit against the directors without first making a demand on them that they remedy the situation. The directors claim that the suit should be dismissed due to failure to make a demand on directors.

(a) Assume that Delaware law applies. What result? _____

(b) Assume that the MBCA applies. What result? _____

77. Hannibal Lechter Foods, Inc., makes a popular meal extender for cannibals, "Manburger Helper" ("... when you need a helping hand.").[1] The corporation is incorporated in (and based in) the mythical state of Atlantis. Robinson Crusoe, a 1% shareholder, believes that the directors are cooking the books; however, they refuse to allow him to see the corporation's books to find out if he's right. Nineteen other shareholders have the same problem. Among them, Crusoe and the other nineteen shareholders own 3% of the corporation's shares. When they sue the corporation in Atlantis state court to enforce their state-law right to inspect the books, the corporation asks that they be required to post bond for the corporation's litigation expenses. The Atlantis security-for-expenses statute is mandatory when the plaintiffs in a derivative suit own less than 10% of a corporation's outstanding shares. Will Crusoe and the other plaintiff/shareholders have to comply with the statute? _____

78. Catherine of Aragon is one of the directors of Henry VIII Dating Service, Inc. In her position as board member, she encourages Henry VIII to acquire another company, Marie Antoinette Cakes, Inc. Unbeknownst to the shareholders or directors of Henry VIII, Catherine is a large, secret shareholder in Marie Antoinette. Catherine honestly (and reasonably) believes that the acquisition, at the proposed price, will be beneficial to Henry VIII. After the acquisition goes through, a Henry VIII shareholder, Anne Boleyn, brings a derivative suit against Catherine, alleging that Catherine violated her duty of loyalty to Henry VIII by not disclosing the conflict. Catherine spends $20,000 litigating the suit; just before it goes to trial, she settles for a payment of $50,000 to the corporation. Henry VIII's charter authorizes indemnification of any director "for any liability which the director may have to the corporation for any breach of any obligation to the corporation, regardless of whether the director shall have acted in good faith." Catherine wishes to have Henry VIII indemnify her for both her $20,000 in litigation expenses and her $50,000 in settlement payments. The corporation wishes to pay these sums to Catherine, but wants to know whether it may properly do so.

(a) Under the prevailing approach, what result? _____

(b) Under the MBCA, what result? _____

(c) Assume now that the case went to trial. The court found that Henry VIII had paid a price that was $50,000 higher than a "fair" price for Marie Antoinette Cakes, and that this was due in part to Catherine's urging of the transaction, coupled with her failure to disclose her secret ownership interest in Marie Antoinette. The court therefore entered a judgment for $50,000 against Catherine in favor of Henry VIII. Catherine now seeks indemnification from Henry VIII for the $50,000 judgment, plus her litigation expenses (now $30,000). Henry VIII is willing to pay these sums. What, if anything, may Henry VIII properly pay her, under the MBCA? _____

---

1. Yes, we know you've seen this cheap pun (and this cheap basic fact pattern) before (p. 192). But we've varied the facts this time.

CHAPTER 10

STRUCTURAL CHANGES

79. Guano Building Supplies Inc. has a thriving business recycling wild bird refuse into building bricks. Guano's board of directors votes to sell all of Guano's assets to the Rin Tin Tin House Construction Company.

    (a) The directors of Guano call a shareholder meeting to vote on the sale. At the meeting, holders of 60% of the corporation's stock are present. 60% of the shares present are voted in favor of the sale. According to the majority rule, has the sale been approved by the shareholders? _____

    (b) Same facts as (a), but now assume that the case is governed by the MBCA rather than by the majority rule. Has the sale been approved by the shareholders? _____

80. Same facts as in prior question. Now, the directors of Rin Tin Tin vote to make the acquisition of Guano. They do not call for a shareholder meeting to vote on the acquisition. Under the majority approach, is the acquisition duly authorized without a shareholders' vote? _____

81. Sampson, Inc., manufactures beauty supplies. It has 100,000 shares of voting stock outstanding. Its board resolves that Sampson should purchase Delilah's Hairdressers, Inc., a chain of beauty parlors. To effectuate the merger, Sampson will issue 25,000 shares of authorized but previously-unissued stock to Delilah's shareholders. Whose shareholders must approve the transaction: Sampson's, Delilah's, both, or neither? _____

83. The Paleolyric Music Publishing Co. owns 92% of the stock of the Tyrannosaurus Lex Publishing Co. Tyrannosaurus's and Paleolyric's boards of directors approve a merger, with Paleolyric to be the survivor. They file a plan of merger with the jurisdiction's Secretary of State, saying that the merger was duly approved. Terry Dactyl, a 2% owner of Tyrannosaurus, seeks to rescind the merger on grounds of lack of a shareholder vote. Assume that Delaware law applies, and that any special procedural requirements have been satisfied. What result? _____

84. Salome founds a successful privately-held company, Seven Veils Dancing Schools, Inc. Seven Veils's board of directors votes to merge the company into the Gypsy Moth Lee Costume Company, with Seven Veils holders getting one share of Gypsy Moth in exchange for each share they hold of Seven Veils. A Seven Veils's shareholder, John Baptist, opposes the merger, because he believes that a share of Gypsy Moth will prove to be worth much less than a pre-merger share of Seven Veils.

    (a) If you represent John Baptist, what would you advise him to do? _____

    (b) What procedural steps will John have to take in order to implement your recommendation in part (a)? _____

(c) Assuming that John takes your advice, and carries out all procedurally-required steps, what is the likely outcome? _____

85. Same basic facts as prior question. Now, however, assume that Seven Veils is traded on the New York Stock Exchange, and has several hundred million dollars of annual revenues. Assume also that John makes a demand for appraisal, and takes all required procedural steps.

(a) If Seven Veils is a Delaware corporation, will John be entitled to appraisal? _____

(b) If Seven Veils is incorporated in a state that follows the MBCA, will John be entitled to appraisal? _____

87. Little Joe gets tired of working at the Ponderosa Ranch, and decides to start up a chain of hotels, Horsepitality Inns, Inc. About 20 other investors join him. A few years later, another chain, Mare-iott Hotels, Inc., a public company, proposes a plan of merger, whereby each Horsepitality holder will exchange his shares for an equal number of shares in Mare-iott. (Mare-iott has 1,000,000 shares issued and outstanding before the merger, and proposes to issue 100,000 new ones to Horsepitality holders in the exchange.) The boards of both companies approve the transactions, and the holders of each company approve the transaction by majority vote. (Mare-iott's holders don't have a formal right of approval under state law, but Mare-iott's board decides to solicit their consent anyway.) Answer the following two questions by reference to prevailing law (as opposed to the law of any particular jurisdiction).

(a) Hoss Cartwright, a Horsepitality holder, votes in favor of the merger. Shortly after the vote, and before the share exchange is consummated, Mare-iott releases very poor quarterly earnings, and Hoss no longer wishes to receive Mare-iott stock in exchange for his Horsepitality stock. Assuming that Hoss acts in a timely manner, can Hoss now assert appraisal rights? _____

(b) Wyatt Earp is a holder of Mare-iott prior to the merger. He votes against the merger. Assuming that he acts in a timely manner, can Earp now assert appraisal rights? _____

88. The Long Silver Company and the Dong Bell Company plan to merge, with Long Silver disappearing and its holders getting .5 shares of Dong Bell for each share of Long Silver they hold. The merger is approved by the boards and shareholders of both companies. Paul Revere, a Long Silver shareholder, votes against the merger (but does not demand appraisal). After the merger is approved, and before it is consummated, Revere sues in state court for an injunction against consummation. Revere's complaint asserts that the Long Silver stockholders are getting far less in assets and in "business value" than they are giving up. Revere's complaint does not make any other allegations of unfairness or wrongdoing on the part of either Long Silver, Dong Bell, or their directors or officers.

(a) If you represent the Long Silver board of directors, what procedural argument should you make in support of a motion to dismiss Revere's suit? _____

(b) Will the argument you make in (a) be successful, under the prevailing view? _____

89. Moby Dick Cruise Lines, Inc. — "Have a whale of a time with us" — has two classes of stock: preferred and common. It has 10,000 shares of nonvoting preferred outstanding and 40,000 shares of common. In order to raise funds, Moby Dick's board votes to authorize a new class of preferred shares with cumulative dividends of $5 a year. The existing preferred shares are noncumulative. At a valid shareholders' meeting, 30,000 of the common shares and 2,000 of the preferred shares are voted in favor of the amendment, and 5,000 of the common shares and 1,500 of the preferred shares voted against. (There were no abstentions.) The applicable statute and the corporation's charter, as a general principle, allow charter amendments based on a simple majority. The charter is silent about what constitutes a quorum.

(a) Assume that because the new class would have rights superior to the preferred shares, a state statute gives the preferred shareholders the right to vote separately on the issue. Under the majority approach, has the amendment been approved? _____

(b) Under the MBCA, has the amendment been approved? _____

90. Big Bad Wolf is the majority shareholder of the publicly-traded Red Riding Hood Grocery Delivery Service, Inc. Wolf doesn't want to share any of the business with the company's minority shareholders. As a result, at a properly-convened shareholders' meeting, he votes to sell all of Red Riding Hood's assets to another of his businesses, the Grandma Costume Company, at a fair price in an all-cash transaction. In documents sent to holders before this vote, Wolf makes full disclosure to the other holders about the value of the business and the nature of the proposed transaction. The founder of the company — Red R. Hood herself — who is now only a minority shareholder, opposes the transaction, because she thinks the delivery business will continue to grow and she doesn't want to be cashed out. In fact, nearly all of the holders apart from Wolf vote against the transaction, because they feel the same way as Red does. But because Wolf holds a majority and votes in favor of the transaction, it's approved. The sale of assets takes place, and Red is left with cash for her shares and no part of the business.

(a) If Red R. Hood sues in federal court to unwind the transaction or for damages, on the theory that Wolf unfairly eliminated all other holders from the ownership of the business, is Red likely to get relief? _____

(b) If Red sues in state court for an unwinding or for damages, on the same theory of unfairness, is she likely to get relief? _____

91. As of January, 2005, Glory Hallelujah owns 2% of the outstanding common shares of a publicly traded defense contractor, the Terrible Swift Sword Corp. Glory doesn't announce her intent to increase her holdings, nor does she solicit any other shareholders to sell to her. However, in February, 2005, Glory goes on a buying binge, snapping up Terrible Swift Sword shares on the open market until her holdings total 8% of the company's outstanding common shares. What step, if any, does federal statutory law require Glory to take, and when? _____

93. Charlie owns 3% of the stock in the Willy Wonka Chocolate Factory, Inc., a public company. He wants to increase his holdings to 6%. On June 1, he makes a tender offer to the other shareholders, seeking 600,000 shares at $5 a share. The offer is to be open one month. After two weeks, only 200,000 shares have been deposited with Charlie. As a result, on June 15 Charlie raises the offer to $8 a share to induce additional shareholders to sell. Coco Nutt has already tendered her 5,000 shares on June 10, in response to the $5 offer. Assuming that Charlie buys some shares at the $8 figure, what price must he pay Coco Nutt for those of her shares that he wants to purchase? _____

94. Mickey wants to take over the Mouse Von Trapp Company, a public company. On March 1, Mickey launches a tender offer of $10 a share for all of Mouse Von Trapp's common shares, the offer to remain open until April 15. On March 15, Minnie tenders her 100 shares to Mickey. On April 1, Pluto launches an offer to all Mouse Von Trapp shareholders at $12 a share. Can Minnie revoke her acceptance and accept Pluto's offer? _____

95. Richie Rich intends to eventually make an offer to purchase a majority of the shares of the Getrich Qwik Food Company. For the time being, however, he contents himself with a spending spree, buying up 15% of Getrich Qwik's common stock on the open market. (He files all required disclosure documents in a timely manner.) Has Richie violated any law by failing to make a formal tender offer and by failing to follow the Williams Act's procedural rules for tender offers (e.g., the rule that offers must be open for at least 20 business days)? _____

96. Queen Victoria is chairman of the board of a publishing conglomerate, Not Amused Publications, Inc., which is publicly held and which is incorporated in Delaware. Queen owns about 3% of Not Amused's common stock. Albert Prince owns Hanover Press, a rival publisher. After first trying (unsuccessfully) to convince Queen Victoria to merge Not Amused with one of his companies, on April 1, 2005, Albert launches a tender offer to Not Amused's common shareholders at $60 per share. (The market price before the tender offer was $40.) As of April 1, Albert holds only a trivial amount of Not Amused stock. In an effort to fend off the attack, the Not Amused board immediately votes to issue to every Not Amused stockholder of record on March 30 a "special call." This special call gives the holder the right to buy an additional share of Not Amused for $1. The special call will become exercisable only if there is a "change of control" in Not Amused, defined as the acquisition of 20% or more of Not Amused stock by a person who, as of March 30, 2005, owned less than 1% of the stock. The call also provides that it may not be exercised by any person who at the time of exercise owns more than 20% of Not Amused. Finally, the call provides that if Not Amused is merged into some other entity controlled by a person who has acquired a more-than-20% stake in Not Amused, the call may be exercised against the surviving entity.

(a) What is the popular name for the anti-takeover device which the Not Amused board has attempted to put into place? _____

(b) Do the shareholders of Not Amused need to approve the device before it becomes effective? (Assume that Not Amused has a sufficient number of authorized-but-not-outstanding shares that even if all the calls were issued and exercised, the number of shares would not exceed the authorized number.) _____

   (c) In what court — Delaware state, or federal — does Albert have the best chance of getting the device invalidated? _____

   (d) What is the likely outcome of a suit brought in the court you identified in part (c)? _____

97. James Bond makes a hostile tender offer for all shares of Her Majesty's Secret Laundry Service, Inc., a Delaware company, at $30 per share. Her Majesty's Secret has no controlling shareholder or group — it's held by the public at large. The directors of Her Majesty's Secret decide that the company is now "in play," and that control will almost inevitably change, one way or another. The board therefore grants a "crown jewels" option to SMERSH, Inc., another public company. Under this option, SMERSH has the right to buy, at a below-market price, Her Majesty's most valuable subsidiary, which owns all the company's washing machines and dryers. (The board of Her Majesty knows that another bidder is not very likely to acquire Her Majesty without this subsidiary.) The board has given SMERSH this option because the board thinks that SMERSH will keep Her Majesty's existing executives in their posts and will treat the existing board members fairly — the board fears that Bond will not do either. The board has also begun to negotiate a merger agreement with SMERSH for the whole company, at a price of $31 (but the negotiations have not yet been completed). Bond goes to Delaware state court to get an order invalidating the option. Will Bond succeed, and why? _____

CHAPTER 11
DIVIDENDS AND
SHARE REPURCHASES

98. In late 2006, Cleopatra founds a chain of pet stores, the "You Bet Your Asp" Stores, Inc. You Bet Your Asp sells 500 shares of its $5 par-value common stock for $10 a share. At the same time, it sells another 500 $5 par value common shares in return for retail space to be occupied by it in the future, worth $2,500 total.

   (a) What is You Bet Your Asp's stated capital (and why might it matter)? _____

   (b) Assume that You Bet Your Asp makes a profit of exactly $0 in its first year of operations, 2007. Assume further that it hasn't yet used the rental space worth $2500. Ignore issues of insolvency. In a state allowing the payment of dividends out of any sort of surplus (whether earned or unearned), how much in dividends may You Bet pay, in early 2008? _____

99. The balance sheet of the 100 Dalmatians Restaurant — don't ask what happened to the 101st dalmatian — looks like this:

Assets		Liabilities & Owners' Equity	
Cash	$300	Current Liabilities	$100
Inventory	$100	Long-term debt	$400
Other Assets	$400	Owners' Equity:	
		Stated Capital	$ 50
		Paid-In Surplus	$100
		Retained Earnings	$150

(a) Assume that the state of Disney, in which the restaurant is incorporated, follows the strict "earned surplus" test for determining sources of dividends. Assume further that the state also uses the balance-sheet test for insolvency. What's the most 100 Dalmatians could pay out in dividends? _____

(b) Now, assume that the state follows the MBCA's rules on when dividend payments are allowed. What's the most 100 Dalmatians could pay out in dividends?

_____

100. Jed Clampett discovers oil on his property, and begins selling it under the auspices of his Clampett General Store, Inc. His balance sheet, prepared by his very conservative accountant, looks like this:

Assets		Liabilities & Owners' Equity	
Cash	$ 50	Current Liabilities	$100
Oil reserves, at cost	$ 400	Long-term debt	$200
		Owners' Equity:	
		Stated Capital	$ 50
		Paid-in Surplus	$ 50
		Retained Earnings	$ 50

Jed has just received an appraisal of his oil reserves, done by an expert. That appraisal shows that the fair market value of the reserves is now $1,000 (compared with the $400 Jed paid to acquire them). Jed would like to declare as big a dividend as possible. Assume that the state's dividend statute allows payments out of any source of capital surplus, whether earned or unearned. Assume also that the balance-sheet method is the state's only test for insolvency.

(a) What change should Jed make to his balance sheet, and how should he go about making that change? _____

(b) Can Jed pay a $600 dividend after taking the step you recommend in (a)?

_____

102. The directors of the Universal Solvent Soup Company declare a $5 a share dividend on the corporation's 1,000 shares of common stock, payable out of the company's cash on hand. Minnie Strone, who owns 50 common shares of Universal Solvent, receives her $250 dividend.

(a) Assume that the company was insolvent at the time of the dividend payment, and that the payment was therefore a violation of state law. Assume further that Minnie had no knowledge of the company's financial position, and thus neither knew nor had reason to know that the company was insolvent. Under the common-law rule, could Universal Solvent's creditors recover the $250 from Minnie (assuming that Universal Solvent refuses to sue her)? _____

(b) Same facts. Now, however, assume that the company was not insolvent at the time of the payment, but that the company had no retained earnings at the moment of payment. The jurisdiction prohibits dividends except out of retained earnings. Again, assume that Minnie did not know, and had no reason to know, that the payment would violate the only-out-of-retained-earnings statute. Under the common-law approach, could Universal Solvent's creditors recover the $250 from Minnie? _____

103. The Shortt Sirkit Electronics Company makes radios and TVs. Joe Electron is the President, and 35%-stockholder, of Shortt Sirkit. Joe decides he wants to lighten up on his holdings of Short Sirkit stock. He proposes to the board that the company repurchase his shares for $20 each, at a time when the public market price is $17. Joe indicates to each director that if that director votes against this proposal, he, Joe, will take this into consideration in deciding whether to renominate the director for re-election the next year. All directors (except for Joe, who abstains) vote in favor of the repurchase, and it goes through. Charles Capacitor, a minority shareholder, brings a derivative suit on the company's behalf against Joe, seeking recovery of the amount by which the corporation's payments to Joe exceeded the then market price. Will Charles succeed? _____

CHAPTER 12
ISSUANCE OF SECURITIES

105. On April 1, the Old King Coal Company incurs a $10,000 liability to the Keepon Trucking Co., for trucking that Keepon did for Old King Coal. On August 1, Old King Coal issues stock having par value of $25,000 to LaBrea Tarpit, in return for property that is worth (as LaBrea knows) only $10,000. On Sept. 1, Old King Coal becomes insolvent. Keepon Trucking sues LaBrea for $10,000, on the theory that Keepon may, as creditor of Old King, recover against LaBrea on account of LaBrea's having received $15,000 of "watered" stock. Assume that in the jurisdiction, the issuance of stock to LaBrea was in fact improper. Assume further that the jurisdiction follows the majority view on all relevant matters, and that there is no statute on point. May Keepon recover the $10,000 from LaBrea? _____

106. Torquemada is a fabulously successful TV producer, his most popular program being "Wheel of Torture." His TV production company, a close corporation called Thumbscrew Productions, Inc., has 2,000 shares of common stock authorized and outstanding. Lucrezia Borgia owns 500 of those shares. Because the company needs more capital, Thumbscrew's board and shareholders vote to amend its articles to increase the company's authorized common stock from 2,000 to 3,000 shares. The board offers all 2,000 shares to Torquemada, at a fair price. Lucrezia would like to buy some of these shares for herself (so her percentage interest in the company won't be reduced). The company's charter is silent on all relevant issues.

(a) What doctrine or property concept is relevant to whether Lucrezia has the right to buy any of the newly-issued shares? _____

(b) Assume that the MBCA is in force. Does Lucrezia have the right to buy any of the newly-issued shares? _____

107. Same basic facts as prior question. Now, however, assume that the corporation's charter expressly awards preemptive rights.

(a) For this question, suppose that the events occur at a time when the corporation's authorized shares still total the originally-authorized 2,000 shares, of which only 1,000 were ever issued (750 to Torquemada and 250 to Lucrezia). Five months after the corporation is formed and the first 1,000 shares were issued, the board votes to sell an additional 500 shares (out of the initially-authorized batch) to Torquemada. Does Lucrezia have a right to buy enough shares to keep her ownership at 25%? _____

(b) Suppose that after the company has raised its authorized shares to 3,000, the board enters into a employment contract with Torquemada, under which Torquemada gets 500 of the newly-authorized shares as compensation, in addition to salary. Does Lucrezia have the right to purchase as many new shares as will keep her percentage of ownership at its prior levels? _____

108. Rocky Raccoon is the sole shareholder of Roadkill Family Restaurants, Inc., a restaurant chain that obtains its ingredients mainly by harvesting them from the nation's highways and byways. Rocky would now like to raise about $2.5 million of additional capital for the company, to fund expansion. He tells you that he has two friends who are multi-millionaires that would like to invest around $1 million each. He says he also has an additional 20 or so friends who are "working stiffs," who each earn under $100,000 and don't have many assets; Rocky thinks that these friends might invest an average of about $20,000 each. A public offering (which would require a registration statement and subject the company to all sorts of SEC regulation) is out of the question at this time, so the money will have to be raised without one.

(a) If you are drafting and structuring the offering, what SEC exemption should you rely on? _____

(b) Does the SEC regulate the types of financial and business disclosures you will have to make to the investors, when you rely upon the exemption you chose in (a)?

_____

(c) Suppose that Rocky tells you, instead, that he only wants to raise the money from his two very rich friends. You and Rocky both want to be sure that the transaction won't be a public offering, so that you won't have to prepare a registration statement. Do you need to find a particular SEC Rule that gives you an exemption from the public offering requirements (and if so, what Rule applies)? _____

ANSWERS TO SHORT-ANSWER QUESTIONS

1.   No. Corporate existence is perpetual, and doesn't depend in any way on the continuity of its shareholders. Therefore, the death, withdrawal, or bankruptcy of any shareholder (even a majority or controlling one) doesn't terminate the corporation.

COMPARE: A *partnership* dissolves when any partner dies, withdraws, or files for bankruptcy, unless the partnership agreement provides otherwise. Uniform Partnership Act § 31(1)(a). This means that, when any one of these occurs, the only authority left in the partners, as to the partnership business, is to wind up and liquidate the business.

2.   Yes: if it's a partnership, Shemp isn't an owner, and, if it's a corporation, he probably is. The rule on transferability of ownership for a corporation is that shares are freely transferable unless they are subject to a written restriction on transfer. (Note that shares in a "close corporation" usually have restrictions on transfer and are therefore similar to a partnership in that respect; that's why we specified that there are several hundred owners, so that this wouldn't be considered a close corporation)

For a partnership, unless the partnership contract provides otherwise, a partnership interest is only transferable with the remaining partners' approval; without it, the transferee cannot become a full partner (e.g., he can't vote). (Keep in mind, however, that if the partnership agreement is silent on the subject a partner can assign his *economic interest* in the partnership, such that the assignee gets the partner's profits from the partnership. But the assignee won't have any other involvement with the partnership, such as the power to vote.)

4.   No. One of the benefits of conducting business as a standard C corporation is that the corporation is a ***separate taxable entity***, such that unless the corporation's income is distributed to shareholders via a dividend, shareholders don't pay tax on corporate income (and, conversely, can't deduct corporate losses).

EXCEPTION: Small corporations may elect to be treated more-or-less like a partnership for purposes of income and losses, such that income and losses are attributed to the shareholders and must be reported on their personal tax returns regardless of whether income is distributed. This kind of corporation is called a "Subchapter S corporation." (Note that the same result — pass-through taxation as in a partnership — can be created by using a limited liability company (LLC), a newer form of organization that is neither a corporation nor a partnership.)

6.   The gift is valid, as long as it's in the corporation's interests (and not purely for McDuck's own personal benefit). The scope of a corporation's powers is determined by its articles and state statutes. Statutes typically allow reasonable corporate charitable gifts. Thus MBCA § 3.02(13) allows corporations to make "donations for the public welfare or for charitable, scientific, or educational purposes." If the amount of the gift were excessive measured by the corporation's financial status, the court might strike it down. But with a $19,000,000 profit, $500,000 (2.5%) is probably reasonable. Note that the fact that McDuck controls the charity in question is relevant to whether the donation was "reasonable," but this fact probably wouldn't change the result. (However, if the charity were a sham, or McDuck was making the gift for purely personal reasons having nothing to do with the corporation's business interests, then the court might strike it down as "unreasonable.")

7.   (a) No. Even though a contract is made in a not-yet-formed corporation's name and for its behalf, the corporation doesn't become liable merely by coming into existence.

(b) Let 'Em's express or implied adoption or ratification of the contract. Let 'Em would be bound if it *expressly* adopted or ratified the contract, say by passing a resolution by the Board of Directors to that effect. Alternatively, Let 'Em would be bound if it *impliedly* adopted or ratified the contract. This might happen if it received the goods and used them (or even kept them very long) rather than returning them. Or, it might happen if the company learned of the contract before the goods were shipped, and didn't notify Wilted not to perform.

8.   (a) Yes, in all probability. When a promoter contracts on a corporation's behalf before the corporation is formed and does not let on that the corporation doesn't exist yet, the promoter is personally liable on the contract. If the corporation is later formed and ratifies the agreement, the promoter would be discharged if the other party manifests a willingness to look only to the corporation (not to the promoter) for performance. (Such a substitution is called a "novation.") Here, there's no sign that Haney agreed (even implicitly) to look only to the company for performance. So Douglas remains liable.

(b) Probably not. If the other party knows the corporation doesn't yet exist, and urges that the contract be signed in the corporation's name anyway, this is strong circumstantial evidence that the other party is expecting to look to the assets of the to-be-formed corporation, not to the assets of the promoter. So unless there's some evidence that this isn't what Haney contemplated (and there's no such evidence here in our facts), the court won't hold Douglas liable.

9.   (a) Disraeli should assert the doctrines of "de facto incorporation" and "corporation-by-estoppel." He'll probably succeed with at least one of these. Under the de facto incorporation doctrine, since Disraeli made a "colorable" attempt to incorporate before signing the lease (he tried his best, and did not know of the problem), the common-law court would probably hold that Sceptered Isle was a de facto corporation, thus shielding Disraeli. Under the common-law corporation-by-estoppel doctrine, so long as Victoria Regina thought it was dealing with a corporation (as the form of Disraeli's signature here suggests), and Disraeli was ignorant of the lack of incorporation, Victoria will be estopped from denying that a corporation existed. So here, too, Disraeli would win.

(b) Disraeli won't be liable under the MBCA, either. The MBCA is usually interpreted as having abolished the de facto incorporation doctrine; it's not clear whether it also abolishes the corporation-by-estoppel doctrine. But MBCA § 2.04 implicitly insulates from liability anyone who acts on behalf of a corporation *without knowing* about the defect in incorporation, so Disraeli qualifies.

10.   Not all of them — she can go after everyone except Happy and Bashful, under both the common-law and modern approaches. When a defectively-formed corporation becomes insolvent, creditors try to go after shareholders directly, citing the defect in formation. In a situation where shareholders knew about the defect and carried on as a corporation anyway, the common law defenses of de facto incorporation and corporation by estoppel aren't available. That's the case here; all the shareholders knew about the defect. Under the modern statutory view, as stated in MBCA § 2.04, personal liability is incurred by anyone purporting to act as a corporation knowing of a defect in formation. However, under both the common-law and modern (including MBCA) approaches, the only shareholders who are liable personally for unpaid corporate debts are those who were active in the corporation's management. That excludes Happy and Bashful from liability, since they were merely passive investors.

11. Wolf will be allowed to seek payment from the pigs personally. As a general rule, corporate creditors cannot seek payment directly from the shareholders of a corporation; the shareholders are protected by the corporate "veil." However, when shareholders don't deserve such protection, creditors may "pierce" the corporate veil and seek payment from the shareholders personally. Mere undercapitalization, without more, won't usually be grounds for piercing the veil. But undercapitalization combined with failure to follow corporate formalities *will* be. Here, the Pigs have committed both sins: (1) they have left the corporation undercapitalized, i.e., unable to pay its bills; and (2) they have ignored corporate formalities — the holding of board meetings, the keeping of records of withdrawals, etc. Since the Pigs have ignored the corporate form when such ignorance was to their benefit, a court will disregard that form now that it's to the Pigs' detriment. As a result, the Pigs will be liable personally for Huff 'N Puff's debt to Wolf.

13. (a) The doctrine of "equitable subordination." Under this doctrine, a bankruptcy court can "subordinate" the claims of insiders, i.e., not pay the insiders anything until all outsiders have been paid in full.

(b) Shemp will likely get 50 cents on the dollar, because there is $40,000 available to pay the $80,000 debt to him. The issue here is whether equitable subordination should apply. If it does, the court will give the entire $40,000 to the outsider, Shemp, and leave the three insiders with nothing. One of the grounds for equitable subordination is inadequate capitalization. The capitalization here was clearly inadequate in light of the fact that the partnership, which undertook the same activities as the corporation, was capitalized for $150,000, and the corporation was only capitalized for $30,000. So the court probably will apply equitable subordination. As a result, the "loans" from Larry, Curly, and Moe would be treated as invested capital, being subordinated to the $80,000 in claims from Shemp, the outsider. Since there's only $40,000 to distribute, Larry, Curly, and Moe would get nothing.

14. No. The issue here is the extent to which an *owner* of a corporation (i.e., a shareholder) may conduct corporate business. Here, that's all Alfred is; he's neither a director nor an officer. The rule is that shareholders have no authority to conduct corporate business; the board of directors has such authority, which it may delegate to officers or subordinates. Thus, a shareholder who is not an officer or director cannot enter into a contract on the corporation's behalf, unless the board has explicitly given him authority to do so. And that's true even where the shareholder owns a majority of the shares (and could therefore replace a majority of the board with a compliant one that would do what he wants.)

15. (a) You should tell her to use cumulative voting. Of course, depending on the state and on what the company's charter says, Carol may not be able to bring this about on her own. (For instance, MBCA § 7.28(c) allows cumulative voting only if the charter explicitly includes it; if Brady Strippers' charter doesn't, then without Mike's agreement Carol can't get the charter amended and thus can't use cumulative voting.)

You should also tell Carol to give *advance notice* to Mike that she'll be voting cumulatively, if you're in a jurisdiction that requires such advance notice. See, e.g., MBCA § 7.28(d), so requiring.

(b) She'll elect one director. Under cumulative voting, there's no limit on how many shares a shareholder can use for any one candidate. The number of shares needed to elect *n* directors is determined by the formula

$$\frac{nS}{D+1} + 1$$

where *S* is the total number of shares voting and *D* is the number of directors to be elected. So to elect one director, Carol would need 26 shares ((100 total shares ÷ 4) + 1). Since she's got 40 shares (120 votes), she'll be able to do this. She'll want to cast at 61 of her votes for her favorite candidate, let's say Marcia. That way, even if Mike spreads his votes evenly (which is how he comes closest to being able to elect all three of his candidates), he'll have only 60 votes for each, so Marcia will finish first, and one of his 3 will then lose to the other 2 in a run-off election. (If he splits his votes any other way, Marcia will finish third, and will take the third seat.)

(c) She won't elect any directors. With straight voting, a shareholder cannot cast, for any single candidate, more votes than the voter owns shares. Thus, in straight voting, although Carol gets 120 total votes, she can't cast more than 40 of them for any single candidate. Mike is, similarly, limited to 60 votes for any candidate. Therefore, the voting will be: Greg, Peter and Bobby, 60 each, Marcia, Jan and Cindy, 40 each, and Greg, Peter and Bobby will be elected.

16. In most states, yes — even though they don't constitute a quorum. Normally, a board election to fill a board vacancy is like any other board action — it must occur at a meeting at which a quorum is present. But to deal with the situation presented in this question, most states recognize an exception: when the number of directors remaining in office is less than a quorum, each vacancy can be filled by a majority vote of the remaining directors. So in such a state, any candidate who got the vote of both of the remaining directors (i.e., a "majority" of the 2 remaining directors) would be elected. See, e.g., MBCA § 8.10(a)(3).

17. (a) No — The business transacted at the meeting was valid. As a general rule, the board of directors may only take action at a properly convened meeting. The two prerequisites of a properly convened meeting are quorum and notice. The issue here is notice. The general rule is that "regular" meetings — i.e., those whose time and place are fixed by the bylaws or prior resolution — don't require notice of time and place. See, e.g., MBCA § 8.22(a) ("Unless the articles of incorporation or bylaws provide otherwise, regular meetings of the board of directors may be held without notice of the date, time, place or purpose of the meeting.") On these facts, the quarterly meetings are provided for in the bylaws. As a result, business at the meeting was valid, even though Wile E. didn't receive particular notice of it.

(b) The meeting would probably be invalid. Most states *do* require that notice of time and place be given to each director for a "special" meeting, i.e., one which is not a "regular" (e.g., quarterly) one. See, e.g., MBCA § 8.22(b) (at least 2 days advance notice of time and place required for a special board meeting.)

19. No. Board action may generally occur only at a duly-noticed board meeting, at which a quorum is present. Most states now treat a director as being "present" if he's part of a tele-phone conference call. But this "exception" to the requirement of a quorum applies only if enough board members to constitute a quorum are all *simultaneously* on the phone, because the purpose is for them to all be able to discuss the matter at once and receive input from each other. The seriatim phone calls here did not satisfy this requirement. Therefore, no quorum was present, and consequently board action has not occurred. Since the facts say that undertak-ing a new crop line requires board approval, Jack can't proceed. (If Jack goes ahead anyway and plants the seeds, then the doctrine of "ratification" may apply.)

20. **(a) Have them sign a unanimous consent to the purchase.** Nearly all states now pro-vide that directors may act without a meeting if they give their unanimous written consent to the proposed corporate action. See, e.g., MBCA § 8.21(a). So all should sign copies of a reso-lution saying that the board approves the purchase.

(b) No. For the "written consent" exception to work, the written consent must be *unanimous*. Thus Giant, by refusing to sign, can force Jack to call a formal board meeting at which a quo-rum is present. That way, Giant will get to make his arguments in person to the other directors — he may get outvoted, but he's guaranteed a chance to speak against the action.

21. **(a) Yes.** Under the MBCA, as in most states today, shareholders can (by ordinary major-ity vote) remove a director from office at any time, without cause. See MBCA, § 8.08(a). (This rule does not apply if the articles of incorporation say that directors may be removed only for cause, but the facts tell us that Libber's charter is silent on this point.) Thus the holders' action here sufficed to remove Arnold even though no cause (like fraud, or gross abuse of discretion) was shown.

Observe that this very scenario — change of control — is the scenario in which the ability to remove a director without cause is of greatest importance. Without such an ability, Washing-ton would have to wait until the expiration of Arnold's term, two years from now, before he would have full control of the board. And, in fact, if a majority of the board were friendly with George III and had the same two years to run, then Washington wouldn't be able to exercise any control over the company for two years even though he was the majority owner! So the power of removal-without-cause by vote of a majority of shareholders is very important to merger-and-acquisition law.

(b) No. Under MBCA § 8.08(d), "A director may be removed by the shareholders only at a meeting called for the purpose of removing him and the meeting notice must state that the pur-pose, or one of the purposes, of the meeting is removal of the director." Since the facts suggest (by the reference to "everyone's surprise") that the notice of meeting did not mention that Arnold's removal would be a purpose of the meeting, the vote was improper. (But Washing-ton could fix the problem at any time, at least under the MBCA. As a more-than-10% owner, he could call a special meeting of shareholders at any time under MBCA § 7.02(a)(2), and state that the purpose was to vote on whether Arnold should be removed. Then, he could cast his votes in favor of the motion and remove Arnold.)

(c) Yes. At common law, directors were only removable for cause; that is, for conduct harmful to the corporation, like fraud, incompetence, or disloyalty. Thus under the traditional rule, Arnold could successfully challenge his removal.

23. **Yes, on either an "implied actual authority" or "apparent authority" theory.** The issue here is whether Betty had authority to bind the corporation. Officers can bind the corporation only if they act within the scope of their corporate authority (unless the corporation subsequently ratifies the officer's action, something that's not relevant to this problem.) There are four types of authority commonly recognized: (1) express actual authority; (2) implied actual authority; (3) apparent authority; and (4) ratification. Here, Betty probably had both "implied actual authority" and "apparent authority."

An officer has "implied actual authority" whenever either: (1) authority is inherent in the particular post occupied by the officer, measured by common business understandings about what people holding that post customarily do; or (2) the corporation, by its own conduct or inaction, has implicitly granted the actual authority to the officer in question. The situation here falls into case (2), because when the corporation on prior occasions allowed Betty to place purchase orders and uncomplainingly paid the bill, the corporation was implicitly giving her actual authority to place such orders. So even if Tuffas hadn't been aware that it was Betty who had placed the prior orders, Frontier would still be bound because it gave Betty implied actual authority.

An officer has "apparent authority" when the corporation indicates to a third person that the officer has authority to act on its behalf, and the third person believes in good faith that such authority exists (whether or not it actually does). So Betty had apparent authority to place the order for hardtack, since Tuffas knew that Betty had placed prior orders with it that the corporation had honored. Therefore, even if Frontier now wishes to change its mind about Betty's authority (or had, unbeknownst to Tuffas, changed its mind before the latest order), Frontier is stuck under the apparent-authority doctrine, because the only issue is what Tuffas reasonably *believed* about Betty's authority, and Tuffas clearly had grounds to believe that Betty's purchase was authorized. (Remember, by the way, that for apparent-authority to apply, the corporation itself, not just the agent, must convey to the third person that the agent has authority. So if there had been no prior orders, and Betty had merely told Tuffas, "I have authority to buy," this would not suffice for apparent authority. It's the corporation's acquiescence in the prior orders by Betty that makes the difference here.)

25. No, because the merger was not mentioned as one of the purposes of the meeting. Shareholders are entitled to notice of both annual and special shareholders' meetings. If the meeting is "special" (i.e., a meeting other than the annual meeting), as is the case here, virtually all states say that the notice must include a statement of the meeting's purpose. See, e.g., MBCA § 7.05(c) ("Notice of a special meeting must include a description of the purpose or purposes for which the meeting is called.") What this statement does is limit the scope of what may be discussed at the meeting, since no unstated business can be transacted at the meeting. Since the notice didn't mention the merger, it can't be discussed.

(No statement of purposes is required in the notice for the *annual* meeting, by contrast. But even as to an annual meeting, if a merger will be discussed, shareholders must be told in advance that this will happen, and must be given the details of the plan. See, e.g., MBCA § 11.04(d). So even if de Gama was making his merger proposal at the annual meeting as opposed to at the special meeting, the merger couldn't be approved without this proposal's having been mentioned in the notice-of-meeting.)

26. You should advise her to call an immediate special meeting of shareholders, at which Sea Hag will move to remove all directors without cause. Most states now allow the holders of a certain percentage of shares to call a special shareholders' meeting at any time. The MBCA allows any holder or holders of more than 10% to do this (see § 7.02(a)(2)). Then, the shareholders can, under the MBCA (as under the law of most states today), remove any director by majority vote, even without cause. So, because the corporation doesn't have cumulative voting, at the meeting Sea Hag can cast all her votes (51% of the total votes cast) to remove all three directors. She can then elect herself to one of the vacancies by majority vote. Then, she can (either as the sole member of the board or as majority shareholder) elect two new directors to fill the vacancies. Thus she gets complete board control without waiting for the prior directors' terms to expire. (If the corporation had had cumulative voting, Sea Hag would only have been able to remove two directors and control the election of their replacements — by the formula on p. 216, she would have had just exactly the 51 shares (153 votes) needed to elect two of three directors, and not enough to elect all three.)

27. (a) No, because there was no quorum for the meeting. Unless the charter or bylaws provide otherwise (which the facts say they don't), a shareholder meeting requires a quorum of at least a bare majority of the outstanding shares entitled to vote on the measures at issue. Since only 49 of 100 shares were present, shareholder action could not validly take place.

(b). Yes, since we're told to ignore the quorum problem. The real issue in this sub-question is whether the fact that less than a majority (i.e., only 49%) of the total shares outstanding voted for the measure prevents the measure from passing. The answer is "no" — all that's required is that a majority of those shares *actually voting* vote for the measure. (States differ in how they treat abstentions, but that's not an issue here.) Since 30 out of the 49 votes actually cast voted for the measure, it passed.

28. Yes. Most states let a shareholder examine the corporation's books and records, provided that this is not being done for an "improper" purpose (e.g., stealing the corporation's secrets so as to compete with it). Confirming or refuting one's suspicions that the books are being cooked certainly qualifies as a proper purpose, so Crusoe should be able to get a court order compelling the company to allow the inspection.

Note that under MBCA § 16.02(c), Crusoe would be allowed to inspect the accounting records, but only if: (1) he made his demand "in good faith and for a proper purpose" (satisfied here); (2) he described with "reasonable particularity" why he wanted to do the inspection (e.g., "I think the books are being cooked," which he could honestly say here); and (3) the records are "directly connected" with his purpose (satisfied here). So Crusoe would get the inspection under § 16.02(c) (and in fact the corporation would probably have to pay his legal fees in getting the court order, under § 16.04(c)).

29. (a) No. § 12 of the Securities Exchange Act ('34 Act), and SEC Rule 12g-1 enacted under it, describe the companies subject to federal proxy rules. A company qualifies if *either*: (1) Its securities are traded on a regulated securities exchange (e.g., NYSE); *or* (2) The company fits *both* of the following requirements: (a) It has assets greater than $10,000,000, and (b) It has 500 or more shareholders of a class of equity securities (e.g., common stock).

The key to this question is that if a corporation isn't traded on a national exchange (as Botch Ewlism isn't), it must have a *class* of stock held by 500 or more people, not 500 or more shareholders all together. That's the problem here: Botch Ewlism has 700 shareholders, but it doesn't have 500 or more holders of any one class. Thus, it's not subject to the SEC's reporting requirements.

(b) No. A company is bound by the SEC's proxy solicitation rules if, and only if, it's required to file financial reports under the '34 Act. So the negative answer to part (a) compels a negative answer to this part as well.

30. Yes — management must send each shareholder material "substantially equivalent" to the material that it would have had to send if it were soliciting proxies. This means that management has to send an *annual report* containing the corporation's financial reports, plus information about the compensation and stockholdings of management and board members, transactions between management and the corporation, and any matter on which there will be a shareholder vote. This information must also be filed with the SEC. So shareholders get as much information about a management-controlled public company as they do about one that is not management controlled. (But remember, the solicitation and filing requirements don't get triggered if the company is not traded on a stock exchange and doesn't have at least 500 holders of some one class of stock — see the previous question.)

32. (a) Yes, probably. Rule 14a-9 of the '34 Act requires that proxy materials be free of misstatements or omissions of "material" fact. Here, the fact that Clampett Oil's directors were all Drysdale's nominees would be likely to influence the Clampett directors' recommendation that the merger be approved. A fact is "material" (so that the proxy materials can't omit or misstate it) if "there is a substantial likelihood that a reasonable shareholder would consider it important in deciding how to vote" (i.e., if the fact would "significantly alter the 'total mix' of available information"). *TSC Industries.* The omission here certainly seems to qualify: a Clampett shareholder would probably give the Clampett board's recommendation much less weight if she knew that the board was controlled by the acquirer than if she didn't know this. So omission of the fact of board domination renders the proxy materials misleading. A federal court has discretion to issue an injunction against the transaction if adequate proxy materials haven't been sent, and there's a good chance the court in this situation would exercise that discretion.

(b) No, probably. The Supreme Court has held that no private recovery for proxy misstatements is available to "a member of a class of minority shareholders whose votes are *not required* by law or corporate bylaw to authorize the transaction giving rise to the claim." *Virginia Bankshares.* Here, since Drysdale controlled a majority of the common stock, and only a simple majority had to approve the transaction, the merger would have gone through even if Ellie May and all other shareholders apart from Drysdale had voted against it. Therefore, the omission didn't cause things to turn out differently, and Ellie May hasn't really been damaged. (If Ellie May had been duped into surrendering her state-law *appraisal* rights — as would be the case in a state that grants such rights to those dissenting from a merger, but denies appraisal where the holder votes in favor of the transaction — then Ellie May might still have a federal monetary claim, on the theory that the omission deprived her of her appraisal rights. That's why the facts tell you that Ellie's appraisal rights weren't affected by her vote in favor of the transaction.)

33. Yes. Rule 14a-8 of the '34 Act allows shareholders to include proposals in management's proxy solicitation materials. There are significant restrictions on this right; for instance, the shareholder must have owned 1% or $1,000 (market value) of the corporation's voting stock for at least a year, and any shareholder can only submit one proposal for any one meeting. In addition, there are many grounds on which management may omit a proposal. (For instance, the shareholder proposal can't be counter to a management proposal on the same subject; it can't relate to electing or removing directors; it can't be insignificant, personal, or relate to ordinary business; and it can't have been voted down in the recent past.)

The exclusion that comes closest to fitting these facts is that the proposal must not relate to the "conduct of the ordinary business operations" of the company. But the composition of 10% of the company's product line would probably be held not to relate to the company's "ordinary business operations," especially in light of the extreme public controversy associated with fur products. (Courts have generally held that where the issue is an ethical, social or political one, it doesn't fall within the "ordinary business operations" ban.) So a court would probably order Cruella to include the proposal.

34. (a) Violations of §§ 302(a)(2) and (a)(3) of the Sarbanes-Oxley Act, triggering a violation of § 906 of the Act. § 302(a)(2) of Sarbanes-Oxley requires the reporting company's "principal executive officer" (Bernie) to certify that "based on the officer's knowledge, the [quarterly] report does not contain any untrue statement of a material fact[.]" And § 302(a)(3) requires Bernie to certify that "the financial statements ... fairly present in all material respects the financial condition and results of operations of the issuer ... for the periods presented in the report." § 906(a) authorizes an up-to-10-year prison term for certifying any statement covered by §§ 302(a)(2) and (3) while knowing that the report being certified doesn't meet the requirements of those sections. (The penalty is up to 20 years for a "willful" violation, whatever that means.)

(b) You'll have to prove (a) that the report was false; and (b) that Bernie knew that the report was false when he certified it. You *won't* have to prove that Bernie ordered anyone else in the company to cook the books, or that he otherwise actively participated in the fraud — it's enough simply that he *knew* of the falsehood(s) when he certified that the report was accurate.

35. (a) Yes. Virtually all courts today hold that voting agreements — including those which, like this one, are of the "agreement to agree" type — are valid and enforceable.

(b) Specific performance, in that Athos's shares will be voted in favor of Porthos's nominee, so that that nominee is sure to be elected. With three directors, under cumulative voting it takes at least 26% of the shares to elect one director. (See the formula on p. 216). So if the court casts Athos's shares in favor of Porthos's nominee, putting 40% of the total voting power behind that nominee, the latter is certain to be elected.

Note that in earlier days, a court was more likely to cancel any votes cast by Athos in violation of the agreement than to order that Athos's vote be cast in a particular way. Such "relief" would be useless to Porthos, because Aramis would still elect the entire board, since Porthos's 20% would not be enough to elect a single director, even under cumulative voting. See *Ringling Bros. v. Ringling,* involving similar facts. Porthos thus does much better under the modern approach.

36. (a) That this is an attempted voting trust, which is invalid because not previously disclosed to the corporation. Under MBCA § 7.30 (as under most modern statutes), "voting trusts" are legal, but only if several quite stringent requirements are met. In particular, "[T]he trustee shall prepare a list of the names and addresses of all owners of beneficial interests in the trust, together with the number and class of shares each transferred to the trust, and deliver copies of the list and agreement to the corporation's principal office." § 7.30(a). Such a trust does not become effective until "the date the first shares subject to the trust are registered in the trustee's name." § 7.30(b). Since the shares here were never registered to Hare as trustee, and the document was never filed with the corporation, if it's a voting trust it never became effective (you would argue on Hatter's behalf).

(b) That the arrangement is a valid voting agreement, not an invalid voting trust, and that it's therefore specifically enforceable. MBCA § 7.31 says that "Two or more shareholders may provide for the manner in which they will vote their shares by signing an agreement for that purpose. A voting agreement created under this section is not subject to the provisions [on voting trusts]." If the court agrees that this is a "voting agreement" rather than an attempted "voting trust," it doesn't matter that the corporation wasn't aware of the arrangement, because there's no requirement of disclosure. If the court accepts this characterization, the agreement will be specifically enforceable.

(c) Probably Hare's argument will prevail, and the arrangement will be specifically enforced. Other than the physical transfer of shares, there's nothing in this arrangement (so far as the facts tell us) that forces the conclusion that this was intended to be a true trust, as opposed to an agreement. So the court will probably conclude that the parties' intent will be better carried out by treating it as an agreement, and enforcing it, than by treating it as a nullity.

37.   Yes, probably. Agreements restricting director discretion in a close corporation are generally valid if they comply with applicable statutes *and* they don't harm creditors or minority shareholders. Here, the agreement between the majority shareholders that they will vote themselves excessive salaries harms the minority shareholders (Dawg and Weasel) by leaving less money for dividends and other corporate activities. (It may also harm creditors — the facts don't give us enough information to know.) Since the agreement harms the minority shareholders, a court will probably hold it invalid. At the very least, this will mean that if either Foghorn or Miss Prissy changes his/her mind about voting the high salaries, the other won't be able to sue. (It's less clear whether Dawg will be able to get a court to intervene if both Foghorn and Miss Prissy continue to vote for the high salaries once the agreement is struck down.)

39.   The company wins. The issue here is whether the bylaw, granting the corporation an option to repurchase shares from its shareholders at book value, is valid even where it produces a price that's much below market value. The general rule is that a restriction on stock transfer is valid if the person taking the shares has notice of the restraint and the restraint is "reasonable." The focus here is on the "reasonableness" element, since the shares are worth four times the option price. However, most courts say that if the mechanism chosen by the parties was reasonable *at the time the method was agreed upon*, the method will be deemed reasonable even though later trends make the price produced by the method very high or low viewed as of the moment of adjudication. Since the facts tell us that the book-value method was reasonable at the time it was adopted, the fact that valuation methods have changed will not invalidate it. Thus even though the method produces a very below-market price now, the restriction is binding. At the very least, the court will allow the company to continue to refuse to recognize the transfer to Walton. If Jekyll is unlucky, the court will hold that Jekyll's notice of intent to sell gave the company a temporarily-irrevocable option to acquire the shares at the $25 price, and will order specific performance by Jekyll.

40.   (a) That the company (and Ricky as controlling shareholder) owes a fiduciary duty

to Lucy to treat her as favorably as it treated Ricky, and thus repurchase her shares at the same $1,000 price.

(b) Yes in Massachusetts; probably not in most other jurisdictions. A few states have in recent years held that a majority stockholder in a close corporation has a fiduciary obligation to each minority stockholder, such that the majority holder must behave in good faith towards the minority holder. If the state falls into this group, it would be likely to agree with this argument by Lucy that the company must repurchase Lucy's shares on the same terms as Ricky's, assuming that its financial condition still permits it to do so. The Massachusetts court in *Donahue v. Rodd Electrotype* so held, on almost exactly these facts. However, *most* courts (including those in Delaware) would probably *not* agree that such a fiduciary obligation exists merely because of the close-corporation context, so Lucy would probably lose in most non-Massachusetts courts.

41. (a) The shareholder. Directors can violate their duty of care through inactivity, as by failing to inform themselves of their corporation's business. They typically can fulfill their duty to keep themselves informed by relying on the advice of experts, such as lawyers and accountants. However, reliance on third parties shields the directors from liability for failure to exercise due care only when the reliance is ***reasonable***. Reliance is not reasonable where the director is on notice of facts or circumstances indicating that the expert is wrong. Here, the directors know that Bully Sheet hasn't met its payroll recently; this flies in the face of Counter's statement that the company could pay a dividend and still meet its financial obligations. Once on notice of facts suggesting that Counter's statement was unreliable, the directors had at least a duty to inquire further, a duty that they did not discharge. Since the payment of the dividend in these circumstances seems to have brought harm to the corporation (by making it further insolvent), the directors are likely to be required to reimburse the corporation for the improperly-paid dividend.

(b) Placing an exculpation clause in the corporation's certificate of incorporation. Del. GCL § 102(b)(7) lets a corporation put into its certificate of incorporation "a provision eliminating or limiting the personal liability of a director to the corporation or its stockholders for monetary damages for breach of fiduciary duty as a director[.]" The provision can't cover a breach of the duty of loyalty or good faith, but it can cover a breach of the duty of care. Since only the duty of care is involved here, such a provision would make it virtually impossible for a shareholder derivative suit to succeed on these facts.

42. (a) You should assert that the "business judgment rule" bars liability. Under the business judgment rule, a director (or officer) who makes a business judgment in "good faith" fulfills the duty of care if the director (1) has no conflict of interest concerning the transaction; (2) is reasonably well-informed about the transaction; and (3) rationally believes that the business judgment is in the corporation's best interests. You can make a pretty plausible case that Letizia's decision to vote in favor of the acquisition satisfied these requirements (see part (b) below).

(b) Letizia will probably win. As to requirement (1), there's nothing in the facts to indicate that Letizia had any conflict of interest regarding the transaction (for instance, the purchase was made from an unaffiliated third party.) As to requirement (2), the long board meeting, Letizia's detailed questions, and her reliance on the accountant's report, seem enough, taken collectively, to have made her "well-informed" about the acquisition. As to (3), Letizia's belief that Napoleon knew what he was doing seems to have been at least "rational," even if not fully "reasonable." Therefore, Letizia probably qualifies for the protection of the business judgment rule. If the court agrees, it won't hold Letizia liable even though an ordinary director of reasonable prudence would probably not have voted in favor of the transaction, based on the facts then known to the board.

44.　(a) No. Delaware, like most states, will not allow a corporation to nullify the duty of care as completely as this clause purports to do. In particular, this clause would absolve a director from liability even if he knew that the corporate action he was approving violated the law, or even if the director was engaging in self-dealing, and most state courts, including those of Delaware, would not allow such a complete waiver of liability. See Del. GCL § 102(b)(7), listing a number of wrongs to which an exculpation clause may not apply, including an act or omission that violates the director's "duty of loyalty," that is "not in good faith," or that involves "intentional misconduct or a knowing violation of law."

(b) Yes. Because this clause requires good faith, and doesn't apply if the corporate action is known to be illegal or constitutes self-dealing, the clause meets the requirements of Delaware law (and probably that of most jurisdictions). See Del GCL § 102(b)(7), discussed in part (a) above.

46.　Yes. The contract will not be voidable on conflict grounds, because a majority of the disinterested directors have approved it after full disclosure.

A conflict arises when a director or officer has split loyalties. Here, the conflict is indirect — four Addams directors are shareholders of a corporation with which Addams Shroud is contracting. The prevailing rule is that such a contract is voidable at Addams's option unless either disinterested directors approve it on full disclosure, shareholders approve it on full disclosure, or it's fair. Most states hold that as long as a majority of the disinterested directors (with a 2-person minimum) approve the transaction, this counts not only as approval, but also as a quorum. See, e.g., MBCA § 8.62(c). Since a majority of the 3 disinterested directors have approved, this condition is satisfied.

47.　The deal isn't voidable, because it was approved by disinterested directors, and, besides, it's fair. The transaction here involves a conflict because Kirk is a director for one party to a contract and majority shareholder of the other. The general rule is that such a contract is voidable unless either: (1) the transaction and conflict are disclosed to directors, who approve it; (2) the transaction and conflict are disclosed to shareholders, who approve it; or (3) it's fair to the corporation. Here, Kirk fully disclosed the material facts of the deal and the conflict to the disinterested directors of Enterprise, who approved it. This satisfies test (1), and is thus in and of itself enough to avoid voidability on grounds of conflict.

In any event, the transaction here was "fair" to Enterprise. A court will generally judge fairness as of the time the transaction was made. (See, e.g., MBCA § 8.61(b)(3)). At the time this deal was made, everything suggested that the deal was fair to Enterprise. So the transaction satisfies (3), and would therefore not be voidable at Scotty's urging even if full disclosure and pre-approval by the board *hadn't* occurred.

48.　(a) Lack of consideration. The issue here is the validity of payments for past services. The general rule from contract law is that such payments are only valid when the basic specifics of the arrangement and the recipient's identity are established *before* the services are rendered (in the form of a contract, a formal bonus plan, or established company practice). Otherwise, such payments are without consideration, since "past consideration" is not consideration at all.

(b) Yes, probably. Mr. Bill was dead before the specifics of the pension were ever worked out, so the pension couldn't have been consideration for his performance of services while alive. Consequently, the court will probably order that the pension not be paid. (Alternatively, the court might say that paying a pension for which there is no consideration is a "waste" of corporate assets, since the corporation receives no benefit from the payment.)

49.   (a) No, because Mike doesn't owe Mona Lisa a fiduciary duty on these facts. The rule as to corporate opportunities is essentially that "insiders" may not exploit an opportunity that rightly belongs to the corporation. Only directors, employees and controlling shareholders will generally be deemed to be bound by the corporate-opportunity doctrine. The mere fact that Mike owns 5% of the shares won't be enough to make him a controlling shareholder (and there's nothing else to indicate he controls the corporation); since he's also not a director or employee, he's free to buy the land without regard to whether it might be a valuable opportunity for the corporation.

(b) No, probably. If Mike were a director, he'd be barred from taking anything that was a true corporate opportunity. But the land here probably wouldn't be deemed to be a corporate opportunity. Where the Key Player is a director (but not an employee), fewer things are deemed to be corporate opportunities. Thus the ALI's *Principles* say that, vis-a-vis a director, something is a corporate opportunity only if the director either (1) learned of the opportunity in connection with performing his duties for the company; (2) learned of it under circumstances where he should reasonably have believed it was being offered to the corporation, not to him personally; or (3) learned of it through the use of information or property belonging to the corporation. Since the facts suggest that Mike learned of the land (and of the routing of the highway) through means that had nothing to do with Mona Lisa or his director-work for Mona Lisa, the land did not represent a corporate opportunity. Consequently, the fact that the land might have been very useful to the company is irrelevant.

(c) Yes, probably. More things are held to be corporate opportunities when exploited by a full-time employee of the corporation than when exploited by an outside director. Thus the ALI *Principles* say that an opportunity is a corporate one if exploited by an employee who knows that the opportunity is "closely related to a business in which the corporation is engaged or expects to engage." Since Mona Lisa is currently engaged in the business of putting up fast-food restaurants on vacant land near highways in fast-growing towns (and has already expressed interest in putting a store in David), this was a corporate opportunity vis a vis a full-time employee. Consequently, Mike was required to offer the property to Mona Lisa first, before buying it himself. (The fact that Mike's area of expertise was sales instead of, say, real-estate acquisitions, won't make a difference.) The court will probably impose a "constructive trust," under which Mike will be treated as holding the property for Mona Lisa's benefit. (Mona Lisa would have to reimburse Mike for his costs before taking control of the property, however.)

51.   (a) That the corporation, through Wendy its President, rejected the opportunity.

(b) Probably not. Most courts do indeed hold that if the corporation rejects the opportunity after full disclosure, the Key Player may exploit the opportunity himself. The real issue here is whether "the corporation" has in fact rejected the opportunity. It's true that the President has rejected the opportunity. But most courts would probably hold that rejection does not occur unless either a majority of the disinterested directors, or a majority of the shareholders, have rejected it. Since no disinterested directors other than Wendy have rejected it, true rejection did not occur here.

(c) Probably not. Although the opportunity is drug-related, Darling's focus — cancer — has nothing to do with a drug that merely helps people fly; Darling's marketing channels might not even be useful in selling the product. Thus, this probably wouldn't constitute an opportunity under the line-of-business test, even though "line of business" is typically interpreted very broadly. Under the interest-or-expectancy test, Darling didn't have any interest or expectancy related to "flying" drugs, nor was such a drug essential to Darling's business. As a result, Peter would probably win with the argument that the opportunity wasn't a "corporate" opportunity at all.

52. (a) That the company was financially unable to take advantage of the opportunity, and thus hasn't been harmed.

(b) Unclear. Courts are split about whether and when the corporation's financial inability to take advantage of the opportunity constitutes a defense to a usurpation-of-opportunity claim. Many courts say that unless the defendant made full disclosure of the opportunity to the corporation in advance, he may not later rely on its probable financial inability as a defense. Courts following this view reason that: (1) if the opportunity is attractive enough, the corporation might be able to raise the funds even if it doesn't already have them on hand; and (2) allowing financial inability to be a defense furnishes a bad incentive to corporate insiders, because the defense's availability discourages the insider from seeking a way to help the corporation raise the funds. Since Peter didn't notify anyone associated with New England Potato about the opportunity before taking it for himself, he won't be able to raise the "financial inability" defense later, under this view.

But other courts, including those of Delaware, don't require advance disclosure as a pre-requisite to a "financial inability" defense. So in those states, Peter's failure to notify anyone at the company before taking the opportunity for himself won't bar his use of the financial-inability defense.

53. Doubleday. The issue here is whether a controlling shareholder can sell his control at a premium — that is, a price above the fair market value of the shares. The *general* rule is that he may, in fact, sell his shares for whatever price he wants. There are exceptions to this doctrine, but none of the exceptions applies here. (For instance, Doubleday has no reason to believe that the buyer will loot or otherwise harm the corporation, Doubleday hasn't explicitly agreed to transfer control of the board as a condition of the deal, and there's no reason to believe that the premium is a diversion of a "collective opportunity.") So Doubleday is within his rights in collecting something extra for his controlling stake, even though he's getting a benefit not available to other shareholders.

54. (a) That Ali Baba knew or should have known that Scheherezade was likely to "loot" the company. Part of a controlling shareholder's fiduciary duty to his corporation is that he cannot sell control to anyone whom he knows or should know will harm the company (e.g., by looting the company's treasury, committing fraud on the corporation after acquiring control, or implementing business policies that would harm the corporation or its shareholders).

(b) Any facts that ought to have put Ali on notice of Scheherezade's intent-to-loot would be helpful. Look for pre-transaction facts known to Ali, such as Scheherezade's exaggerated interest in the corporation's liquid assets; any demand by her that control be transferred to her immediately following the closing; any sign that she had only a negligible interest in the corporation's operations; or evidence that as Ali knew, Scheherezade had engaged in similar self-dealing with corporations she'd bought in the past. (Her mere payment of a substantial premium for control, by contrast, would be only a *weak* indication that she might intend to loot the corporation.)

55. (a) That the document constituted an illegal "sale of office." A director or group of directors, like any other shareholder, can normally sell for a "control premium." However, a director cannot baldly sell "his office," i.e., his directorship.

(b) Yes, probably. Since the 7% stake bought by Evil would not normally have given her control of the board, and since the purchase agreement here was expressly contingent on the sellers' resignations and votes for Evil's board nominees, it's hard to imagine a more blatant sale of a directorship. So the court will probably order the selling directors to disgorge the control premium either to the corporation or (preferably) directly to the shareholders other than Evil. (If the 5 selling directors owned, and were selling, a *majority* of the shares, then probably no sale-of-office would be found; that's because Evil would have been able to get control of the board eventually, even without the resignations and succession votes by the sellers. The same would probably be true if the selling directors were selling Evil a "working majority.")

56. (a) SEC Rule 10b-5. That rule (roughly) makes it unlawful to "employ any device, scheme, or artifice to defraud . . . in connection with the purchase or sale of any security."

(b) Yes. A person commits insider trading in violation of Rule 10b-5 if he (1) has a special relationship with the issuer of stock (e.g., he is an "insider" of the issuer), and (2) buys or sells the issuer's stock, while in possession of information that is (3) material and (4) non-public. Aquaman, as president, was an insider of the corporation whose shares were being bought (Wet Dreams), so Aquaman satisfies (1) and (2). Information is "material" if a reasonable investor would consider it important in deciding whether to buy or sell the shares. Information that in fact increases a company's share price from $1 to $50 is clearly "material" (satisfying (3)). The Oxygum invention hadn't been known to investors generally when Aquaman made his purchases, so the information about the invention was "nonpublic" (satisfying (4)). As a result, Aquaman is liable for insider trading in violation of Rule 10b-5.

57. No, because Charlie didn't trade in Good shares before the acquisition was made public. The rule on insider trading is that insiders may not *trade* in the company's stock while in possession of material inside information. 10b-5 does not require the prompt disclosure of material non-public information: the company and its insiders may delay disclosure indefinitely so far as the Rule is concerned, so long as they don't buy or sell in the interim. This is the "disclose or abstain" rule. Here, Charlie abstained. Thus, he can't be liable to Olive.

58. Yes. An SEC Rule enacted in 2000, Rule 10b-5-1, forecloses Squishy's defense. The Rule starts by saying that Rule 10b-5 prohibits trading "on the basis of" material nonpublic information. But 10b-5-1 then defines "on the basis of" to *mean "was aware of"* the information at the time of the purchase or sale. Since Squishy was "aware of" the info when he sold, he's liable, even if the "motivation" for his sale was his need for house-acquisition funds rather than the inside info. (10b-5-1 would have given Squishy a "safe harbor" if, before he got the lower-earnings news, he had irrevocably committed to sell the shares as part of a pre-planned trading program, such as a commitment to sell a certain number of shares at the beginning of every quarter regardless of market conditions. But there's no indication on our facts that Squishy qualified for this safe harbor.)

59. No — Cindy Lou Hoo loses, because only purchasers or sellers of the affected securities can be plaintiffs under 10b-5. More precisely, a person can only be a plaintiff if she bought or sold the company's stock *during the period of non-disclosure. Blue Chip Stamps v. Manor Drug Stores.* Since Cindy didn't buy or sell any Hohoho stock during the period when the insider-trading was occurring — July 2 through July 14 — she can't recover, no matter how clear it is that Santa in fact violated 10b-5 (and it's very clear here that he did).

60. (a) That the non-public information was not "material." Insider trading violates Rule 10b-5 only if the defendant bought or sold while in possession of "material" non-public information. Cole can make a plausible argument that because there was only a 30% chance that the site would be commercially viable, the news about it wasn't material.

(b) No, probably. Information is "material" if there is a "substantial likelihood" that disclosure of that information "would have been viewed by a reasonable investor as having significantly altered the *'total mix'* of information made available." A 30% chance that a coal company's proven reserves will at least double would almost certainly be viewed as significantly altering the "total mix" of information about the company's prospects.

61. No, because Bond had no disclose-or-abstain duty. Bond did trade on the basis of material, nonpublic information. However, that by itself doesn't violate 10b-5. Instead, the only people subject to liability are pure insiders (directors, officers, controlling shareholders, employees), temporary insiders (accountants, lawyers, investment bankers, etc.), misappropriators, and tippees (those to whom an insider knowingly discloses inside information in breach of a fiduciary duty). Bond fits none of these descriptions. Instead, what he did was, essentially, to obtain market information by chance. It's perfectly OK to trade on the basis of such information. See, e.g., *SEC v. Switzer.*

If Goldfinger had *known* that Bond was listening, and had intended to give Bond the information so that Bond could make money by trading the company's stock, then Goldfinger would be a tipper and Bond would probably be liable as a tippee. But since Goldfinger didn't even know that Bond was listening, Goldfinger is not a tipper and Bond is not a tippee.

62. Probably not. Here, Brenda is not herself an insider in Cooper Printing, so if she's liable at all it would be as a tippee. A tippee's duty to disclose or abstain derives from the liability of his tipper (here, D.B.) A tipper is only liable for the disclosure if the tipper is breaching his fiduciary duty to the issuer's shareholders by making the disclosure. Furthermore (and this is the not-so-obvious step), the tipper will be deemed to be breaching his fiduciary duty only if he "personally will benefit, directly or indirectly, from his disclosure." *Dirks v. SEC.* If D.B. had expected Brenda to make money from trading on the tip and give him a portion — or even if D.B. had just intended to make a pecuniary gift to Brenda by giving her information on which he expected her to trade — D.B. would be in breach of his fiduciary duty, and Brenda would be derivatively liable if she realized that D.B. was violating his duty. But here — where the facts tells us that D.B. has no idea that Brenda will use the info for personal gain — D.B. hasn't violated any fiduciary duty, so Brenda can't be derivatively liable no matter how bald-faced her conduct may have been.

63. $50,000 — 10,000 shares x $5 profit per share. Congress has given certain types of claimants an express private right of action for insider trading, under the Insider Trading and Securities Fraud Enforcement Act of 1988 (ITSFEA). Under that Act, damages "shall not exceed the profit gained or loss avoided in the . . . transactions . . . that are the subject of the violation." Therefore, Lady M. is limited to the *lesser* of her own lost profits (50,000 x $5, or $250,000) and the defendant's gains ($10,000 x $5, or $50,000).

RELATED ISSUE: Say the plaintiff had been the *SEC*, not a private plaintiff like Lady Macbeth. The SEC could seek, among other remedies, *treble damages* under ITSFEA — the SEC is not limited to recovering the defendant's actual gains made or losses avoided. (These damages would go to the Treasury.)

66. Neither. Rule 10b-5 prohibits (among other things) misstatements and omissions of material fact "in connection with the purchase or sale of any security." When D knowingly makes an affirmative misstatement of material fact to P about a security, and this induces P to buy or sell that security, P can recover from D for a 10b-5 violation even though D never bought or sold the company's securities, and even though D was not a company insider and didn't learn any nonpublic fact by means of a breach of fiduciary duty on the part of a company insider.

If you got this question wrong, it's probably because you confused suit based on affirmative misrepresentation (which is what we have here) with a suit based on *insider trading*. If P's claim is that D has insider traded, then P must show both: (1) that D bought or sold the issuer's stock while in possession of material nonpublic information; and (2) that D was either an insider of the issuer or learned the information by means of a breach by someone of a fiduciary duty. But neither of these requirements applies to suits based on affirmative misrepresentation. So here, since McCheese knew that she was making an incorrect statement about McSpeedy's earnings, she's violated 10b-5 and Sylvester can recover. Thus in the garden-variety "fraud by a broker" scenario, the broker has typically violated 10b-5.

67. (a) A claim under § 16(b) of the '34 Act, to recover short-swing trading profits. Under this section, if an officer (or director or 10% owner) of a publicly-traded company buys and then sells (or sells and then buys) the company's stock within a 6-month period, all profits must be paid over to the company.

(b) Yes. Joker, as president, is obviously an officer of Metropolis. Since he bought shares on March 15, and sold 1,000 of them on June 15 (less than 6 months after purchase), he's automatically liable under §16(b). The fact that he had no actual insider knowledge is irrelevant.

(c) $5,000, payable to Metropolis. The computation is simple, in this instance: on the 1,000 shares Joker sold, he made a profit of $5 per share, so he must disgorge the entire $5,000 profit to Metropolis. However, the plaintiff's lawyer will be entitled to reasonable attorney's fees out of this sum, with the corporation receiving only the balance.

68. Yes; if the corporation itself doesn't pursue a § 16(b) claim against an insider, any shareholder can do so, regardless of when he became a shareholder. Thus, the fact that Judicata wasn't a shareholder either at the time Fairy Godmother made her purchase or at the time she made her sale doesn't matter. Note that the lack of any "advance purchase" requirement gives attorneys an incentive to keep up with trades by insiders: such trades have to be reported to the SEC, and are then publicly disclosed. So an attorney can view the public record to spot a §16(b) violation, buy a few shares (or have a friend buy shares) in the corporation in question, press a § 16(b) suit derivatively, and collect attorney's fees.

70. Yes. § 16(b) prohibits in-and-out purchases and sales of corporate securities by insiders, who can be directors, owners, or 10+% shareholders of the issuer. As the previous question shows, 10%-owners won't be covered unless they occupy that status both at the time of purchase and the time of sale. But the rule is different for directors or officers: these are covered by §16(b) if they hold that director or officer status at *either* the time of sale *or* the time of purchase. Since Calvin was a director at the time he sold the 1,000 shares, he's liable under §16(b) (and will have to pay his $5,000 profit over to Hobbes).

71. $2,000. This is true even though Einstein lost $500 overall on his trades during the 6 months! § 16(b) makes insiders (and a President, as an officer, is clearly an insider) liable to the corporation for short-swing profits from trading in the corporation's stock. The court will match purchases and sales according to a *lowest-in, highest-out* formula, and will consider only those matches that produce profits. Here, Einstein's "lowest in" is the 1,000-share lot he bought June 1 at $5. His "highest out" is May 1, when he sold 500 shares at $8. Matching 500 of the June 1 purchase against the May 1 sale results in a $1,500 profit (500 x $3). His next "highest out" is the 500-share sale at $6 on July 1; matching this sale against the remaining 500 shares from the June 1 purchase (at $5) results in a $500 profit (500 x $1). Any matching that produces a loss is ignored. Thus, Einstein's "profits" within a six month period are deemed to be $2,000, which he owes to the corporation.

72. (a) You'd rather it be direct. A derivative suit has to jump many more procedural hurdles. For instance, demand has to be submitted to the board, and in most states if the board makes a reasonable inquiry and concludes that the claim has no merit, the court will probably terminate the action. Also, the plaintiff often has to post security for expenses, and the court has to approve any settlement. A direct action typically does not suffer from any of these shortcomings.

(b) As direct. A case is a derivative suit only where the primary harm is to the corporation, not the individual plaintiff shareholder. Here, Donnay is complaining of an injury to her personally as a shareholder (failure to pay her dividends), not an injury to the corporation. The vast majority of derivative cases are against directors and/or officers for breaching their duties of care and loyalty to the corporation (e.g., wasting assets, self-dealing, excessive compensation, usurping a corporate opportunity). That isn't what happened here. In general, a suit alleging that insiders have taken an action whose motive or principal effect was to injure a minority shareholder will be treated as direct.

73. (a) That demand would be futile, because the claim is that a majority of the board has breached its duty of care, and the board will almost certainly conclude that a claim of board-wrongdoing has no merit. It is indeed true that if the court becomes convinced that demand would be futile, the court will excuse the demand. It's also true that in general, if the complaint charges a majority of the board with wrongdoing, the court is more likely to find demand to be futile than where only one board member, or a non-board-member, is charged with wrongdoing. However (as discussed in part (b) to this answer), a Delaware court is likely to conclude that the wrongdoing charged here is not serious enough to excuse demand.

(b) No, probably. Delaware makes it very difficult to have a suit treated as demand-excused. The fact that a majority of the board approved the transaction doesn't, in and of itself, mean that demand on the board would be futile (says Delaware). Demand will not be excused unless P shows in advance a reasonable likelihood that the board either: (1) was not disinterested or not independent; or (2) was not entitled to protection of the business judgment rule for its approval.

There's no evidence of (1) (lack of disinterestedness or independence) on these facts. As to (2), the slightly-high price was not enough to make the board's approval "irrational," which is what would be required for an informed and distinterested board to lose protection of the business judgment rule. So the case will be dismissed until Manny makes a demand on the board. In other words, a charge that a majority of the board has violated its duty of care (as opposed to a charge that it has violated its duty of loyalty) will generally not be enough in Delaware to make the case demand-excused, unless there's substantial evidence of gross negligence or true irrationality. (A New York court, by contrast, would probably excuse demand here, merely from the fact that a majority of the board is charged with breach of the duty of care.)

74. (a) The demand will be excused, so the case won't be dismissed. As the prior question indicates, the main exception to the requirement of a demand on the board is where demand would be futile. Although Delaware makes it harder than most states to get a finding of futility, a claim (backed by some evidence) that a majority of the board has violated its duty of *loyalty* will suffice. Here, that's the case: all the directors have been offered lucrative consulting contracts with Munchkinsoft, in return for which they seem to have violated their duty to seek the best deal for the Seven Dwarfs' shareholders. As a result, Snow White needn't fulfill the demand-on-directors requirement.

(b) The demand must be made. The MBCA, in § 7.42(1), requires that a demand be made on the board in all cases, no matter how futile it would be. (On the other hand, once the demand is made and the plaintiff waits the 90 days required by § 7.42(2), the court won't dismiss the action even if the board so recommends, unless the court believes that the independent directors have "determined in good faith after conducting a reasonable inquiry upon which [their] conclusions are based that the maintenance of the derivative proceeding is not in the best interests of the corporation." MBCA § 7.44(a). So if the directors do a complete whitewash, the court will let the action proceed.)

77. No, because the suit isn't derivative, it's direct. Security-for-expenses statutes generally require that "small shareholder" plaintiffs in derivative suits post a bond (or other security) for the corporation's litigation expenses, which the plaintiff will have to pay if he loses. Not all states have such statutes; however, even in the ones that do, only *derivative* suits are covered, not direct ones. Here, Crusoe and the other shareholders are claiming that their *own* right to inspect the corporation's books has been violated; they aren't claiming that the corporation itself has been wronged. Therefore, the claim is direct, not derivative, so the security-for-expenses statute won't require the plaintiffs to post a bond (or other security) for the corporation's litigation expenses.

78. (a) The \$20,000 in expenses, but nothing towards the \$50,000 settlement amount.
The vast majority of states do not permit a corporation to indemnify a director or officer for a settlement payment made by the defendant to the corporation at the conclusion of a derivative suit. The reason is that if indemnification were allowed, there would be a circular recovery — the corporation would be receiving the settlement with one hand and paying it out again with the other hand as indemnification. However, most states *do* permit the defendant to be indemnified for his litigation expenses, if the derivative suit has been settled.

(b) Same as in part (a) (\$20,000 for expenses, only). Under MBCA § 8.51(d)(1), "a corporation may not indemnify a director: (1) in connection with a proceeding by or in the right of the corporation, except for ***reasonable expenses*** incurred in connection with the proceeding if it is determined that the director has met the relevant standard of conduct under subsection (a) . . . ." So no matter what Catherine's conduct was, she can't recover the settlement itself, since this is a "proceeding by or in the right of the corporation" (i.e., a derivative suit.) (The *court* still has discretion to *order* indemnification, under the "fair and reasonable" test of § 8.54(a)(3), but it's unlikely that the court will use this discretion, and the corporation may not make the indemnification payment without a court order.)

On the other hand, Catherine probably *can* recover the litigation expenses. These are clearly "reasonable expenses incurred in connection. . . ." The issue is whether Catherine's conduct met the requirements of § 8.51(a). That subsection requires that she have: (1) conducted herself in "good faith"; and (2) "reasonably believed . . . in the case of conduct in [her] official capacity, that [her] conduct was in the best interests of the corporation." The facts tell us that (1) is satisfied, and her belief that the acquisition would be a good one for Henry VIII probably means that (2) is satisfied as well. Therefore, Catherine can probably recover her litigation expenses.

(c) Nothing. MBCA § 8.51(d)(2) prohibits the company from indemnifying a director "in connection with any proceeding with respect to conduct for which [the director] was ***adjudged liable*** on the basis that he ***received a financial benefit to which he was not entitled***, whether or not involving action in his official capacity." This applies here: the court has found a breach of the duty of loyalty, leading to an unduly high price being paid, which price was shared in by Catherine. Therefore, without a court order the company may not even pay Catherine's litigation expenses, let alone indemnify her for the judgment. (The court might still order that Henry VIII reimburse the expenses, under § 8.54(a)(3), if this would be "fair and reasonable"; but the court does not have discretion to order indemnification for the judgment under any circumstances, under that same provision.)

79. (a) No. In most states, a sale of substantially all of a corporation's assets must be approved by a majority of the corporation's *outstanding stock* — not just a majority of those present at a validly convened meeting. Here, only 60% of the shares were represented at the meeting, so a 60% approval represented only 36% of Guano's outstanding shares. As a result, the sale hasn't been approved by the shareholders and can't be carried out.

(b) Yes. MBCA § 11.04(e) requires only a majority of those shares actually voting, as long as a quorum (1/2 of eligible votes) votes. Since 60% of those voting voted yes, and since more than half of all eligible shares voted, that's enough under the MBCA, even though fewer than half of all eligible shares voted yes.

80. Yes. In virtually all jurisdictions, the shareholders of a corporation that acquires another corporation's assets do not have to approve the transaction.

81. Both. In virtually all states, if a company's shareholders will give up their existing shares in return for shares in some new entity, that company's shareholders must approve the transaction. (In other words, in a merger the "merged" company's shareholders must approve.) Again in most states, the "default" rule is that the shareholders of the company which is "buying" assets in exchange for its shares must approve, as well. (In other words, the holders of the surviving party to the merger must approve.) See, e.g., MBCA § 11.03(a). There are some exceptions, but none applies here.

83. Dactyl will lose, because no shareholder vote is required in a short-form merger. Delaware, like many states, recognizes the "short-form merger" — that is, a scenario by which a corporation owning at least 90% of another corporation merges that corporation into itself. In such a merger, neither corporation's shareholders get a vote, on the theory that such a vote would be meaningless. Instead, only the boards of the two corporations need approve the merger. See Del. GCL § 253. Since Paleolyric owns more than 90% of Tyrannosaurus, the short-form merger provision is available, and Paleolyric properly took advantage of it. (The protection that Dactyl gets is the right to an appraisal of his shares. See GCL § 253(d); § 262.)

84. (a) Demand appraisal of his shares. Nearly all states allow an unhappy shareholder in a merging company to demand appraisal of his shares, provided that he does not vote in favor of the merger. The basic idea is that the merging company will be required to buy the dissenter's shares at their fair market value, rather than forcing him to accept the surviving company's stock.

(b) Submit a demand and deposit his shares. John will have to submit a written demand that the company purchase his shares for fair value. In many states (e.g., Delaware — see Del. GCL § 262(d)(1)), this demand must be made in writing *before the vote on the merger occurs*. John will also probably have to deposit his shares with the company at the time he makes the demand (so he can't sell the surviving-company shares at a profit if the price runs up, thus playing "heads I win, tails you lose").

(c) The merged company will have to buy John's shares for their fair market value, judged as of the time of the merger. If the company and John can't agree on what that fair price is, a court will ultimately decide.

85. (a) No, because Seven Veils is publicly-traded. Delaware, like a number of states, denies appraisal rights as to public companies. Specifically, Del. GCL § 262(b)(1) denies the right of appraisal to holders of any company that is either traded on a national stock exchange, listed on NASDAQ, or held of record by more than 2,000 people. In other words, in Delaware, holders of publicly-traded companies don't get appraisal rights (on the theory that such a holder can simply sell his shares in the open market for what the market views as their fair value, so he doesn't need the "escape hatch" of appraisal). Since Seven Veils is listed on the NYSE, that fact alone means that John doesn't have appraisal rights.

(b) No, because Seven Veils is publicly-traded. The MBCA was amended (in 1999) to furnish a "publicly-traded" exception similar to those existing in many states (see (a) above). Under MBCA § 13.02(b)(1), no appraisal rights exist if the class of stock in question is listed on a national stock exchange or NASDAQ (or meets certain other "liquidity" standards).

There is an exception for certain transactions thought to pose conflict-of-interest problems, like management buyouts, but this exception does not apply here.

87.   (a) No. In virtually all jurisdictions, the cardinal rule is that a holder who votes in favor of the merger cannot later assert appraisal rights. Indeed, in many jurisdictions the holder not only can't vote in favor, but has to announce his demand for appraisal *before* the vote is even held. See, e.g., MBCA § 13.21(a); Del. GCL § 262(d)(1).

(b) No. The general principle is that only holders who were entitled by law to vote on the merger may assert appraisal rights. (There are exceptions, such as for a minority holder of a subsidiary in a short-form merger, but no exception applies on these facts.) Because this was a "whale-minnow" merger (i.e., Mare-iott's shares outstanding would increase by less than 20% as the result of the merger), Mare-iott shareholders didn't have a legal right to approve, even though Mare-iott's board decided to solicit their approval anyway. Therefore, under the prevailing view Earp as a Mare-iott holder would not be permitted to demand appraisal.

88.   (a) That appraisal is the exclusive remedy, thus foreclosing an injunction.

(b) Yes, probably. Most states make appraisal the exclusive remedy when the shareholder's contention is merely that the proposed transaction is a bad deal for him or for the company in which he is a holder. So Revere's claim that Long Silver and its holders are not getting equivalent value would be foreclosed, under the prevailing view. It will make no difference that Revere did not in fact ask for appraisal: he was entitled to ask for it, so this becomes the exclusive remedy even though he didn't avail himself of it.

89.   (a) No, because it didn't receive a majority vote of the preferred shares. The issue here is the percentage by which nonvoting shares must approve an amendment to the articles when they are entitled to vote on such an amendment. The majority rule is that, if a class of nonvoting stock is entitled to vote on an amendment (as is the case here), a *majority of that class* must approve the amendment. Here, although a majority of the *total* outstanding shares approved the amendment — 32,000 out of 50,000 — only 20% of the outstanding preferred shares approved it (2,000 out of 10,000). As a result, the preferred shares as a class didn't approve the amendment. Thus, the amendment has not been adopted.

(b) No, because although a majority of those preferred's voting voted "yes," no quorum of the preferreds was present. Under MBCA § 10.04(a)(5), holders of a class of stock have the right to vote as a separate voting group on a change to the articles of incorporation if the change would "create a new class of shares having rights or preferences with respect to distributions or to dissolution that are prior or superior to the shares of the class." The proposed change here, by creating the new class of cumulative-preferred shares, would create a class that is superior to the non-cumulative preferred with respect to the payment of distributions (since dividends are a form of distributions). Therefore, § 10.04(a)(5) gives the existing preferreds the right to vote as a separate group. Now, MBCA § 7.25(c) says that when a separate voting group votes, the measure passes if a majority of those voting in the group vote for the measure. However, that is true *only if a quorum of that voting quorum* — that is, a majority of the votes in that voting group — *is present*. See MBCA § 7.25(a). Under § 7.25(a), second sent., a quorum of a voting group consists of a majority of the shares outstanding of that voting group, assuming that the charter does not provide otherwise (and the facts tell us that the charter here does not provide otherwise). Therefore, for the quorum requirement to be satisfied,

5,001 shares of preferred must have been "present" (i.e., voting for or against or abstaining). Since only 3,500 voted or abstained, no quorum was present. Consequently, the fact that a majority of those preferreds voting voted "yes" is irrelevant — the preferreds didn't validly give their approval, and without their separate approval the measure couldn't pass.

90. (a) No. Federal laws governing takeovers and proxy solicitations essentially protect only against fraud and inadequate disclosure, not against substantive unfairness. Thus If Wolf had engaged in deceptive conduct, Red could have challenged the freezeout under Rule 10b-5, or under the proxy solicitation anti-fraud rules. But since Red's claim is merely that she's been unfairly excluded from the business, federal law gives her no remedy.

(b) It depends on the state. Some states follow the Delaware approach, and require that a freezeout — that is, any transaction cutting out minority shareholders — need only meet the "entire fairness" test. Here, the fact that Red got a fair price for her shares, after adequate disclosure, probably makes the transaction "entirely fair" to her. Other states (e.g., New York), however, require — in addition to fairness — a valid "business purpose" for a corporate freezeout. Courts following this latter approach typically hold that a majority holder's mere desire to eliminate minority holders is not a valid "business purpose." In such a court, therefore, Red might well succeed either in getting the transaction unwound or at least in getting money damages from Wolf.

91. Glory must file a statement of ownership within 10 days of the time she became a more-than-5% owner of Terrible Swift's common stock. SEC Rule 13d-1(a) says that if a person becomes a more-than-5% owner of any class of stock in any publicly-traded company, the person must file a statement of ownership on Schedule 13 within 10 days of the time the person acquired that status. So Glory must file a 13D, showing the number of shares she owns, the date of acquisition, and other information. The fact that Glory did not conduct a "tender offer" is irrelevant to the 13D filing obligation. (If Glory *had* conducted a tender offer, then she would have had to make disclosures even before acquiring the shares in connection with the tender offer; but these disclosures would have been on a different form, 14D-1, and pursuant to different rules, grouped under Regulation 14D under the '34 Act.)

93. $8 per share. Under the "best price rule," if the consideration offered in a tender offer for a target's shares is increased, the increased price must be paid to all the target's shareholders who accepted at the earlier, lower price. As a result, Charlie will have to pay Coco an extra $3 a share. '34 Act, § 14(d)(7).

94. Yes. Under SEC Rules enacted pursuant to the Williams Act, a shareholder who tenders to a tender offeror may revoke the tender, and withdraw the shares, at any time so long as the offer remains open. See Rule 14d-7. Since Mickey's offer remains open, Minnie may revoke and tender her shares to Pluto up until April 15.

95. No, because Richie has not made a tender offer. The Williams Act doesn't explicitly define tender offers. However, courts and the SEC cite eight elements (not all required in any given situation) in deciding whether a person has made a tender offer: active and widespread solicitation for a substantial percentage of the stock at a premium over market price, a firm price, an offer for a limited time and contingent on the tender of a fixed number of shares, an offer that is publicly announced before or during a buying spree, and the placing of pressure on shareholders to sell. The most important elements are the fixed price of the offer and its limited time.

The only element present here was the buying spree. A court would almost certainly conclude that Richie's widespread open-market buying, in and of itself, wasn't enough to constitute a tender offer. Such a conclusion would be consistent with Congress's intent to protect shareholders from making hasty, ill-informed choices — on these facts, with private purchases and no actual offer to buy control at a particular price at a particular time, no real pressure on shareholders existed. This would be true even if Richie told the world that he expected to someday seek control. (Note that since Richie's purchases put him over 5%, he was required to file a Schedule 13D ownership statement, and on that statement was required to disclose that he intends some day to attempt to acquire control.)

96. (a) A "poison pill."

(b) No. Generally, the issuance of shares is within the control of the board, as long as the shares are within the "authorized" number (which must normally be set in the charter, and which requires a shareholder vote to amend). Indeed, that's a big advantage (from the target's board's perspective) of a poison pill plan — since no shareholder approval is typically needed, the board can act quickly, and on its own. (If holder approval were needed, the holders might well vote down the plan, since it reduces their chance of getting a premium price from a hostile bidder.)

(c) Delaware state court. Nothing in the federal securities laws generally bars a target company from using defensive measures, especially where the target's management has not solicited shareholder consent to the measure. (If Not Amused had solicited shareholder approval of the call options, and had made misstatements or omissions in the materials accompanying the solicitation, then there *would* be a federal securities-law violation, which could be addressed in federal court.) Any relief that Albert is to obtain will have to come from Delaware state court, and will have to derive from Delaware law.

(d) That the call will be struck down as an unreasonable barrier to a hostile takeover. In evaluating anti-takeover measures taken by a target's management or board, the Delaware court considers four factors: (1) whether the target's board had reasonable grounds for believing that the raider posed a danger to the corporation's welfare; (2) whether the defensive measures were "reasonable in relation to the threat posed"; (3) whether the board acted in good faith and after reasonable investigation; and (4) whether the measure was approved by a board a majority of whose members were outside (as opposed to employee) directors. If the court finds that the answer to all questions is "yes," the court generally gives the defensive measure the protection of the business judgment rule (and upholds it without second-guessing its substantive merits); but if the answer to one or more questions is "no," the court will make the target's management carry the burden of showing that the transaction is "entirely fair" to shareholders, something management usually can't do.

As to (1), there is no evidence on these facts for Not Amused's board to have any special fear about what Albert will do to operations. As to (2), Albert can make a very strong case that the call plan here was not "reasonable in relation to the threat posed" — the call seems to be a "preclusive" one (one which will make it very unlikely that Albert will go through with his tender offer, because of the horrible consequences to him if he does), and a preclusive measure will almost always be found to be unreasonable. As to (3), the fact that the board has acted "immediately" suggests that they didn't do much investigation about what Albert's offer really means for shareholders, and are acting mostly to protect their own posts. Therefore, even if the board satisfied (4) (the facts don't tell us whether it did), the court is very likely to conclude that the call plan should not receive the protection of the business judgment rule. In that event, the court will probably go on to find that the plan is not "fair" to Not Amused's shareholders, because it will probably prevent them from having the opportunity to be bought out at a premium. Consequently, the court is likely to invalidate the plan.

97. Yes, probably, because the board has not treated both bidders equally. Once the management of a Delaware company decide to sell control of the company, the board bears the obligation to get the highest price for shareholders. This obligation normally means that the board must treat all bidders substantially equally, rather than favoring one (because a bidding war normally offers the best chance to get top dollar for the company). This is the "level playing field" rule. On these facts, it's quite clear that the board of Her Majesty is trying to steer the sale to SMERSH instead of to Bond, even though Bond might well be willing to offer more than the $31 price that SMERSH is talking about. So the Delaware court will probably invalidate the crown-jewel option, and order Her Majesty's board to negotiate equally with both Bond and SMERSH.

98. (a) $5,000 — that is, 1,000 shares outstanding multiplied by $5 par value. Stated capital (a/k/a legal capital) is the par value per share multiplied by the number of outstanding shares. Here, the par value is $5 and there are 1,000 shares outstanding, making $5,000 in stated capital. The remaining $2,500 paid for the shares (in cash or prepaid rent) would be "paid-in surplus." The "stated capital" figure might matter because in most states (regardless of their precise rules on when dividends may be paid), dividends may not be paid "out of" stated capital. That is, a dividend cannot be paid if following the payment, the company's net worth (assets minus liabilities) would be less than its stated capital. So here, prior to operations, the company could not make a payment that would cause its net worth to go below $5,000.

(b) $2,500. The company has an "earned surplus" of $0 (i.e., it has a lifetime total of $0 in "retained earnings"). However, it has an "unearned surplus" of $2,500. This unearned surplus comes entirely from the "paid-in surplus," that is, the amount by which the company collected cash or property for share-issuance in excess of the $5,000 stated value. This paid-in surplus is, of course, represented by the $2,500 in pre-paid rent that's shown as an asset on the company's books.

So in a state — like Delaware or New York — that allows dividends to be paid out of either earned or unearned surplus, a dividend of $2,500 could be paid. (On these facts the company probably doesn't have *cash* to pay out the $2,500 dividend. But it could borrow the $2,500 from a bank, and then pay that cash out as a dividend, because this would just "use up" the value of the prepaid rent. This might leave the company "insolvent" — in the sense of "unable to pay its debts as they come due" — which is why the question tells you to ignore any issue of insolvency. Note that in virtually all states, regardless of your surplus situation you can't pay a dividend if the payment would leave the company insolvent.)

99. (a) $150 — that is, the amount in the retained earnings account. Under the "earned surplus" test, a dividend can only be declared to the extent of the contents of the retained earnings account, which represents the accumulated but undistributed lifetime profits of the business.

In addition, the facts tell us that the dividend is further restricted in that it can't leave the corporation insolvent, with insolvency to be measured by the balance-sheet test. Under this standard, the dividend won't be allowed if, after it's paid, the corporation's liabilities would exceed its assets. Since paying a $150 dividend would leave the corporation with $650 in assets and $500 in liabilities, payment is not prohibited by the balance-sheet test. (After the dividend is paid, the cash account would be left with $150, and the retained earnings account would be empty.) Notice, by the way, that if the state allowed dividends to be paid from paid-in surplus as well as from retained earnings, this would leave another $100 for dividends, since after payment the company would still have $550 in assets and $500 in liabilities.

(b) $200, probably. Under the MBCA test, § 6.40(c), a corporation must essentially meet two tests of solvency (but no tests relating to surplus). First, a dividend can't reduce the company's assets below its liabilities (using any fair measure of assets, including fair market value). Second, the company must be able to pay its bills as they mature (the so-called "equity," as opposed to balance-sheet, test for insolvency.) The pay-bills-as-they-mature standard more or less means that the company can't deplete its cash below its current liabilities. Under the MBCA, then, 100 Dalmatians could pay out $200 in dividends (since its cash is $200 more than its current liabilities, and its total assets exceed its total liabilities by $300). (Actually, if the company could show that it would soon collect additional cash — say from receivables — in time to pay already-accrued liabilities, the dividend might be ok even if it would leave cash on hand at less than current liabilities. Conversely, if the company knew that it would be receiving a huge bill soon that it couldn't pay when due, the fact that the company would, today, be left post-dividend with more cash than current liabilities, would not protect it. But "cash greater than current liabilities" is at least a good first *approximation* of whether the company is "able to pay its debts as they mature.")

100. (a) He should have his board declare a "revaluation surplus" of $600. For purposes of dividend statutes, most states probably permit a corporation to "write up" its assets from their "historical cost basis" to their "current market value." This should typically be done by a resolution of the board of directors.

(b) Yes. After the revaluation surplus is declared, (and before the dividend is paid) the balance sheet will look like this:

Assets		Liabilities & Owners' Equity	
Cash	$ 50	Current Liabilities	$100
Oil reserves, at market	$1,000	Long-term debt	$200
		Owners' Equity:	
		Stated Capital	$ 50
		Paid-in Surplus	$ 50
		Retained Earnings	$ 50
		Revaluation Surplus	$600

The corporation can now pay dividends out of three types of surplus: paid-in surplus ($50), retained earnings ($50), and revaluation surplus (the difference between historical cost and market value, or $600), for a total of $700. If Jed wants to pay $600, the capital-surplus test doesn't block him. He'll have to borrow the money (since he doesn't have enough cash). If he borrowed the full $600 (as long-term debt), and used this to pay the dividend, his balance sheet would now look like this:

Assets		Liabilities & Owners' Equity	
Cash	$ 50	Current Liabilities	$100
Oil reserves, at market	$1,000	Long-term debt	$800
		Owners' Equity:	
		Stated Capital	$ 50
		Paid-in Surplus	$ 50
		Retained Earnings	$ 50

Since the company's assets ($1,050) still equal or exceed its liabilities ($900), payment of the dividend did not violate the balance-sheet insolvency test, so the dividend was legal in this jurisdiction. (In a state following the "able-to-pay-debts-as-they-mature" test for insolvency, the dividend probably wouldn't be legal, because the corporation now has $50 in current assets, and $100 in current liabilities.)

102. (a) Yes, even though she wasn't on notice that the dividend was illegal. The issue here is whether an innocent shareholder can be required to repay a dividend that is paid by an insolvent corporation, even if the shareholder does not know, or have reason to know, of the insolvency. The majority approach at common-law is that the company (or its creditors) may recover the payment despite the shareholder's lack of guilty knowledge or even lack of negligence. As a result, Minnie can be required to repay the $250 she received, even though she had no reason to know anything was amiss at Universal Solvent.

(b) No. Where the problem is not the corporation's insolvency, but merely its surplus status, the majority common-law approach is that the stockholder can be required to disgorge only if she *knew* that the payment was improper.

103. Yes, probably, because the repurchase was not for a proper purpose. In general, a corporation has the right to repurchase its shares. And there is no general rule that the corporation must treat all shareholders equally in making such a repurchase. (So, for instance, most courts say that a privately-held corporation can repurchase the controlling holder's shares for a fair price while refusing to do the same for the non-controlling holders.) But most courts say that the corporation must be acting for a valid "business purpose" when it makes a repurchase, and that the transaction must not violate the rules against self-interested transactions. The purchase here seems to have no valid business purpose, merely the purpose (on Joe's part) of enriching him, and the purpose (on the board's part) of staying in power. Since the board was not "independent" and "disinterested" when they voted, the court will probably treat the purchase as being a self-interested transaction, and therefore probably won't give the directors' decision to repurchase the benefit of the business judgment rule. Consequently, the court will probably hold that the repurchase violated Joe's duty of loyalty to the corporation, and that the repurchase was not fair to the other stockholders. In that event, the court will order Joe to disgorge his profits (or will even rescind the entire transaction).

105. No. Not all courts recognize any common-law right on the part of a creditor of an insolvent corporation to recover against a recipient of "watered stock." Of those courts that do recognize such a right, most apply the "holding out" or "misrepresentation" theory. Under this theory, only a creditor who has *relied* on the corporation's (false) implied or express assertion that all shares were issued for at least par value may recover. Here, Keepon extended credit to Old King Coal *before* Old King Coal even issued the stock to LaBrea. Therefore, Keepon could not possibly have relied on any express or implied assertion by Old King Coal that no watered stock had been issued. Since Keepon didn't rely on any assertion, it can't recover anything from LaBrea. (But there may be a statute, or case law, letting *Old King Coal* or its trustee in bankruptcy recover from LaBrea for the amount of "water.")

106. (a) The doctrine of preemptive rights. A preemptive right is a right, sometimes given to a corporation's existing shareholders, permitting them to maintain their percentage of ownership in the corporation by enabling them to buy a portion of any newly-issued shares. If preemptive rights applied here, Lucrezia would be guaranteed the right to buy 25% of any newly-authorized batch of shares, at the same price as was offered to anyone else.

(b) No. The MBCA, like many modern statutes, follows an "opt in" approach to preemptive rights. That is, stockholders don't have preemptive rights unless the articles of incorporation specifically confer such rights (as opposed to an "opt out" approach, under which holders have such rights unless the charter says that they don't). See § 6.30(a). Since the facts say that Thumbscrew's charter is silent on all relevant issues, Thumbscrew has not "opted in," and there are no preemptive rights. Therefore, the board can choose to offer all the new stock to Torquemada. (Where there are no preemptive rights, and the price is fair, courts generally say that the board can offer the stock to whomever it wishes.)

Notice that the facts say that the stock is being issued to raise needed capital. If this had not been true — if the stock was instead being issued solely to increase Torquemada's control — a court might hold that there was no "valid business purpose" for the issuance, and that Torquemada had used his control in violation of a fiduciary duty to the minority holders. In that event, even without preemptive rights the court might strike down the issuance to Torquemada, or order that Lucrezia be permitted to participate pro rata.

107. (a) No. Preemptive rights generally do not apply to shares that are part of the initially-authorized shares at the time the company is formed. Some states provide that after a certain lapse of time, the initially-authorized-but-unissued shares do become subject to preemptive rights. But virtually no state would make this happen in as little as the five months specified in the facts. (MBCA § 6.30(b)(3)(iii) makes it happen 6 months from the date of incorporation; NY BCL § 622(e)(5) makes it happen after 2 years.)

(b) No. Shares that are issued in exchange for property or services generally are not deemed to trigger preemptive-rights schemes.

108. (a) Rule 505 under the '33 Act. SEC Rule 505 allows a company to raise up to $5 million. There can be any number of "accredited" investors (those having a net worth of more than $1 million or income of more than $200,000 in each of the past two years), plus up to 35 non-accredited investors. The 20 "working stiff" friends thus qualify as non-accredited investors.

(b) Yes. You'll have to obey the pretty precise disclosure requirements laid out in SEC Rule 502. Some of the financial information (e.g., the balance sheet) will have to be audited.

(c) No. §4(2) of the '33 Act exempts from the registration requirements any transaction that does not involve a "public offering." Certain SEC Rules give a "safe harbor," by preventing certain transactions from being public offerings; Rule 505, discussed above, is one such. But a transaction can also avoid being a public offering just by complying with judicial decisions that define "public offering." An offer to a very small number of very rich people would almost certainly be held by a court not to be a public offering. Therefore, Rocky can make his offer to his two rich friends, and take their money, without complying with any particular SEC Rule. The advantage of this non-Rule-based approach is that Rocky won't have to comply with any particular SEC-defined disclosure requirements (as he would if he went with SEC Rules 504, 505 or in some instances 506).

MULTIPLE-CHOICE QUESTIONS

Here are 24 multiple-choice questions. They have been created especially for this book, and are built mainly on the fact patterns from some of the questions in the *Law in a Flash* Corporations flash-card set published by Aspen Publishers.

1. On April 1, 2008, Marc Antony and Brutus signed an agreement with Caesar, a promoter for Roman Empire Corporation, whereby Marc Antony and Brutus each agreed to purchase 500 shares of $10 per share par value stock. This contract was made prior to the time Roman Empire Corp. was formed; Roman Empire Corp. was then formed on June 1. On July 1, just before the board of directors of Roman Empire was to affirm the subscription agreement, Marc Antony advised the board that he was repudiating the agreement. The board affirmed the subscription agreement on July 2, and Brutus immediately paid for his stock. The agreement was silent about whether, or for what time period, it was irrevocable.

   Assuming that the MBCA is in force, which of the following statements about Marc Antony's liability under the agreement is most likely correct?

   (A) He is not liable, since he revoked prior to acceptance of the contract by the corporation.
   (B) He is liable, because the corporation was formed prior to his attempted repudiation.
   (C) He is liable, because by operation of law the agreement was irrevocable at the moment the board affirmed it.
   (D) He is liable if and only if he failed to notify Caesar of his repudiation.

2. Bill and Ted decided to open up a travel agency, Bill & Ted's Excellent Adventures. They decided that the business should be operated as a corporation, so they drew up articles of incorporation and put them in the company safe-deposit box, intending to file them with the state soon. They then purported to carry on the business as a corporation, putting an "Inc." after the business name and keeping the company records and finances separate from their own. They forgot to file the incorporation papers, and in fact never made any filing of any sort with the state.

   Alas, the agency's debts soon exceeded the resources that Bill and Ted were willing to put into it, and the agency stopped doing business, at a time when it owed $10,000 to Adventure Airlines. The jurisdiction has enacted the MBCA. Are Bill and Ted liable for the agency's unpaid debt to Adventure Airlines?

(A) No, because the agency is a corporation, by operation of the de facto corporation doctrine.

(B) Yes, because the agency is a general partnership, for the debts of which the partners are personally liable.

(C) No, if Adventure thought it was dealing with a corporation.

(D) Yes, because a corporation's shareholders are secondarily liable if the corporation cannot pay its debts.

3. Gilligan's Island Tours, Inc. (GITI), runs one-day cruises. Its articles of incorporation list only one corporate purpose, which is "the operation of one-day cruises to nearby islands." Realizing that a desert island to which it sails would make a great resort, the chairman of the board of GITI, Skipper, signed a land sale contract on the corporation's behalf to purchase the island from Mary Ann, its record owner. Before closing, Mary Ann changed her mind. GITI brought suit to compel Mary Ann to go through with the sale. Mary Ann has examined GITI's charter, and has noticed the cruises-only purposes clause; she therefore asserts as a defense that the proposed transaction would violate GITI's charter.

Which of the following best summarizes how Mary Ann will fare with this defense?

(A) Mary Ann will win under the common law, but lose under the MBCA.

(B) Mary Ann will lose under the common law, but win under the MBCA.

(C) Mary Ann will lose under both the common law and the MBCA.

(D) Mary Ann will win under both the common law and the MBCA.

4. The Attila the Hun Wrecking Company has a wholly-owned subsidiary, Attila's Army-Navy Surplus Stores, Inc. Army-Navy is run as a separate corporation, with its own board of directors (most of whom are also directors of Wrecking Co.) Army-Navy observes all corporate formalities, such as the holding of board meetings, the keeping of minutes, segregation of funds from those of Wrecking Co., etc.

Wrecking Company, through its domination of Army-Navy's board, has always caused Army-Navy to sell Wrecking Co. product at Army-Navy's cost; these sales from Army-Navy to Wrecking Co. account for 90% of Army-Navy's total sales. Now, because Army-Navy does not have sufficient gross profits, it can't pay a creditor, the Bambi Freeze-Dried Venison Co. Bambi is seeking payment from the Wrecking Company directly. Can Bambi recover from Wrecking Company?

(A) Yes, because Wrecking Company unfairly prevented Army-Navy from conducting its operations in a way that would produce enough profits to satisfy Army-Navy's creditors.

(B) No, because a parent is normally not responsible for the debts of its subsidiary, and no exception to this rule applies here.

(C) Yes, because a majority of Army-Navy's board members were also members of Wrecking Company's board.

(D) Yes, because a parent corporation is responsible for the debts of its subsidiary if the parent effectively controls the business decisions of the subsidiary.

5. Spencer Christian is a member of the board of Pitcairn Travel Agency, Inc. Captain Bligh, another director (and majority stockholder), called a special meeting of the board of directors to discuss changing the location of the annual meeting from an island in the South Pacific to a town in the Midwest, since this would be far more convenient for the company's directors and shareholders. Christian didn't receive notice of the meeting (though all other directors did). However, Christian happened to be at company headquarters when the meeting started. He therefore sat in and offered his opinion — he was hotly against the move. A majority of the directors (all directors were present) voted for it, however. Christian then judicially challenged the change, claiming that the meeting was invalid because he didn't receive clear and timely notice of it. What result, under the MBCA? (Assume that there are no quorum issues, and that Pitcairn's charter and bylaws are silent about advance notice of meetings.)

   (A) The meeting was invalid, because a special meeting of the board is not valid unless preceded by advance notice to all directors of the meeting's date, time and place.
   (B) The meeting was valid, because even apart from Christian a quorum of directors got the notice and was present.
   (C) The meeting was valid, because Christian waived any objection by participating in the meeting.
   (D) The meeting was invalid, because all board meetings, whether regular or special, must be preceded by advance notice to all directors of the meeting's date, time and place.

6. Melmac Phlegm Industries, Inc., has a board of directors with five members. Alf was elected to the board. He was not an especially impressive board member (he constantly made off-the-wall comments and rarely said anything intelligent), but he didn't do or say anything that would have been cause for removal in the jurisdiction. Two major stockholders duly called a special stockholders meeting for the stated purpose of removing Alf from the board. A quorum of stockholders was present and voted. By a vote of 1,000 to 800, the shareholders voted to remove Alf, even though his term had one year left to run. Was Alf validly removed from the board? (The corporation's charter is silent on the issue of whether a director can be removed by shareholder vote without cause.)

   (A) Yes, whether or not the corporation's charter authorizes cumulative voting.
   (B) Yes, if and only if the corporation's charter authorizes cumulative voting.
   (C) No, whether or not the corporation's charter authorizes cumulative voting.
   (A) No, if and only if the corporation's charter authorizes cumulative voting.

7. Dr. Seuss was the corporate secretary for the Sam I Am Company. The company's office manager usually handled the arrangements for the annual meeting of

shareholders, and had the express authority to make all necessary contracts regarding the arrangements for the meeting. However, this past year the office manager, Bartholomew, had an oobleck virus and couldn't make up the meeting arrangements. Dr. Seuss stepped into the void. Among other tasks, he looked through the yellow pages and hired the Cat N. Hat Caterers to provide two hundred servings of green eggs and ham. (No one else at Sam I Am knew that Dr. Seuss was ordering food for the meeting.)

The meeting took place as scheduled. At the meeting, most of the directors, officers, and shareholders ate the green eggs and ham. When Cat N. Hat sent its bill, Sam I Am refused to pay, claiming that Dr. Seuss, as corporate secretary, had no power to bind the corporation. What result?

(A) Sam will win, because there is no doctrine under which Dr. Seuss' action in hiring Cat N. Hat was properly authorized.

(B) Sam will lose, under the doctrine of apparent authority.

(C) Sam will lose, under the doctrine of implied actual authority.

(D) Sam will lose, under the doctrine of ratification.

8. Elvis Presley, Richie Valens and Janis Joplin formed a record company, Rock Platters Inc. There were 100 shares outstanding. Elvis owned 51 shares, Richie 30 and Janis 19. At the annual shareholders meeting, Richie and Janis showed up, but Elvis didn't. (Nor did Elvis give anyone else his proxy). At the meeting, Janis introduced a motion to change the company's principal business to the operation of an Internet Website, oldies.com. Nothing about Janice's motion was mentioned in the notice of the shareholders meeting. Both Richie and Janis voted their shares in favor of the motion.

Assume that Janice's proposal was a proper subject for shareholder action, even without any prior board action on the proposal. Also, assume that the company's charter and bylaws are silent about all issues relevant to this question. Is the corporation now authorized to change its principal business?

(A) No, because there were not enough shares represented at the meeting.

(B) Yes, because a majority of the shares actually voting supported the proposal.

(C) No, because less than a majority of the outstanding shares voted for the measure.

(D) No, because notice of the proposal was not included in the notice of the meeting.

9. Sarah Connor owns shares in the Terminator Wrecking Company. Terminator's annual meeting is to take place on June 1st, and has a record date of April 15th. On May 1st, Sarah took out a loan with the Cyborg Bank, pledging as collateral her Terminator shares. Cyborg insisted on being granted a proxy as a condition for the loan, so Sarah granted the proxy. The proxy says, on its face, that it is irrevocable until Dec. 31. Sarah then paid off the loan in full on May 20th. Sarah has now showed up at the Terminator annual meeting, intending to vote her shares. Cyborg Bank has sent a representative as well, claiming that it has an irrevocable proxy and is entitled to vote the shares. The MBCA applies. Who gets to vote the shares?

(A) Cyborg, because a proxy that conspicuously states that it is irrevocable is in fact irrevocable.

(B) Cyborg, because the proxy stated that it was irrevocable and the proxy was coupled with an interest.

(C) Sarah, because the loan was paid off.

(D) Sarah, because a shareholder proxy is revocable by the shareholder even if the proxy states otherwise.

10. Carl Icant, a corporate raider and activist, has owned .5 % of the stock of Macrosoft Corp., a large software producer, for 2 years. Icant's stock is currently worth $3 million. Icant has in a timely manner submitted to Macrosoft a 250-word shareholder proposal to be included in the proxy materials that Macrosoft sends to shareholders in advance of the upcoming annual meeting. The proposal resolves that management be urged to release a greater number of Internet-based products, and fewer desktop-software products. State law on all matters is in accord with the law of most states. Must Macrosoft include the proposal in its proxy materials?

(A) No, because Icant does not own enough Macrosoft stock.

(B) No, because Icant's proposal relates to the conduct of the ordinary business operations of the company.

(C) No, because the proposal is not a proper subject for action by stockholders under state law.

(D) Yes, because Icant has owned more than 1% of the company's stock for more than one year, and the proposal does not fall within any exclusion from the federal shareholder-proposal rules.

11. The Lady Macbeth Suicide Hotline, Inc., is a close corporation with 1000 shares outstanding. Macbeth owns 700 shares, and Banquo owns the remaining 300. (Banquo bought 100 of his shares from another shareholder in 2000, and the remaining 200 directly from the company in 2004.) At the 2001 annual meeting, Macbeth voted his 700 shares to amend the bylaws to grant the company a right of first refusal on any subsequent stock transfer. Banquo voted the 100 shares he then owned against the amendment. The amendment passed. Due to an administrative oversight, the 200 shares Banquo purchased in 2004 did not have the share-transfer restriction noted on the certificate, as the bylaw required to be done. (Nor do the 100 shares Banquo bought in 2000 have the restriction on them.)

Now, Banquo wants to transfer his 300 shares to Fleance, who's willing to buy them for $100 a share. The company has learned about the proposed transfer, and seeks a judicial declaration that its right of first refusal applies to all Banquo's shares. Under the prevailing modern approach, as to how many of Banquo's shares, if any, does the company's right of first refusal apply?

(A) To all 300 shares, because a properly-enacted bylaw amendment granting a right of first refusal to the corporation applies to all proposed transfers occurring thereafter.

(B) To all 300 shares, because by voting at the 2001 meeting, Banquo is deemed to have consented to any share restrictions implemented at that meeting.

(C) To 200 shares, because the bylaw amendment does not apply to the 100 shares Banquo bought prior to the date of the amendment.

(D) To no shares, because the 100 shares were bought by Banquo before the bylaw amendment, and the 200 shares were not labelled with the restriction.

12. Lillian "Mama" Carlson was chairman of the board of Cincinnati Communications, Inc. (CCI), whose sole asset was radio station WKRP. Lillian ruled WKRP with an iron fist, dominating the other seven board members. Sosumi Inc., a giant Japanese communications company, offered to buy CCI for $50 a share. CCI was currently trading on the NYSE at $39 a share. Lillian wanted to accept the offer, but realized she needed board approval. At a special board meeting called on one day's notice, Lillian made a 20-minute presentation about the offer. She didn't supply — and the directors didn't request — a valuation study or a written copy of the purchase terms. After her presentation, and following 5 minutes of discussion, she called for a vote. The directors unanimously approved the sale. The board submitted the sale to a shareholder vote shortly thereafter, with their recommendation in favor of approval. The shareholders approved it. Thereafter, a minority shareholder, Bailey Quarters, sued the directors for violating their duty of care to the corporation, asserting that the value was closer to $80 a share. The directors denied liability.

Assume that Quarters is correct that another bidder could have been found who would have paid $80. Assume further, however, that it was rational for a director to believe, based on the facts as the directors knew them at the time they voted, that the Sosumi offer was the best offer available at the time. What's the most likely result in Quarters' suit?

(A) The directors will win, because based on the facts as they knew them, the decision to sell to Sosumi was rational.

(B) The directors will lose, because they made their decision without a reasonable level of information about the transaction, and because their overall conduct was not reasonably prudent.

(C) The directors will win, because the business judgment rule will shield them from having a court review whether their decision was in fact in the corporation's best interests.

(D) The directors will lose, because their decision was not the best one in light of the availability of another bidder who would have paid substantially more.

13. Mr. Haney was one of six directors of the Green Acres Produce Company. Green Acres was interested in expanding its acreage in nearby Hooterville. Mr. Haney told the chairman of Green Acres Produce, Oliver Wendell Douglas, that a 100-acre tract

of land in Hooterville, owned by the Hooterville Limited Partnership, was available for $10,000 per acre. Douglas confirmed with Hooterville's general partner (someone other than Mr. Haney) that this was so. Douglas then decided that the property would be a good buy, and brought the proposed purchase to Green Acres' board of directors. Mr. Haney was not present at the directors' meeting where the land purchase was discussed. The other five directors approved it unanimously. Unbeknownst to the other board members, Mr. Haney was one of the limited partners in the Hooterville Limited Partnership (he owned a 25% economic interest in the partnership). No other board member of Green Acres had any conflict.

A minority shareholder of Green Acres has now found out about the proposed purchase, and has sued to prevent its consummation, on account of the fact that Mr. Haney was arguably on both sides of the transaction. There is convincing evidence that the fair market value of the land is only $7,000 per acre.

Will the court issue an injunction against the completion of the transaction?

(A) No, because the transaction was approved by a majority of the five disinterested directors.

(B) Yes, because a transaction in which one or more directors have a conflict may be enjoined if the transaction is substantively unfair to the corporation.

(C) Yes, because the transaction is unfair to the corporation and has not been authorized by disinterested directors (or all shareholders) following disclosure of the conflict involving Mr. Haney.

(D) No, because the directors' decision is protected by the business judgment rule.

14. Alexis Colby is a director (but not an employee) of the Prime-Time Suds Oil Company, a well-capitalized full-service oil company. Because Alexis is proud of being exceptionally knowledgeable about the company's affairs, she annually (and at her own expense) takes a tour of some of Prime-Time's properties. While at one of those properties, she learned from the property's manager that mineral rights were available for an adjacent parcel that Alexis thought had promise for oil. Alexis secretly bid to buy the mineral rights on that parcel for herself, won, drilled, and found oil. As Alexis knew at the time she placed her bid, the rights were ones on which Prime-Time would probably have placed a serious bid (at least equal to Alexis' bid) had Prime-Time's board known about the opportunity. The jurisdiction follows the "line of business" standard for measuring when something is a corporate opportunity.

Prime-Time, citing the corporate-opportunity doctrine, has sued Alexis to the profits she made on the parcel. Will Prime-Time recover?

(A) No, because Alexis was a director, rather than an employee, of Prime-Time.

(B) Yes, because Alexis learned of the opportunity while acting in connection with company business.

(C) No, because Alexis paid for the trip to South America herself.

(D) Yes, but only if Prime-Time shows that it would probably would have been willing and able to purchase the rights had it known about them.

15. Jeff Bazooka was a 55% shareholder, and board chairman, of the NASDAQ-listed Nile Corp., an Internet bookseller. The fair market value of Nile's stock on NASDAQ at the time in question was $20. Bazooka decided he wanted to give up the online book business and go into something really lucrative — being an Internet venture capitalist. Ebuoy, an online seller of boating supplies, offered to buy Bazooka's shares for $30 each, if he was willing to sell all of them. Bazooka accepted the offer. As part of the sale, Bazooka agreed to resign as board chairman immediately, and to cause any directors who were friends of his to also resign, so that Ebuoy could use its voting majority to appoint a majority of the board without waiting for the directors' terms to expire normally.

The sale took place, and Bazooka and a majority of the board immediately resigned as planned, allowing Ebuoy to take control of the corporation. Nile's minority shareholders have sued Bazooka on behalf of Nile, seeking a pro rata part of the $10-per-share premium he received for his shares over fair market value. Who wins?

(A) Bazooka, because as a general rule a controlling shareholder may sell his position for a control premium, and no exception to this rule applies here.

(B) The plaintiffs, because as a general rule a controlling shareholder may not sell his position for a control premium that is not made available to other shareholders.

(C) The plaintiffs, because in a tender offer the same offer must be made to all shareholders.

(D) The plaintiffs, because Bazooka effectively agreed to sell control of the board of directors, a breach of Bazooka's fiduciary obligation to minority shareholders.

16. Jim Kirk was president of Tribble Trouble Inc. ("TTI"), a closely-held corporation with 20 shareholders. TTI owned a tribble ranch, on which it raised fuzzy little tribbles that were sold as exotic housepets. On August 1, Kirk phoned Mr. Spock, a neighbor who was also a TTI shareholder (he owned 1,000 shares), and told him that the ranch was having breeding troubles, making the outlook for profit very poor. Kirk encouraged Spock to sell Kirk Spock's 1,000 shares for $50 each. At a face-to-face meeting the next day, August 2, Spock sold Kirk the shares at the $50/share price. In reality, the tribbles were reproducing like rabbits, and Spock's shares would really have been valued at $200 each on Aug. 2 by an investor who knew the full facts. Spock found out about Kirk's lie on Sept. 1. By that date, due to additional favorable developments, the stock was trading in private transactions among the 20 shareholders at $300 each. That same day, Spock gave Kirk a Vulcan neck pinch, and simultaneously filed a 10b-5 claim against him in federal court. How much, if anything, will Spock recover?

(A) Nothing, because rule 10b-5 does not apply to non-publicly-traded companies.

(B) Nothing, because 10b-5 does not apply where no instrument of interstate commerce is used in connection with the transaction.

(C) $150,000, the difference beween what the stock was really worth on Aug. 2 and what Kirk paid Spock.

(D) $250,000, the difference between what the stock was being traded at on Sept. 1 and what Kirk had earlier paid Spock.

17. Ariel, believing that seaweed is likely to become a major food source, bought 5,000 shares of publicly traded Little Mermaid Sea Harvests, Inc., on March 1. The shares cost $5 each, and her 5,000 shares represented 5% ownership of Little Mermaid. Ariel had no other connection with Little Mermaid. On April 1, Ariel bought another 10,000 shares at $6. On May 1, the U.S. government announced substantial government support for seaweed-based food products. Little Mermaid stock soared to $15 a share. On May 2, Ariel bought another 1,000 shares at $15. On May 15, Ariel sold all her 16,000 shares at $20. A §16(b) claim has been filed against Ariel on behalf of the corporation. How much, if anything, will Ariel owe?

(A) Nothing.
(B) $5,000.
(C) $145,000.
(D) $220,000.

18. Peter Pan was a shareholder of the Fairy Dust Pharmaceuticals Corp. Three of Fairy Dust's five directors, Wendy Darling, Tinkerbell and Captain Hook, arguably usurped a corporate opportunity of Fairy Dust's by buying a drug patent for Quick-Acting Fairy Dust from a third party. Peter Pan, intending to file a derivative suit against Darling and Hook, made a demand on the directors first as required by the applicable statute. The directors then voted to appoint a special litigation committee of the board, comprised of a retired judge, Oliver Motor-Holmes, and a retired doctor, Jack Kevork. (Neither Holmes nor Kevork had anything to do with the acquisition of the Quick-Acting patent.) Holmes and Kevork abstained from the vote to appoint them to the committee.

After a thorough investigation of the facts, the committee recommended that Fairy Dust not pursue a claim. Peter Pan then filed the derivative claim anyway. The directors responded by filing a motion to dismiss, citing the committee's recommendation in support of the motion. The court, conducting its own preliminary review of the documents, has concluded that the corporation probably has a valid claim against Darling and Hook for usurpation of opportunity. Under the MBCA, should the court honor the committee's recommendation and dismiss the action?

(A) Yes, because the recommendation of a special litigation committee is entitled to the protection of the business judgment rule if the committee thoroughly investigated the facts.

(B) No, because process by which the special committee was appointed did not ensure the independence of the committee.

(C) Yes, because all members of the special committee were independent, and did their work in good faith after reasonable investigation.

(D) No, because despite a contrary recommendation by a special committee the court should allow a derivative action to go forward if the court believes that the derivative claim is likely to prevail at trial.

19. Sampson, Inc., manufactures beauty supplies. At the time in question, it had 100,000 shares of voting stock outstanding. Its board resolved that Sampson should purchase all of the stock of Delilah's Hairdressers, Inc., a chain of beauty parlors. To effectuate the merger, Sampson planned to issue 10,000 shares of authorized but previously-unissued stock to Delilah's shareholders in full compensation. Under Delaware law, whose shareholders must approve the transaction?

(A) Both companies' shareholders.

(B) Only Sampson's shareholders.

(C) Only Delilah's shareholders.

(D) Neither Sampson's nor Delilah's shareholders.

20. Seinfeld, Inc., a privately-held producer of TV sitcoms about nothing, was controlled by Jerry Seinfeld and Cosmo Kramer. The board of Seinfeld voted to sell all the company's assets for cash, to Friends, Inc., a rival sitcom producer. The plan of sale called for the company to reinvest the cash received into a coffee shop on the Upper West Side of Manhattan. A majority of Seinfeld shareholders approved the transaction. George Costanza, a minority shareholder of Seinfeld, voted against the transaction and gave prompt notice that he wished to have the company buy his shares for fair market value. Seinfeld, Inc. refused to do so. Which of the following states the correct result under the law of Delaware and under the MBCA?

(A) George wins under Delaware law but loses under the MBCA.

(B) George loses under Delaware law but wins under the MBCA.

(C) George loses under both Delaware law and the MBCA.

(D) George wins under both Delaware law and the MBCA.

21. Alexis Colby wanted to take over the Carrington Oil Company, a public company with 1 million shares outstanding. She didn't own any Carrington stock and intended to launch a tender offer for 51% of it. She was concerned, however, that, as soon as she announced her tender offer, her rival, Krystal Carrington, would make a rival bid. To minimize the possibility of this, Alexis announced on March 1 a tender offer for 510,000 shares @ $20, the offer to expire relatively quickly, on March 10. This tender offer also provided that "all tenders are final," i.e., that once a holder tendered into the offer, the tenderer could not withdraw the tendered shares from the offer. On March 8, when only 200,000 shares had been tendered, Alexis announced that the offer was being amended to an offer to buy 310,000 additional shares (beyond the 200,000

already tendered) @ $25, with the revised offer to expire on on March 15. The amended offer made it clear that anyone who had tendered by March 8 would receive the lesser ($20) amount.

Which of the following violated federal law?

I.   Alexis' initial decision to have the March 1 tender offer expire on March 10.

II. Alexis' statement that all tenders would be final.

III. Alexis' later decision to pay $25 to the later tenderers while paying $20 to the early tenderers.

(A) I, II and III

(B) I and II only

(C) II and III only

(D) I and III only

22. The Jacques Cousteaudian Houseboat Cleaning Service, Inc., was formed. The amount that the shareholders actually paid for each share was equal to the share's par value, $10. For the first three years of the corporation's existence, it lost a total of $75,000. In its fourth and fifth years taken together, however, the service cleaned up, to the tune of a $30,000 profit. During Year 5, declaring a $1,000 dividend would have left the corporation solvent (regardless of the test used for solvency). Just before the end of Year 5, the directors declared a $1,000 dividend.

Which of the following statements is correct about the propriety of declaring the $10,000 dividend?

I. Under the majority approach, the dividend was properly declared.

II. Under the Delaware approach, the dividend was properly declared.

(A) I and II.

(B) I only

(C) II only

(D) Neither I nor II

23. Torquemada wanted to buy 100 shares of newly-issued Spanish Inquisition Co. stock. The stock was worth $10,000. As payment, Torquemada gave Spanish Inquisition a document signed by him, which said, "In consideration of 100 shares of SI stock to be issued immediately, I promise to perform for SI inquisitorial and torture services equal in value to at least $10,000. The services shall be performed, on the schedule requested by the company, over the next 2 years."

Which of the following is a correct statement about the propriety of the share issuance?

    I. The share issuance was proper under the majority approach, such as that of New York.

    II. The share issuance was proper under the MBCA.

(A) I only.

(B) II only.

(C) I and II.

(D) Neither I nor II.

24. Elvis Presley is the sole shareholder of Heartbreak Hotel, Inc., a hotel chain that gives a 50% discount to anyone who has recently been jilted by a spouse or significant other. Elvis would now like to raise about $3.2 million of additional capital for the company, to fund expansion. He tells you that he has three friends who are multi-millionaires that would like to invest around $1 million each. He says he also has an additional 6 friends who are underpaid lawyers earning between $70,000 and $150,000 each, and who each have assets of less than $500,000. None of the lawyers are especially sophisticated in business and financial matters (they're all personal injury lawyers). Elvis thinks that these lawyer friends might invest an average of about $30,000 each. A public offering would be too expensive, so Elvis wants to raise the money without one.

Which of the following SEC provisions, if any, would allow you to do the fundraising without conducting a public offering?

    I.   SEC Rule 504

    II. SEC Rule 505

    III. SEC Rule 506

(A) I alone.

(B) II alone.

(C) II and III.

(D) Neither I, II nor III.

ANSWERS TO
MULTIPLE-CHOICE QUESTIONS

1.   **C**   It's true that at common law, subscription agreements are normally revocable by any subscriber. But the MBCA changes this result. MBCA §6.20(a) says that a subscription entered into before incorporation is irrevocable for six months unless the agreement provides for a longer or shorter period, or all subscribers agree to revocation. Since the agreement was silent on the issue of revocation, and since Brutus did not join in the request for repudiation, the six-month rule applied, and the agreement was therefore irrevocable until Oct. 1, 2000. Since the agreement was board-ratified within that period, it became binding at the moment of ratification. Therefore, **C** is correct.

Because the agreement was irrevocable for six months, **A** is wrong. **B** is wrong because the formation of the corporation did not cause the corporation to affirm the subscription agreement, and the issue is whether the agreement was still in force (as a kind of offer) at the moment it was "accepted" by the corporation. **D** is wrong because the giving of notice of repudiation to the promoter is irrelevant to whether a subscription agreement is revocable.

2.   **B**   A corporation can only be formed by the filing of articles of incorporation with the state. See MBCA §2.03(a) ("Unless a delayed effective date is specified, the corporate existence begins when the articles of incorporation are filed.") All people who purport to act as a corporation, knowing that there was no proper incorporation, are jointly and severally liable for all liabilities created while they so act. MBCA §2.04. Since the facts make it clear that Bill and Ted knew that the corporation wouldn't come into existence until they filed the articles, §2.04 makes them personally liable. They will be treated as a general partnership, since that's the legal entity that is deemed to arise when two or more people work together for profit and do not qualify for some other legal entity.

The MBCA effectively abolishes the doctrine of de facto corporation (see §2.04, which has that effect); therefore **A** is wrong. Under MBCA §2.04, as explained above, those who purport to act as a corporation knowing they are not incorporated are personally liable. Nothing in the MBCA changes this result merely because the counter-party thinks that it's dealing with a corporation; therefore, **C** is wrong. **D** is wrong because it states an incorrect general rule about liability — if the corporation is properly organized, the shareholders are *not* secondarily liable if the corporation fails to pay its debts (indeed, that's the principal purpose of incorporation).

3. **A** At common law, transactions prohibited by the corporation's charter were said to be "*ultra vires*" ("beyond the power"), and were often treated as being unenforceable either by or against the corporation. So here, at common law Mary Ann would probably wriggle off the hook because of the purposes clause.

But under the MBCA, Mary Ann would lose for two reasons, even though the articles of incorporation limit the corporation's purpose to running cruises. First, under MBCA § 3.02, unless the charter provides otherwise, every corporation has "the same powers as an individual to do all things necessary or convenient to carry out its business and affairs . . ." Under sub-section (4) of 3.02, the powers automatically (unless the charter says otherwise) include the right to "purchase . . . real or personal property . . ." The mere fact that the only listed purpose here is the operation of cruises would not be enough to trigger the "otherwise provided in the charter" provision, and thus not enough to make the proposed acquisition here beyond the corporate powers.

Second, even if the charter expressly said that the corporation's purposes were *only* the operation of cruises, or expressly said that the corporation was not permitted to buy real estate (thus triggering the "charter provides otherwise" clause in § 3.02), the ultra vires doctrine *still* wouldn't work here. That's because, according to § 3.04(a), "Except as provided in subsection (b), the validity of corporate action may not be challenged on the ground that the corporation lacks or lacked power to act." Assertion of *ultra vires* by a third party whom the corporation sues for enforcement of a contract is not one of the exceptions listed in (b). (Nor, by the way, would assertion of the defense *by* the corporation, if the third party sued it for enforcement of the contract, be such an exception.)

So Mary Ann wins under the common law, but loses under the MBCA, making **A** correct and **B**, **C**, and **D** incorrect.

4. **A** In a parent-and-subsidiary context, running the subsidiary for the parent's benefit rather than for the subsidiary's own benefit is likely to be grounds for piercing the corporate veil, especially where this has the effect of stripping all profits from the subsidiary. This makes perfect theoretical sense in that, if the parent is unwilling to view the subsidiary as a separate corporation for profit purposes, it ought not to be able to take advantage of the subsidiary's corporate "veil" so as to avoid the subsidiary's liabilities. Therefore, Wrecking Company will be liable for Army-Navy's obligations, making **A** correct.

As to Choice **B**, it's true that a parent is not *normally* responsible for the debts of its subsidiary; but the "running the subsidiary for the parent's benefit" scenario is, as detailed above, one of the exceptions to the general rule. **C** is incorrect because overlapping directors between a parent and a subsidiary, without more, will not lead to a piercing of the corporate veil. Similarly, **D** is incorrect because the mere fact that the parent effectively controls the business decisions of the subsidiary (as is normally the case with a wholly-owned subsidiary) is not, without more, enough to pierce the veil and make the parent liable for the subsidiary's obligations — only if there is some misrepresentation of the true relationship, or some manifest unfairness in preserving the corporate boundaries, will the parent's veil be pierced.

5. **C** For "special" board meetings — i.e., those whose time is not fixed by the bylaws or prior resolution — all directors must receive clear and timely notice of the meetings (which includes the date, time, and place of the meeting). Here, Christian didn't receive notice, so if he hadn't attended a court would allow him to challenge the board action. However, Christian waived the requirement by showing up at the meeting and not making a prompt objection to the lack of notice. See MBCA § 8.23(b) ("A director's attendance at or participation in a meeting waives any required notice to him of the meeting unless the director at the beginning of the meeting (or promptly upon his arrival) objects to holding the meeting or transacting business at the meeting and does not thereafter vote for or assent to action taken at the meeting.") Therefore, the vote was valid, making **C** correct.

As to choice **A**, it's true that a special meeting must normally be held on at least 2 days' notice of time & place (see MBCA §8.22(b)); however, as described above Christian's participation in the meeting without objection constituted a waiver of the lack of notice. **B** is incorrect because the presence of a quorum (and the giving of notice to a quorum) does not excuse the requirement that the company's give *every* director notice of the special meeting. **D** is incorrect not only because of Christian's waiver, but also because that choice incorrectly says that prior notice is required for regular board meetings. (Under MBCA §8.22(a) and (b), notice is required only for special, not regular, meetings).

6. **B** Whether the jurisdiction authorizes cumulative voting makes all the difference. If cumulative voting is not allowed, then most jurisdictions provide that a director may be removed by a shareholder vote if and only if the number of votes cast to remove him exceeds the number of votes cast not to remove him (see, e.g., MBCA §8.08(c), so providing); by this standard, Alf can be removed.

On the other hand, in nearly all states if the corporation *has* authorized cumulative voting, a director cannot be removed without cause if there are cast against his removal enough votes to have elected him under cumulative voting. (If this were not the rule, the majority could always remove minority-chosen directors, defeating the whole purpose of cumulative voting.) See, e.g., MBCA § 8.08(c). Here, there were 1800 shares voting, and the board has 5 seats. Therefore, we use the formula for the number of shares which one must control in order to elect one director:

$$\frac{S}{D+1}+1 \ ,$$

where S is the total number of shares voting and D is the number of directors to be elected. By that formula, Alf could have been elected so long as at least the following number of shares voted for him:

$$\frac{1800}{6} + 1 = 301$$

Since the 800 shares voted against Alf's removal were more than 301, Alf got enough support to have elected him to the board, so he won't be deemed to have been removed.

The lack of cause doesn't matter — nearly all jurisdiction allow removal of directors without cause, unless the charter provides otherwise. (See, e.g., MBCA §8.08(a).)

7. **D**   The issue here is a corporate officer's ability to bind the corporation. Even though an act is unauthorized at the moment it occurs (and that was the case here, as we'll see below), it can become authorized after the fact, if the requirements for "ratification" are met. Ratification occurs when the corporation either expressly adopts the unauthorized act (e.g., by passing an explicit resolution adopting the act) or implicitly indicates, by conduct or inaction, that it approves of the action. The most common way in which a corporation implicitly indicates its approval after the fact is by *retaining the benefits* from the transaction. Here, by allowing its employees to attend the event and eat the green eggs and ham, Sam I Am implicitly ratified the contract. Therefore, the company became liable, making **D** correct.

As a general rule, corporate secretaries by virtue of their post alone have no authority to bind a corporation, certainly not to a purchase order. And as of the moment that Dr. Seuss placed the order, Sam I Am had not done anything to make Dr. Seuss think that he had such authority (no superiors even knew he was making the food arrangements); therefore Seuss did not have implied actual authority, making Choice **C** wrong. Nor did Sam I Am make any communication to Can N Hat that could reasonably have led Cat to think that Dr. Seuss had authority; therefore, Seuss did not have apparent authority. (No statement by the agent alone can give rise to apparent authority — the corporation as principal must somehow give the third party reason to believe the agent has authority, if apparent authority is to apply.) Consequently, Choice **B** is wrong. And since ratification applies, Choice **A** is wrong.

8. **A**   Unless the charter or bylaws provide otherwise (which the facts say they don't), a shareholder meeting requires a quorum of at least a bare majority of the outstanding shares entitled to vote on the measures at issue. Since only 49 of 100 shares were present, there was no quorum, and shareholder action therefore could not validly take place. Therefore, **A** is correct.

The fact that less than a majority of the total shares outstanding voted for the measure would not by itself have prevented the measure from passing; therefore Choice **C** is wrong. For this same reason, Choice **B** would be correct had a quorum been present; but the absence of a quorum prevents **B** from being correct. Choice **D** is wrong because under most statutes (see, e.g., MBCA §7.05(b)), notice of the annual meeting need not contain a description of the purposes of the meeting (though notice of purposes *is* required for a *special* meeting).

9. **C** The normal rule is that a proxy is revocable unless it's **coupled with an "interest."** This is true even if the proxy says that it's irrevocable. One of the ways in which a proxy can be coupled with an interest is if the stock is pledged as collateral for a loan. See MBCA §7.22(d)(1). That was the case here, so Cyborg is correct in the sense that the proxy it received *was* irrevocable. However, if the interest with which the proxy is coupled is *terminated* — e.g., in the case of a collateralized loan, the loan is paid off — then the proxy is automatically revoked. MBCA §7.22(f). As a result, Sarah's entitled to vote her own shares.

Choice **A** is incorrect because even a proxy that states that it's irrevocable is revocable if not coupled with an interest. MBCA §7.22(d), first sent. Choice **B** is incorrect because, although it correctly states a generally-applicable rule, there is an exception when the coupled interest is terminated, which happened here. **D** is incorrect because a proxy that conspicuously states that it's irrevocable and that's coupled with a still-existing interest is in fact irrevocable.

10. **B** Under SEC Rule 14a-8(i)7), a shareholder proposal may be excluded from the corporation's proxy materials if if relates to the "company's ordinary business operations." That's the case here — the quantity breakdown between a software company's Internet- and desktop-based products would almost certainly be held to relate to routine business operations.

A is incorrect, because a shareholder who owns either 1% or $1,000 of a company's common stock (and has done so for at least one year) is entitled to submit a shareholder proposal; Icant qualifies. **C** is incorrect because, although most states hold that that shareholders don't have the power to *require* the board to conduct operations in a particular way, most states do allow shareholders to *urge* or *recommend* particular action, so the "not a proper subject for action by shareholders under state law" ground for exclusion (SEC Rule 14a-8(i)(1)) does not apply. **D** is wrong because, as stated earlier, there is an applicable exclusion, namely the relates-to-ordinary-business-operations exclusion.

11. **C** The modern approach is to refuse to apply the restrictions to shares issued before the restrictions were adopted. For instance, MBCA § 6.27(a) provides that "A restriction does not affect shares issued before the restriction was adopted unless the holders of the shares are parties to the restriction agreement or voted in favor

of the restriction." So the restriction does not apply to the 100 shares that were issued to Banquo before the restrictions were enacted, since Banquo did not vote in favor of the restriction.

On the other hand, the restriction probably *does* apply to the 200 shares that Banquo bought after restriction was imposed, even though the shares were not marked; that's because Banquo had actual notice of the restrictions, and thus under most statutes can't benefit from the absence of a restrictive legend on the share certificate. (See, e.g., MBCA §6.27(b), saying that where there is no restrictive legend, the restriction "is not enforceable against a person without knowledge of the restriction" — this would almost certainly be read to mean by negative implication that the restriction *is* enforceable against a person *with* knowledge.)

12. **B**   Directors have a duty of care toward the corporation, which they can violate either through inactivity or negligence. Under the "business judgment rule," a director who makes a business judgment in good faith fulfills the duty of care (even if the decision is objectively a bad one) if she meets three requirements: (1) she has no conflict of interest concerning the transaction; (2) she is reasonably well-informed about the transaction; and (3) she rationally believes that the business judgment is in the corporation's best interests.

The problem is that here, the directors have almost certainly not met requirement (2), that they be reasonably *well-informed* before taking the action. The fact that the directors didn't have a valuation study or see a copy of the acquisition agreement, the shortness of the advance notice to directors, the lack of discussion at the meeting — all of these things indicate a lack of reasonable information on the part of the board.

Since the board doesn't qualify for the protection of the business judgment rule, the question becomes whether the board's decision demonstrated "due care" or reasonable prudence. Since another buyer could have been found to pay $80, selling for $50 probably wasn't reasonably prudent. Therefore, the board will probably be held liable to reimburse the corporation for the money that was left on the table. See *Smith v. Van Gorkom*, 488 A.2d 858 (Del. 1985), so holding on roughly the same facts. So **B** is correct.

A is incorrect because it wrongly turns solely on what the board in fact knew — the protection of the business judgment rule is not available to directors who do not make reasonable efforts to gather reasonably-sufficient information relating to the decision (as explained above), even if the directors make a decision that's reasonable in light of the limited information known to them. **C** is incorrect because, as explained, the directors' lack of information deprived them of the benefits of the business judgment rule (though had the rule applied, **C** correctly states what the rule's effect would have been). **D** is incorrect because it implies that where the business judgment rule doesn't apply, the directors will be automatically liable if they fail to make the best available decision; that's not a correct statement, since even without the business judgment rule the directors will only be liable for a lack of reasonable prudence, and a decision that is other than the best-available decision is not necessarily a decision that was imprudent.

13. **C**   This was a director-conflict situation: Haney was a director of the buyer, and he also had a sufficiently large financial interest (25%, or $250,000) in the subject of the transaction that his impartiality can reasonably be questioned. (See, e.g., ALI Principles § 8.60(1)(i), making it a direct conflict where the director "has a beneficial financial interest in or so closely linked to the transaction and of such financial significance to the director . . . that the interest would reasonably be expected to exert an influence on the director's judgment if he were called upon to vote on the transaction.")

When a director has a conflict of interest involving a corporate transaction, there are three ways to avoid the transaction's voidability on conflict grounds: (1) full disclosure and disinterested director approval, (2) full disclosure and shareholder approval, or (3) overall fairness. But the conflict won't be deemed to have been "disclosed" unless the disinterested directors (or shareholders) knew *both* the nature of the transaction *and* the *nature of the conflict*. Here, the disinterested directors didn't know that Haney was a significant partner of the selling entity, so they didn't know of the "nature of the conflict." Therefore, there wasn't true disclosure, and the approval by the disinterested directors will be irrelevant. (It's also irrelevant that Haney didn't vote on the proposed transaction — as long as there was a conflict between Haney's role as director of Green Acres and his role as partner in Hooterville, the conflict rules apply, requiring disclosure.) **C** is correct because it correctly explains that none of these 3 ways of avoiding the conflict problem applies.

A is incorrect because the fact that the transaction was approved by a majority of the five disinterested directors is not sufficient to immunize it: the disinterested directors' vote performs such an immunization function only if, as described above, the directors voted after reasonable disclosure of the existence and nature of the conflict. **B** is not correct because, although an unreasonably high price arguably makes the transaction unfair to the corporation, even an unfair transaction can be immunized by a vote of disinterested directors (or shareholders) following disclosure, and choice B falsely falsely ignores the possibility of such an immunization. **D** is incorrect because when directors engage in a transaction in which one of them is acting under an undisclosed breach of the duty of loyalty, the business judgment rule doesn't apply. (The business judgment rule applies only to asserted breaches of the duty of care, not to breaches of the duty of loyalty, which is what we have here).

Observe, by the way, that if the transaction were "fair" to the corporation, the court would probably approve it even without the prior disclosure. (But the facts tell you that the price is quite high, thus making it probably unfair.) Also, note that even *after the dissident shareholder filed suit*, under most conflict statutes it would not be too late for Haney to make full disclosure, and procure a truly informed approval by the disinterested directors. (See, e.g., Off. Comm. to MBCA § 8.62(a)). Such an after-the-fact vote would suffice to immunize the transaction from a court-issued injunction or an award of damages.

14. **B**   The rule as to corporate opportunities is essentially that "insiders" may not exploit an opportunity that rightly belongs to the corporation. An opportunity is less likely to be found to "belong" to the corporation when exploited by a non-employee director than when exploited by a full-time employee. But even in the director situation, if the director found the opportunity *in connection with company business (or by use of company-owned information)*, the opportunity will generally be held to be a corporate one. Since at the time Alexis learned of the South American opportunity she was visiting company properties in connection with her role as director, and since it was a company employee who told her about the opportunity, it seems fair to conclude that Alexis learned of the opportunity both in connection with company business and by use of the company's (i.e., its employee's) information. Therefore, the opportunity was a corporate one, which Alexis improperly usurped.

A is wrong because, although directors are less likely to be found to be corporate-opportunity-usurpers than are full-time high-level employees, even a director may be found to be a usurper under the special circumstances (e.g., use of corporate information) detailed above. Similarly, **C** is wrong because, if the special circumstances such as use of corporate information are present, a director can be liable for taking a corporate opportunity even if the director paid for all associated expenses. **D** is wrong because it imposes too high a burden of proof on the company — so long as the company can show that the opportunity would have been of serious interest to it, the company need not further show that it probably would have been willing and able to take advantage of it. (If Alexis could show that the company probably *wouldn't* have been able and willing to take advantage, this might have been a successful affirmative defense).

15. **A**   The issue here is whether a controlling shareholder can sell his control at a premium — that is, at a price above the fair market value of the shares. The *general* rule is that he may, in fact, sell his shares for whatever price he wants. There are exceptions to this doctrine, but none of the exceptions applies here. So Bazooka is within his rights in collecting something extra for his controlling stake, even though he's getting a benefit not available to other shareholders. Thus **A** is correct.

B is incorrect because it states a "rule" that is not a rule at all (and that is, indeed, just the opposite of the correct rule). **C** is wrong because Ebuoy has not made a tender offer; it has simply bought Bazooka's shares in a private-market transaction. **D** is wrong because, while it's true that a "sale of directorships" is unlawful in some circumstances, it is not unlawful for a majority stockholder and his designees to resign from the board as part of a sale of the majority block. (If

Bazooka had had a small, but controlling, position, the resignations might have been unlawful if they were arranged as part of the sale, since that would be permitting Ebuoy to gain a level of control that it otherwise couldn't have gotten as owner of Bazooka's block.)

16. **C** This is a scenario in which 10b-5 has been violated, because Kirk has made an "untrue statement of a material fact" (the misstatement about the company's prospects), and the statement was made "in connection with the purchase or sale of any security." Therefore, Spock is entitled to damages in a civil action, measured as the amount needed to put plaintiff in the position he would have been in had his trade been delayed until after the misrepresentation was corrected. In the case of a sale by plaintiff based on an unduly pessimistic statement by the insider, the moment as of which that computation done is normally the moment the statement was made — so courts award the difference between the "true" value of the stock at the moment of the misstatement and the price actually received by the plaintiff. This makes **C** correct.

A is incorrect because it is simply a misstatement of the law — 10b-5 applies to transactions involving any "security," whether publicly-traded or not. So the fact that TTI is privately-held is irrelevant. **B** is incorrect because, although it is (roughly) correct as a statement of law, the statement doesn't apply to these facts. That's because Kirk used the telephone as part of his scheme, and the telephone is considered to be an instrument of interstate commerce. **D** is incorrect because courts have virtually all rejected the argument that a defrauded seller should be able to obtain damages based on the true value (or price) as of some post-deception date, such as the date suit was filed; the reason is that the choice of date would be very speculative and hard to fix — so it's the value on the date of the deception that counts.

17. **B** § 16(b) makes certain people engaging in purchases and sales of a corporation's securities within six months liable to pay any profits on those transactions to the corporation. The people covered are directors, officers, and 10+% shareholders. The issue here is whether (and as of when) Ariel fit the 10+% shareholder profile, since she was a 15% owner when she sold her shares. The Supreme Court has held that neither purchases that occur before a person is a 10% holder, nor the purchase that *lifts* a person over the 10% threshold, count under §16(b), even if the person is a 10% holder at the moment of the later sale. So neither the initial 5,000-share purchase (which made her a 5% holder when it was over), nor the 10,000-share purchase (which lifted her from 5% to 15%) counted, since she was not a 10% holder just before either purchase. On the other hand, Ariel *was* a 10% holder just before the final 1,000-share purchase, so she has to disgorge the $5-per-share profit she made on those shares, since she sold those shares within six months of buying them.

C is wrong because it would impose liability on Ariel for the 10,000-share purchase (10,000 shares @ $14/share profit, or $140,000) as well as for the $1,000-share purchase ($5,000), and she's not liable for the former purchase for the reason described above. **D** is similarly wrong, since it would incorrectly impose liability for both the 5,000-share purchase (5,000 shares @$15, or $75,000) and the 10,000-share purchase, as well as for the properly-covered 1,000-share purchase.

18. **B**   When the plaintiff in a derivative suit makes a demand on directors, the directors needn't make their own decision on whether to pursue the claim. They can, and often do, leave the decision in the hands of a "special litigation committee." When they do so, and the committee recommends that the corporation not pursue the claim, the issue becomes whether the committee's recommendation is protected by the business judgment rule (in which case the motion to dismiss the claim will be granted). The MBCA, like nearly all such statutes, requires that before the business judgment rule will apply to the recommendation of a special committee, each member of the committee must be independent from the defendants, and must not have any interest of her own in the transaction under attack (i.e., each must be "disinterested"). To further guarantee independence, the MBCA requires that the committee be selected by majority vote of the independent directors. See MBCA § 7.44(b)(2). Since the facts say that the only directors who voted to appoint Holmes and Kevork were the very same three directors who have been accused of the improper transaction, this requirement was not satisfied, and the recommendation of the committee must therefore be disregarded. Consequently, the suit must be allowed to proceed.

A is wrong because a special committee's recommendation is entitled to the protection of the business judgment rule only if the committee satisfies the requirement of independence, and this one doesn't for the reasons described above. (By the way, even if the committee *had* met the independence requirement, its recommendation would still entitled to deference only if the committee made its determination "in good faith after conducting a reasonable inquiry upon which its conclusions are based..." See MBCA §7.44(a).) **C** is wrong because the fact that the committee members were independent is not enough, if the ones who appointed the committee members were not independent, as described above. **D** is wrong because under the MBCA, if a properly-constituted committee recommends dismissal after a procedurally-proper investigation, the recommendation *must* be followed by the court even if the court thinks the action has merit.

19. **C**   Ordinarily in a merger, the shareholders of both the surviving and the disappearing company must approve. However, a different rule applies where the merger is what is sometimes called a ***"whale-minnow"*** merger, i.e., a merger in which the acquiring company is so much bigger than the to-be-acquired corporation that the former's shares outstanding won't materially increase. That's because the impact on the surviving corporation's shareholders isn't deemed great

enough to give them a vote. In most jurisdictions, if the survivor's shares outstanding won't increase by more than 20%, the survivor's shareholders don't have to approve; Del. GCL § 251(f) follows this majority rule. Here, Sampson had 100,000 voting shares before the merger and only 10%, or 10,000, more voting shares after the merger. As a result, Sampson's shareholders aren't entitled to a vote.

20. **B** The question is asking you whether George has appraisal rights under the relevant law. Under Delaware law, the shareholders of a company that sells all of its assets (whether for cash or for some other property, such as shares of the acquirer) do *not* have appraisal rights. See Del GCL § 262(b) (giving appraisal rights only to holders of "a constituent corporation in a merger or consolidation" — an asset sale is not a "merger" or a "consolidation"). Therefore, even though George will effectively be forced into ownership of a business (coffee shop) that's quite different from the one he expected to be owning (sitcom producer), he's locked in.

On the other hand, MBCA § 13.02(a)(3) gives stockholders of a company that's selling all or substantially all of its assets a right of appraisal. There's an exception if the company is selling for cash and plans to distribute the cash to holders within one year after the sale, but this exception doesn't apply here. So (for the reasons suggested by the last sentence of the prior paragraph), the MBCA gives George the right to force Seinfeld, Inc. to buy out his shares for cash at their fair market value.

21. **A** All three of Alexis' actions violated the federal Williams Act. As to **I**, the Williams Act says that tender offers must be left open for at least 20 business days. SEC Rule 14e-1(a) under the '34 Act. Thus, regardless of Alexis's concerns about Krystal, she can't make a ten-day offer. (Note, by the way, that it's just this kind of competition that the 20-day rule is designed to encourage, so that shareholders will get the best possible deal.) As to **II**, under SEC Rule 14d-7, a shareholder who tenders to a tender offeror must be permitted to revoke the tender, and withdraw the shares, at any time so long as the offer remains open. As to **III**, under the "best price rule," if the consideration offered in a tender offer for a target's shares is increased, the increased price must be paid to all the target's shareholders who accepted at the earlier, lower price. '34 Act, § 14(d)(7).

22. **C** As to **I**, the statement is false. Most states still impose an "earned surplus" restriction. That is, in most states dividends may only be paid out of "retained earnings" (a/k/a "earned surplus"), i.e., the profits which the corporation has accumulated since its inception. Jacques Cousteaudian doesn't pass this test, because it has negative retained earnings (i.e., over its lifetime, it's lost a net of $45,000). Even in a more liberal state allowing payment out of "unearned sur-

plus," the company still couldn't pay the dividend, because there is no paid-in surplus (since holders only paid par for their shares), and there is no other source of unearned surplus.

As to **II**, the statement is true. Del. GCL § 170(a)'s "nimble dividends" provision allows payment of dividends — even if there is no surplus — if the dividend is paid "out of [the corporation's] net profits for the fiscal year in which the dividend is declared and/or the preceding fiscal year." Since in Years 4 and 5 the company has earned a net of $30,000, the company could actually pay the entire $30,000 as a dividend in Year 5, at least as far as the surplus (as distinguished from insolvency) test goes. So the $1,000 payment is allowable, even though there is no earned or unearned surplus. (But if the corporation just broke even in Years 6 and 7, it could no longer declare even the $1,000 dividend, because this would no longer be from the "current or preceding fiscal year" — the provision is called "nimble" dividends because the board has to act promptly after earning the money.)

23. **B**   The issue, of course, is whether Torquemada has supplied adequate consideration for the shares. As to **I**, the majority approach — followed in New York and Delaware, among others — is that a contemporaneous transfer of property or services is valid as consideration, but that an unsecured *promise* to supply cash, property or services *in the future* is *not* valid. See, e.g., N.Y. BCL § 504(a) ("Consideration for the issue of shares shall consist of money or other property, tangible or intangible, or labor or services *actually received by or performed for the corporation . . .*") Since Torquemada has supplied only his unsecured promise to perform the services, rather than the services themselves, under the prevailing view Torquemada has not supplied adequate consideration, and Spanish Inquisition may not validly issue the shares. Thus I is not a correct statement.

As to **II**, MBCA § 6.21(b), unlike the prevailing approach, allows a very broad range of things to suffice as consideration for share issuance. In particular, that section says that if the board so authorizes, consideration may consist of "contracts for services to be performed." Since Torquemada has bound himself contractually to perform the services, his agreement constitutes valid consideration, making II a correct statement.

24. **B**   All of the Rules cited — Rules 504, 505 and 506 — are part of Regulation D, which supplies various exemptions to the public-offering rules. Therefore, any offering that qualifies under any of these Rules is exempt from the registration requirements imposed on public offerings. As to **I**, Rule 504 is limited to raising $1 million or less, so it won't work. As to **II**, Rule 505 allows the raising of up to $5 million, as long as there are no more than 35 purchasers. The interesting thing about 505 is that it doesn't require that the purchasers be "accredited" or sophisticate in business/financial matters, so the presence of the unrich and financially-unsophisticated lawyers won't be a problem. Therefore, Rule 505 will work.

As to **III**, Rule 506 imposes no dollar limit, but every purchaser must either be an accredited investor (essentially, a person worth more than $1 million, or having an individual income greater than $200,000 per year or with his/her spouse $300,000 per year), or have "such knowledge and experience in financial and business matters that he is capable of evaluating the merits and risks of the prospective investment." So this requirement rules out 506, because the lawyers don't qualify.

ESSAY EXAM QUESTIONS & ANSWERS

The following Essay Questions are taken from the Corporations volume of *Siegel's Essay & Multiple-Choice Questions & Answers*, a series written by Brian Siegel and published by Aspen Publishers. The full volume contains 25 essays (with model answers), as well as 100 multiple choice questions. (The essay questions were originally asked on the California Bar Exam, and are copyright the California Board of Bar Examiners, reprinted by permission.) The book is available from your bookstore.

QUESTION 1

Starco, stockbrokers, in attempting to market 1,000,000 common shares to be issued by Durmac, offered 500,000 shares to the Ennis Corp. at $50 per share. Already the owner of a substantial interest in Durmac, Ennis's financial condition was such as to make a large, immediate acquisition of additional shares of Durmac desirable.

Ennis's by-laws provided that a quorum consisted of five out of its seven directors. After due notice to the four resident directors, but without notice to the three non-resident directors, a special emergency board of directors' meeting was held. Resident directors Almon, Barnes, and Chester with a proxy executed by Grabe, the fourth resident director, attended the meeting. Also present was Webster, a non-resident director. The directors present unanimously voted to purchase 400,000 additional Durmac shares. Upon conclusion of the meeting, Webster signed a waiver of notice.

Immediately following the meeting, Ennis purchased and paid for 400,000 shares of Durmac stock at $50 per share.

At their next regular meeting, attended by all directors, the board voted unanimously to ratify the action taken at the special emergency meeting.

Before the actual offering of Durmac shares to Ennis, Starco had offered, for one day only, a few thousand shares of the new Durmac shares at $42 each, cash, to a few select persons. Among the offerees was Almon, who purchased a total of 2,000 shares for his own account. Almon subsequently disposed of these shares at a substantial profit. However, by the time Ennis shareholders became aware of the foregoing facts, the market price of Durmac shares had declined sharply.

1. Was the acquisition of Durmac shares by Ennis a proper corporate action? Discuss.

2. Are any of the Ennis directors liable to their corporation for the decline in value of Durmac shares? Discuss.

3. What, if any, is Almon's liability to Ennis for profits he made on his purchase and sale of Durmac shares? Discuss.

Do not discuss federal statutory securities issues.

ANSWER TO QUESTION 1

1. Acquisition of Durmac ("D") shares by Ennis:

It could be contended that the vote on the acquisition of D stock was improper because (1) not all of the directors were noticed (only four of the seven were sent notice), and (2) there was not a quorum (only 4, rather than the required 5, directors were present).

As to the latter contention, it could be argued that (i) Almon should not be counted, since he was interested (i.e., owned shares of D stock), and (ii) directors usually cannot give their proxies to other directors to vote at a board meeting (and so Grabe's vote should not be counted). Thus, only three directors were present for purposes of a quorum. (Additionally, a special rule exists in almost all states providing that, if a majority of the disinterested directors approve the transaction, this number will constitute a quorum. In that case, four disinterested votes in favor out of a total of six disinterested directors would have been sufficient. However, since there were only three legally-cast disinterested votes if Almon's vote is excluded, even under the special rule there would have been no quorum.)

Notwithstanding the foregoing, since the decision to purchase D's stock was unanimously ratified at the next regular board meeting, the corporate action was properly taken. While Almon should have disclosed his interest and refrained from voting on the D stock purchase, his failure to do so is probably not be an adequate basis to avoid the purchase. The resolution would still have passed 6-0, even if he had abstained.

2. Liability of Ennis directors for the decline in D's shares:

Under the business judgment rule, a corporate director is required to exercise the due care with respect to corporate matters as he would with respect to his own assets. The facts are silent as to whether Almon or the other members of the Ennis board should have realized that the market price of D shares could decline sharply. It is also unclear as to whether Almon had any special basis to perceive the subsequent decline in D stock. If Almon was aware of the possibility of an imminent decline in D's shares, he probably had a fiduciary obligation to disclose such information to the board of directors of Ennis. If he failed to do so, and such data could have dissuaded the board from making the acquisition, Almon would be liable to Ennis for the losses resulting from the decrease of D stock.

Assuming the decline in D stock was the result of market conditions which could not reasonably have been perceived by the board of Ennis, the latter group has no liability to its shareholders. On the other hand, since Ennis was expending $2,500,000, the board of directors may have violated the business judgment rule by making such a major expenditure without a thorough investigation of D.

Assuming the board of Ennis violated the business judgment rule, the two non-resident directors and Grabe could probably not successfully defend against liability. Non-resident directors are ordinarily held to the same standard as local directors, and Grabe waived notice of the meeting. Also, all of the directors later ratified the action taken at the emergency meeting.

3. Liability of Almon to Ennis for the purchase and sale of D's shares:

Ennis could attempt to recover from Almon under the "corporate opportunity" doctrine.

Under this theory, a director is obligated to refrain from gaining any personal advantage to the detriment of his company as a consequence of information derived through his corporate position. Thus, the board of Ennis could contend that Almon should have (1) advised it of the possibility of purchasing D stock at $42 per share, and (2) permitted Ennis to purchase the shares at that rate.

However, the facts are silent as to whether (1) the offer to Almon was made as a consequence of the latter's position at Ennis, (e.g., Almon may have simply been on a mailing list of wealthy individuals), and (2) Almon had reason to believe that D stock would subsequently be offered to Ennis at a higher rate. Assuming either inquiry is answered in the negative, Almon has no liability under the corporate opportunity doctrine.

In summary, Almon probably has no liability to Ennis.

QUESTION 2

Art has been president of Exco, a publicly held corporation with net assets of approximately $50 million, for the past six years. Exco manufactures computers. Two years ago, Art negotiated an agreement for the purchase by Exco of all of the outstanding shares of Yang, Inc., a privately held maker of computer components, for $5 million cash. The purchase was made about one and one-half years ago. At the time, other members of Art's immediate family were holders of the outstanding shares of Yang. This information was not known except to Art, Yang's management, and Bob, an Exco director.

Art negotiated Exco's purchase of Yang stock and executed the purchase agreement on behalf of Exco, relying on his authority as its president. Before the purchase documents were signed, Art discussed the proposed acquisition individually with Bob, Curt, and Don. Curt and Don are Exco directors who, with Art and Bob, comprise a majority of Exco's seven-person board of directors. Bob, Curt, and Don each told Art that he approved of the transaction.

After the purchase of Yang stock by Exco, at the next regular meeting of the Exco board one month later, Art informed all of the directors of the acquisition. While some questions were asked, there was no vote on the acquisition at the meeting. Except for Bob, no Exco director was informed of the previous ownership of Yang stock by Art's family members. Since Bob believed the acquisition was beneficial to Exco, he never mentioned to any of the other Exco directors his knowledge of the prior ownership of Yang stock by members of Art's family. The existence of such prior ownership could, however, have been discovered by a review of Yang's corporate records.

Since the stock purchase by Exco, Yang has been consistently and increasingly unprofitable. At the annual Exco shareholders meeting two months ago, Art, Bob, Curt, and Don were not re-elected as directors. Last month, Exco's new board replaced Art as president.

1. Can Exco rescind the purchase of Yang stock? Discuss.

2. Can Exco recover damages for Yang's unprofitability from any or all of the following:

    a. Art? Discuss.

b. Bob? Discuss.

c. Curt and Don? Discuss.

ANSWER TO QUESTION 2

1. Can Exco ("E") rescind the transaction?

There are three independent theories pursuant to which E could attempt to rescind the transaction with Art's family (the "Sellers").

Breach of fiduciary duty

Where a director has a personal interest in a transaction which his corporation is considering, he is ordinarily obliged to (1) disclose that interest to the entire board of directors, (2) refrain from voting upon it, and (3) disclose any information indicating that the transaction may not be in the corporation's best interests. A transaction involving a director's immediate family would probably constitute a "personal" interest. While it is unclear from the facts whether or not Art believed the transaction was not in E's best interests, he clearly failed to meet the initial two requirements.

It will be difficult for Art to successfully claim that the transaction was subsequently impliedly ratified by a majority of the board (e.g., when Bob, Curt and Don advised him that they approved of the transaction), since (1) there was never a formal vote upon it, (2) he and Bob never disclosed to the other members of the board that the Sellers were members of Art's immediate family, and (3) there is no clear majority in favor of the purchase if Art's vote is discounted. Of these problems, (2) is the most important, since ratification requires a full disclosure of the underlying facts, including the facts that demonstrate the conflict.

Lack of authority

The President ordinarily oversees the day-to-day operations of a corporation. While this officer usually has the power to bind the corporation in routine transactions, a five million dollar acquisition (constituting 10% of E's assets) would probably not be within this implied authority.

SEC Rule 10b-5

Under SEC Rule 10b-5, it is unlawful to employ any scheme to defraud another in connection with the purchase or sale of a security. If it could be shown that (1) Art had reason to know that the Yang stock was overvalued, or (2) Sellers knew (or should have known) that Art was effectuating the sale for the purpose of paying them an excessive amount for their Yang shares, the transaction is probably violative of SEC Rule 10b-5; *Superintendent of Insurance v. Bankers Life & Casualty Co.*, 404 U.S. 6 (1971).

Under rescission (1) E would tender the Yang stock back to the Sellers, and (2) the Sellers would return the purchase price of the shares to E.

Sellers could contend that rescission (an equitable remedy which is discretionary with the court) is not appropriate, since (1) laches is applicable (i.e., E's board was informed of the transaction one and one-half years ago, and yet no action has been taken), and (2) Yang's decreased profitability may be due to actions undertaken by E or subsequent market conditions.

Unless E can show that (1) the decline in value of Yang stock was not due to market conditions, or (2) the Sellers knew that Art was deliberately paying them an excessive purchase price, rescission will probably not be granted.

2.

a. Can E recover for Yang's unprofitability from Art?

In addition to the theories described above, a derivative action against Art might also be sustained under the business judgment rule (i.e., a director must exercise the due care with respect to corporate matters as he would with regard to his own assets).

It is unclear from the facts as to whether Art investigated the transaction with the thoroughness which a five million dollar acquisition deserves. Assuming (1) he did not, and (2) the price paid by E was excessive, E could probably recover (under the business judgment rule and the other theories described above) from Art the diminishment in the value of Yang stock between the (1) time of purchase, and (2) trial. This amount would be reduced to the extent, if any, that Art could show that Yang's decreased profitability was due to mismanagement by E.

b. Can E recover for Yang's unprofitability from Bob?

The discussions above with respect to the business judgment rule and (for the most part) a director's fiduciary duties would be applicable to Bob. Although Bob did not conduct the transaction, he was probably under a fiduciary obligation to disclose Art's conflict of interest to the entire board (even though Bob, in good faith, believed the transaction to be beneficial to E). No action would lie under SEC Rule 10b-5 against Bob, since the scienter (desire or intent to deceive the corporation) element is lacking.

c. Can E recover for Yang's unprofitability from Curt and Don?

The discussion above with respect to the business judgment rule would be equally applicable to Curt and Don. Since the transaction had not been consummated at the time they were originally informed of the prospective acquisition, they (presumably) could have prevented its consummation.

QUESTION 3

Gasco is a State X Corporation involved in the petroleum industry. Its stock is traded on the New York Stock Exchange. Its board of directors hired Media, a public relations firm, to campaign against the passage of a State X ballot proposition to use gasoline tax receipts for the development of a statewide public transit system. The contract provided that Gasco's financing of the campaign should not be made public by Gasco or Media.

A group of Gasco shareholders, calling themselves Citizens Against Pollution (CAP) learned of the contract. They submitted to Gasco management, for inclusion in the next proxy statement and for presentation to the Gasco shareholders at the next shareholder meeting, proposals to:

(1) remove from the Gasco board those directors "who voted to authorize the Media contract or otherwise sought to prevent passage of the gasoline tax proposition";

(2) hire an auditor to go over Gasco's books; and

(3) consider the use of non-polluting cleansing products in all company-owned gas stations.

CAP has complied with all SEC procedural requirements.

A State X statute requires public disclosure of all corporate expenditures "designed to influence the outcome of issues to be decided by public ballot."

Pursuant to a valid Gasco by-law, only three of the nine Gasco directors are to be elected at the next shareholder meeting. The Gasco charter provides that the board of directors may, by majority vote, remove a director for "sufficient cause."

Discuss and decide the following:

1. Is management required to present the CAP proposals to the shareholders and include them in the proxy statement?

2. If adopted at the shareholder meeting, would the proposals be binding on the board of directors?

3. If a new Gasco board repudiates the Media contract, may Media nevertheless have it enforced?

ANSWER TO QUESTION 3

1. Management's obligation to present the CAP proposals to shareholders and include them in the proxy statement.

Since Gasco's stock is traded on a national exchange (e.g., the NYSE), it is subject to the proxy rules promulgated under Section 14 of the Securities Exchange Act of 1934. Under Rules 14a-8(a), a shareholder is ordinarily entitled to submit, for inclusion in management's proxy solicitation, proposals which he intends to present at the upcoming shareholder's meeting. However, there are several exceptions to management's obligation to include such materials.

a. *Proposal to remove directors who authorized Media contract and sought to impede the gas tax proposition.*

Management may omit a proposal if, under the laws of the corporation's domicile, it is not a proper subject for shareholder action. It is unclear from the facts as to whether stockholders can remove a director in this state. We are advised only that Gasco's charter provides that the board may remove a director for sufficient cause.

Nevertheless, in most jurisdictions there is a common law right of shareholders to remove directors for cause. However, "cause" typically exists only if a director has committed fraud, waste, or otherwise overtly misused his position. This standard is arguably satisfied by the directors' deliberate effort to circumvent the State X statute requiring disclosure of corporate expenditures made for the purpose of influencing public ballot measures.

However, the directors could contend in rebuttal that, unless this law provides for significant criminal penalties in the event it is violated, removal is not proper. They were only attempting to promote corporate objectives by preventing action which would presumably make Gasco's business less profitable.

While a close question, unless the directors' actions were criminal in nature, their removal is probably not a proper subject for shareholder action.

b. *Proposal to hire an auditor to review Gasco's books.*

The directors could assert that retaining auditors to review the corporation's books is a matter which relates to the "conduct of the ordinary business operations" of the company, and therefore should be excluded.

However, given the board's deliberate effort to avoid the State X statute, the request for an independent party to determine if there was other misconduct by Gasco seems appropriate.

Thus, the directors can probably be compelled to include this proposal in their proxy materials.

c. *Proposal to require non-polluting products only in company-owned gas stations.*

Directors may omit a proposal if it relates to a "personal claim or grievance." It can be argued that this proposal is nothing more than a general environmental grievance which reflects the personal views of the complaining shareholders.

The stockholders could respond that, even if the proposal emanates from the desire to have an environment free of pollutants, it nevertheless relates to an aspect of Gasco's general business policy. The courts and the SEC have shown a tendency to require inclusion of proposals that relate to major ethical, social and political issues that have a tangible link to the corporation's affairs. The use of non-pollutants in company-owned gas stations would place Gasco on the cutting edge of environmentally-conscious energy companies, which would arguably constitute a unique advertising appeal to its consumers.

Therefore, the most likely result is that the directors must include the proposal because it relates to major social/political issues with a tangible link to the company's affairs.

2. Binding effect of proposals.

As already discussed, unless there has been a serious criminal violation, dismissing the directors for involvement in the Media contract is probably not sufficient "cause." Thus, it is not includible nor is it binding upon the directors. Additionally, if it were includible, it would still not be binding, because a director must ordinarily have an opportunity to defend his actions and obtain judicial review of an unfavorable decision.

It might also be argued that, since only three of the nine directors are to be elected at the shareholder meeting, removing all of the directors (assuming the decision to enter into the contract with Media was approved unanimously) would result in there being no management of Gasco. However, Articles of Incorporation ordinarily provide for interim appointments or elections if a director is removed. Thus, the six vacancies could be filled by the three newly elected directors soon after the meeting.

The proposal to have an auditor review Gasco's books relates to verifying past conduct of the directors, and should be binding upon the board.

The third proposal, if found to have some tangible link to the corporation's affairs, would be includible but not binding upon the board. Management decisions are the exclusive province of the directors.

3. The contract with Media.

Two arguments can be made that this agreement is unenforceable.

First, it might be asserted that the contract is ultra vires, since it requires Gasco to do something which is contrary to law (e.g., refrain from disclosing corporate spending which is designed to influence public ballot issues).

However, a court could simply strike the illegal provision and permit the balance of the contract to stand. This remedy seems appropriate since the provision, having become known, has ceased to have any effectiveness.

Second, Gasco might argue that it and Media are in pari delicto with regard to an illegal provision, and therefore the contract is unenforceable. However, since the provision was presumably inserted at Gasco's insistence, a court would probably not permit Gasco to evade its contractual responsibilities under these circumstances.

Thus, Media can enforce the contract.

SUBJECT MATTER INDEX

This index includes references to the Capsule Summary
and to the Exam Tips, but not to Q&A or Flow Charts.